ISLAMIC HUMANISM

Islamic Humanism

LENN E. GOODMAN

OXFORD
UNIVERSITY PRESS

2003

OXFORD
UNIVERSITY PRESS

Oxford University Press
Oxford New York
Auckland Bangkok Buenos Aires Cape Town Chennai
Dar es Salaam Delhi Hong Kong Istanbul Karachi Kolkata
Kuala Lumpur Madrid Melbourne Mexico City Mumbai Nairobi
São Paolo Shanghai Taipei Tokyo Toronto

Published by Oxford University Press, Inc
198 Madison Avenue, New York, New York 10016

www oup com

Library of Congress Cataloging-in-Publication Data
Goodman, Lenn Evan, 1944–
Islamic humanism / Lenn E Goodman
p cm
Includes bibliographical references and index
ISBN 0-19-513580-6
1 Islam and humanism. 2. Islam and social problems 3. Human rights—Religious aspects—Islam 4. Philosophy, Islamic I Title
BP190 5 T78 G66 2002
297 2'6—dc21 2002071525

9 8 7 6 5 4 3 2 1

Printed in the United States of America
on acid-free paper

For Bernard Lewis

Preface

This book is the product of some forty years' study of Arabic and Islamic thought and culture. I wrote my first essays on Ghazālī, Ibn Khaldūn and Ibn Ṭufayl in the 1960s, my first book-length treatments of Maimonides and the Ikhwān al-Ṣafā in the 1970s, and a number of comparative thematic studies of Jewish and Islamic philosophy and literature in the 1980s. In the '90s I published *Avicenna*, a philosophical appreciation of one of the greatest of the Muslim philosophers, and I began the studies of Arabic universal history writing that are reflected in chapter 4. I wrote *Islamic Humanism* during my sabbatical year in 2001, supported by a Fellowship from the National Endowment for the Humanities and a supplemental Research Scholars Grant from Vanderbilt University. Throughout the writing, my bride, Roberta Goodman, has stood at my side. My recent philosophical study, *In Defense of Truth: A Pluralistic Approach*, was dedicated to her, quite fittingly, in view of the insight and integrity she shows in her work, in her relations, and in her character. The present book is dedicated to Bernard Lewis, the doyen of Arabic and Islamic studies, whose erudition, wit, insight, and versatility as a historian and a scholar of literature are exceeded only by his forthright courage in behalf of truth and understanding in a realm where half-truths and misdirections too often prevail.

Islamic Humanism was written for Oxford University Press. It is my third title for them (after *God of Abraham* and *Judaism, Human Rights and Human Values*). All were prepared under the astute editorship of Cynthia Read. Fred Denny of the University of Colorado in Boulder, after serving as an anonymous external reader of the preliminary text, made known his identity and expressed his profound understanding of the project I had in hand. He and another reader who remains anonymous made many helpful suggestions, which I have taken to heart.

The first chapter of this book grew from the embryo of the Halmos Lecture I gave in Tel Aviv in 1988. Sasson Somekh, who holds the Halmos Chair of Arabic Literature at Tel Aviv University was my host. A friend since our D. Phil. studies together at Oxford, he encouraged the project that led to the present book, from its inception. I began the relevant work on the interplay of sacred and secular themes in Arabic literature under a fellowship at the East West Center in Honolulu and published an early version in Mustansir Mir's festschrift for James A. Bellamy. The underlying essay is much revised and expanded here.

The second and third chapters grow out of essays I wrote for Brian Carr and Indira Mahalingam, the founders of the journal *Asian Philosophy* and the editors of the *Companion Encyclopedia of Asian Philosphy*, where I first tried out some of the language and ideas that are developed here.

The final chapter began its life as my keynote for the international conference on the uses of history at the University of Denver. The conference, organized by Seth Ward, was sponsored by the Institute for Islamic/Judaic Studies, founded by Stanley Wagner and led by S. D. Goitein and William Brinner. It was my privilege to co-chair some of that institute's meetings after Professor Goitein became unable to travel. The work of the institute, which resulted in the publication of several conference volumes and the formation and strengthening of important cross-cultural friendships, was terribly important to me. I attended that last conference to present my keynote (again much expanded and revised here) in October 1996, only days after the death of my first wife, Dr. Madeleine Goodman. I will not forget the strength imparted to me when the Jewish participants joined their voices to mine when I said kaddish in her memory.

The many scholars whose studies, texts, and commentaries contribute to the understanding that underwrites the present book are cited in the notes and bibliography. Among my own contemporaries, teachers, colleagues, friends, or simply authors of superb monographs and essays, particular mention should be made of M. A.-H. Ansari, Mohammed Arkoun, A. F. L. Beeston, J. N. Bell, Clifford Bosworth, Michael Cook, Herbert Davidson, D. M. Dunlop, A. A. Duri, Majid Fakhry, Walter Fischel, Sir Hamilton Gibb, Lois Giffin, S. D. Goitein, Gustave von Grunebaum, Dimitri Gutas, Andras Hamori, Nicholas Heer, George Hourani, Stephen Humphreys, Toshihiko Izutsu, Tarif Khalidi, Joel Kraemer, Bruce Lawrence, Ilse Lichtenstadter, Richard McCarthy, Muhsin Mahdi, James Monroe, Roy Mottahedeh, Eric Ormsby, Frank Peters, Fazlur Rahman, Franz Rosenthal, Everett Rowson, Abdulaziz Sachedina, Ahmad Shboul, M. A. Sherif, Yedida Stillman, Richard Walzer, John Wansbrough, Charles Wendell, Brannon Wheeler, and John A. Williams. From somewhat earlier generations: A. J. Arberry, Miguel Asín Palacios, Henry Farmer, Ignaz Goldziher, Paul Kraus, David Margoliouth, Adam Mez, R. A. Nicholson, Joseph Schacht, William Montgomery Watt, A. J. Wensinck, and Constantine Zurayk.

As I reflect on this little constellation of thinkers who have themselves reflected on the cosmopolitan and humanist traditions of Islam, I'm reminded of a story told me by another student of Islamic thought and civilization, on his return from lecturing in countries with large Muslim populations. He was often asked during that overseas assignment how long he had been studying Islam. His account of his several decades of study invariably provoked the same response: "Then what are you waiting for?" That, in turn, brings to mind the mild irony of Ibn Ṭufayl, who writes of his fictive mystic Absāl's motive on his first encounter with Ḥayy Ibn Yaqẓān, who had grown up on an equatorial island without human contact: When he saw "that Ḥayy did not know how to talk, the fears he had felt of harm to his faith were eased, and he became eager to teach him to speak, hoping to impart knowledge and religion to him, and by so doing to earn God's favor and a greater reward."[1] But Absāl learns that Hayy's independent thoughts and meditations have already brought him to an understanding of the deeper truths that Absāl's own religion sought to symbolize. That discovery itself is revelatory for Absāl: "The eyes of his heart were unclosed. His mind caught fire. Reason and tradition were at one within him. All the paths of exegesis lay open before him. His old religious puzzlings were solved; all the obscurities clear. Now he had 'a heart to understand'" (Qur'ān 3:7).

Contents

Abbreviations and Short Titles

AJAS	*American Journal of Arabic Studies*
AOS	American Oriental Society
ED	Saadiah Gaon, *K. al-Mukhtār fī 'l-Āmanāt wa-'l-I'tiqādāt,* The Book of Critically Chosen Beliefs and Convictions
EI	*Encyclopedia of Islam*, 2nd edition.
Guide	Maimonides, *Dalālat al-Ḥa'irīn*, The Guide to the Perplexed
Ihya'	Ghazālī, *Iḥyā 'Ulūm al-Dīn*, Reviving the Religious Sciences
IJMES	*International Journal of Middle Eastern Studies*
JAOS	*Journal of the American Oriental Society*
JHP	*Journal of the History of Philosophy*
JPS	Jewish Publication Society
JQR	*Jewish Quarterly Review*
JRAS	*Journal of the Royal Asiatic Society*
JNES	*Journal of Near Eastern Studies*
MEJ	*Middle East Journal*
Mishkāt	Tibrīzī, *Mishkāt al-Masābiḥ*
NE	Aristotle, *Nichomachaean Ethics*
TF	Ghazālī, *Tahāfut al-Falāsifa*, The Incoherence of the Philosophers
TT	Ibn Rushd (Averroes), *Tahāfut al-Tahāfut*, The Incoherence of the Incoherence

ISLAMIC HUMANISM

Introduction

Oppression comes from the heart. It begins in fear and loathing of what one finds within, inclinations too frightening to be acknowledged. Externalized, these unwholesome or unwelcome desires are projected on the mythic other, the depersonalized, dehumanized members of some exotic or rival group. Are such projections the source of racist persecution and religious violence? I doubt that bigotry has a single source. But projection and the denial behind it form one source of its violent energies. The same destructive dynamics are found in every culture. And if we view religions not from the heights for which they reach but from sea level or below, watching the dalliances of their leaders and the actions and reactions of their adherents, we can find the same forces and potentials in every religion. They do not always rise to the surface, but they show their faces and their teeth often enough to give religion itself a bad name.

It's hard to set one's heart on *any* ideal while shaking off fanaticism. Even harder, perhaps, to forge the bonds of group allegiance that sustain a tradition, without invidious reference to a mythic other whose image is exploited to keep insiders centered on what they are about. Just as phonemes are marked by contrasts with fixed alternatives, human groups are often held together by the wires drawn from the sketched figures of those deemed alien, base, wicked, unchaste, or unclean. Such images are not inevitable, but they are handy and can draw the eye in the shrill marketplace of identities and ideals. Religions, like states, need an inner check against such invidious characterizations. Few of us are so fortunate as to be seen in quite the joyous visage that we carry about with us once we have purged the looking glass of all that is unpleasant and assigned the rime and ugliness to those others who are now, ironically, expected to admire us.

Some years ago, when I was teaching in Hawaii, we had a visit from the chairman of a sister department in Pakistan. The visitor was warmly welcomed and invited to speak in the philosophy colloquium and at the East West Center, where the hope was that he would speak for philosophy as practiced in Islamic lands. But this last expectation embarrassed him. He was a tall man, handsome, grey haired, Oxbridge trained. He wore chinos, a blue blazer and a paisley foulard tie. During his stay he confided in me that the discomfort he felt was not confined to this visit. At home too he was hearing requests for Islamic approaches to philosophy. "What do they want from me," he asked when we were alone, "to use the names of Zayd and ʿAmr in my examples instead of Smith and Jones? To open every lecture with a *basmallah*? To teach Shariati and Mawdudi?"

The pressures are not to be made light of. Perhaps in part they expressed a hunger that many Muslims feel for knowledge and appreciation of their own civilization and its all but legendary achievements. Every Western historian knows that between classical antiquity and the modern age, "the Arabs"—Muslim thinkers and scientists, in fact of many backgrounds but most often writing in Arabic—brought to the West a new knowledge of philosophy, mathematics, astronomy, and medicine. But did an Avicenna or an Averroes make any large or lasting original contributions? Or were such figures just a bridge to be crossed and left behind, transmitting, perhaps, a somewhat muddled impression, say, of Aristotle, that remained to be corrected in the Renaissance? Most academics do not know quite how to answer that question, and many Muslims know less. Ethnic pride might press for knowledge, for a heritage, even for answers to life's great questions, from the great names of the past. People may itch for information about exotic cultures, but they also hanker for roots and rootedness. That was an appetite our visitor did not feel quite prepared to meet, not philosophically, although plenty of popularizers and militants seemed more than ready to answer in his stead.

I hazarded a suggestion. Pakistan, after all, has undergone decades of constitutional turmoil in search of a polity that would respect Islamic principles and values. It has not yet found its way to a stable and modern recasting of those ideals. There is contention, of course, over just what it is that modernity legitimately demands—and also, over the authentic content of Islam. Perhaps one of the distinctive marks of modernity is its demand that each of us, as individuals and as members of a community, must decide what to make of our received traditions. One strength of philosophy, and of historical cultural studies, is that explorations in these areas can open up our minds to options and ways of thinking that we have not confronted. We can learn from the intellectual, moral, spiritual, and artistic successes and failures of the past. And we can conceptualize and reconceptualize our own identities in terms that are neither dictated by past achievements and experiments, nor uninformed by them. Facing my colleague's dilemma, it occurred to me that Fārābī in the tenth century confronted a situation in many ways like his own.

A profound encounter with Greek science, logic,[1] and philosophy led Fārābī to see Islam itself as something both alien and intimately familiar—a unique phenomenon, yet part of a class about which generalizations could be framed. Gaining a standpoint that was both shaken and steadied by the awareness of multiple cultural and religious options, and by the ability to conceive many more that spilled beyond the bourne of historical experience, Fārābī could appropriate the received tradition critically. Seeing it with new eyes, he could formulate its teachings in a way that made them cohere with the balance of his understanding. Generalizing, he went on to rough out a philosophy of culture that was pertinent to his historical moment and to moments both earlier and later than his own. Ibn Khaldūn, in his own way, did the same. I asked my visitor what he thought of teaching Fārābī, or Ibn Khaldūn, if not for recipes then for kinship, as partners in a conversation that has never really ended. Both of these men, after all, were social thinkers of world historical stature. Each had addressed the question of an Islamic polity. Fārābī, in particular, had brought to bear a penetrating grasp of logic and metaphysics in his effort to make sense of the religion to which he loyally adhered. My visitor was unversed in the thought of either figure. He was surprised that I imagined medieval thinkers might contribute to social discourse, let alone to metaphysics or epistemology, in the last years of the twentieth century.

Yet the crisis of modernity is not a new phenomenon. The philosophers who wrote in Arabic, the ones we call medieval, called themselves modern (*muta'akhirūn*). They meant by that to express their sense of difference from the ancients. So did many of the Arabic poets, who labored to situate themselves vis à vis an older tradition. They, like all of us, confronted problems of critical appropriation. The past seemed alien to them, but not utterly foreign. There was always something they could cherish as their own, no matter how archaic its words might sound or how far afield its roots might spread. For the poets, that older heritage lived in the pre-Islamic odes. The new poets, those who really were poets, knew that they could not copy the old odes, since theirs was not the experience so vividly reflected in the old nomadic lays. But neither could they ignore the earlier literature, or slight its achievement. For the philosophers, the vista was wider, and the past, glimpsed over one's shoulder, stretched back more deeply. Its landmarks were the writings and sayings of the ancient Greeks and the scriptural verses of the faith. The ideas still spoke to them, but the idiom belonged to another age. Arabic writers could not compose Platonic dialogues, any more than the Romans could. Qur'ānic language too could never be their own. The words were still warm, but no longer molten. The dicta needed to be forged anew if they were to be taken up as implements for living and not just kept as relics of the past, like the campfire embers that the nomad poets had rekindled only in memory.

The moderns could hear and chant Qur'ānic verses, but they could not speak them, not for themselves. Perhaps that helps explain the Muslim idea of the inimitable Qur'ān. To make the scriptural words their own, these medieval moderns needed new ways of understanding the old tropes. They drew aid from the shared experience of other scriptural monotheists. Indeed, if the proper work of translating was done, there were allies to be found even among the ancient Greeks, the old Persians, and writers of Sanskrit. In recognition of their shared ideal, the monotheists called one another *muḥaqqiqūn*, exponents of the truth. For Muslims, Jews, and Christians had the same God, called

Allah in all three faiths. The Arabic word is formed by adding the definite article to the generic term for a deity. It means the one God. For the definite article here has the same force that English speakers assign by capitalizing when the God of monotheism is meant and not some mere object of veneration.

The philosophers and theologians among the *muḥaqqiqūn* borrowed freely from one another's arguments and imageries. They expressed respect for the theological values and concerns that led their rivals, within or outside their own confessions, to conclusions at variance with their own. Differences of language, culture, or belief meant much less to thinkers trying to make monotheistic sense of life and the world than did the affinities that might yield a useful insight. As the work of translation went forward, any reader of Arabic could access the ancient philosophical, scientific, mathematical, geographical, medical, and even historical texts. Thinkers wrote commentaries, critiqued, pirated, and continued one another's works. Their writings pursue a dialogue that continues across the boundaries of language and creed and down the generations.[2]

Was the new work derivative? On the contrary, its relation to the past made it synthetic and creative. The glory days of philosophy in Islam, the rise of great literature, science, and scholarship, the invention of new disciplines and genres, were the days when Islamic civilization and culture were challenged by new ideas. Thinkers pushed themselves to originality, because they were so eagerly assimilating new and often alien materials. Conquest had something to do with that expansive spirit. So did conversion. But there was also conversation. In the Muslim conquest, as in so many others, the conquerors were in some respects the conquered. And converts could hardly forget utterly all that they had once known. So the converts were in some ways the converters.

Unquestionably, the spread of Arabic language and Islamic beliefs and practices followed the routes of conquest and the resulting social, economic, political, and military dominance. But the efflorescence of medieval Islamic culture was not simply a matter of imperial success. It was in small principalities, after all, and not just the vast Islamic empires, that some of the most important advances in the sciences, the humanities, and the arts were achieved. Warfare did bring cultural contacts, in the long struggle with Byzantium, the conquest of Iberia, Iran, and much of India, the engagement with the Crusaders. But trade and travel, dialogue, polemic and apologetic were also broadening. Great conquerors could prove their liberality and petty princes their stature by sponsoring works of history and poetry, philosophy and science. What mattered was the attitude: Knowledge, art, and wisdom were eagerly appropriated, from every source, grasped with all the proprietary zeal of newfound heirs. The constant, among men of learning and their sponsors, if we trace the vitality of Islamic civilization at its most vital, was that eagerness to learn. Decline sets in not just when the floods of conquest reach their highwater mark, but when the tides of interchange subside.

Like all postcolonial peoples, Muslims in general and Arabs in particular look back with pride today on the heady days of their early history. Often they blame the fading of that past not on the optical illusion that imparts a rosy glow to what is all but out of sight, but on foreign domination—as if to say: *our* conquests were great, even godly achievements; *theirs* were brutal, godless acts of aggression. But history reveals more than enough brutality and corruption of motives, more than enough sublimation of worldly aims into sacral crimes, more than enough cruelty, ignorance, and exploitation, to be shared.

If one single factor fostered genuine greatness in the achievements of classical Islamic civilization—in philosophy, in the sciences, in medicine, and in humanity's moral and spiritual quest—that factor was not the military or economic power that fueled and funded the Islamic conquests, nor even the spiritual message that gave them their battle cry. For the religious message was a recasting of ancient monotheistic ideas, and the imperial resources, fiscal, administrative, political, and intellectual, as in any empire, were the resources that the new regime brought under its tent. Rather, what made for greatness—a greatness whose spiritual and intellectual achievements are still appropriable and worthy of appropriation today—was the way in which those resources were integrated, cultivated, put to work. That is, what gave greatness to Islamic civilization in its heyday was its self-confident openness to what was of genuine value in the achievements of predecessors and contemporaries. What makes Islamic culture a lesser presence in the world today is a lesser openness, a loss of confidence, a crabbed defensiveness and chafing chauvinism grounded in insecurity.

There was reaction against the early openness of Islamic culture, suspicion of the exotic, not just for where it came from but for where it might lead. In theology and law, a fear of reason and its potentials for abuse pushed to close down the early openness and stifle the humanistic themes that had marked the birth of these disciplines within Islam. Ramparts were thrown up aiming to fence off a closed community. In Islamic piety there was a fear of the burgeoning traditions of music, the dance, and mysticism—a reaction against decadence, not all of it imagined. In historiography there was a turn toward positivity. Even in philosophy, as the loyal adherents of the Aristotelian and Neoplatonic tradition circled the wagons for defense, there was a turn toward the scholastic, ossifying and desiccating what the would-be philosophers sought to keep alive.

The cultural reaction still goes on. The enemy is now called American or European civilization, or capitalism, or the West. It was concern with this sort of reaction, in part, that sparked the anxiety of my Pakistani colleague, and it was with this sort of reaction in mind that I commended the writings of Fārābī, not as a talisman but as a text preserving the philosophical efforts of a thinker who had faced reaction in his own time and had done some real thinking about the critical appropriation of traditions, Islam in particular. I thought it might do some good for Muslim students to read a little of Fārābī's work.

Why Fārābī in particular? In part, because his reasoning will stun complacency and challenge nostrums. In part, for the same sort of reason that we ask students to read Plato's *Republic*. Fārābī has thought hard about Plato's claim that philosophers must be kings, unless kings can somehow acquire the insight of philosophers (*Republic* V 473D; cf. VI 484D). He welds that idea to Aristotle's related thesis that a person of practical wisdom (*phronesis*) must have not just skill in choosing means conducive to his ends but also wisdom in choosing the right ends. Responding to Aristotle's striking claim that "a man cannot have practical wisdom unless he is good," Fārābī argues that the true legislator is a philosopher. For only a philosopher has the insight to legislate wisely. Imagine saying that not to a class of *madrasa* learners but to university freshmen and sophomores in Karachi or Kabul, who have grown up thinking that politics and wisdom are somehow opposites, that statesmanship is force or cunning, or connections, that worldly wisdom is inevitably selfish or self-serving; and spiritual wisdom, inevitably unworldly and naive—or fanatic. But *madrasa* students are not stupid, although they may be stultified by rote and arbitrary discipline. So imagine teaching Fārābī's views to *madrasa* students too. Why should they be left to imagine that the only laws are those that come from one reading of the Book, enforced and underscored by public beatings of women whose chadors do not hide enough of their bodies or men whose beards do not hide enough of their faces?

Fārābī argues that the true philosopher is a legislator, since legislation in service to the common good is the ultimate fulfillment of the philosopher's role. The philosopher is not an ivory tower recluse but a person of action and counsel. A ruler who lacks philosophy, Fārābī argues, will fail, for want of understanding of the general conditions of human felicity and the particular conditions of felicity in the diverse nations of humanity. A philosopher who does not legislate is an armchair theorist. For how can theory be perfected without implementation? Implementation, we notice, is enmeshed in the particularities of language and culture. So it demands experimentation, and an acknowledgment of change.

A society that makes no use of the philosopher in its midst, Fārābī urges, has only itself to blame. That philosopher remains the rightful *imām* all the same. But a thinker who builds theories in the abstract yet cannot communicate them to the populace and so put them to work, is a false philosopher—not a counterfeit like the one who misses the truth and legislates against the common interest, but an unfulfilled intellectual, who does not harvest the fruits of philosophic insight. We all need to extend what knowledge we have into the governance of our lives. But the philosopher's charge goes further. Having learned the discipline of self-governance, a philosopher fails critically if he fails to effectuate his understanding by introducing it to others "in the measure of their capacity." Such private or armchair philosophers come to regard philosophy itself as useless.[3] With them, in a way, it is.

The philosopher, Fārābī argues, will have all the virtues. For without them he cannot act on his insights. He is the true ruler—prince, thinker, and *imām*.[4] He governs legitimately because the moral and intellectual virtues are united in him, which is the same as to say, because of his capacity to integrate the society he governs, bringing its beliefs and practices into harmony with each other and into line with the demands of goodness and truth. Such a prince "occupies his place by nature and not just by will." His subordinates govern and administer because of their particular virtues and strengths, not simply because they are chosen or have chosen to do so.[5]

To effectuate his insights the prince relies on language and habit. He explains and instructs, using argument but also symbols, which translate pure ideas into images for the benefit of the masses, who do not typically think conceptually (cf. *Republic* VI 494A). He also teaches in a more practical way, aiming at the formation of character, arousing and instilling habits of resolution, discipline, and enthusiasm, which lead individuals to act as though "enraptured," spontaneously performing right actions on the basis of the virtue they have acquired. In the well-ordered society, philosophy and religion support one another in pursuing the common good—philosophy, through concepts; religion, through beliefs: "Wherever philosophy gives an account based on intellectual apprehension or conception, religion gives an account based on imagination. Wherever philosophy uses proof, religion uses persuasion."[6] We can see the staying power of religions here. For persuasion is more flexible than what may look like proof. But notice that the durability of religion rests on the protean character of symbols, their ability to take on new meanings in new contexts.

Symbols, in Fārābī's account, speak for beliefs, and beliefs stand in for ideas in the public mind. Some symbols are universal, but many are best suited to the outlook of a given nation.[7] The same might be said of certain habits and even virtues. Are there habits proper to the training of the philosopher? Indeed there are, since philosophers need all the virtues, above all, the intellectual habit that will enable them to rule.[8] But philosophy is more universal than religion. Its discoveries rise above local symbolism.

Adapting Aristotle's remarks about the natural supremacy of the civilized, Fārābī claims that a legitimate ruler will have military as well as pacific virtues.[9] Indeed Fārābī justifies aggressive warfare "to conquer nations and cities that do not submit to doing what will give them the happiness man is made to acquire. . . . The warrior who pursues this purpose is the just warrior, and the warfare that pursues this purpose is just and virtuous warfare."[10]

One of the detriments of the Platonic and Aristotelian insistence on preferring objective to subjective happiness is that it becomes possible, as in that last argument, to infer that felicity can be forced on human beings. Fārābī sees an analogy here with parental responsibility. But, unlike our liberal tradition, he argues that a ruler's responsibility for forming the characters of his subjects (and potential subjects!) must be greater, not less than a parent's in forming the character of his children.[11]

Yet the argument does not entail, indeed does not allow mere military self-assertion: It justifies offensive warfare, but only in behalf of civilizing ends. So it covers the institution of *jihād* in a generic way, just as Aristotle justified the institution of slavery in a generic way. It allows, even promotes "civilizing" wars—not just by one's own group! But it excludes wars that are only nominally or notionally fought in behalf of a civilizing mission. Fārābī's own forebears came into the Islamic fold through Islamic wars. But our university and *madrasa* students might have some hard questions to ask themselves and one another about the borderline between civilizing and exploiting or enslaving others, and about the shadowy area in intent and consequence that falls between a civilizing mission and a chauvinist or imperialist adventure. Standing guard at the gateway to that shadowland is a principle often less honored in practice than in the breach, the Qur'ānic (2:256) principle of "no compulsion in faith." Fārābī's argument allows for ethos-forming institutions, but not for the enforcement of dogmas. The acceptance of ideas depends entirely on demonstration or persuasion.[12]

Laws and symbol systems, Fārābī argues, will vary in appeal and effectiveness over time. Some have immediate value, some are of only temporary worth, some should be recorded for posterity. The best can guide nations without much change of goal, "except over long periods."[13] Fārābī stops short of assigning permanence to any mere institution or set of words, as distinguished from the underlying ideas. The reason for this striking qualification to the Islamic doctrine of the eternity of the Qur'ān is plain: Aristotle had traced laws to the work of practical wisdom and intelligence (*NE* X 9, 1180a 22), but Fārābī sees practical wisdom at work in concrete situations. Laws are far more general. For situations are unique. But laws are also far more particular than their backgrounding principles. Legislation is the work of imagination, and therefore mutable.

Fārābī departs strikingly from Plato (*Republic* VII 519E) in holding that leadership is not a sacrifice but a fulfillment for the philosopher. Without it, he is frustrated, debarred of *philosophical* fulfillment.[14] Rhetorical persuasion and social legislation are proper work for philosophers, and the poetry that Plato both feared and praised for its power over the human heart can be found doing its persuasive work in scripture. Religion, Fārābī explains, is founded on similitudes, imagery that bodies forth the unseen in sensory metaphors. Religion symbolizes the ultimate realities—God and the incorporeal beings that mediate between God and nature—as political figures, their actions as edicts. The ontic hierarchy is painted in images of rank and order, spatial position or temporal precedence. The powers of nature are drawn as though they were human faculties. Prime matter is water or the abyss, nothingness is darkness. Happiness is pictured in the images that enliven the dreams of the vulgar.[15]

Finding an enduring worth in Fārābī's account of culture and religion does not mean somehow putting on Fārābī's fur hat and Central Asian cloak or trying to dance to the music he is said, in legend, to have loved and played so well.[16] No one, I trust, will rush from a reading of Fārābī to a campaign for philosophical monarchy. But the idea of the philosopher king remains a powerful tool of analysis, because it raises to high relief the core questions of political legitimation. Is it judgment or lineage, faith or philosophy, gender or education, wealth or insight that legitimates authority?

There are questions to be raised about Fārābī himself, of course. He knew that religious discourse can be projective. But the same thought might be turned upon his own philosophical constructions. Don't Fārābī's cosmic hypostases, with their delegated powers, reflect the feudal hierarchy of rule and fealty just as much as the panoply of angels whose order he sought to explain? Aren't Fārābī's spheres and the disembodied minds that steer them also a projection? And doesn't Fārābī's political thinking, like Aristotle's, gain some of its sense of drama from a tension between critique and glorification? When Fārābī calls the philosopher the *imām* and legislator, he can mean that the thinker is the rightful ruler. For he does treat all others as usurpers, as if to imply a radical, Platonic critique of all political institutions that fall short of true philosophy. Or is Fārābī suggesting that the mere possession of effective authority somehow legitimates a legislative role, since all political effectiveness presumes a philosophic base? Is Fārābī's theory no more than a gussied up version of the divine right of kings? Is that what is meant by saying that the prince and all his officers hold sway by nature and not simply by will? For most of his life Fārābī did not serve at the courts of princes, but he did end his days at the Ḥamdānid court of Sayf al-Dawla (d. 967) in Aleppo. To what extent must we discount his words as the same sort of tribute that a poet like Mutanabbī paid to that aggressive and rapacious prince?

The ambivalence of conceptual radicalism and the ambiguity of its dicta about actual regimes run all the way back to the Sophists. For Thrasymachus can turn his notion that justice is the interest of the stronger to either side of an argument about the status quo. He can make of it a radical critique of self-serving by the powers that be. Or he can transform it into a Machiavellian rationale for whatever anyone has the power to do. Even moderate thinkers like Aristotle and Locke drink from both sides of the cup, legitimating authority by its power but cautioning would be tyrants with a Platonic warning, that power abused tends to its own ruin. More radical thinkers, like Hobbes or Hegel, sometimes grow tipsy on the ambivalence latent in their radicalism. They seem at once to justify more earnestly and warn more gravely than their moderate counterparts. In the most radical–a Mao or Mussolini, Lenin or Gentile–the ambivalence becomes schizoid, tolerating and justifying everything and nothing.

Fārābī participates in one of the more moderate forms of this ambivalence. He is not the philosopher to resolve it.[17] Yet just because he sees Islamic institutions like *jihād* and the Qur'ān itself through eyes that have read Plato and Aristotle, his efforts at critical appropriation grow far more perceptive and valuable than they would be had he cleaved more closely to the mold framed by our cultural relativists and studied the institutions of his day from within, not departing from the repertoire of categories they seem to generate. We cannot assign Aristotle or Plato any absolute edge on objectivity, as if their prejudices amounted to reason and the reasonings of others, outside their ambit, were mere prejudices. It is the power of Socratic analysis, Platonic dialectic, and Aristotelian logic that makes Greek thinking no longer merely Greek but universal; and it is through that universality that we can expose even Greek prejudices as prejudices. Yet alien assumptions can cast a clearer and sharper light than local sources alone. Qur'ānic imagery can be both grasped and weighed when it is recognized as imagery. It can only be marveled at when confined to its own terms. *Jihād* can be assayed globally and concretely when its rationale is voiced conceptually. Otherwise, it remains opaque.

My colleague from Pakistan mentioned Mawdudi and Shariati. The contrast of a philosopher like Fārābī with an ideologue like Mawdudi (ca. 1903–1979) shows just what opacity means here. The founding amīr of the *Jamāʿat-i-Islāmī*, the movement that battled to make Pakistan an Islamic state, Mawdudi was a man in reaction to what he saw as the decadence and febrility of the West: liberalism, secularism, humanism. He did study the texts of Ibn Khaldūn, but what he drew from that well was not a way of thinking critically about history but an affinity for the ways in which religion might be used to weld a more powerful and wider-reaching political bond than mere kinship or ethnicity could forge.[18]

Seeking to reaffirm the sovereignty of God in an all-embracing *Sharīʿa*, Mawdudi campaigned for delegation of "all administrative matters and all questions about which no explicit injunction is to be found in the *Sharia*" to "the consensus among the Muslims . . . capable and qualified to give a sound opinion on matters of Islamic law."[19] This is not the place to weigh Mawdudi's rationales for a polity that would make nonparticipatory citizens of all *dhimmīs*. Nor can we explore here his notion that clericalism is the purest democracy–or that the state exists to execute God's will. What matters here is that Mawdudi has left that will opaque to analysis, and all accredited expressions of it opaque to critique.

In Fārābī's frame of discourse reason has opened up a space for critical thinking. One can ask about the meaning of Qur'ānic symbols and their adequacy in representing what they portend. One can ask about the legitimacy of any campaign that purports to strive in the path of God. Alien categories call forth a deliberative and speculative objectifying of what is received or proposed. Critical appropriation is possible because rejection is possible in principle and reinterpretation is invited in practice, allowing the received to be made over and made one's own. Confining the same symbols and institutions within their own terms brackets them within the bonds of referential opacity and renders them ultimately inscrutable. They may be embraced or rejected, but only impulse remains to judge.

If Muslims today should read Fārābī, it is not because he is "their own"—as though Muslims can fathom only what issues from their own "world." Rather, they should study Fārābī because he brings to seemingly familiar experiences and institutions an outlook foreign enough to cross-light well worn habits and ideas, giving even the familiar a somewhat exotic appearance. But that makes critical consciousness possible, and critical consciousness makes the habitual and familiar actively appropriable.

Compare the work of Ali Shariati (1933–1977), the outspoken lay forerunner of the Iranian revolution.[20] Shariati does not speak from the common identity of the *muḥaqqiqūn*. A student of the romanticizing orientalist Louis

Massignon and of Franz Fanon, whose *Wretched of the Earth* he translated into Farsi, Shariati naturalized his teachers' socialist ideals by projecting them on a gilded Shīʿite past.[21] Islam, he finds, gave the monotheistic idea of *tawḥīd*, a new "degree of signification," indeed, a new meaning. That turns Fārābī on his head: Ideals change, but symbols are eternal. We are not told how what is contextualized and articulated in a single idiom and framework somehow becomes more universal than the values it expresses. But the thrust becomes clear when the new meaning of monotheism is spelled out: It "gives man certainty and a sense of security and inner tranquility; it also makes him responsible for the welfare of his own self and the society in which he lives . . . *tawḥīd* embodies all the manifestations of religious faith in the spiritual as well as material life of man." It eliminates greed, fear, ignorance, the causes of all corruption, distortion, and immorality.[22] This is not a critical or receptive response to religious teachings but an anodyne proffered, along with an attempt to shape the content of faith by touching all the bases, promising attention to all needs, moral, spiritual, material, individual, and social: "Thus Shariati points out that when he takes the question of belief in One God seriously, it is not in order to engage in theological or philosophical argument about it; more correctly, it is an attempt to comprehend the spirit of history and existing sentiments regarding this affirmation in every age."[23]

Yet Shariati's historicism is not quite as catholic as, say, Condorcet's. He is the enemy of the akhunds, the popular preachers of Iran, if they were tools of the colonialists; and he is the enemy of all Safavid history, although it was the Safavid, dervish dynasty, beginning with their rise to power in 1500, that made Iran so thoroughly a Shīʿite country as it is today. Like Mawdudi, Shariati sets up a small patch of sacred history soon after the Prophet's death, as a screen on which to project his social ideal. For Mawdudi this is the reign of the four *rāshidūn* caliphs; for Shariati, it is the regime of ʿAlī and his immediate descendants and followers. Patrice Lumumba enters the pantheon of martyrs, but many a Sunni saint cannot.

When we consider Avicenna in chapter 3, we will see how his engagement in the sort of disciplined inquiry that Shariati seems inclined to dismiss as mere logic chopping aims directly for the heart of what monotheists mean when they affirm God's absoluteness. Avicenna binds together core ideas of scriptural monotheism with the rationalism he imbibes as an active philosopher and scientist. Shariati, by contrast, seeks the bedrock of authenticity in "the spirit of history" but fails to make contact with a fellow Persian of less than fifty generations past and reduces the living faith of his countrymen to a kind of cosmic security blanket, answering to the needs of all constituencies, sacred or profane.

One more twentieth-century thinker might be mentioned here. Sayyid Quṭb (1906–1966) was a leader of the Muslim Brotherhood in Egypt. His writings, including a widely circulated and much excerpted thirty-volume commentary to the Qur'ān, have touched Muslims throughout the world. Like Mawdudi, whose work deeply affected him, and like Shariati, whom he influenced in turn, Quṭb fails to rise above ideology. He does not draw from his own heritage that intellectual scope and catholicity of spirit that Ghazālī says made him "thirst from an early age to apprehend the true natures of things" and scorn to rely on blind faith in authority (*taqlīd*).[24]

Like Fārābī, Quṭb was very much a political writer. Unlike Avicenna he never held high state office. His program for the Muslim *umma* was formed not by conceptual desiderata but largely by reaction to the British posture in the Middle East in World War II, by a hankering for a rotogravure past, and by the culture shock of a stay in the United States in 1948–50. He wrote with horror of the influence of Darwin, Freud, Marx, and the Kinsey Report. He told of a church dance he had witnessed in Greeley, Colorado: "Every young man took the hand of a young woman. And these were the young men and women who had just been singing their hymns! Red and blue lights with only a few white lamps, illuminated the dance floor. The room became a confusion of feet and legs: arms twisted around hips, lips met lips, chests pressed together."[25] The widespread American support for the establishment of the state of Israel was just one more sign that the West was lost. Quṭb took refuge in Islam from his early faith in secular nationalism, joining the Muslim Brotherhood around 1951. Close to the Free Officers whose coup brought Gamal Abdel Nasser to power in Egypt in 1952, Quṭb broke with the junta over their secular bent. After several bouts of imprisonment, he stridently charged all Muslim societies with being not Islamic at all but *jāhilī*—because they were Westernized: "This is the most dangerous *jāhiliyya* which has ever menaced our faith. For everything around is *jāhiliyya*: perceptions and beliefs, manners and morals, culture, art and literature, laws and regulations, including a good part of what we consider Islamic culture."[26] As Emmanuel Sivan and Bernard Haykel have shown, it was Rashid Rida and Mawdudi who framed the equation of Western culture with the pre-Islamic barbarous age, the *Jāhiliyya*. Sayyid Quṭb made the inference to action: Secular Muslim nationalists were apostates, liable, in principle, to the death penalty. Charged with treason and with plots to assassinate Nasser and stage a coup d'etat, Quṭb was executed in 1966.

Mawdudi had worked as a journalist, but Quṭb began as a poet and literary critic. What the two men had in common was their militant vision of Islam. Ghazālī too, to name just one thinker of the classic age, saw in Islam an all-embracing way of life. But Quṭb's Islam was not the lambent faith of a Ghazālī, who took absolute trust in God to be the highest expression of surrender to God's will.[27] Ghazālī argued, against Aristotle, that there is no proper mean in pride. Utter humility is the optimum for man. But Quṭb replaces that outlook with a truculent triumphalism that appeals to Western guilt over colonialism, even as it demands worldly rule:

> Truth and falsehood cannot coexist on earth. When Islam makes a general declaration to establish the lordship of God on earth and to liberate humanity from the worship of other creatures, it is contested by those who have usurped God's sovereignty on earth. They will never make peace. Then [Islam] goes forth destroying them to free humans from their power . . . the liberating struggle of jihad does not cease until all religion belongs to God.[28]

Quṭb's political use of religious ideas has been compared to Latin American and Afro-American liberation theology.[29] The rhetoric is familiar, but the affirmation that God's enemies will never make peace is a theological and juridical warrant for perpetual *jihād*, and the claims made in the name of that *jihād* are distinctive in their totalitarianism. Quṭb, like Mawdudi, holds all human sovereignty to be usurped. Of Islam, Quṭb writes:

> This religion is a universal declaration of human liberation on earth from bondage to other men or to human desires. . . . To declare God's sovereignty means comprehensive revolution against human governance in all its perceptions, forms, systems and conditions and total defiance against every condition on earth in which humans are sovereign. . . . This declaration means the extraction of God's usurped sovereignty and its restoration to Him.[30]

Yet the faithful are qualified to exercise God's sovereignty over their fellow humans. The Sufi idea that the great *jihād* is a fight for self-mastery drops out of sight. So does the worry of the Ikhwān al-Ṣafā'[31] that religion is debased and corrupted by subordination to what they call its younger sibling, politics. The Qur'ān does proclaim that there is no compulsion in religion, but Quṭb wrings a qualification to this categorical safeguard, from the obligation to combat those who oppose the way of Islam. This he takes to mean that the mission of Islam is the destruction of all secular authority. All who actively resist Islamic dominance—by legislating, for example—must be brought down. The notion is a harbinger of Osama bin Laden's thinking[32]

Are such theocratic claims common to all monotheistic faiths? Christianity, despite the temptations of triumphalism, preserves its early fear of secular power and relegates to Caesar that which is Caesar's. The Hebrew Bible asks its hearers to love God with all their hearts, all their souls, and all their might. But it also insists that the law is here on earth, not in heaven or across the sea. It must be interpreted and appropriated as human hearts and minds direct.[33] And Rabbinic doctrine holds that the law, even of an alien or secular state, is law.

Nor does Islam, despite its many epochs of aggressive militancy, universally see itself as engaged in a struggle for world domination. Abdulaziz Sachedina cites the caliph ʿUmar's acceptance of Arab Christians within the Muslim *umma* as an early precedent for religious pluralism in Islamic communities.[34] He interprets the Islamic concept of the *fiṭra*, or underlying human nature, as an endorsement of the view that all humans have a basic moral sense that grounds the dignity with which we are endowed from the creation, as taught in the Qur'ān. On this basis, Sachedina argues for toleration and intercommunal respect as Islamic norms well grounded in the principles of the *Sharīʿa*. Normative Islam, he argues, can authorize no public sanctions in matters of faith and spirituality. Civil and criminal penalties come into play only in the realm of interpersonal obligations, where practical matters legitimately pertain to public policy. But, as Salman Rushdie writes, "The restoration of religion to the realm of the personal, its depoliticization, is the nettle that all Muslim societies must grasp in order to become modern."[35]

Reactions against fatalism and against the modern panaceas of socialism and ultranationalism, Sachedina urges, along with xenophobic responses to European colonialism, have provoked a tunnel-vision version of Islam that excludes the mechanisms of toleration needed in the framing of a civil society. Demagogues sensitive to the impact of such reactions, he argues, have marketed and commoditized the faith, transforming it into a sheer militancy, exampled, in the extreme, in the devastation wrought by Islamic suicide bombers, the foot soldiers and cannon fodder of bin Laden's universal *jihād*. The September 11, 2001, attack on the World Trade Center and the Pentagon was an outgrowth of such extremism, and, we might add, an effort to pander to it and further inflame it. In Sachedina's eyes, for this reason, the terroristic attack had another victim beyond the innocent thousands who were killed and injured. It was an assault on Islam, by assailants who dared to arrogate to themselves the judgment that belongs to God alone.

There is a Muslim institution of *jihād*. Like many institutions from the past, it stands much in need of rethinking in the present age. Thus Fazlur Rahman wrote: It is historically unacceptable, as some modern Muslim apologists have done, to pretend that the expansionist *jihād* of early Islam was purely defensive. Yet "it is only the fanatic Khārijites who have declared *jihād* to be one of the 'pillars of the Faith'":

> Other schools have played it down for the obvious reason that the expansion of Islam had already occurred much too swiftly in proportion to the internal consolidation of the Community in the Faith. Every virile and expansive ideology has, at a stage, to ask itself the question as to what are its terms of coexistence, if any, with other systems, and how far it may employ methods of direct expansion. In our own age, Communism, in its Russian and Chinese versions, is faced with the same problems and choices.[36]

To acknowledge that there may be spatial or temporal boundaries even to Islam is to recognize the distinction between generic *islām*, service to God's will, and institutional Islam, a culturally concrete way of articulating such service. It is to recognize that there are limits in all human articulations of values, no matter how universal the underlying ideas. It is to recognize, with Fārābī, that not every system is ideally suited for every people and environment. That is an admission that Sayyid Quṭb and his present day followers are not prepared to make: Unless all power is subordinate to Islam, Quṭb held, the legitimacy and authenticity of God's revelation has been affronted–indeed, impaired.

Ghazālī's celebrated critique of causality, like Quṭb's polemic in behalf of Islam, is an affirmation of divine sovereignty, meant to liberate the human spirit from dependence on all things less than God. Like Quṭb, Ghazālī finds a practical significance in this theme. But that does not add up simply to a demand for hegemony. Ghazālī is far more interested in the spiritual and moral struggle for self-conquest than in the worldly struggle for dominion–even in the name of his own faith. One who fully recognizes God's sovereignty, by Ghazālī's lights, is one whose hope and fear rest in none but God, who has risen above dependency on earthly things. Such a person has achieved the true reliance upon God (*tawakkul*) that is the practical expression of the highest form of monotheism, that sees God in all things.

Seeing God in all things need not mean denial of the reality of things distinct from God. For human beings are distinct from one another and from God, Ghazālī argues, by the differences in their histories and the contents of their minds. Nor does this ultimate phase of monotheism exclude the efficacy of proximate causes. Ghazālī denies only their necessity. He preserves what matters spiritually and metaphysically in the Islamic discontent with proximate causes not by denying that winds blow across the seas or that ships sail upon them. That would be to deny the Qur'ān's appreciation (2:164, 14:32, 16:14) of God's bounty in providing the seas for navigation. What Ghazālī affirms is simply the dependence of all causes upon God. Proximate causes act not by a power of their own but by a borrowed power. That is what the Qur'ān itself said (17:66, 22:65) of the sailing of ships upon the seas. To deny the work of wind or waves would trivialize God's act within them. To negate the moral personhood or spiritual subjecthood of others, we must add, is the same affront, as Ghazālī recognizes when he lays out the rights and duties attendant on spiritual brotherhood and friendship.[37] Ghazālī does not deny the action of the pen or the hand that moves it, but only that they act alone. What radical monotheism calls for, he reasons, is that we affirm, as he does, following the Neoplatonists, that the powers and strengths, characters and dispositions of things come to them from Above.[38] If such claims issue an imperative, its chief force for Ghazālī, is upon the self, as a command to seek self-mastery and self-perfection. In regard to others, we may infer, it authentically evokes only the imperative to recognize their God-given subjecthood.

The morally sensitive person is not the one who feels his own injuries most sharply and voices his own grievances most tellingly but the one whose sensibilities are most catholic and who is most able to conceive and articulate the joys and pains of all, himself included, in a system of mutual recognitions and respect. Similarly, it is a distinctive feature of world religions, of which Islam is surely one, that they relate their adherents not only to the natural cosmos but also to a social world in which their own constructions–their customs, rituals, myths, and narratives, even legislative systems–have a part, but not the only part. The distinctive feature of a sect is that its claims but not its sensibilities are universal.

Quṭb's perverse articulation of the idea of liberation, which seeks to impose on others what he and his followers would feel as oppression if others imposed its counterpart on them, lacks that elemental tact which is the root of the ethical teaching in Islam, as in all world religions worthy of the name. Quṭb casts Islam in the role of a sect or faction, untrue to its founding prophetic spirit. The rhetoric is Muslim, but the intentions are all too transparent, and all too human. For, contrary to Shariati's premise, it is not words or symbols but ideas and values that are universal—as Fārābī, among other Muslim thinkers, clearly and cogently proposed.

When I sat down to write this introduction, the Ṭālibān rulers of Afghanistan had begun to fire rockets and artillery to destroy the monumental Buddhas of Bamiyan. These figures in stone had overlooked a valley in the Hindu Kush for well over a thousand years. The smaller of the two, some 115 feet high, dated from the later third century. The larger, from the fifth or sixth century, rose to over 170 feet. Both works predated the founding of Islam. Both were emblems of the Buddhist ideals of their makers, but also of cultural fusion: The elder, in its style, bore the legacy of the conquests of Alexander, who built a city at Kandahar, where the Ṭālibān began and ended their own conquests of the land. The younger was a scaling up of an Indian Buddha. The two works were precursors of the Buddhist colossi of China and Japan. Before this book reached its readers, these ancient deep reliefs were dust. Their destruction was among the final boasts of the regime of Mullah Muḥammad Omar, which banned women from almost all nondomestic working roles, cast a veil of repression across one of the proudest and fiercest lands on earth, and cowed or coopted many of the same people who stood tall not so many years ago against the seeming invincibility of the Soviet Union.

The Ṭālibān obliterated images throughout Afghanistan. Their culture minister strode through the museum of Kabul, shattering the relics of an ancient heritage. The destruction extended to the ruins of Ai-Khanum, where archeologists had discovered Greek statuary and inscriptions of Delphic wisdom transcribed by colonists in the Hellenistic age. The delicate stuccos of Hadda were smashed. So were the seventh century life-sized images of a king and queen from Fundukistan. The statue of Kanishka, the long dead Kushan ruler, from Surkh Kotal; coins bearing the profiles of Bactrian kings; murals from the Islamic period that adorned the pleasure palaces of Maḥmūd of Ghaznā; hunting scenes from the palace of Masʿūd III; a Ghaznavid copper dish adorned with mythical creatures and Qurʾānic verses–all these were marked methodically for destruction. Irreplaceable artworks were spirited away, purloined or protected. The fate of many is unknown.[39]

As the national army of Afghanistan set about its work of destruction, looters and smugglers of art began to look almost like rescuers. Crowing over the demolition at Bamiyan, the Ṭālibān culture minister pronounced: "It is easier to destroy than to build." That simple truth, once stated with sardonic discontent by John Steinbeck, now proved prophetic, even monitory: "The statues are objects only made of mud or stone," lovers of art and others who cherished the monuments of history, were told.[40] Even as the destruction went forward, Osama bin Laden was disseminating his own message and his visage throughout the world, using videotapes that were somehow exempt from the anxiety about, say, the royal images preserved on ancient Bactrian coins. And the leaders of al-Qāʾida, under the protection of the Ṭālibān, were setting living targets in their sights and plotting the coordinates of loftier monuments.

The intense fury and impatient publicity of the Ṭālibān attack on cultural treasures that were theirs to preserve revealed clearly that more than mud and stone was at stake in the eyes of the attackers. With the help of hindsight, we can now see that the shelling and smashing of sandstone in March 2001 was the *Kristallnacht* of the Ṭālibān. The smashed images were emblems of vanquished faiths and lost civilizations. But they were emblems of humanity as well. Their destruction was a lashing out in anger. In theory, the very existence of these images in stone was a desecration of the human image and thus an affront to God. But, as the midrash asks, can one deface the king's coinage without an affront to the king? The images targeted stood for our common humanity, and when spring had changed to fall, humanity itself became the target, on a more global scale.

Muhammad Omar, the Ṭālibān leader, had laid claim to the caliphal title *Amīr al-Mu'minīn,* Commander of the Faithful. He had made himself a hero by doing battle with the Soviets and suppressing the warlords who contended with one another in their wake. Now, in April 1996, Muḥammad Omar had boldly grasped an ancient cloak thought by his countrymen to have belonged to the Prophet and displayed it to a crowd in Kandahar that trembled at the sight.[41] He was literally claiming the mantle of the Prophet. In that same month Osama bin Laden returned to Afghanistan, an exile from Arabia and Sudan. Flattering the pretensions of the newly ascendant Afghan leader, he swore allegiance to Muḥammad Omar as his caliph, the legitimate guardian of the holy cities of Mecca and Medina and rightful ruler of Muslims throughout the world. Even other Muslim theocrats were his enemies. But neo-Nazis in America, Basque terrorists in Spain, IRA killers in Great Britain could be allies. The Muslims of Indonesia, China, Bosnia, and the Philippines were called to fall in line behind their new leader, or fall before him. Just as the Ṭālibān fighters and their Qā'ida confederates and shock troops had broken the seeming invincibility of the Soviet Union, their cohorts had bloodied the United States in Senegal, bombed American embassies in Africa, and sunk the USS Cole in Yemen. Recovery of Jerusalem, first conquered by Arab armies in 638, was an interim aim of the rising new power. Beyond that lay destruction of the State of Israel, which had set history running backwards, rolling back the Islamic tide. But ultimately, the aim was not regional or local. The new *jihād* would be global. And only notionally would it be fought as a war of liberation.

Muslim militants can trace their frustrations with history to an era long before the founding of Israel or the heyday of European colonialism. Nor are the grievances of a revanchist movement like that of the Ṭālibān confined to issues of national sovereignty, affirmed as a universal principle in the face of imperialistic aggression. For Islamic imperialism is still celebrated as a moment of triumph, now lost to treachery or internal weakness and lack of resolve, a moment whose recapture is desperately grasped after. As Cantwell Smith explained years ago:

> If one truth of earthly Islam is that its programme worked for a time well, another is that it was only for a time. As others of man's civilizations have done across the centuries, the Arab civilization rose, flourished for a period—and declined. The fall of Baghdad in 1258 marks the formal end of the once tremendously successful Arab empire. The Mongol invasions that fall epitomizes certainly dealt the Arab world a devastating blow. Many millions were killed;

> whole areas were laid utterly waste; and political rule in the centre of the Muslim world passed into the hands of barbarian infidels. Yet the date is but a symbol. Arab culture flourished for another two centuries and more in areas unravaged by the Mongols, notably Cairo and Spain. On the other hand, it can be argued that the conquest gave the *coup de grâce* to a civilization already past its prime.[42]

For the Arab kingdom had ceased to be Arab in any strict sense, in demography, culture, or leadership, long before the Mongol conquests. The ʿAbbasid caliphs of Baghdad had been creatures of their Turkic solidiery and majordomos for over three hundred years before Genghis Khan's grandson Hulagu laid waste the city. And medieval Muslim historians, as we shall see, could trace the falling away from the pristine ideals of an Islamic polity all the way back to the origins of the Islamic state, in compromises made not only by Muḥammad's successors but by the Prophet himself, as he sought to forge a state from the airy substance of his revelations.[43]

Nor was all lost. The Mongols themselves were Islamized in time–in fifty years in the Islamic lands–just as China bent them to the ways of its ancient civilization. And Islamic culture did grow and flourish, change and adapt, despite the internecine dynastic struggles; the poverty and inflation, plague, drought, and famine; political and moral corruption; and yes, foreign incursions and defeats that were so much at odds with the once triumphal vision of the past and yet more triumphal expectations for the future. But sacred history seemed to make that past a living reproof to the present and a call to arms in behalf of a proud new future.

Sayyid Quṭb equated his struggle against Nasser with Ibn Taymiyya's thirteenth century call to arms against the Mongols. And, like Ibn Taymiyya, he saw the remedy to the evils of his times in forceful and forcible resistance, not just against external foes but against internal laxity, permissiveness, moral weakness, spiritual compromise. As Cantwell Smith sums it up:

> The fundamental *malaise* of modern Islam is a sense that something has gone wrong with Islamic history. The fundamental problem of modern Muslims is how to rehabilitate that history: to set it going again in full vigour, so that Islamic society may once again flourish as a divinely guided society should and must. The fundamental spiritual crisis of Islam in the twentieth century stems from an awareness that something is awry between the religion which God has appointed and the historical development of the world which he controls.[44]

To spirits like Quṭb's it seemed plain that what was needed was militancy and mobilization for the faith. As the twentieth century gave way to the twenty-first, Osama and the cutthroats of al-Qāʾida took that message to heart and laid their plans to take back the flow of history and restore it to the channels in which God so clearly intended it to flow. The new tactic was to unite Muslims in enmity not just against Israel or their own too-secular regimes but by finding a more formidable common foe in the United States. Any defeat of that Great Satan, they reasoned, would bring pride and new power to Islam. The *mujāhidīn*, purified of the alien dross that had polluted and confounded their minds, would bring America to its knees and drive a stake through the heart of the beast that spewed forth so much corruption. Many infidels would be slain, and victory would win over many souls, finally ending the contretemps that had allowed the West to seem the model of modernity and pattern of civilization. The stationing of American troops in Arabia—women among them—exposed the Saudi monarchy as unfit defenders of the holy places and unworthy beneficiaries of oil wealth. But it also exposed the United States as an invader, thus a rightful target of *jihād*. Dreams of air crashes among cohorts not yet privy to the details of bin Laden's plans were proof from heaven that al-Qā'ida's murderous scheme was favored by God. It was the execution of His will.

Among the militants' allies was Sheikh Omar ʿAbd al-Raḥmān, the blind Egyptian cleric convicted in the 1993 plot to bring down the World Trade Center. That attack would have created some fifty thousand casualties, had the truck bomb left in the building's garage done its worst. Al-Qā'ida, well financed and well manned by a global network of support, was the force to finish the job. Under its umbrella, Osama bin Laden brought together militant Islamist cells and movements in sixty countries. The leader of the Egyptian Islamic Jihād, which had compassed the assassination of Anwar Sadat, now stood at bin Laden's side. Egypt had been subtly turned by that assassination. But nothing seemed to arouse or disrupt the stolid United States. Planes were hijacked, bombed, ditched. The beast just flicked its tail, flung a few cruise missiles, bargained with Lybia for an operative or two, opened inquiries. The United States might be stunned momentarily, but it was not dismayed. It was hardly aware of the *jihād*. Long focused on its Soviet adversary, America seemed barely to notice the manhood of Islam. Training, dedication, religious zeal, planning, even where purity might falter, would correct all that. Islam needed young men, skilled, willing to die. The United States would be reduced. Its mighty economy would spin out of control, its populace would grieve and tremble, its military would be bruised and baffled, its judges would stumble amongst their law books, its polity would fall in upon itself in a screeching babble of mutual recriminations. God's rule and plan would be manifest once again, and His name would be exalted.

The purist slogans and puritan demands of the Ṭālibān, then, masked a more worldly and a deadlier quest. The name denotes seekers, students, seminarians. It connotes a quest for truth that is the goal of any sincere Muslim. But hidden within the spiritual goal was a lust for power, and a bloodlust that sanctified itself with the name of God and veiled itself with the vision of everything holy. The *jihād* of the Ṭālibān would reach beyond iconoclasm. Their assertions of power, their anger and externalization of all that they found hateful within would reach beyond domestic repression. With an appetite for worldly domination whetted by blood in the anti-Soviet campaign, the Ṭālibān alliance with al-Qā'ida plotted out a goal so megalomaniacal and far fetched that it was hardly credited even by those who stood in the cross hairs. But the aims seemed credible to those who set them forth. For they were promulgated in the name of the Sovereign of the Universe, whose grace had favored the early conquests of Islam. God Himself would succor and second the murderous schemes framed in the name of His compassion.

Islam is no mere cover here. The quest is sincere. But the name of Islam is sullied; and the idea it stands for tainted by the motives of the fighters who have stood to defend its honor and glory. Their intent is saturated with anger, hatred, and sublimated doubts and fears. The malaise Cantwell Smith spoke of, arising from the sense that history has gone wrong, has found an answer in the claim that only bloodshed can restore control of history to the God of history. And that perception creates a peculiar political dynamic in the lands of Islam. In the West, revulsion with the wars of religion gave birth to liberalism and the ideals of a secular commonwealth, open society, and pluralistic comity. Extreme positions have come to seem marginal, heretical. Moderation is deemed safe, stable, and stabilizing. Hence the idea of a lunatic fringe: Extremes are irresponsible, even crazy, not normative, not even normal–hardly likely to attract a mass following. But in Islamic lands the sense that something has been lost to Islam that needs to be restored has given mass appeal to extreme claims. So Islamic revolutions, all the way back to the first such movements, have made restorative and even apocalyptic claims. Their mass appeal has grown not just from frustration, deprivation, or defeat, but from a sense of guilt or shame, transmuted into blame and anger and alloyed with a resolve to be (or find) God's chosen instrument in setting the world to rights and restoring the honor and supremacy of Islam.

Muslims today face a choice—a host of choices, in fact—among rival and competing understandings of Islam. Apologists will repeat the nostrum that the very word Islam means submission to the will of God. Its connotations, they remind us, are those of peace. For the word is cognate with the Arabic *salaam*, and the Hebrew *shalom*. But is submission to the will of God to mean a spiritual acceptance freely chosen? Or is peace here to be a peace imposed? In speaking or thinking of the will of God, are Muslims to understand that will in worldly terms, as a matter of the world's domination by those who are chosen, or who choose themselves as God's earthly instruments? Do those who struggle for God's kingdom on earth pursue the kingdom rather than the God whose will they profess, and too readily forget that the kingdom God chose, in giving freedom to His creation, was sovereignty over those who choose their own way, not dominion over the coerced or intimidated?

One side of the choice facing Muslims throughout the world today is all too familiar from the daily headlines. It is the Islam of the Ṭālibān and al-Qāʾida, the Islam of hands severed for theft,[45] adulterers stoned, prostitutes shot, homosexuals crushed under bulldozed walls. It is the Islam that promotes genital mutilation of Muslim girls, condones slavery in Africa, and foments the persecution of non-Muslims from Egypt to Indonesia and the Philippines. It is the Islam of Ayatollah Khomeini that put a price on Salman Rushdie's head for the writing of a novel. And it is the Islam that demands suppression of the free flow of ideas, especially the ideas of Muslim progressives. For this is the Islam that condemned the sociologist Saad Eddin Ibrahim, leader of the Ibn Khaldun Institute, for advocating coptic rights and other political reforms like the registration of women for the vote,[46] and that branded Nasr Abū Zayd, an editor of the *Encyclopedia of the Qur'ān*, as an apostate and forced the dissolution of his marriage, in response to his efforts to read the Qur'ān as a literary text. It is also the Islam that back in the 1960s put a price (not a million dollars but a mere twenty-thousand, and so, perhaps, not worthy of a headline) on the head of Fazlur Rahman, a faithful and traditional Muslim thinker who had dared to utter a thought at variance with accepted dogma–allowing that Muḥammad might not have anticipated quite everything that would occur within his polity in the wake of his demise. We cannot pretend that this Islam is inauthentic, that it has no mass following and no genuine historical roots. It is authentic and most often earnest—deadly earnest—and neither stupid nor naive. It is repressive and unworthy. But it is Islam.

There is another Islam, tolerant, pluralistic, cosmopolitan without triumphalism and spiritual without repression. It too is an authentic expression of Islamic ideals, and a worthier expression of the compassion and generosity that flow through the Islamic texts and traditions, as they do through the texts and traditions of the sister religions of Judaism and Christianity. This book is about that other Islam, an Islam that does not typically make headlines. It is subdominant today. Historically, it has often been suppressed. But over the centuries its spirit has inspired marvels of art and literature, philosophy and law. It has been a leaven to institutions that have allowed and encouraged human beings and their communities to flourish. This other Islam is not purist and xenophobic. Like any civilizational phenomenon, it has been nourished in part by practices and ideas that sprang up elsewhere and that took on new and creative forms in their interactions with the ancient and familiar. It is an Islam that many Muslims are looking for and that some have never heard of. In some ways it is an Islam that remains to be invented. Part of my purpose in this book is to put Muslims as well as non-Muslims in touch with a few of the materials and ideas that might be relevant in that work of rediscovery and reinvention.

Islamic humanism is neither an oxymoron nor a redundancy but a theme, a possibility, an authentic strand of meanings and values to be discovered in a rich, often neglected past, a religious and philosophical way of being that individuals and communities can build on in the present and the future. Like all things human this too is fallible and subject to corruption. (For even the most perfect ideal can be corrupted in an instant by false, self-serving, or self-deceiving motives). The work of appropriating, rebuilding, and redefining the ideals of Islamic humanism is not mine. That is a task for committed Muslim thinkers and leaders. But it can only be done in an atmosphere of far freer thought and exploration than presently prevails in Muslim countries.

There are precedents aplenty for both freedom and repression in the Islamic past. The Buddhas of Bamiyan, after all, were long familiar to Muslims. Some of the statues there were destroyed when the place was raided by Yaʿqub b. Layth, the founder of the Saffārid dynasty, in 871. Yāqūt describes the shrine that remained, "supported on columns illuminated with pictures of every kind of bird created by the Almighty, most wondrous to see," and the "mighty idols carved out of the mountainside from top to bottom. One is called Surkbud and the other Khingbud (Red Buddha and Gray Buddha). They say there is nothing else like them in the world." The attitude here was one of interest and marvel. The final destruction came much later, awaiting more modern techniques of artillery and propaganda.

Muslims first came to the Indian subcontinent in 712, and Maḥmūd of Ghaznā made annual raids into the Punjab from 997 to 1030. The Buddhists, who once maintained ten monasteries and a thousand monks at Bamiyan, have long vanished from the place. But the memory of the Muslims who drove them from these lands survives in Buddhist scriptures, in the *Kālacakra-tantra*, which Jan Nattier describes as "the only genuinely apocalyptic text that has ever been accepted into any Buddhist canon."[47] The text, an angry scar of exile and devastation, pictures a cosmos very different from that of mere empiric history, and "contrary to all realistic expectation," it envisions a great victory and sustained (but not eternal) flourishing by (a somewhat Hindu influenced) Buddhism in the distant future. Tellingly, this scripture pictures the prophet of Islam and other monotheist figures, including Moses and Jesus, as demonic serpents. The impact of Islam is reduced to a few barely recognizable names and an unmistakable taste of bitterness. Muslims here are remembered not as bearers of a great civilization and still less as servants of the most Merciful and Compassionate, but as persecutors and destroyers. They are blown up to otherworldly proportions but then blown away in the visionary reaches of apocalyptic time. When Muslims today make choices in interpreting their own faith they are choosing their own Islam, as a way of life for themselves as individuals and as members of a community that makes its home among the other communities of this planet. But their choices include many that will affect how Muslims and the teachings they profess and hold most sacred will be viewed by those around them and remembered, a thousand and more years from now.

What the present book seeks are some of the threads of Islamic humanism in the past. My aim, in part, is a fuller picture of Islamic civilization than the headlines and the headline makers can convey. But I am also hoping to promote or provoke a fuller self-understanding among Muslims, and among others too, who are interested, intellectually and pragmatically, in the possibilities and pitfalls of a religiously constructed or religiously inspired way of life. That is a human quest of relevance to us all, and one in which all of us can learn from one another's failures and successes–and from discovering how to discriminate the pitfalls from the possibilities. It is perhaps in a similar spirit that the Ikhwān al-Ṣafā' describe their ideal man as: "Persian by breeding, Arabian in faith, Ḥanafite [thus, moderate] in his Islam, Iraqi in culture, Hebrew in lore, Christian in manners, Damascene in piety, Greek in the sciences, Indian in contemplation, Sufi in intimations, regal in character, masterful in thought, and divine in insight."[48] I see a cosmopolitan spirit here that is authentically Islamic. That is the spirit of Islamic humanism. The loveliest verse in the Qur'ān, the famous Light verse, is framed on a recognition that transcendent goodness and beauty bespeak just such a spirit:

> God is the light of heaven and earth. The likeness of His light: It is as if there were a niche, and within it a lamp, a lamp enclosed by glass, a glass that gleams like a star. It is fed from a blessed olive tree of neither the East nor the West, whose oil all but gives light even when untouched by flame–light upon light. God guides to His light whom He pleases He coins the symbols for mankind. For God knows all things. (Qur'ān 24:35)

Let me say a little now about what's in this book, and about what it is not. The book has four chapters. The first explores the interplay of sacred and secular themes in Arabic literature and Islamic faith. It opens with some thoughts about the sacred and the secular in general, and it focuses on the Qur'ān, on Arabic poetry and music, and Muslim attitudes and responses to those elements of Islamic culture. It speaks of Islamic dress, sumptuary laws, and sumptuous displays of wealth and power whose vehicle is clothing. It speaks of wine and mysticism, warfare and the hunt. It speaks of the celebration of love as a secular value that finds a prominent place in Islamic religious literature, not only as a metaphor of the mystic quest but also as a counterweight to that quest, set out by Muslim theologians and jurists of the most traditionalist stamp in their efforts to quash erotic mysticism and all that it stood for in their minds. The chapter includes my own translation of what is widely regarded as the finest of the pre-Islamic odes, the *Mu'allaqa* of Imru' al-Qays. The poem brilliantly encapsulates the spirit of the *Jāhiliyya*. It becomes a paradigm of some of the values that Muslims would contend with, whether their own spirit leaned toward the sacred or the secular, or toward the various modes of synthesis by which the two might be interwoven. The chapter turns in the end to Hamadhānī and a sampling from his *Maqāmāt*, the delightful and satirical picaresques that anticipate the flavor of Cervantes, Bocaccio, and Chaucer.

Our second chapter is devoted to Islamic ethics. It speaks of the texts and contexts in which Islamic ethical norms and values were classically articulated, in scripture and tradition, theology, law, literature, mysticism, and philosophy. At the level of theory, the chapter considers theological treatments of moral agency and responsibility. At the level of practice, it examines the work of the *muḥtasib*. the marketplace inspector, and the norms set out for his enforcement, which were meant to give expression to Islamic values in the context of daily life. The chapter considers some of the efforts of Muslim jurists and jurisdictions to institutionalize the Qur'ānic obligation to enforce decency and ban wrongdoing–the task that the Ṭālibān so notoriously assigned to a government agency. Against this background the chapter considers a key figure in the humanistic tradition, the Persian ethicist Miskawayh, who built a system of virtue ethics on the foundations afforded by the Qur'ān, drawing his materials from Arabic literary and historical culture, Aristotle's ethical philosophy, and the Persian courtier tradition. Of special interest to us is the transformation of that system when adopted and adapted to the pietist ethos of Sufism by the great Muslim theologian al-Ghazālī.

Chapter 3 is about metaphysics and epistemology. Like the previous chapter it begins with the Qur'ān and Islamic theology and considers the views of literary humanists like Miskawayh and Hamadhānī about the nature of knowledge, for example. Individual and shared insights and even presumptions are interesting and instructive here, but metaphysics and epistemology, in the end, call for the efforts of professionals, and most of the chapter is devoted to the views and arguments of the philosophers–their responses to the Greek texts they read in Arabic translation, and their efforts to forge a synthesis of the values they found most credible at the confluence of the Greek and Arabic philosophical traditions. The core problem about being examined here centers on its necessity or contingency, eternity or creation. The core problem about knowledge is the possibility of theory, necessary truth, as it was classically called, or lawlike generalization in the more apologetic sounding language in use today. These are still living issues, and the syntheses framed by the great Muslim thinkers, Kindī, Rāzī, Fārābī, Avicenna, and the rest still speak to us. Indeed, despite the strangeness of the tools these workers brought to their task–ideas about the Active Intellect, or the ultimate contingency of an eternal world–we find that the discussions of the Islamic philosophers can illuminate our own paths philosophically, partly because these thinkers share with us in the problems they address, but not always in our underlying and unquestioned assumptions.

I deal with literature in this book because it is the seed bed for the individuality of spirit that is critical to humanism of any sort, and because literary culture (as Miskawayh recognized) is a source and vehicle of values of refinement and reflection, detachment, moral criticism, and self-cultivation. I deal with ethics for its powerful affinity with the humanistic project in general, and for the very special affinity of virtue ethics to that project. I deal with Islamic theology because its debates enshrine the values of a civilization, including many that are humane and humanistic—the Muʿtazilite ideas of individual moral responsibility and accountability, for example, or the Muʿtazilite treatment of the ancient (Stoic and Aristotelian) idea that our own actions can enhance or constrict our degrees of freedom, or the Muʿtazilite idea that God Himself is answerable to the standards of justice and fairness that we humans can articulate. But equally relevant to our humanistic focus is the more orthodox Ashʿarite idea that one cannot and should not attempt to pry open the hearts of our fellow human beings to test the sincerity of their faith, or the Ashʿarite idea that life itself may fail to live up to our human standards of justice and fairness. Fārābī's philosphical affirmation of human free will is a landmark of humanism.[49] But so, in a very different way, is Ghazālī's artful sowing of the seeds for recognition of an open future, the outspoken empiricism of his refusal to accept the logicist and naturalist determinism of the authoritative philosophical tradition of his age.

It is not my intent in the brief sampling that this book can contain, to attempt to reconcile all the spirits it finds in contention, or to adjudicate among them. Some of that work may form an agenda for future workers in philosophy, Muslim and non-Muslim (since the problems are of universal import). I am content here for the most part to call attention to the materials, the ideas they voice and the issues they broach. One book could not do this comprehensively, but I want to show what sort of timber for construction can be found, and to set out an invitation to others to explore, interpret, and describe, but also to construct.

The final chapter of the book is an extended survey of the growth of Arabic universal history, that distinctive genre that follows historical events from the creation down to the author's own times. The chapter reflects a bit on the problems of historiography in general and describes the evolution of Arabic historical writing from the earliest anecdotal and genealogical accounts to the great chronicles of Ṭabarī and others, to the encyclopedic and digressive works of Masʿūdī, to Ibn Khaldūn's *Muqaddimah*, and the universal history of Rashīd al-Dīn. It is the catholic and cosmopolitan spirit that emerges in this literature that registers it in the ranks of humanistic writing–the desire for a universal chronology, the appetite for knowledge of cultures, realms, and epochs other than one's own. Miskawayh emerges here once again, along with some of the Mamluk historians, who made their historical work a vehicle for social criticism and critical reflection. And Ibn Khaldūn stands out among the thinkers who sought to find a meaning in history, not in the sheer ebullience of conquest but in the patterns of human life, the rise, decline, and fall of dynasties and regimes.

The humanism considered in this book is not the same as the humanism of the Quattrocento, nor is it the humanism of our twentieth-century secularists. Even Rāzī, a hands-on clinician and a skeptic as to special revelation, is a theist and a creationist. I count him as a humanist for his independence of mind, his striking affirmations of progress, individualism, and intellectual equality. Miskawayh, with his courtly and literary values, his scholarly tastes, pragmatic interest in the past, and commitment to character and its refinement, comes closer to the Renaissance ideal, which in many ways he anticipates. But he too is a committed Muslim, valuable to Muslims today less for his courtly ethic than for showing another way in which commitment to Islam conjoins with values distinct from those that claim a lock on Islamic ethics and outlooks today.

Secularity plays a role in Islamic humanism, both within and outside the religious sphere, as we shall see. But Islamic humanism is not typically secularist. Even Hamadhānī, the most irreverent of the Muslim authors considered here, is committed to Islamic seriousness in his own way, as we see in chapter 3. Like many a satirist, from Aristophanes onward, he is rather conservative in outlook, and our analysis finds the *Maqāmāt* playing a vital role, beyond their sheer delight, in puncturing pretensions and exposing hypocrisies.

Perhaps part of what binds together figures like Miskawayh, Fārābī, Avicenna, Hamadhānī, Ibn Ṭufayl and Ibn Khaldūn is their ability to examine the tradition they live in, to look at it both sympathetically and critically, and to select, develop, and combine values and ideas that are conducive to human understanding, human growth, and human flourishing. There is nothing hidebound and scholastic here. Old traditions are taken up and examined eagerly, ideas devoured with gusto, made whole, made new, made over.

Another book or several more could have been written about the scientists of Islam—Bīrūnī, Ṭūsī, Ibn al-Ḥaytham. Many more could be written about the philosophers who are in play here but not comprehensively explored. I have hardly touched on the humanism latent in Islamic art, especially in the Persian miniature tradition. With the literary figures I have barely grazed the surface. Ḥarīri deserves a book of his own. So does Ibn al-Muqaffaʿ, or Abū ʾl-ʿAlāʾ al-Maʿarrī. And I could go on. But the point is not to be encyclopedic but to cite a few of the landmarks that might help a reader chart a course, and to mark out a certain trend that deserves not just to be studied but to be followed up on—not mimicked, but not lost.

That leads me to a few words about what this book is not. It is not a whitewash, an apologetic or sheerly celebratory history. It is not, in fact, a history at all, but one philosopher's appraisal of some widely varied articulations of values, sacred and secular, that intertwine, support, and nourish one another, borrow and steal from one another, and occasionally seek to smother one another, never with perfect success. Neither secularity nor theocracy is seen here as "the answer" for Muslims, or for anyone else. Indeed, one of the findings of our explorations is that these two seeming opposites, like so many polarized extremes, meet and often couple behind the scenes. Secularism can become a religion of sorts and put on many of the airs that secularists most despise in the religions against which they rebel. And theocracy, as experience reveals, can be brutally secular in its goals and methods. The life of the human spirit has no worse enemy. Equilibrium is what must be sought. But equilibrium, in any living system, is dynamic, never static. It must be constantly recalibrated and restored.

Islamic humanism has a long and sometimes splendid history. But if pursued as an option for today, it does not come ready made, and this book offers neither a recipe nor a prescription. It is not a recipe, because a way of life needs to be built in the living, created by individuals and communities, not just espoused. A formula can always be perverted, or ignored. For the same reason, this book is not a prescription. It is those who make a path who determine ultimately where it will lead. Besides, our researches into the humanistic history of Islam uncover ideas and resources that are treasures perhaps, but tinged with rust and ergot, and themselves tainted with ambiguity. Humanism too has its dark side, as Muslim mystics and militants know all too well. The task of forging a new and humanistic Islam lies with thoughtful and progressive Muslims. The alembic is in their hands. It does not belong to the interpreter.

Worldliness is not always an antidote to obscurantism. It may be its goad and irritant—as the Medicis were the irritant of Savonarola—or it may be its cynical counterpart. And spirituality can be a blind for passivity, and worse. But as we seek to follow the tangled skein of values and ideas that Islamic thinkers and writers articulated in their attempts to reconcile individuality with community, originality with tradition, responsibility with liberty, art with experience, and knowledge with understanding, I think we shall be tracing threads that progressive-minded Muslims will be interested in taking up and knitting together today. And others, who seek understanding and a common ground with a faith that they find worthy of respect, although it will never be their own, may welcome an encounter with the riches and the problems, the past and the potentials, of that faith and the civilization to which it gave birth.

I

The Sacred and the Secular

A falcon swoops and pinions a dove in midair. There are divine energies here, and mythic thinking marks them with its distinctive fusion of natural with magical powers. Not that mythmakers fail to see distinctions. Myths can make the keenest discriminations.[1] But mythic discourse does not so willingly dissolve the aura cast by its sacralizing gaze. It savors the extraordinariness of the extraordinary. By cycles of ritual, story, dance, poem, and song, cultures retell and seek to relive those moments that so trap the gaze or arrest the mind—to mime the bear or deer or monkey, become the god that animates the game, paint the walls with torsos and evocations of the animal energies discovered in the field.

It is in such efforts that art, science, and religion take their birth. They are not at first clearly demarcated. Not that myth is false or frightened science. We do not catch the essence of religion by dismissing it as unliberated art. Nor do we understand science by scouting it as religion made prosaic. But there is an overlap. The heart of the scientific hunger to understand and the artistic itch to speak or sing or paint the highlands of experience do not so readily abandon the religious desire to celebrate and recapture the lost vision, to see it once again, from safety. Neither science nor art ever wholly loses the sense of wonder that is the matter and root of all religious feeling.

Uniqueness, of course, is irreducible. Its moment is killed by analysis. Setting a backdrop to his own tale, Melville explains in his chapters on the painting of whales that to see a drawing, or a stuffed carcass in a museum, is not to see a whale.[2] Schematic renderings are crude, fantastical, scaled down to the point of falsity. Cuvier, "brother to the famous Baron," painted "not a Sperm Whale but a squash." Others, of more experience or livelier imagination, show whales in action—"though in some details not the most correct." The painted board of a stump-legged beggar near the docks at Tower Hill begins to convey something when it mutely narrates how the "kedger" lost his leg. The cartoon drawings of the amputee's placard show "as good whales as were ever published in Wapping." This man has seen a whale.

The bulk and danger of the whale may demand a canvas as broad as the northern and Antarctic skies. Moving from pictorial to natural representations—from the whales of prehistoric barrows and rock formations, to the whales found by the prepared eye in the "topmost heaven," Melville shows how romantic poets and transcendentalist painters could find intimations of immortality in nature and divine brushwork in the Arabian desert or Niagara. But he also reveals how kindred sensibilities might find divinity itself in an instant and project natural powers beyond the cave walls and barrows of human art and up to those topmost heavens.

Religion protects its moments by setting its cynosure at a vanishing point, beyond the mere things of nature. The falcon is not entombed in any feathered corpse. It flies upward to become a god—no mere image but a spirit, in excelsis, beyond capture or control. Yet that very rise, which lifts objects beyond the ordinary, yields secularity too, as its precipitate. For it leaves the natural object bereft, reduced to ordinariness. The basalt falcon becomes the prize in some camp treasure hunt, a token goal in a film noir that cynicism will empty of treasure and of mystery.

Repetition too yields secularity. Just as science demands reproducibility, ritual can routinize religiosity in its drive to institute powerful but fleeting emotions. Whether in high church formalism, devotional legalism, drugged gropings after ecstasy, hypnotic *dhikrs*, wild glossolalias, or maenad bacchanals, the demand to *handle* and control the extraordinary undercuts the very summit that is its goal.

All religions look with awe upon some thing, event, or pattern. They differ in their varieties of response, in allocating that awe and seeking to preserve and transmit it without loss. The worshiper rocks to and fro, as one midrash puts it, drawn to the warmth and light of the flame but scorched if drawn too close.

Secularity poses special problems for monotheists. They press the idea that religious awe belongs only to the highest. But they also seek fascinated mastery of the peaks their quest may open to view.[3] The central monotheist theme is this: that being, goodness, life, insight, and inspiration—all things of real worth—stem from God, *although* no mere thing exhausts divine perfection. The falcon, eagle, or lion may be emblems, but they never comprehend divine power itself. Even to touch or know or represent that Absolute demands divine initiative, a miracle of grace or faith, incarnation, or revelation.

Monotheistic ethics submits all human actions and desires to God's will. But God's absolute intent is made explicit, humanly relevant, and humane only by the presumption that God is honored in the recognition of creaturely deserts—that God, to put it anthropomorphically, desires His creatures' well-being, in keeping with their capacities and needs. Hence the ethical impact of the idea that creation is God's work and that we humans are created in God's image. Still, creaturely goods are not gods. If only God is Absolute, no mere intent or aspiration holds absolute worth or merit. The idea of human rights may be anchored or smashed and wrecked upon that rock.

By denying the absolute value of natural objects, experiences, and desires, monotheism constantly risks emptying them of all value. Zen, by contrast, the most secular and aesthetic of religious traditions, finds a kind of absolute in the idea of emptiness. It builds an ethic and an ethos on the discipline of emptying the mind to house its daily lodgers while curbing attachment to any of them. Thus, by indirection, it inures mind to the paradox of the extraordinariness of the ordinary.

Zen shares a certain ascetic penchant, then, with the monotheistic traditions. Both look beyond the sensation of the moment. But the beyond of Zen arises dialectically, from the negation of the particular as such, much as a painting needs an object to orient the infinitude of negative space. Monotheism, for its part, looks beyond the particularity of the moment—first, ethically, to the next moment, and then, further, to eternity.

Both Zen and monotheism pursue an unnamed and unnameable boundlessness. But for monotheists the Infinite is a reality mirrored and refracted in created things. For Zen initiates, emptiness locates the depth behind the myriad things. The risk is fetishism, complementing the yawning sense of absence and hunger for the absolute that is the shadow side of monotheism.

When Kawabata visited the Kahala Hilton (as it was then called) he saw the beauty of the sunlit glasses stacked by the poolside bar. Mundane objects became an occasion, through their orderly arrangement, their crystal lattices, their natural and artificial glory—if the word is not too suggestive of an epiphany. Later, busloads of visitors from Japan trooped dutifully to the spot.[4] Rather than discover the wondrous in their own mundane, they pursued Kawabata's vision—as though their Nikons could give them his eyes. The procession became a ritual almost—at once sacralized and routinized.

Monotheism finds significance in all things, not in isolation but as expressions of divine creativity—God's pleasure, or perhaps displeasure. Paganism holds ultimate value closer to home, but at a cost. For it keeps its values free and independent of one another, in some measure. But autonomous values may conflict, and likely will. In a mythic scheme, definition is won by contrast and contrast is dramatically projected as conflict. Life is a value in paganism, but so is death. Kindness is celebrated, but so is cruelty. Intensity advances its own claims. For all values either flash their own flavors or point elsewhere—and thus propose integration, subordination to a system, hierarchy beneath an absolute. If autonomous values are to be preserved, as romantics might prefer, a premium is placed on vividness. Contrast becomes a value in itself, and violence may follow. Intensity becomes the badge of authenticity. Tragedy is then the highest art; and paradox, the most profound philosophy.

Secularity need not careen to the orgiastic. Confucianism is a case in point. But secularity has this in common with paganism: that it prizes values insofar as they are not subsumed in some Ultimate. So the multiple and disparate interests of secularity, even if well mannered, may seem misdirected to the monotheist. Disparate values are cherished, for their moment—elegance, pleasure, fun, fashion, discipline, honor, sport, seduction, vengeance, virtuosity, bravado, sprezzatura, fame, and other aesthetic modes. Not all are wholesome or conducive to human flourishing. And none will be valued as highly by the rest as it is by its own lights and appetites.

It is the short weight of such values when judged against one another that gave Socrates the opening he needed for corralling in a common scheme all such recalcitrant values that would lay claim to any real worth. This Socratic dialectic, refined to a method by Plato and Aristotle and made a system by later thinkers, casts into sharp relief the moral posture implicit in monotheism. For it is a defining thesis of monotheistic ethics that such values as pleasure, risk, experience, even knowledge, or ascesis, or filial piety are soundly weighed only if judged extrinsically. They do not come off well as absolutes.[5]

Yet, through a paradox of monotheism or a perversity in secularity, monotheistic religions seem to feed upon and egg on their rivals, autonomous, secular pursuits. Spurning or neglecting secular concerns only gives them an identity and an animus. But trying to set them into an overarching value hierarchy can assign them canonical legitimacy. Equilibrium is elusive.

Focus and Distraction

Islam originates as a particularly earnest monotheistic creed, born from the visions and admonitions of the Arab prophet. Muḥammad was deeply troubled by the recklessness and unconcern he saw around him. Ecstatic experience confirmed his moral vision, and an angelic voice gave it the shape of inspired poesy, in images of judgment against his fellow Meccans' way of life. He inveighed against their moral laxity and what he called distractedness. They practiced infanticide (Qur'ān 6:152, 17:31), buried daughters alive (Qur'ān 81:8, 16:58–60). And they wore revealing clothing, drank wine, played games of chance (Qur'ān 24:31, 60; 33:59; 6:152; 2:216, 5:90). The revelatory condemnation of wine and of *maysir* gambling arrows reflected no merely utilitarian concern with alcoholism or self-impoverishment.[6] It voiced a demand for cohesion and a warning against forgetfulness: "The Fiend desireth only to strew strife and enmity amongst you with wine and arrow-shuffling—to distract you from mindfulness of God and worship. Will ye cease and obey God, and obey His Emissary, and be ware?" (Qur'ān 5:91–92).

Focus is demanded in a community of believers. The intoxicated are polluted, unfit for prayer (Qur'ān 4:43). But the theme of distraction, extends more broadly. Man's thoughts, the Sufis argue, belong properly to God. Thus Ibn Ṭufayl (ca. 1105–1185/6) equates failure of concentration on the thought of God with the alienation of infernal chastisement.[7] What is at stake poetically is admission to the hereafter. Metaphysically, for Ibn Ṭufayl, that means eternal and ecstatic communion, *ittiṣāl* with God's ultimate unity.

Yet, as if in mockery of the Qur'ān itself, Hamadhānī (968–1008) makes wine and dandified clothes symbols and paradigms of youthful joy and antinomian abandon.[8] Muḥammad's antipathy, as described in the canonical sources, to music and dance, silken garments, secular song and poetry, thematize a zeal for direction of the mind toward God.[9] Yet forbidden fruits taste all the sweeter. The persona that Jāḥiẓ (ca. 776–868/9) sets in motion in his burlesque apology for the trade in song girls voices openly what must have seemed a common sotto voce rationale: Why should puritanical denials tempt a passion that can be lawfully sated? If song girls distract from the thought of God, don't many other things—talk and food, drink and pleasure gardens, venery and the chase—in both senses of those terms?[10] The solemnity of the warnings cast the faith in somber hues and color forbidden pleasures with a rebellious purpose, along with their tinctures of delight.

Naḍr b. al-Ḥārith, a wealthy Qurashite, opposed Muḥammad's mission. The owner of song girls and perhaps of books acquired in his merchant travels to Iran, he cited the mighty monarchs of Persia to discredit the Prophet's accounts of vanished nations that had failed to heed God's call. He was captured in battle against the Muslim forces at Badr and executed, according to tradition, by the Prophet's own hand, or at his orders by ʿAlī. His memory is kept alive in a threnody ascribed to a surviving daughter or sister, and he becomes a sort of secular patron of song and the lute. For it is Naḍr, they say, who brought the lute to Mecca.[11] Singing will be proscribed and many lutes smashed in the name of Islam, but the Prophet is said to have regretted Naḍr's slaying, and the variant stories as to who wielded the sword express such regret, at least on the part of those who told the tale.

Poetry and Music

Poetry enjoys an ambiguous status in Islam. It is not forbidden. But, as a patterned mode of discourse, where pattern is a vehicle of art and art can militate for autonomy and for control of content, poetry is clearly suspect. Muḥammad vehemently rejected the name of poet (Qur'ān 36:69, 69:40–41). But the poetic qualities of the Qur'ān are evident—placing the Prophet on much the same uneasy footing as Plato, who also feared the dominance of artistic values over the claim of truth. Fakhr al-Dīn al-Rāzī (1148/9–1210) artfully dissolved the dilemma by appealing to the spontaneity of Muḥammad's inspired discourse: The Prophet's art was not contrived but compelled—as unpremeditated as the rhymed and metrical exclamation he made when his toe was wounded in battle. But the difficulty persists. For the special authority of spontaneity is a literary distinction, indeed, a romantic topos older than the Hellenistic age, when even Skeptical philosophers gave credit to the spontaneous responses of body or mind.[12]

In the Qur'ān (26:224) we read: "Those who stray follow the poets" and in the *ḥadīth*, of Bukhārī and Muslim: "Better a belly full of rot than a belly full of poetry."[13] Yet the Prophet is quoted as finding wisdom in poetry, even magic in eloquence. He encouraged poetic satire of his enemies and detractors, although he deplored extravagant rhetoric in general.[14] He listened entranced, the traditions report, to the poetry of Abū 'l-Ṣalt, who never became a Muslim, and when he heard Labīd's half-line, "All things but God are vain," exclaimed that no truer words were ever spoken, by a poet.[15] But the hemistich, by the author of one of the Seven Golden Odes later avowed to have been suspended at the Kaʿba, was mated with another, developing its elegiac theme: "And all that is fair must perish." To this ʿUthmān b. Maẓʿūn, is said to have objected violently: "You lie! The joy of Paradise will never cease!"[16] The emotive demands of Labīd's poem were countermanded by a higher authority.

Even internally Labīd's line struck a paradox: Its words purport to recognize no worth but God's, yet as they are spoken they enunciate their own value as well. Words rhymed for the faith might harbor spiritual value; and satires hold pragmatic worth. But there is a joy in satire, and in all poetic power, that is quite distinct from the joy of heavenly union.

The Prophet, it is said, softened toward poetry when Labīd embraced Islam. Labīd, for his part, is said to have withdrawn his poetry on hearing the Qur'ān. Avowedly secular poetry remained suspect for its content, of course. But even sacred poetry broached values distinct from the Highest. And wasn't poetry at large, by its very nature, secular, following where feelings beckoned to words? The words of the old poets in particular, recorded and remembered, rekindled feelings that were by no means trapped in amber. But they added layers of nostalgia as the decades and centuries passed. As Tarif Khalidi writes:

> *Jahili* poetry, often embedded in stories relating to the lives of the poets, was collated and provided with commentaries in literary anthologies of the 3rd–4th/9th–10th centuries. . . . the past is recreated or evoked in a manner which the Qur'ān was later to brand as *jāhilī*, even while it shared with this poetry certain terms to describe and situate that past. This poetry speaks to us in many moods: epic or lyrical, tragic, ironic or nostalgic. . . . Youth is always recalled in sorrow.[17]

Transmuting ambivalence into elegy, the culture adopts almost the same tone toward its own youth as do the poets whose memories and longings it enshrines.

Music is at once more abstract and more sensuous than poetry. The ascetic side of Islam frowns on it, and more sternly on dance. Drama does not thrive in the house of Islam, although present in the Shīʿite passion plays of Kerbala.[18] Representational painting will flourish in Iran, and with lesser brilliance in the courts of early Arab monarchs and later Mughals, Ottomans, and other dynasts.[19] It is found among Muslims in India, Turkey, China, Central Asia, and Africa, but most often as a court phenomenon, celebrating warfare, love, or the hunt. These secular themes recur in the miniatures that adorn Iranian epics and line the walls of Arab pleasure palaces. Religious themes are touched in Islamic art, but often with a self-conscious, almost guilty modesty. Or they are sublimated in geometrical motifs of austere complexity or ornate splendor, eloquently suggesting the inadequacy of line or form to a supernal subject.[20]

In Sufi art, modesty yields to a puckish, quietly antinomian lilt, the full-faced youth swaying gently to music he alone can hear, a wine cup held openly in his hand. In the mosque, images give way to words. Icons fail, but calligraphy blooms, and words become iconic, leaping from the walls and the manuscript page. Here again the secular lurks in the aesthetic, as fancy yields to fantasy in the elaborate Ottoman *tughras* that declare the many titles of a monarch in resplendent gold and lapis lazuli. Tile work is brilliant. Carving is a tour de force, but sculpture is stillborn. Ballet or opera, alien and uncountenanced.

Dance is generally deemed un-Islamic, ruled unlawful by the jurists, although no text or tradition expressly forbids it, and the traditions of Bukhārī's *Ṣaḥīḥ* explicitly permit it on the day of the Great Festival.[21] But gravitas turns the Qur'ānic (17:39) admonition "Walk not proudly" into a proof text against dancing, which Muslim purists and puritans pointedly apply to the ecstatic *dhikr*s of the Sufis.

ʿĀ'isha, it is said, was rebuked by Abū Bakr, for listening to two female singers.[22] Nāfiʿ is reported to have learned from Ibn ʿUmar, a companion of the Prophet, to follow Muḥammad's example by putting his fingers in his ears on hearing the sound of a musical pipe.[23] *Ḥadīth* is not alone, of course, in confounding music with noise. Gilson speaks of music almost as an assault. He cheerily quotes Kant's "priceless observation" from the *Critique of Judgment* "on the impertinence of those who sing spiritual hymns in their homes during family devotions without considering the noise they inflict on their neighbors." Music may be the most agreeable of the arts, Kant allows, but even that renders it suspect, as "enjoyment rather than culture," since it "involves neither concepts nor definite ideas." To which he adds: "if we measure the value of the fine arts against the culture which they impart to the sentiment, and against the enlargement of the faculties which must be combined in judgment for cognition, then music immediately passes into the lowest place among the fine arts . . . because it brings only sensations to bear."[24] So "music is sure to see itself despised by those who judge art by knowledge. As Voltaire said: 'One sings what is too silly to be said.'"[25] Yet, silly as they are, I don't think anyone has set those last words to music. The words show more a blind spot in Gilson and a bald spot in Kant than any real insight into art or culture. Gilson is plainly moved by prejudice, partly sectarian—distaste for Protestant family worship; and Kant, similarly, by amusement at the Schwarmerei he so disliked in Pietism. Only contrast Gilson's glowing remarks about statuary: "When statues are carried in a pageant, the spectacle can take on a hallucinatory beauty, which invariably produces a strange effect, like the Spanish statues that swing gently to and fro with and almost living grace when they are borne in religious processions."[26] Invariably? I don't think that's quite what a Muslim observer would have felt, say, not long after the Reconquista, on witnessing some fiesta procession in Spain.

A Sufi exponent of musical spirituality, responding to the Islamic condemnation of music as noise, acutely sets apart "assaultive" from "nonassaultive" music: "The first . . . produces an agitation. . . . The second . . . has the effect of transporting the listener to some other place," perhaps "to the presence of God."[27] Even so, partly for its sensuality, and even more for its emotive effects, music remains suspect in Islam.

Ibn Abī Dunyā, the subject of the only obituary recorded by Ibn al-Athīr for the year 894, was tutor to two ʿAbbāṣid caliphs and wrote over a hundred works, including a series of seven Censures: of the world and worldliness (*al-dunyā*), of the vicious passions (envy and ire), of loose language (slander and obscenity), and of the implements of distraction (intoxicants and instruments of diversion). The last of the series, *Dhamm al-Malāhī*, the Censure of Toys, devotes some ten folios to the condemnation of vocal and instrumental music.[28] Citing numerous *ḥadīth*s, it links music and its tools with wine and gaming, racing pigeons and sexual license. Some of the direst warnings of the Final Judgment aim at those who keep song girls and indulge in related forms of decadence and debauchery. Music is vicious, precisely because it is a distraction: One man grew so devoted to his song girl that he gave up the mosque altogether. Ibn Masʿūd destroyed musical instruments with the same vehemence that Carrie Nation used against saloons. It is the devil, he said, who makes a man sing as he rides—perhaps playing on the notion that riders sang to ward off spirits. But the worry, again, is distraction: The devil gains access because the song has not mentioned God—and if one sings poorly, bowing to the devil is next! Chess, Ibn ʿUmar reasons, is worse than backgammon, because it is more absorbing. Song, for the same reason, is worse than poetry. As in Kant and Gilson, cognitivism abets austerity. But the real fear is lest music become a sensuous vehicle for autonomy of spirit.

Music, it would seem, then, even when tolerated, could never be cherished in Islam.[29] And it is true that Islamic culture does not afford to the temporal abstractions conveyed in music by tone and timbre the same acceptance that it gives, say, to the geometrical abstractions of mosaic or faience. Nor do we see classically the kind of secular spirituality attaching to Islamic music that has arisen in the West among devotees of the symphony. Indeed, the smashing of musical instruments and breaking up of musical parties are paradigm cases of what the classical Muslim jurists take to be ordained by the religious obligation to "ordain what is right and forbid what is wrong" (Qurʾān 3:104).[30] Yet, despite the censorious traditions, music thrives at the heart of pivotal Islamic institutions. And beneath the spiritual meanings it bears in such contexts, wear and rubbing may occasionally expose impulses other than the purely spiritual.

The *samāʿ* or mystical concert is a stimulant to Sufi ecstasy. Often accompanied by rhythmic movement or dance, the *samāʿ* is never a purely passive affair. There is always at least mental participation, and typically a joining in the chanting, in active quest for the higher states that are the mystic's goal. *Samāʿ* gatherings are not normatively held for the pleasure of the music. Yet sensuous values are present, legitimated by the sacred setting. So Sufis have long warned against secularization (or resecularization) of such events. The music, the dancing, the celebratory meal may turn a *dhikr* into a party, a paganizing trance-dance ritual, or today, a performance for the tourists.

Persian secular poetry has long been fitted to the *samāʿ*, made over by the assignment of metaphorical meanings to its imagery and then marked with the distinctive rhythms and forms of the Sufi repertoire. The mystic virtuoso

Ibn ʿArabī, seeking discipline, urges that the *samāʿ* should keep to Qurʾānic texts. But the ever practical Ghazālī prescribes religious poetry rather than Qurʾānic texts, lest the familiar words of scripture dim the liveliness of the experience.

Perhaps derived by "a sacralization of the secular concert and a sublimation of *ṭarab*," the emotional, even bodily response to poetry and song,[31] the Sufi *samāʿ*, never wholly loses its aura of sensuous or emotional excess. The institution spread rapidly from ninth century Baghdad to Isfahan, Shiraz, and the great province (or little empire) of Khurasan. The *samāʿ* came of age in Persia, spread by Persian disciples of such mystics as Nūrī and Junayd. Most of the early writers about it were Persians too. Widely accepted in countries of Islamic culture, it took hold most firmly where Persian influence was strongest—in Turkey and India particularly.

Niẓām al-Dīn al-Awliyāʾ (d. 1325) loved poetry and favored the devotional *samāʿ*, which helped him propagate his Chistī Sufi order from Uttar Pradesh to Rajasthan, Gujarat, Bihar, Bengal, and the Deccan. But his chosen successor, Naṣīr al-Dīn Maḥmūd Chiragh-i Dihlī (d. 1356) took a different tack. He relaxed the Chistī demand for strict obedience of acolytes to their *pīr*s and abolished the controversial prostrations of these aspirants before their guides, giving prominence to law, scripture, and *ḥadīth*, in place of music. An ascetic from his youth, he was indifferent even to the most spiritual poetry and, as Bruce Lawrence puts it, lukewarm at best in assaying its spiritual worth to others. He criticized the pretensions of *ḥajjī*s and never made the pilgrimage himself, modestly arguing that neither had his master. Even while that master lived, tradition records, Maḥmūd left an assembly where a woman sang and played the drum, saying that this was not in keeping with the *sunna*. The master's approval was not enough. A practice must be vouched for by the Qurʾān or *ḥadīth*.[32]

The more heavily Chistī spirituality leaned on music, the more elaborate grew the defenses of the *samāʿ*. One apologetic turns the tables on arguments from distraction: It is those who impugn the *samāʿ* who are distracted, by their very detachment; the listener is wholly absorbed. Critical questions may come from the lips and speak of reason, but their answer, could it be given, would come from the heart and speak of love.[33] The tension remains. For as the Sufis themselves say, the listening at the core of the *samāʿ* might be selfish or soulful, a response of one's nature, or a response of the heart.

There are no real condemnations of music in the Qurʾān, only rejections of vain or idle talk (23:13, 25:72, 31:5, 38:55). These must be worked up into proof texts with the help of a few tenuous suggestions, say, about the voice of Iblīs (17:66) and more general remarks: "Will ye laugh and not weep, making merry?" (53:60–61). In context, that last seems to aim at those who did not hearken to the Prophet's message as seriously as he hoped. Taken more broadly, it is a call to high seriousness and still says nothing about music.[34] Yet the application was plain enough to jurists in search of a legislative hook. And the defenders of music had little more to go on—only vague remarks about gladness and a preference for the beautiful over the harsh and ugly

(30:14, 31:18, 35:1, 39:19). Against the tradition that Muḥammad condemned the use of song girls, Ghazālī could cite a rival *ḥadīth*, also on the authority of ʿĀ'isha, offering the assurance that the Prophet himself had listened to two song girls at her house. Muḥammad, it was said, joined in a work song while helping dig trenches at Mecca. But the four first caliphs, we read, all disapproved of listening to songs or other music, so the strict legal school of Iraq banned it, although the school of Medina did not.

As the poet Ibn ʿAbd Rabbihi argued (860–940), if song is unlawful, then so is Qur'anic chanting. Henry Farmer, the celebrated scholar of Islamic music, chuckles at the acrobatics jurists went through to distinguish the two.[35] For, as Ibn Qutayba notes, the cantillation of the Qur'ān is musically indistinguishable from singing. But that cantillation was far too entrenched to be drawn into the vortex. Even its designation, *taṭrīb*, which would normally connote an excessively emotive tremolo, did nothing to inhibit the practice. Ibn Qayyim al-Jawziyya called it simply the spoonful of sugar that helps the medicine go down, and the worries of the jurists were subdued in the understanding that cantillation was perfectly acceptable, as long as it did not obscure the sense of the divine message.

But music did not confine itself to the *samāʿ* and Qur'ānic *taṭrīb*. The professional singers, instrumentalists, and song girls of the *Jāhiliyya* did not disappear on the rise of Islam, and the great philosophers of Islam, Kindī, Rāzī, Fārābī, Ibn Sīna, and Ibn Bājjah all wrote treatises on musical theory. Ibn Ṭufayl, a founder of the so-called "Andalusian revolt" against Ptolemaic astronomy, is said to have remarked cheerfully when he lined up for his pay at the (nominally puritanical) Almohad court: "If they're in the market for musical theory, I can supply it."[36] A word, then, about song girls, and then about musical theory and practice.

There were free professional singers in Arabia at least as early as the seventh century, but song girls (*qaynāt*, *qiyān*) were typically slaves, highly trained in musical entertainment and highly valued by those who marketed them for sale, or for hire in lavish entertainments.[37] The institution probably had deep pre-Islamic roots among the tribes and in the taverns, at various levels of elegance or commonness. Two song girls were used in early propaganda against Muḥammad, and executed for their trouble. But the institution survived and flourished at Mecca and Medina. The banning of wine thinned the ranks of the singers far more than the condemnations of early Muslims. But the Islamic conquests swelled their numbers, as entrepreneurs sought to add value to the slaves acquired as booty, by training them in music. The fabulous prices commanded by the finest of these women soon became the stuff of legend. Schools and music masters vied to meet the demand for *qaynāt* in the newly built garrison cities of Iraq, and later in Baghdad, Cordova, and Seville. Specialized dealers used their *qaynāt* to gain wealth, protection, patronage, and influence.[38] Some of the slave songstresses became celebrities as poets, wits, or performers, or as the mistresses of powerful men, or mothers to caliphs. Some were given their freedom, one was the subject of a biography. There was a chorus and even an orchestra of *qiyān*.

Song girls were sought after for their charms and not just for their talents. But there was piety among them, despite the role in which they were cast, and doubtless at times in response to the demands of that role. Many of the singers had vast repertoires of poetry, and some were learned in literature and the sacred sciences as well. Some were free, and many were not baubles of the court but tavern workers, as in the past. Lacking the respectability of free matrons and wives, the *qiyān* enjoyed a certain mobility that was withheld from others. They wore colorfully dyed clothing, unlike the natural colors seen in the home. And they were encouraged to engage in repartee with the men they were supposed to entertain, albeit never as equals. The institution of the *qaynāt* retreats with the retreat of slavery in modern times, and egalitarians could hardly mourn for it deeply. But comparable roles persist today, and the secular entertainments at which the *qaynāt* were adept survive in the repertoire of those troupes of women who entertain at family feasts even today in Moroccan cities.

Musical theory was the province of philosophers, who were also often physicians and scientists. Kindī (d. 867) is exemplary in this way. His work on music adopts a cosmological perspective, relating the Pythagorean mathematical system of musical tones to the seasons and elements, the compass points, humours, days of the week and heavenly bodies. The same neoplatonizing approach, based on a quest for the deep foundations of the psychological and even therapeutic value of music, was popularized in the essays of the Sincere Brethren of Basra and survives in traditional Islamic literature about music down to modern times.

A rival, Aristotelian scheme is found in Fārābī. And Avicenna "brusquely dismisses" the cosmological approach, and its Neopythagorean numerology.[39] But the contrast is not simply between the spiritual and the naturalistic. For the Sincere Brethren introduce the idea that sound is propagated spherically; and Fārābī, for his part, ranks musical instruments by their approach to the human voice. His musicology is noted for its logical rigor, but his focus on theory does not obscure his interest in the practical art of music making. That combination recurs in Ḥasan al-Kātib's *Kamāl Adab al-Ghinā'* (late tenth or early eleventh century), which preserves fragments of the lost musical work of Kindī's disciple al-Sarakhsī (ca. 835–899), along with discussions of the etiquette and aesthetics of performance practice.

Ṣafī al-Dīn al-Urmawī (d. 1294), the father of the Systematist school of Islamic musical theory founded a method of notation based on inscribing musical values at various points on a circle. The system was perfected by Quṭb al-Dīn Shīrāzī (1236–1311), a physician, astronomer, and philosopher known as "the polymath" (*al-mutafannin*). A student of Naṣīr al-Dīn al-Ṭūsī, Quṭb al-Dīn became a *qāḍī* under the Ilkhānid Mongol rulers of Persia and influenced his sovereign's conversion to Islam. Retiring to Tabrīz, he avidly studied *ḥadīth* and lived the life of a Sufi—ascetic but rather relaxed in his religious observance, loving wine and chess, performing his devotions in the mosque, but "sitting among the scorners." He played the *rabāba*, a small viol, and was skilled in conjuring tricks.[40] His life displays the tangled skein of many of the secular threads of humanism in Islam.

Musical theory and practice unite again in the work of ʿAbd al-Qādir al-Marāghī (d. 1435) a celebrated composer and performer whose Persian writings reflect the traditions of practice in the music of his day and whose influence persists down to the present. He describes some forty musical instruments, including Indian and Chinese examples that reflect the varied interests and the multicultural windows of a cosmopolitan artist and thinker.

Citations against music can be found in all four Sunnī schools of law, but three of the four founders of those schools are reported to have enjoyed it. Ḥujwīrī, an exponent of Sufism (d. 1072–77), tenders the widely offered explanation: The fault lies not with music but with the behaviors that customarily accompany it. Abū Sulaymān al-Dārānī (d. 830), an ascetic known for his weeping in worship, argues in the same vein: Music adds nothing new to the heart but only stirs up what is already there. Dhū ʾl-Nūn (ca.796–860), the Nubian freedman who rose to be a major early Sufi, admits that mere sensuous listening lists toward heresy. But at its core, he urges, music is God's stirring of the human heart to seek Him.

Abū Ṭālib al-Makkī (d. 998), in the same vein, describes music as a slippery rock of sensuality for the ill-prepared but no danger to the steady minded, if it is used not for mere amusement but for spiritual growth. Junayd (d. 910) had warned that love of music is a mark of laziness in Sufi novices—as though music opened a shortcut to higher states.[41] But Ghazālī follows Makkī, the author whom he mentions first among the Sufis whom he studied when he was seeking his way out of the thicket of despond into which his doubts had cast him. Prizing experience over theory and valuing Sufism for its grounding in practice, he opens the use of music to Sufi novices as well as steady-minded veterans. Daqqāq, a Moroccan Sufi and younger contemporary of Ghazālī's, might have his worries that ecstasy could foster unbelief, if the inexperienced are carried away by sensations of divine indwelling. But in Ghazālī's view the fault lay not in music but in bad theology. One might outgrow the need for spiritual stimulants, but they are not themselves improper, as long as one avoids instruments with profane associations and follows the path under proper guidance.[42]

With Ghazālī's approval, then, the melody unheard beneath the sensuous surface of music could become a metaphor for the progress of the soul. As the mystic poet Ibn al-Fāriḍ (1181–1235) put it, in gnostic mode, music reminds us of our true home and so helps free us from the flesh. That argument offers, in effect, an answer (unself-consciously Platonic) to the somber advice of Abū Naṣr al-Sarrāj (d. 988), who held that music does not help prepare a man for death.

Ghazālī's wiser and more moderate approach is much the same as his stance toward logic and mathematics, holding onto the device and condemning only what might accompany it. Granted the *Sharīʿa* condemns certain instruments for their association with vicious company and debauched practices—wine, gambling, female impersonators. Yet what is not explicitly forbidden is permissible. It is not unlawful to sing what would be lawful if merely spoken. "Whenever joy is permissible, so is the stirring up of joy." And likewise with courage, resolution, love, or longing, including the love of God.

From the references to Sufi music and dance in Ghazalī's *Iḥyā'* and his praise of Sufi practice as an avenue toward resolution of the speculative dilemmas that had triggered his spiritual crisis,[43] it is not hard to discern that Sufi music played its part in resolving that crisis. With the authority that gave him the title *Ḥujjatu 'l-Islam*, the Proof of Islam, Ghazālī more than repaid the debt by defending music juridically and philosophically, not only when spiritually employed but in any licit context. Analyzing song into its elements, each of which he finds permitted by tradition, Ghazālī concludes that the traditional authorities deem song no different from poetry, or ordinary, unornamented speech. Pointing to the Qur'ānic thesis that the embellishments found in nature are the work of God (35:1), he argues that song is just such an embellishment. Music, like erotic behavior, may need to be regulated, but it is not disapproved by the Law. And neither is "dancing and the beating of tambourines, or playing with hide shields and darts, or looking on at the dancing of Abyssinians and Blacks on occasions of joy."[44]

A Muslim contemporary of our own age argues in much the same vein:

> The idea has gained popularity somehow, that Islam, as a religion, is against the fine arts and that music is prohibited by the *Sharīʿa*. The fact of the matter is that jurists have shown strictness in this regard only to avoid waste of resources. But this strictness has nothing to do with the *Sharīʿa*. It is based on judicial discretion. Anything that may lead to evil through excess and abuse can be curtailed by judicial discretion. But this can never change the reality of the *Sharīʿa* and its true prescriptions. On this the Qur'ān (7:30–31) says: "Say: Who has forbidden the ornament of God which He brought forth for His servants, and the good things of His providing. . . . Say: My Lord has forbidden only indecencies, inward and outward, and sin, and unjust insolence, and that you associate with God that for which He sent down no authority, and that you say concerning God such as you know not."[45]

The modernist author, Abū 'l-Kalām Āzād, addresses some of the same arguments that troubled Ghazālī. He differs from the classical authors in four respects: He generalizes, to include the fine arts at large; he cites economic rather than moral constraints; he focuses more on secular pleasures as an adornment to human life and less on Sufi practice; and he writes with one eye cocked toward a non-Muslim public, or toward secular-minded readers who might be seduced from Islam by the thought that theirs is a dour faith. So he blames not puritan jurists of the past but critics (and extremists?) in the present for misconstruing the Islamic ethos and intent.

But in Ghazālī's time, as in our own, not every authority was convinced by such defenses. Music remains problematic in Muslim countries, and in Muslim law it was classically disputed whether one who breaks a lute, a tabor, pipe, or cymbal must reimburse the owner. Abū Ḥanīfa takes the affirmative, since instruments are articles of lawful commerce. But their use is not so clearly countenanced. And two of Abū Ḥanīfa's followers, Abū Yūsuf and Muḥammad, dissent from his view, pressing for greater zeal.[46] Makkī and Ghazālī struggled with the traditions, but Mālik did make it a duty to return a newly acquired slave girl on discovering that she could sing, and Shāfiʿī frowned on music, chess, and backgammon—"all the games that people play. For play is not the practice of the pious or the manly."[47]

Dress and Display

Still manliness is not always the aim in view. The Qur'ān (7:26) plays at the interface of poetry and prose when it informs its hearers that God "bestowed clothing on you to cover your shame and put you in fine feather, but the garment of piety is the best."[48] Utility here stands alongside modesty and ornament as the warrant for deeming clothing a divine gift. But piety trumps all of these, with an impact that arcs back to touch the matter of ornament. So we read in the *ḥadīth*: "Whoever wears a silk garment in this world shall not wear it in the next." But note the structural symmetry. Such patterns, as Oscar Wilde knew long before Levi-Strauss, are the topiary frame of wit—itself a secular value.

Islamic traditions about clothing are as variegated as the fabrics they address. Some of the ideas come with the booty of conquest, some are of domestic manufacture. There are traditions urging that silk should be cut up for women's veils. Others allow silks for men suffering from a skin inflamation. The broad consensus is that silken clothing and gold jewelry are fit for women's wear but too luxuriant for men. Yet exceptions can be made: a signet ring for men, for example. One *ḥadīth* has it that silk is best sold; another that it should be burnt; others allow a small amount for trimming. Both the Prophet and his wife ʿĀ'isha are said to have worn various colors. A Paris MS of Ḥarīrī's *Maqāmāt* dated to early-thirteenth-century Syria shows Pilgrims "wearing *Iḥrām* garments that are dyed in subdued hues"—not in the now obligatory white.[49] Ibn ʿAbbās is quoted with the advice: "Eat what you like and wear what you like as long as you avoid two things: prodigality and pride," a sentiment much echoed. But elsewhere we are cautioned that a plain white garment is suitable for meeting God, in mosques or in the grave.[50]

Muslim jurists have their work cut out for them when they turn to sewing a coherent legal doctrine from the patchwork of counsels preserved in *ḥadīth*. The dislike of luxury is plain. Gold rings, silver cups, silk, satin, brocade—even tanned leather is proscribed in various traditions.[51] The reasoning is plain once again: Luxury, or even fancy, distracts. Muḥammad, it is said, was given a spotted silk mantle; but, finding it distracted him in prayer, he cast it aside and would not wear it again.[52] Yet just such distractions become delights to dandies, whose variegated silks are caught still fluttering in the pages of Hamadhānī's thousand-year-old *Maqāmāt*.

A man who trails his garment rakishly, Muḥammad warns in one *ḥadīth*, trails his hem in Hell. In a more credulous variant, one such decadent was swallowed up by the earth.[53] He who attracts mortal eyes here will not be looked on by God in the Hereafter.[54] Yet what is condemned in this world is a reward in the next: "He who drinks from a silver cup drinks hellfire";[55] but the meed of the heedful, "their recompense for what they have borne—a garden and silk" (Qur'ān 76:12).[56] The images are brilliantly limned: "God will bring those who have been faithful and done righteously into gardens, under which rivers flow, where they are allowed armlets of gold and pearl, and their clothes will be of silk" (22:23).

Some Muslims preferred not to wait. As Yedida Stillman writes:

> The idea of austerity in male attire quickly gave way in the century following the Prophet's death, with the rise of a leisured class in the Islamic Empire. Only ascetic pietists still wore simple clothing, and they eventually came to be known as Ṣūfīs because of their plain wool (*ṣūf*) garments. The Muslim bourgeoisie, on the other hand indulged itself with garments made from every conceivable type of luxury fabric and justified their indulgence with countertraditions expressing the permissibility of wearing silk, brocade, satin, and the like. In the words of one such countertradition, "When God bestows benefaction upon one of his servants, He wishes the physical sign of that benefaction to be visible on him."[57]

Stories of the luxurious garments of the Umayyad court may be meant by later comers to discredit the ousted dynasty. But the art of the era shows that Umayyad luxury was no fiction. And we note that clothing was a target, precisely because it was a mode of self-expression and a ready vehicle of excess. Neither the obloquy nor the ostentation ended with the Umayyads.

The richly bordered garments that Arab monarchs bestowed on favorites, poets, musicians, philosophers, and potentates, evolved into a secular ceremonial. By 'Abbāsid times *tirāz* meant not just embroidered fabric but robes of honor (Arabic *khilā'*, cognate with the English gala) presented on court occasions and bearing suitably ornate and precious designs, often inscribed in gold thread running through the silk.[58] Production of such fabrics, since they bore the ruler's insignia was, like the coinage, typically a royal prerogative, and a prince's court had its own factory and artisans dedicated to the purpose.

Tirāz bespeaks pomp, as Ibn Khaldūn explains. It is a mark of authority and a sign of favor, sharing the éclat of power. Pre-Muslim dynasties, Ibn Khaldūn writes, used figural borders that might include images of the king. Muslim rulers substituted their own names, along with auspicious phrases. Most dynasties followed the practice, and its elaboration became an index of prosperity. But the early Almohads abandoned *tirāz*, "because they had been taught by their imām, Muḥammad b. Tūmart al-Mahdī, the ways of religion and simplicity. They were too austere to wear garments of silk and gold. . . . Their descendants in the later years of the dynasty, however, re-established it somewhat, although not nearly as splendidly as it had been.[59] The inscription, worked in gold, might well be a pious phrase. But, as Ibn Tūmart saw, the subtext too readily took control. Indeed, both the medium and the message bespoke secular values: elegance, virtuosity, royal favor, sovereign authority. Fabulous sums were spent on court dress. The gold thread in a single military robe could cost 500 gold dinars, and in 1122, as Stillman learns from Maqrīzī, 14,000 robes were needed for a single court event.[60]

The dialectic does not stop there. In Fāṭimid Egypt the garments of a Shīʿite imām, who was imbued with divine light and the charisma of infallibility, themselves acquired *baraka*, and *ṭirāz* fabrics began to show up in large numbers as burial garments. The Fāṭimid court, not slow to note the market potential of its franchise, developed a special line of *ṭirāz* for sale to the public. The sale of luxury garments to the bourgeoisie became a significant source of revenue to the court, and bogus inscriptions soon appeared, presumably from unauthorized manufacturers, much as prestige brands are pirated today.[61]

By Mamluk and Ayyubid times, vesting with a *khilāʾ* was the name for investiture in office. In Cairo, Alexandria, and Damascus government workshops still turned out court dress. But the fine garments were now also privately produced. The *khilā'* market of Ibn Khaldūn's Cairo bustled with dealers. Hunting scenes were featured on one design, an emblem of secularity. As uniforms grew increasingly standardized for the military and for civil servants in the Turkic regimes, clothing all the more marked the man. Only the *ʿulamāʾ* eschewed the *khilāʾ* and its distinctive *ṭirāz* bands. Black robes and a turban, the garments of austerity, had become their uniform.

Social status is not a religious value. But where religious values are held high, a devotional posture can enhance social status. Hence Ghazālī's concern over the worldly use of spiritual gestures.[62] Two social divisions of greatest concern to classical Islamic societies were strongly underscored by dress: that between women and men, and that between Muslims and non-Muslims, the *dhimmī*s, the tolerated or "protected" communities of the People of the Book. Turbans, sometimes called "the badge of Islam" were a mark of Muslim male dignity and gravitas. Veiling was an expression of female dignity and chastity, at least among urban, as opposed to peasant or beduin, women.

The veil was and still is most commonly seen (by both advocates and detractors) as a religiously mandated expression. But many values lend it support, not a few of them tinged with secularity. For the reserve that the veil and other forms of covering announce is a mark of respectability. The resumption or reimposition of veils for women in Islamic societies today bears nationalistic as well as pietist overtones, and the two often interpenetrate. But 40 percent of the educated Egyptian women interviewed in one study explained that they went veiled or wore "Islamic dress" because it was the latest fashion. The currency of that fashion in turn is an expression of cultural identity and of resistance to values and lifestyles often seen as threatening and foreign. Neo-Islamic dress, "a full- length loose gown, or a longsleeve loose shirt and a full-length skirt, or loose slacks with an overshirt extending below the waist, sometimes a long light overcoat, and a head scarf . . . or wimple . . . has become a sort of pan-Islamic uniform."[63] The message, in part, is one of assertive unavailability. So it carries a feminist subtext, but without recourse to the language of liberated or confrontational sexuality. And again, Islamic or *Sharʿī* dress can express rebellion against "often liberal, pro-Western, middle-class parents, or in a more political form, against secular, modernizing, but undemocratic governments."[64] But what can be a matter of personal choice and communal self-affirmation in an open and pluralistic society all too readily becomes a matter of oppression in a closed society, or one in which social pressures are seeking to force closed a door—to light and open air, to jobs, education and opportunity, to personal expression and social interaction—that might otherwise have opened.

In medieval times the veil could be emulated by non-Muslim women, and the turban meant as much to a respectable non-Muslim as a business suit might mean to a European today. Garments bore too powerful a valence to be left untouched by invidious markings. In Mamluk Egypt, for example, social stratification was sharply signaled: "*Dhimmī*s were so-to-speak color coded by their outer garments. Beginning with a decree issued in 1301/700, Christian men had to wear a blue turban, Jews a yellow one, and Samaritans, a red one, in clear contrast to the white *ʿimāma* worn by Muslims. Christian, Jewish, and Samaritan women were required to appear in public in a blue, yellow, or red *izār* [wrap], respectively."[65]

Sharīʿa law under Islamic regimes ruled that *dhimmī*s were not to ride horses, bear arms, or emulate Muslim dress. They must wear a thick cord-like belt, short cropped hair, and special headgear. Often there was a patch or badge, sometimes specified to bear the image of an ape for Jews and a pig for Christians. Neck rings of lead or iron might be required, to distinguish non-Muslims at the baths, and at times even a brand or tattoo. Repeatedly the restrictions were relaxed, often on the community's payment of huge indemnities. But they were regularly reimposed at the demand of the *ʿulamāʾ* or the mob, in keeping with the Qurʾānic (9:29; cf. 2:61) demand that non-Muslims be humiliated.

Such regulations do not speak for the humanism of monotheistic ethics. But the sumptuary rules that S. D. Goitein calls an "obsession pestering Muslims almost throughout their entire history" do reveal the interplay of secularity with religious exclusivism. They signify intolerance and triumphalism, but they are also "a sign of the excessive importance attributed to clothing and the status it confers" in Muslim societies.[66] Just as robes of honor can become ends in themselves, so can the invidious differentiation of credal commitments and communal engagements. Status, in Islamic norms, is based on piety. And that means Islamic piety. So a Muslim (marked by clothing) becomes a socially superior being; a *dhimmī*, a social inferior. Since the external so readily displaces the internal as the focus of attention, the value system that the sumptuary laws were supposed to regiment is now inverted: Status becomes the end, piety and the signs of piety and affiliation become the means. Such inversions are a risk in any attempt to objectify what is of moment spiritually. The effort to institute a seemingly authentic norm has undercut more central and more universal norms. The issue remains for Muslim thinkers and leaders to address.

Dunyā and Dīn—in Wine, War, and Love

Secular values raise their heads in the very heart of Islamic norms. They may rival religious values, offering a release from perfect earnestness and magnifying their intrinsic appeal through claims upon the love of freedom and the delicious delight of the forbidden. They may be coopted by religiosity, and they may exploit its energies in turn—from within, by turning religious projects to secular ends, and from without, by antipathy and mockery. What we must not ignore in these dialectics is the valuation placed on the secular by the faith itself, which prizes asceticism yet treats sensuous delight as a divine gift, which ascribes all power to God yet seeks mastery in God's name, which denounces wine and gambling but promises wine in heaven (47:16) and gambles this world for a heaven whose pleasures would be damnable on earth.[67]

There is a chiasmus here. So far as wine goes, Kathryn Kueny's study of the semiotics of wine in Islam, blames a deep ambiguity in the nature of wine. She finds a cultural ambivalence that she traces to the physiology and phenomenology of intoxication.[68] But this may be to describe the effect rather than name its cause. For to speak of an ambiguity is already to presume an ambivalence. And the account is also awfully general. Many cultures celebrate or condemn, regulate or restrict wine and other intoxicants, often simultaneously. The distinctive Islamic response is colored by the role of wine in pre-Islamic Arab culture, the ethos of the tavern and wine garden and the values they fostered, values that Arabic poetry will articulate well into the Islamic age and that the laws and discourse of Islam will both react against and appropriate.

Wine, to the pre-Islamic poets, was "red as the blood of sacrifice."[69] But just as these poets did not balk at appropriating sacred images to their secular purpose, when they boasted their manly strength, love of pleasure, dogged determination, bitter but unbending resolution before the blows of fate and the threat of oblivion, so the Prophet did not hesitate to use their sensuous imagery for his own higher and more ordered, if more didactic purpose.

Following in the footsteps of Mary Douglas, Kueny notes that the Qur'ān treats wine and other intoxicants not only as a threat but as a blessing and a sign of grace.[70] On Judgment Day, nurslings will be forgotten, babes aborted, men will seem drunk.[71] But the wine so freely passed and poured in the gardens of the Qur'ānic paradise, does not intoxicate or inebriate.[72] It does not cloud the mind or arouse debauched behavior. It leaves no hangover. Cooling wine becomes the emblem of heavenly bliss; and the scalding, bitter drafts reserved for the denizens of Hell become the emblem of their torments.[73]

As Kueny shows, the Qur'ānic revelations as to wine follow a progression, from the open acceptance of Sura 16 (v. 67), to the announcement that wine and gambling hold both sin and benefit, "but the sin is greater than their profit" (2:220), to the demand that believers turn out sober for prayer (4:43), to the admonition to shun wine and gambling as satanic abominations, barriers to felicity (5:90–91).[74] The *ḥadīth* knows that wine was not always forbidden. It was banned at a specific juncture, as the Prophet's companions are asked to recall in later years. But the *ḥadīth* makes of the Qur'ānic admonition a categorical prohibition with legally defined boundary conditions, penal sanctions, and corollaries in the laws of purity and commerce.[75]

Wine bears a meaning in the culture the Prophet grew up in; it acquires a heightened meaning in his own discourse. That heightening assures the prominence of wine in rebellious and antinomian gestures. The ambivalence that the Qur'ānic verses never wholly suppress intensifies in poetry, giving impact to the Sufi poet's wine imagery and piquancy to the ambiguities that secular poets and decadents play with after the rise of Islam.

The general problem is not unique to Islam. It is a fragment of the larger issue faced by all teachings that seek to reorient humankind toward higher values and yet make incentives or rewards, stages or phases, standards or criteria of the familiar goods that we human beings pursue. The secular trinity of pleasure, wealth, and honor raise pure and arbitrary freedom as their banner. They resist the moral monist's recasting of freedom as responsibility and reject the reduction of autonomous sensations and excitations to mere tokens. Dialectically, some would say diabolically, secular values reassert their power. For imagination will not be still. Even God, right, and immortality must speak in sensuous and thus secular terms when rhetoric sets them before the tribunal of popular imagination. With a wizened and perennial smile, imagination will remark that its best audience, the *vulgus populus*, knew all along what was really good.

The intellectual and spiritual soul, which pietists and contemplatives picture as locked in earnest debate or deadly combat with the selfish ego, for which imagination speaks (and would prefer to do the thinking), begs to disagree. It knows of higher goals, prefigured in the absolutes of moral judgment—a higher freedom than arbitrary choice and capricious action, a higher joy than sensuous delights. It even knows a higher impulse in the *vulgus populus*, which it hopes to shape into a holy mass. Yet it is powerless to picture the goods it promises without surrendering its thoughts to its adversary, imagination.

The true focal point is God. In the prophetic imagination of Islam at its point of origin that means the reality of judgment, God's justice sternly confronting human frailty.[76] That vision casts all other sights into stark relief, exposing the worthlessness of all merely worldly concerns. On Judgment Day the oblivious and distracted will be jolted into awareness. Their gaze, in the striking image of the Qur'ān, will be turned about and redirected. Suddenly it will dawn on the benighted that they have bought dear and sold cheap, that temporal distractions have lost them eternal bliss and cost them eternal pain.[77] In every revival of Islam and every attempt to recapture its pristine prophetic message, the same vivid contrast reemerges, between worldliness and religion—*dunyā* and *dīn*. It is Ibn Ṭufayl's burden when he recasts an old saw: This world and the next are "like two wives; if you make one happy you make the other miserable."[78]

Radical monotheism is exclusive. It can be jealous not only of other gods but of any rival commitment. Islamic rigor and its sometime rival, sometime ally, mysticism, are vigorously, militantly theocentric. They seem to speak for the sternness of a God of perfect justice. Yet the God of monotheism is also merciful, *most* merciful, in the epithet most frequently invoked in Islam. His mercy is evident in His theophany, the grace of His creative act and providence, above all, in His sending prophetic admonishers to the wayward and distracted, calling them back to allegiance, allowing repentance and surrender, *islām* to His will.

Here we strike the root of a cardinal paradox engendered by the tension between monotheism and secularity: In Islam, as in the other faiths, this world is often imaged as an antechamber; its values are taken to serve those of the next. Time remains the enemy, as it was in the pre-Islamic poets. But they saw time as inexorable, unforgiving fate. Monotheism proposes that time can be defeated. It boasts that death itself shall die. The world cannot win the resulting contest—except by distractions. Yet transcendence too cannot win at the world's game, except by the world's own means. So Islamic otherworldliness, when it turns to that game, can be very worldly—seemingly must be, if the profession and propagation of Islam are to achieve their worldly goals. Muḥammad was a political and military as well as a religious leader, and from his immediate successors and their rivals to the "seventy odd" splinter groups of the faith—the Shīʿites, Khawārij, ʿAbbāsids, Almohads, Almoravids, Mahdists, and Wahhābīs, to the followers of Khomeinı, Qaddafi, and bin Laden today—every major Muslim movement in history has claimed political as well as spiritual authority, and many have used military and other coercive means to win their claims, even as they used spiritual inspiration to legitimate their temporal authority.

That *jihād*, construed as military contest aimed at the expansion of Islam, should be counted a central institution of Islam reflects the worldly claims made by Islam in behalf of otherworldly aims.[79] Islam does seek allegiance in this world. Even the word *islām* bears more than a hint of triumphalism. It does connote pacification as well as submission to God's will—peace under God's dispensation, as the Muslim authorities understand it—much the sense that 'peace' had, say, in the *pax Romana*. Yet early in Islamic history Muslims saw that warfare is a project fraught with values inimical to those of monotheistic morals and spirituality, and a potent source of secularity.[80] Faith fueled the Crusades as a project to remake the world in God's plan, but it also fanned a lust for conquest. And later it breathed exhaustion with the carnage of crusading and bred the pacifism of the anti-crusading movement, whose spirit can still be heard in its songs in praise of another, less ambitious peace. In Arabic literature too the same piety that demands the hegemony of religion over politics bespeaks a striking rejection of conventional notions of *jihād*.

The Sincere Brethren of Basra picture the representatives of humanity defending man's dominion over nature by boasting that the sons of Adam worship one God. The king of the jinn, who adjudicates the animals's case against the humans, asks how it is, if all men worship one God, that human sects are so divided; and if all seek the same Goal, "Why then do they slay one another?" A "reflective Persian" answers: "This does not arise from faith, for 'There is no compulsion in faith' (Qur'ān 2:257); rather it comes from the institution of faith, that is from the state," religion's younger and lesser brother, which needs power to establish a religion, but perverts that power by making it an end in itself, seeking domination through religion. Such corruption of the spiritual impulse is all too palpable at the present moment. Blood lust, anger, envy, and fanaticism desecrate the very name of Islam, distancing where they have not eclipsed, its spiritual goal. True *jihād*, as the Sufis say, is self-mastery, and the really precious sacrifice is self-sacrifice.[81] Here the Ikhwān sublimate Islamic militancy, in keeping with the Sufi ideal and the dictum of *Pirkei Avot* (4.1), "Who is a hero? He who quells his inclination."[82]

Turning from thoughts of war and militancy to a more peaceful focus of literature, consider romantic love. Here is a home for the secular par excellence. For lovers create a cosmos in their coupling. They are impatient of external bounds to their attachments. Yet all monotheistic religions are active in regulating erotic relationships—with whom they shall be formed, when, how, and for what duration. The religions are guided by ideas of the worth and dignity of the human person[83] but also by concerns for offspring, social structure, hygiene, and the uses and postures of the human body, created in the image of the Divine.

Poetry pursues interests of its own, the lure of sentiment and promise of impact. It celebrates the sensual, heightening and modulating the emotive impact of sensuality by setting it into dramatic conflict against risk, enmity, interference, and the most implacable of foes, time. The Arabic *nasīb*, the amatory opening of the pre-Islamic *qaṣīda*, was defined by its fixation on these themes. It reaches for a single limpid but complex emotion—romanticism loves emotive complexity—that of lost love, a love lost first to circumstance and ultimately to time. The Sincere Brethren catch the echo of this elegiac tone, applying it to their own spiritualizing ends, when they ascribe snatches of its poetry to the owl. He understands humankind, for

> he lives in their abandoned dwelling places, decayed buildings, and dilapidated castles. Having studied the ancient ruins of mankind, he has learned the lessons of ages past. . . . He fasts by day and weeps and worships by night. Often he admonishes mankind and calls them to recollection with his laments for bygone kings and vanished nations, declaiming stately elegies. . . .
>
> Where are the monarchs of old
> Who ranged from ʿUdhayb to Dhū Afrād?
> What hope have I if the halls of Muḥarriq are ruined . . .
> And the turreted towers of Shaddād?[84]

Hamadhānī, the greatest secular satirist in Arabic, pays tribute to Imruʾ al-Qays (d. ca. 550), the poet prince and legend-laced quester to avenge his father's murder, for creating the topos of the abandoned campsite. Abū 'l-Fatḥ al-Iskandarī, Hamadhānī's rogue hero, echoes a line of Imruʾ al-Qays's most famous *qaṣīda* on the opening page of the *Maqāmāt*: "He was the first of all those who halted to grieve at abandoned encampments. Now *that's* 'setting out early, birds still in their nests'!" [85] In the "Jurjān Encounter," Abū 'l-Fatḥ, as usual in disguise, strikes a metaphor worthy of Imru' al-Qays himself. The rogue, in the guise of a wretch jaded by vagabondage, recalls his babe, left at home—"Like a bangle of silver, lost and left cracked / On the lea by maids of the tribe."

Here is a taste of the poetry of Imru' al-Qays, his "Golden Ode" or *Mu'allaqa*, one of the seven odes recognized as early as the eighth century as the finest examples of pre-Islamic poetic art and thus, in the strict sense, a pre-Islamic classic. I translate as follows:

Stop, that we three may weep, recalling a lover
 At a campsite where the twisting dune falters
Between Dakhūl and Ḥaumal,
 Tūdih and Miqrāt.

The traces are not yet erased
 By the weaving upon it of south and north winds,
Although you can see oryx dung cross its barrens and hollows,
 The tracks dotted through it like pepper grains now.

As I did on the morn of the day her tribe left,
 So I stand once again,
And I watch as they load, like a colocynth splitter
 From among the acacias.

And my friends standing with me,
 Their beasts over against me,
Say: *"Don't perish now—*
 Take heart, Pull together."

But my cure is my tears
 That fall in profusion.
And what good are tears
 Shed over cold tracks?

"So wept you before over little Ḥārith's mother,
 And before that, for her neighbor, Umm Rabāb at Ma'sal."
When either arose the musk wafted from them
 Like the breath of the East wind, pungent with cloves—

And the teardrops of longing
 Streamed down my breast,
'Til the width of my swordbelt
 Was wet with my tears—

"And had you not many a fair day with them—
 Not least, that day that you spent in the vale of Juljul—"
And the day that I hamstrung my mount for the maidens!
 Oh, the pack to be carried with my camel gone!

While they played with the meat,
 Tossed the fat back and forth—
From one girl to another,
 Like fringes that dangle on twisted raw silk.

And the day that I climbed into ʿUnayza's litter—
    "And she said to you, 'Now what! You're making me walk!'"
And she said, with the saddle leaning off with us in it—
    'You've ruined my camel. You get down, Imru' al-Qays—'

And I said to her, 'Just keep on going, loosen up on the reins.
    Don't hold back one more taste of your juicy red fruit.
You're no different from others I've come to with child,
    Or distracted from nursing year old babes decked with charms.'

When the child cried behind her,
    She would turn part way toward him.
But the part underneath me—
    That part never turned.

Yet one day on the brunt of a sand slope,
    She turned chaste—
Broke it off with an oath
    That could not be undone.

Ah, Fāṭima, gently now with your teasing.
    If you must cut me off, then be fair.
Loathe me if you will, but untangle our clothing.
    Then shed me and go free.

Are you dazzled because
    The love of you slays me,
And whatever you order
    My heart must obey?

Your eyes shed no tear
    But to strike my heart's depths.
With two darts from those eyes,
    I am hit fatally.

There's an eggshell pavilion
    Where none hoped for entry
That I've dallied in gaily
    Taking unhurried pleasure—

Slipped past watchers and kinsmen,
    Avid to hail the dawn of my death—
As the Pleiades showed themselves in the heavens,
    Their rising unfurling a gem studded sash.

At the curtain when I entered,
    She had slipped off her clothing,
All but her nightdress, ready for sleep.
    'Great God! You're incorrigible!'

Then I lifted her up,
    And I walked,
She trailing a broidered hem down behind us,
    Erasing our steps.

Clear of the compound, swallowed up in the trough
    Of the waves of the dune,
I drew her head to me,
    Caressing the hair of her temples.

She swayed to me,
    Slender of thigh and sweet ankle
Willowy, white, and not overblown,
    Breasts gleaming like mirrors.

Turning, she showed me
    Her full and smooth face,
Eyes like a doe's glance,
    Guarding her fawn,

And her neck like the neck of an oryx—
    Not overlong,
When she gracefully shows it—
    And not unadorned.

The hair wreathing her back,
    Twisted up and coal black,
Plaited locks tumbling down from her comb,
    Thick as dates on a palm.

Hair twisted upwards,
    And curls wandering down,
Doublets and loose tresses,
    Knots coming unwound.

Waist lithe as my reins,
    And as supple and slender—
And a leg like papyrus
    Bending down to the water.

Motes of musk scintillate
    Just over her bed,
As she sleeps through the morning,
    Leisurely, still undressed.

She gives with indulgence—
    Fingers light as the sandworms—
Or a toothpick of tamarisk,
    Never heavy or coarse.

She lights up the gloom
    Like the bright candelabrum
Of a monk in his cloister,
    Locked away in his prayers.

On her like would the calmest eye gaze with delight,
    Pleasure turning to ardor,
As she stands, virginal,
    Between girl's bodice and woman's—

Like the virginal white,
    Fed on water unsullied,
Of a first ostrich egg,
    Slightly muddled with yellow.

Let men other and blinder
    Take consolement for youth.
My heart will never
    Betray the passion I've known.

Haven't I shouldered down enough men to attain you,
Beaten off enough foes—
Every one as attentive
And as honest as I in his blame!

O night, like a wave of the sea,
Swelling your tresses upon me
Like curtains of cares
To oppress—

I've told you before
When you spread your loins on me
And mounted up lazily,
Slow on my chest:

"O tedious night,
Make way for the dawn!"
But what good is dawn
When it rolls slow as you?

Ah, what a night—when each star
Seems bound by a line to Mt. Yadhbul,
And the Pleiades, tied in their stalls
By cables of linen to silent stone slabs.

The waterskin strap I've set on my withers,
Low down as a packhorse, for many a tribe,
Cutting through barren gulleys
Bald as any ass belly,

While the wolf howled like a wastrel,
Disconsolate, and disowned.
And I've said to him, 'Wolf, why do you howl?
No one would get rich in choosing between us—

We both, when we've caught somewhat,
Seem apt to lose it.
He's the loser who plows
Your furrow—Or mine.'

Setting out early,
Birds still in their nests,
I've been off bagging game
On a great threadbare hulk,

Charging and wheeling, headlong over heels,
Hurtling together, down from above,
Like one giant boulder
Cast down by the flood.

He's a bay, and his backcloth slips off him
Smooth as rain from a pebble washed by the stream.
Slender but feisty, he pounds when he's riled
Like a great copper cauldron that's set on the boil.

Steady he flows when the game starts to dribble,
Their hooves kicking clods from the rough trodden ground.
The lad slides down off him like a garment slipped off—
A coarse load, though light, for such a fine perch.

That horse runs like a child's top
    Passed on a string
From one hand to another,
    The thread stretched between.

He's got flanks like a fawn
    And legs like an ostrich.
He lopes like a wolf
    And trots like a fox.

Solidly made—check his stance from behind,
    His tail mounted square in the gap of his legs,
Blocking it richly,
    Reaching just off the ground.

His back, when he turns,
    Square as the grindstone for colocynth buds,
But smooth as the stone
    Where a bride pounds her spices.

Spattered blood at his throat
    Like tinctures of henna
Matting curly blond hair,
    At his neck's forward thrust—

There, just before us—
    The herd of gazelles,
The females milling giddy,
    Like maids in long skirts!

Turned tail, they scattered, strung out in a line,
    As beads fall from the necklace
Of a swell of the tribe
    When laid on too heavy by uncles on both sides.

I glued him to the leaders,
    Still pursed up together—
An unbroken mass,
    The stampede passed below.

So we took two at once,
    A buck and a doe,
Not a drop of sweat on him
    To wash down his flanks.

Then the cooks were long at it,
    Browning and roasting,
Toasting and grilling,
    Boiling up a quick stew.

Only later, while resting, did somebody notice,
    Long after the day's long events had been done—
He had stood there—
    Our eyes could hardly embrace it—

He had stood through the evening
    In clear sight, with the saddle
And bit still upon him,
    Waiting to be let go

Friend, do you see the lightning out there?
Did you see how it spread,
Flickering fast as hands flash
In the blossoming stormclouds!

Or was it a hermit's light
Flared in the valley,
Its twisted wick guttered
As he makes free with oil?

There I sat with my two friends
On the ridge between Ḍārij and ʿUdhayb,
Contemplating what lay out there beyond us,
And what lay behind and ahead.

And now the storm's signposts of lightning stood over Qaṭan on the right,
Its left flank mounting up over Sitār and Yadhbul,
Drenching Kutayfa as it passed—turning up on their beards
The great trunks of acacia,

Passing on to Qanān,
Sending down by its spray
The white footed goats,
By every path downward.

At Taymāʾ not one trunk of palm was left standing—
Not one clump of reeds, unless buttressed with rocks.
And Thabīr, its great top swathed in those seas,
Was a man huddled up in a cloak of striped cloth.

By morning the peak of Mujaymir
Was snarled like a spindle—
Debris knotting its slope,
Borne by the flood and the storm,

Whose flow had flung down on the desert
The wrack of the mountain,
As a Yemeni merchant
Unbales his goods.

That morning the songbirds seemed drunk with spiced wine;
And the wild beasts drowned in the night,
Washed down in the flood from the uplands,
Looked like onions plucked up from the ground.

To the Muslim scholars who pored over the usages of the pre-Islamic poets with a view to fine tuning their glosses of the language of the Qurʾān, the old poetry represented the pure Arabic of desert speech[86] but also the pure hubris of the desert ethos, the ethos of the *Jāhiliyya*, the days and ways of barbarism. And the Muslim scholars were not wrong. The *Muʿallaqa* of Imruʾ al-Qays is a tour de force in miniature of the romantic canon: the sense of loss and destiny, the relishing of sentiment for its own sake, of erotic passion, danger, laughter, proud prowess and rejection, the thrill of sport and of risk taking for its own sake, pride of power, and projection of one's freedom and pride onto one's beast, the intimacy and loyalty of fellowship, the blind power of the elements as metaphor of the wild freedom the poet loves, and simultaneously, symbol and agency of the destruction he fears.[87]

Even the seemingly incongruous image of uprooted onions at the poem's close finds its place in the romantic canon as a kind of secular memento mori. Writing of this bit of iconography as a pictorial device and without obvious reference to Imru' al-Qays's kindred usage, Kenneth Clark translates the image into words:

> Roots and bulbs pulled up into the light give us for a moment a feeling of shame. They are pale, defenseless, unself-supporting. They have the formless character of life which has been both protected and oppressed. In the dark their slow biological gropings have been the contrary of the quick resolute movements of free creatures, bird, fish or dancer, flashing through a transparent medium, and have made them baggy, scraggy and indeterminate. Looking at a group of naked figures in a Gothic painting or miniature we experience the same sensation. The bulb-like women and root-like men seem to have been dragged out of the protective darkness in which the human body had lain muffled for a thousand years.[88]

Clark finds in the bulbous Gothic nude an alternative tradition to Greek ideals of nudity. For Imru' al-Qays, similarly, the passive, naked, vegetative images of violation with which the poem ends strikingly set off the active, sensuous forms of his hunting vignette and the lithe beauty of his lively nude word portrait. These images of vitality are made more vivid by the contrasting images of death, and tinged with a romantic poignancy by that backlighting.

Modern scholars find in pre-Islamic poetry an articulate conspectus of the values of the pre-Islamic age, emblematic of all that Islam has done and undone.[89] But the Islamic preservation of that poetry means that we must also reckon with what Islam has never done: It has not erased the fascination of the secular themes of love and conquest, fight and flight. Indeed the puritan strain in Islam heightens that fascination. Romantic themes are absorbed—assimilated or unassimilated or semi-assimilated—to the spirit and ethos of Islam. Their claim to life demands it, and Islam can scarcely gainsay them.

But subtler dialectics are at work alongside the dynamism of recalcitrant motifs. For the pre-Islamic poets boasted on two levels, we have suggested: first, openly, of their prowess or vertu (*muruwwa*); but also, between the lines, of the art that evokes their own emotions and the emotions they choose to conjure in the minds of others. So the subtler autonomy of art joins the outspoken insouciance of romantic values—mastery of horses, hounds, women, enemies, and rivals.

Bāqillānī (d. 1013) is testy when he sets out to criticize Imru' al-Qays. He thinks the *Muʿallaqa* far overrated. Focusing on the *nasīb*, he judges the poetry gross, overly concrete, offensive, implausible. But his critique moves ahead, line by line, as a literary commentary must. He appeals to formal criteria: Imru' al-Qays is prolix, repetitious, redundant, awkward. His language is forced. He swings wildly from elevated to low diction. His composition is disjointed, lacking in harmony, or even coherence. His thoughts are inconsistent; his style, unrefined. He pads his lines reaching for rhythms, adds details to no seeming purpose, undercuts his own claims with faulty transitions, antitheses, anticlimaxes. His images are commonplace, even vulgar or cheap; his wording, plain, weak, at times even effeminate, rarely original.[90]

Bāqillānī does not spare Imru' al-Qays's morals. He exploits the poet's self-betrayal while blaming his ill judgment in exposing himself: "His habit of depraving women need not imply their attachment to him . . . on the contrary, it should entail that they are repelled . . . by his levity, foul habits and base doings. He is so openly obscene that the noble minded would loathe the like of him and scorn even to speak his name. . . . Everything that he says of himself makes him contemptible, foolish, and indecent, and were better left unsaid."[91] Yet Imru' al-Qays knows his own charm. His art may seem crude to Bāqillānī; his "line" may sound trite as well. Still, he did not seem to want for lovers, before and after time overtook him.

Bāqillānī is an Ash'arite theologian and a fighter, the author of our oldest fully extant handbook of Muslim theological polemics (*K. al-Tamhīd*). His critique of Imru' al-Qays belongs to another classic work of his, on the Inimitability of the Qur'ān. His aim is to show how God's prose outstrips the overesteemed secular poetry whose standard bearer is the *Mu'allaqa* of Imru' al-Qays. Bāqillānī knows that he cannot destroy Imru' al-Qays's poetic authority simply by attacking his morals—even from the high ground lent him by the Qur'ānic condemnation of adultery, along with theft and murder (25:68, 60:12; cf. 24:2–3, 17:32). He must tackle the poet as a poet. His aesthetic is no more congruent than his morals with that of Imru' al-Qays. His is a different age with a markedly different sensibility. He looks for a seamless continuity in the ancient ode, which he surprisingly does find in the sacred text. That appraisal rests in part on love of the well-remembered scriptural verses, in part on the Ash'arite image of the Qur'ān as an eternal, cosmic reality. But the appeal is to continuity, ultimately an aesthetic category.

The dialectics of the polemic force this resort to literary standards. To discredit the poetry, Bāqillānī must undercut its claims to originality, concision, authenticity, and charm. He will play off Imru' al-Qays against the poets of his own day and even offer the old roué pointers on the proper way to write seductively, without loss of dignity (ad v. 17). He cannot undercut the poem without quoting and glossing it in extenso, acknowledging its fine points, and touring its images and effects, whether charming or disconcerting. But in this he succumbs to the secular subtext, the autonomy of the poet. Morally, he judges Imru' al-Qays as his post of *qāḍī* would suggest.[92] Aesthetically, he judges harshly, unfairly, but by standards that poetry itself projects, not excluding the vividly self-proclaimed standards of Imru' al-Qays's celebrated ode. Here *dīn*, the faith, bows to *dunyā*, the world. Almost losing sight of his chosen aim of using secular poetry to show off the inimitable art of revelation, Bāqillānī puts the Qur'ān to work in behalf of literary criticism, citing one of the sacred verses—each of which is called a portent by the faithful—to expose a flaw in Imru' al-Qays's diction.[93]

Transformed as it was by the coming of Islam, Arabic love poetry did not disappear. In some ways it transformed Islam, even from the outset. For a faith that would call young men to lay down their lives battling in God's path needs more to offer than the seeming abstraction of peace within the Absolute.[94] Muḥammad painted pleasure gardens, running with wine and water, milk and honey, as a reward for his warriors (Qur'ān 47:15). From the start these were symbols (*amthāl*—see 14:24, 16:75, 30:58, 60:10–11, 2:26, 29:43); but symbols, as poets have known at least since the earliest tales of Pygmalion, can come to life and captivate even their creators.

The perfect complement to the heavenly gardens and lush rivers were the fair, dark-eyed maidens, who, as tradition elaborated the theme, will welcome fallen warriors, and all the faithful men of Islam, with the embrace of long awaited true loves. The *Ḥūr* or houris, promised as mistresses, appear in the Qur'ān beginning in the Meccan period, (Qur'ān 44:54, 52:20, 56:10–40). Faithful women receive no male counterpart. For symbols always have an audience implicit. The *Ḥūr* are complaisant virgins with swelling breasts, like of age (to their husbands, thirty-three, the age of Jesus at his death). Their maidenhead is constantly renewed, tradition adds. ʿĀ'isha, the prophet's witty wife and erstwhile child bride, is said to have groaned on hearing this last, but she was reassured that in Paradise there will be no pain. The Qur'ānic litany, punctuated by the refrain: "Which of your Lord's favors do ye call a lie!" sets the scene elegantly: "Two gardens . . . of spreading branches . . . in them two fountains plashing . . . with every kind of fruit in pairs . . . lying on couches cushioned in brocaded silk, the fruit of both gardens near to hand. . . . And there maidens of downcast glance, untouched by man or jinn . . . like jacinth or coral. . . . Is the reward of goodness aught but good? (Qur'ān 55:46–60, cf. 62–77).

The maidens are prizes. They are called rewards—objects of ultimate conquest.[95] But they are made of dream stuff. Shākir b. Muslim describes their welcome, holding themselves out before each faithful arrival: "How I've longed for you!" When they speak, as they do in the traditions, they laughingly compare themselves to mere earthly wives.[96] In Ibn Wahb (743–813) the houri chides: "Wretched man, why did you not forswear such loves as these, that compared to mine last but a night or two."[97] How can mere reality compete with fantasy?

The perfection of the houris grows hyperbolic in tradition: Formed of saffron, amber, musk, or camphor, with skin so fair it is transparent, the paradisaical maidens are adorned with jewels. Their pavilions, each hollowed from a single pearl, house seventy beds and seventy couches. Jesus has a hundred houris at his disposal. Men will enjoy their houris as often as they have done good deeds, or as many times as the days they have fasted in Ramaḍān. Thus the *ḥadīth*: "A martyr has six privileges with God: He is forgiven his sins on the shedding of the first drop of his blood; he is shown his place in paradise; he is redeemed from the torments of the grave; he is made secure from the fear of hell and a crown of glory is placed on his head, of which one ruby is worth more than the world and all that is in it; he will marry seventy-two of the *ḥūrīs* with black eyes; and his intercession will be accepted for seventy of his kinsmen."[98]

As the Prophet matures, the *Ḥūr* recede into the background Qur'ānically, displaced in the later *sūrahs* (2:23, 3:13, 4:60, 13:23, 36:56, 43:70) by the beatified wives of the elect. But they do not fade from popular imagination or the religiosity that responds to the longings of that imagination. Since they both answer and displace an earthly sensuality, the *Ḥūr* naturally take on many of its tonalities. Accordingly, as Charles Wendell argued, one does not understand the houris by searching for foreign "influences." The key, rather, is in the *ḥadīth* attributing to the Prophet the self-revelatory words: "I am the most Arab among you." Following the lead of Josef Horovitz, Wendell shows that the white complexion of the *Ḥūr* is described in the same terms that pre-Islamic poetry applied to the beloved. Their goblets and brocades are borrowed from the song girls and cup bearers of the old poems of wine and love. The fair skinned and beautiful attendants that once moved gracefully among the pleasure gardens of the *Mu'allaqāt* and *Mufaḍḍaliyyāt* have slipped quietly into the Qur'ānic paradise.[99]

The welcome that the houris offer their battle-scarred lovers[100] reveals the vehicle of that transformation: The risk and energy of battle have been sacralized, and so has its reward–now universal, but still sensual. A poetic convention has become an eschatological promise and, in time, a theological dogma, complete with its own *balkafa*, fleshing out the cosmography of Islam. Ulysses' long awaited embrace with Penelope, the peaceful climax of the tumultuous dangers of the *Odyssey*,[101] is transfigured into a moral expectation for every faithful follower of the Prophet. But it is no longer the beleaguered wife who waits but a full-bosomed virgin, who emerges into reality from the avowed symbolism of revelation (Qur'ān 47:3, 15; 14:18, 26). The image holds sway by the sheer power of its beauty, as though this were a pagan theodicy, an oasis Valhalla and not a promise from the moral emissary of the One God.

The interplay of secularity with spirit grows more complex. For in Sufism the heavenly beloved, who has long awaited the release of her mortal hero from the embrace of his worldly love, becomes an archetype of the mystic's goal, a metaphysical persona who guides the soul—eternal, universal, yet his alone. Asín finds here the antecedent of Dante's Beatrice. In the *Epistle of Forgiveness*, a version of the heavenly journey of the Prophet, written "with a touch of irony so delicate as to be almost imperceptible," the blind poet Abū 'l-Alā' al-Ma'arrī "censures the severity of the moralists as contrasted with God's infinite mercy." Abū 'l-'Alā' "seeks to show with literary skill that many of the libertine and even pagan poets, who finally repented, were pardoned and received into paradise." The celestial maiden sent by God to welcome the weary wayfarer at the gates is the beloved of Imru' al-Qays![102] In Ibn 'Arabī the maidenly idée fixe remains powerfully erotic.[103] And for many Sufis the erotic becomes not the mere symbol but (as it was in Plato) the paradigm of that love by which the mystic yearns toward the divine.

Such love, with its delectable confusion of heavenly and terrestrial eros, sets a second star in the firmament, paired with the one star by which faith offers to guide one's course. Does the earthly erotic merely hint of divine love? Or is it somehow constitutive? Mystics may hang themselves on this ambiguity, and poets may relish it. So three topoi emerge: divine love symbolized by the earthly erotic, divine love subsumed or consumed in earthly eros, and a quasi-antinomian play on the ambiguity.[104]

Similarly, Islamic wine poems, like the corresponding paintings, may be allegories of divine intoxication, evoked as a forbidden worldly taste. But they may be subtle toyings with ambiguity. Or they may be mere wine poems, none too sublimated celebrations of the pleasures of the vine, now touched with an air of rebellion against the stringencies of Islam. Ibn al-Fāriḍ's famous *khamriyya* figures the 'obligatory' joys of mystic union on the illicit joys of wine, echoing the antinomian wine poems of Abū Nuwās (747–893)—who played in turn with religious themes in his secular poetry.[105] As the literature expands and the topoi rigidify, symbolism sometimes rests in the eye of the beholder. But even when the intent is clearly spiritual, it is hard to keep some eyes from straying from the higher sense to the image itself, or to the artistic act of symbolization.

The mystic poets of Islam move beyond the secular fascination with the play of ambiguity and the titillation of a sensuous or willful rebellion. Many promote confusion of erotic and spiritual intentions as a *sub*jective correlative to the pantheistic confusion of identities, human and divine, that is the great theme of their work. Their aim is to evoke that intoxicated state, beyond restraint, where ecstasy connotes union.

But Muslim purists typically abhor the erotic figuring of the divine. Cautious, if not adamant against mystic intoxication and its poetic devices, they quash its antinomian ambiguities by making love verses of their own. Their literary celebrations of love are sequined with rhyme, meter, and other decorations whose appeal is formal, aesthetic, and often sensual. The aim is to fight fire with fire, secular love against the mystic erotic confusions that supply the language of pantheistic libertinage. The resulting art and inquiries may be secular in manner and matter. But the motive is religious: the removal of all confusion between the sacred and the profane.

Thus among the celebrants of secular love we find Ibm Ḥazm of Cordoba (994–1064), poet, historian, jurist, author of the first systematic work in Arabic (or, it is said, in any language) on comparative theology. Widely recognized as one of the most original minds of medieval Islam, Ibm Ḥazm was clearly one of the most loyal.[106] He codified Ibn Dā'ūd's Ẓāhirī (literalist) doctrine of Islamic law and applied it systematically in the religious sciences. The son of a *wazīr* at the Umayyad court, he was raised among court and harem intrigues and saw the fall of his father's party's fortunes, exile and imprisonment in the legitimist cause, banishment, military service as *wazīr* to ʿAbd al-Raḥmān IV, capture and release, an interlude of writing, enthronement of a bosom friend as ʿAbd al-Raḥmān V, a brief new term as *wazīr*, the assassination of his patron, further imprisonment, a third stint as *wazīr* under Muʿtadd, the ultimately deposed last Umayyad caliph of Cordoba, a ten-year refuge in Majorca, and a long and stormy maturity of polemical scholarship.

Attacking Mālikī jurists as time servers and the ʿAbbādids of Seville as usurpers, Ibn Ḥazm was banned from teaching regular classes but continued to take disciples brave enough to befriend him. At his death he left some four hundred of his own works to his son. Like other Muslim literalists, he was suspicious of reason.[107] He criticized even the idea of logical impossibility, arguing that human notions of logic are subjective—and, just that, merely human notions, dependent on discursive thinking and the fragile thread of memory. His anticipations of Descartes' and Kant's criticisms of the faith of naive rationalism rest on a limpid yet rambunctious religious faith: What is absolute is neither nature nor the mind of man but God alone, a sheer, commanding will. It is the same faith that makes Ibn Ḥazm a fountainhead of the tradition of courtly love in his celebrated *Neckring of the Dove* (*Ṭawq al-Ḥamāma*), written apparently in the 1020s at Jativa after his release from capture in the battle for ʿAbd al-Raḥmān IV before Granada.[108]

The book is an essay on love—its signs and symptoms, phases, feelings, stratagems and changes—the gamut of romantic courtship, with its sighs and glances, loyalties and betrayals, secrets, hints, adversaries, trysts, triumphs, and disappointments. There are chapters on love at first sight, love letters, persons who fell in love while asleep and others who fell in love only after long acquaintance. The enemies of love include the Reproacher, the Slanderer, and the Spy. The work ends with a promised exaltation of continence and exhortation against sin. But every phase of love is lovingly described and recapitulated in poetry from the author's own *diwān*. Continence, for Ibn Ḥazm, is not mere detachment but the hard-won renunciation of those who have known and pursued love avidly, using every device of a worldly courtship and experiencing every emotional nuance and twinge of grief, separation, union, and forgetting, sensations cherished in reflection and canonized in art, as they were in anticipation.

Of the romantic and poetic values enunciated in Ibn Ḥazm's "delicate anatomy of chivalrous love," Gibb remarks: "It is strange that it was this same Ibn Ḥazm who, belonging to the narrowest school of Islamic theology, devoted much of the rest of his life to bitter attacks on his theological opponents; the sharpness of his tongue, which became proverbially linked with the sword of the tyrant al-Hajjāj, eventually forced him to give up political life and brought about his practical excommunication."[109] Von Grunebaum credits this curious collocation to the richness of the Islamic world and the versatility of its polymath authors.[110] But an explanatory hypothesis is perhaps less circular: Ibn Ḥazm offers secular love in place of the sublimated and unsublimated eroticism of the mystics. To those who found a spiritual meaning in erotic longings, Ibn Ḥazm offers a naturalistic alternative. This too may spiritualize love, by promoting courtliness. But the goal is to keep spirituality clear of sublimated emotions and theology clear of the metaphysics that artful theosophists and poets fathered upon those emotions—the monistic metaphysics of erotic mysticism. Love wins autonomy here not despite a puritan sensibility but at its behest.

Ibn Ḥazm himself labels *The Neckring* a secular exercise, calling it a recreation licensed by the sacred permission and encouragement of purely playful pastimes. He writes (after suitable *isnāds*): Abū 'l-Dardā' said, "Recreate your souls with a little vanity, the better to hold fast the truth." "A righteous and well approved father declared, 'The man who has never known how to comport himself as a cavalier will never know true piety.'" The Prophet himself said, "Rest your souls from time to time; they rust the same as steel does."[111] Here Islamic legalism and traditionalism declare their distance from the God-intoxicated excesses of those Sufis who claim to make God all yet seem in the same breath to wish to make man God and to throw over the traces of moral reserve, piety, and traditional belief and practice.

But Ibn Ḥazm uses a lateral approach, not a frontal attack like Bāqillānī's. The key words in each line of one of the erotic mystic poems of Ibn al-Fāriḍ might as well be chapter headings for Ibn Ḥazm: separation, reunion, loneliness, disquiet, anguish, memory, recollection, yearning, passion, joy, conquest, visitation.[112] Ibn al-Fāriḍ may echo the desert poets and their imitators, even borrowing almost every one of Mutanabbī's rhyme words in one composition,[113] but Ibn Ḥazm scorns the old poetry. Appealing to urbanity and courtly sophistication, he dismisses Imru' al-Qays and his ilk in tones of literary ennui: "Spare me those tales of Bedouins, and of lovers of long ago! Their ways were not our ways, and the stories told of them are too numerous in any case. It is not my practice to wear out anybody's riding beast but my own. I am not one of those who deck themselves out in borrowed plumes."[114]

Ibn Ḥazm's strategy, rooted in Ẓāhirīte theory is pursued by the later Ḥanbalites, especially the school of Ibn Taymiyya. For the Ẓāhiriyya were early exponents of secular love, and Ibn Taymiyya's followers expand his vehement opposition to monistic mysticism and mystical eroticism into a whole library of loving elaborations of the autonomous sensibilities of the erotic. All of their topoi are prefigured in Ibn Ḥazm.

Ibn Dā'ūd of Iṣfahān (868–909), the son and successor of the founder of the Ẓāhiriyya was a systematic and rational (at times even permissive) opponent of all reliance on human reason in elaborating Islamic law.[115] He stridently opposed pantheistic mysticism and was a signatory to the *fatwa* that led in time to the execution (in 922) of al-Ḥallāj, the mystic who had scandalously proclaimed *Anā al-Ḥaqq*, "I am the Truth." Ibn Dā'ūd was also the first Muslim to convey a tradition (on the authority of his father) ascribing to the Prophet the romantically appealing notion of martyrdom for love: "He who loves and keeps his secret, remaining chaste and forbearing, will be pardoned by God and consigned to Paradise."

Ill when he related this *ḥadīth*, Ibn Dā'ūd died, soon after, of his own concealed love for the youth to whom he had dedicated his magnum opus. So he reportedly confessed on his deathbed.[116] Passionate debate swirled for generations among the jurists and theologians around the story of his death and the figure of the martyr of love. But the topos had a much longer afterlife. For the new *ḥadīth* alloyed chastity with yearning and death. In the theme of unconsummated and consuming love the poetic literalists of Islam, by fusing piety with pathos, had forged a perennial prick to romantic delight, the all-too-medieval literary convention of Platonic love.

Ibn Taymiyya (1263–1328), as we mentioned in our introduction, was a leader of Muslim resistance to the Mongol invasion. An ardent ritualist, he sought to curtail the use of hashish, holding it an intoxicant, despite the seeming silence of the *Sharīʿa* on the subject, and he combated arbitrary use of the formula of triple (i.e., absolute) divorce as an abuse of the Law's intent. His strident antagonism to the quest for mystical union and the Sufi cult of saints makes him the godfather of all Islamic purists who find sensuality in Sufi *dhikr*s and fear pantheism in Sufi meditations. But it also made him godfather to the Ḥanbalite tradition of secular love.

Sufi leaders repaid Ibn Taymiyya's bitter enmity in kind and saw to it that he was persecuted.[117] He died imprisoned for his violent opposition to Sufi beliefs and practices. Monism and pantheism were among his chief charges against the mystics. They in turn accused him of corporealism. But he claimed to oppose both anthropomorphism (*tashbīh*) and abstractionism (*taʿṭīl*) in theology. He took refuge in saying that he described God as He described Himself in His Book. The author of a lost refutation of Ibn Tūmart, the founder of the Almohad movement, and of an extant *Refutation of the Logicians*, Ibn Taymiyya confessed that in his youth he was swayed by the works of Ibn ʿArabī. But that was before he detected their insidious heretical bent.

His teachings on love strove to follow the dogma championed by Aḥmad b. Ḥanbal (d. 855) that the dicta of the Qur'ān and Traditions should be accepted without inquiry or qualification (*bi-lā kayf*). So he opposed the Ashʿarite endeavor to reduce God's attribute of love to that of will. He defended love between man and God but attacked Sufi erotic monism as antinomian and ultimately blasphemous. Early Muslim mystics had struggled with the idea that only God is worthy of human love, and Ibn ʿArabī had suggested that human passion is of a piece with mystic love. But Ibn Taymiyya argued that human love is loyal and obedient only when it knows (as Aristotle might have said) its object, its means, motives, and occasions. There are different kinds of love, and the faithful should know better than to confuse wife with sister, or the love of God with eros.[118] The secularization of human love was a natural corollary of Ibn Taymiyya's position, and his disciples vividly delineate and go on to celebrate human love, aiming, in the first instance, to clear the mind of the moral and spiritual confusions retailed by the poets and the apologists of Sufi inebriation.

Ibn Qayyim al-Jawziyya (1272–1350), Ibn Taymiyya's principal disciple for sixteen years, accompanied him through his imprisonments and tortures. During the master's final imprisonment, both men wrote books, conversed, and prayed to keep up their courage. The disciple's *Rawdat al-Muḥibbīn, The Lovers' Garden*, is a thoroughgoing exposition of secular love, exploring divine love as well, but dismissing mystical eroticism. "Prolific but sensitive," Ibn al-Qayyim—whose father had superintended the Jawziyya *madrasa* of Damascus and who had himself flirted with unorthodoxy in his youth—brought together his master's anti-Ashʿarite and antimonistic polemics with ascetic and literary themes to forge what Bell calls the "definitive and most eloquent" statement of the Ḥanbalite doctrine of love.[119] Practical training in mysticism and erudition in the literary sources, emulation of Ibn Taymiyya's legal and theological doctrines, and appreciation of his ideal of spiritual warmth (in lieu of "incarnationist" ardor or "unificationist" *Schwarmerei*) made Ibn al-Qayyim the ideal elaborator of his master's approach. He knows that love belongs to God alone but vigorously refutes what he sees as the dangerous Sufi reading of that exclusivity and offers his own reconstruction of the goals and avenues of mysticism.

The *Rawdat al-Muḥibbīn* takes its outline and much of its material from *The Censure of Passion* by the moralist Ibn al-Jawzī (d. 1200). But it reverses the censorious current, treating secular love positively—as a "Garden of Delights." Sexual love is a legitimate facet of human experience. Its value is assured by clarity as to its distinctness from the spiritual love of God, with which it is consistently compared but never merged.[120]

Dropping the pedigrees of his traditions, Ibn al-Qayyim applies reasoned argument, anecdote, and entertainment single-mindedly to his task. Not that he has surrendered to the lure of philosophy or succumbed to the charms of literature. He is not a romantic. Indeed, he disapproves of Ibn Dā'ūd's martyrdom to passion.[121] But he sees a need to entertain as well as instruct—to instruct by entertaining. He knows that his didactic aim will fail if his work is merely didactic. He must expound the autonomous charms of human, natural love[122] if he is to preserve the higher love, of God, from subsumption into a hypocrite's rationale for sensuality or a self-deceiver's surrogate for spiritual fulfillment.

Ibn al-Qayyim's naturalism is vigorously anti-Platonic. He struggles against the courtly notion that 'love is destroyed by union' and celebrates licit unions, where love is intensified by usage—not, as in Ibn Dā'ūd, sanctified by abeyance. Profoundly secularized, love is now an end in itself, not a tragic triumph of obedience.[123] Rather than swamp the love of God in sensuality or worse, Ibn al-Qayyim makes an ally of amorous autonomy—for the sake of Heaven.

But such purity of motive is hard to sustain. Ibn Abī Ḥajala (1325–1375) was a Sufi but an intense admirer of Ibn Taymiyya and a virulent foe of monistic/erotic mystics like Ibn ʿArabī. He polished his style in a series of *maqāmāt* but asked to be buried with his *qaṣīda*s in praise of the Prophet. The collection echoed the style but rejected the erotic and monistic Sufism of Ibn al-Fāriḍ. Ibn Abī Ḥajala's *Anthology of Ardor* (*Diwān al-Sabāba*), which collected matter from predecessors like Ibn Ḥazm and Ibn Dā'ūd, became one of the most widely read Islamic works on love. Its contents—dealing with chaste love, love at first sight, sleepless nights, martyrs and victims of love, love notes, rivals, jealousies, and the like—are said to have influenced Stendahl.[124]

Something of a latitudinarian in personal practice, Ibn Abī Ḥajala, according to one detractor, was a Shāfiʿite to the Shāfiʿites, a Ḥanafite to the Ḥanafites, and a traditionist to the traditionists. More fairly, perhaps, he is called a Ḥanafī by rite but a Ḥanbalite in outlook. A follower of Ibn al-Qayyim, he lost the passionate balance that writer had struggled to maintain in behalf of licit union, betrayed by a sensuous eye, which his poetic tastes egged on. He was, as Bell puts it, "an amateur of delicately phrased indecencies" and delighted in verses praising the breeze that exposed the beauties of a sleeping boy by blowing aside his clothing.[125] The Ḥanbalite motive persists, but innocent delights seem now to give way to guilty pleasures.

As for Marʿī b. Yūsuf al-Karmī (d. 1624), his reverent intellectual biography of Ibn Taymiyya is a fitting companion to his book on love. He sums up centuries of discussion by quoting all the authorities and seeking peace among the parties. The pious erotic secularists are no longer to find fault with the erotic mystics. The Sufis, by now triumphant, have become at once less threatening and more sober seeming. Latter day militants of Ibn Taymiyya's stamp, such as the Wahhābīs of Saudi Arabia, will still oppose the Sufi cult of saints and the *dhikr*. But Karmī was a Ḥanbalite of more diplomatic cast. He accepted Ibn Dā'ūd's *ḥadīth* sanctifying the martyrs of love and sought to patch up the old Ḥanbalite quarrel with Ibn ʿArabī. Drawing heavily on his predecessors for literary material and formal structure, he quietly dropped troublesome traditions in the interest of reconciliation. Calling Muḥammad the "lord of lovers" and "mainstay of the enamored," he benignly opens his discussion of love with warm endorsements of licit union. Like many of his predecessors, perhaps more than most, he seems ready to surrender to his material, which all along had been agitating for autonomy, if not control. He sees no harm in closing his treatment with a generous selection of his own verses on love.[126]

The exponents of literalism in love and law spotlight the androcentric cast of traditional Islamic society. Since the *sunna* permits four wives and unlimited concubines, there remains a sanctioned place for courtship and courtliness toward single women even among mature and married men, despite the tension between "cavalier" behavior and the more austere ideals of chastity. Further, homosexuality is a widespread concomitant of the seclusion and engrossment of women. It takes on culturally articulate forms as social barriers rigidify between the sexes, as is candidly attested by Ibn al-Nafīs (ca. 1210–1288), the traditionalist theologian and physician who discovered the minor circulation.[127] Ibn al-Jawzī's denunciations of Sufi pantheism were intimately bound up with censure of homosexuality. For Sufi sublimations on pantheistic themes were often perfused with homoerotic images. Drawing on the Hellenistic thesis of Arabic love literature that "love is an illness conveyed by a glance," Ibn al-Jawzī's *Censure of Passion* condemns the Sufi custom of gazing at the lovely faces of beardless youths (that is, disciples), whose visages, in the charged atmosphere of Sufi poetry, became visible images and apparitions of the Indwelling Godhead. Here, in Ibn al-Jawzī's eyes, blasphemy was piled on decadence.[128]

Some Ḥanbalite love literature clearly seeks not just to bring the erotic imagery down to earth but also to turn the gaze toward what the conservatives saw as objects of more red-blooded interests. But boys came far more readily to hand than girls, and the shift from censure to fascination was a tempting holiday for writers, who might titillate even where they condemned. The Ḥanbalite constant, however, was the censure of Sufi pantheism.

Play, the Hunt, and the Freedom of the Dandy

We have poetry and music, clothing, wine, love and war. But what of sport, and play? The hunt was perhaps the most concerted of secular activities in classical Islamic societies, as in other medieval cultures. A rival to love, a counterpart to war, it was, as we have noted, a favorite topic in secular poetry and painting. Here was a showplace of manly skills and virtues, a place for thrill and risk, and for marvel at animal grace in the quarry and in one's horses, hawks, and hounds. Yet, secular as it was, the hunt held an ancient religious significance, of which R. B. Serjeant found traces even in twentieth-century hunting in Hadramaut. The living evidence is seconded by ancient petroglyphs and inscriptions, the literary accounts of sacrificial customs, and the ritualized dancing and display that are still linked to the hunt. Even in the twentieth century, tribal hunters worried that some moral taint might rob them of an ibex—or that absence from the hunt might delay the rains.[129] Serjeant notes the ironic self-deprecation of the South Arabian townsmen: "The artisans and petty tradesmen (*masākīn*), said my shaikh in Tarīm, love hunting, and in former times they were very much given to it. There was, perhaps still is, a saying amongst them, 'The hunt is the sixth Pillar of Islam.'"[130] The Sayyid *ʿulemāʾ* voiced irritation, calling the hunt pagan and primitive. Didn't some hunts offer propitiatory sacrifices to the jinn? Weren't there indecent goings on, waste of resources, mingling of the sexes, abuse of animals, neglect of religious duties? The ancient pagan gods may be shrunk to sprites and spirits, but the autonomous values of the hunt continually reassert themselves: "A shout on the mountain," one saying went, "is better than a chest full of goods at home."[131] The hunt, here, is both secular and secularized. For secularization defangs pagan beliefs and practices, softening them into customs or superstitions. But paganism is also custom given voice. And customs die hard.

Muslim princes and the wealthy squirarchy, the *dihqān*s of Iran and their counterparts in other lands, hunted with hawks or falcons, gazelle-hounds (salukis), cheetahs and caracal lynxes. Islamic law allowed for the ritual slaughter of captured game, making its consumption licit. The jurist al-Damīrī (1341–1405) wrote at length about the pertinent rules in his encyclopedic *Life of the Animals*. And the poet, secretary, physician, and astrologer Kushājim (d. ca. 961), a fixture (and master chef) at the court of the Ḥamdānid monarch Sayf al-Dawla, compiled an extensive work on hunting, incorporating many of his own poems on the subject along with goodly selections of an earlier prose work, perhaps dating to Umayyad times.

The cheetah hunt was adopted by the Lakhmid vassals of Sassanian Iran in pre-Islamic times. Among Islamic dynasties, the sport came into vogue among the Umayyads, and it is not hard to see why.[132] Cheetahs are high maintenance beasts in captivity. Each generation required fresh capture in the field, since cheetahs could be bred only in the wild and must train their own young to stalk and hunt. The beasts need elaborate taming and training to hunt from horseback. But what could be more impressive than a cheetah perched on a prince's pillion and leaping from the crupper to course a gazelle? Conspicuous waste, to use Veblen's term, joined with virtuosity and élan to give the cheetah hunt its panache. The ʿAbbāsid, Fāṭimid, and Mamluk rulers displayed cheetahs in their parades as emblems of opulence and power, and the cheetah hunt spread (among the wealthy) throughout the Muslim East, persisting down to modern times. Expenses for the requisite entourage led some afficionados into bankruptcy. But the poets (including Abū Nuwās) celebrated the cheetah's lightning charge, and religion licensed the sport. For cheetahs do not mangle their prey, so the captured game is *ḥalāl*, as long as the slaughter is reserved to the knife and the name of God is spoken as the cheetah is released. What was once an accommodation to dietary needs here becomes a bow to sport and the secular emblems of social status.

Franz Rosenthal ascribes the Islamicate interest in hashish to the love of play.[133] Here too the secular declares itself. Generally taken in pill form, hashish was objectionable for its distracting effects, spiritually and materially. Yet it was sought after, perhaps for the attitude of unconcern it induced, an unfocused euphoria that mocked and often parodied pious earnestness. Hashish might seem to open doors to mystic experience, but its very use made Sufi ecstasies suspect. For, even if it could not be classed with wine, it led to permissive ways and open flouting of established norms and values.

The tension between spiritual earnestness and secular restiveness emerges more creatively in wit. Jāḥiẓ (ca. 776–868/9), the great essayist, as Pellat writes

> was shocked by the needlessly stiff attitude of some of his contemporaries, and from the start he set out to justify laughter, which he associated with life, and jocularity, stressing its advantages so long as it was not exaggerated, and showing that Islam was a liberal religion which in no way enforced reserve and severity; from there he went on to attack the boredom bred by most writings, which, in his opinion, were too serious, and he suggested a leavening of a little *hazl* [fun] in even the most severe speculations.[134]

But Hamadhānī, who called himself The Innovation of the Age and who poked fun at Jāḥiẓ himself, among many other individuals and types, took a more frontal approach.

To give up the gods for monotheism is, after all, to give up the idea that somewhere, between the interstices of events or even at their roots, someone or some thing is peering out at us and laughing. The God of monotheism is earnest, sometimes deadly earnest, and the life laid out by monotheist culture, law, and ethics is earnest too. It has a goal and purpose. Even its tragedies have meaning, and its ironies aim at teaching us our frailty and mortality, redirecting our gaze beyond trivial, mortal concerns. Does monotheism leave no room for the absurd?

Clearly the ironies of disappointed hopes and specious pretensions can be heightened, not negated, by earnest homilies and ritual decorum. So monotheism begets satire just as paganism breeds cynicism. Indeed monotheism can breed cynicism too, as it breeds skepticism, by the very loftiness of its claims. For cynicism shrinks moral claims that look overblown in the same way that skepticism casts its shadow of doubt over all complacent claims to knowledge.

Bill Alfred used to point out how false it is to say that there is no Christian tragedy. As Faustus shows, tragedy can open no deeper pit than eternal damnation. Similarly, it is false to suppose that there is no Islamic farce, or parody, or satire.[135] In every genre of epic, lyric, narrative, folktale, theater, or balladry—wherever high or low language gives liveliness to speech—there is room for mockery. The Marx Brothers knew that. The more earnest the expostulations, the deeper the sighs, the finer the sensibilities, the more ludicruous do they become when mocked.

Hamadhānī knew how to mock. He drew upon urbanity to mock rusticity even as he used the naturalness of vulgar speech, street argot, and slapstick, to mock urbanity itself. If there was serious intent in his mockery—and I do not doubt that there was—that intent defied the laws of gravity and will not be found in the handbooks of theology or tradition but in the smiles between the lines.

The *maqāma* was a thing of Hamadhānī's own invention much imitated in his wake. His fifty-two surviving tales in the new genre mingle the values of poetry and prose to form a medium that seems to typify their author's dissatisfaction with established literary conventions–not to mention the settled norms of his milieu. The tales give punch to their poetry by situating it in the narrative embrace of incident. And they naturalize the lyric, by making it an element in the action, much as modern musicals seek to naturalize their use of choreography and song.

The focal figure of Hamadhānī's *maqāmāt*, Abū ʾl-Fatḥ al-Iskandarī, is a rogue and confidence trickster, a master of disguises, respecter of no one and nothing but verbal skill and pyrotechnic wit. The narrator, a named persona, comes to admire Abu ʾl-Fatḥ's poetic brilliance and spontaneity, to imitate his tricks and vie with his virtuosity. But, of course, Abū ʾl-Fatḥ is inimitable. Nothing about him is constant but his inconstancy; nothing real but his roles.

The "Bishr Encounter," the last in Hamadhānī's collection, omits all mention of the now familiar Abū ʾl-Fatḥ, yet preserves a formal unity with the rest, since it is still framed by the raconteur, ʿĪsā b. Hishām. James Monroe has shown how this *maqāma* forms a minuscule mock epic, violating in turn every canon of the ʿAntar-type of heroic cycle.[136] Bishr is a pragmatist about love, concupiscent rather than ethereal. He paid nothing for his bride, a slave girl; and she returns his disdain by urging him to marry his prettier cousin. Rejected by that girl's father, he affronts the code of tribal honor by harassing her kinsmen (who are, of course, also kinsmen of his own). Setting out to capture the thousand camels that will win his new love's hand, he slays a lion (first hamstringing his horse for balking at the lion's sight—shades of Imruʾ al-Qays's camel!), then composes a love poem about his prowess and mocks heroic convention by carrying his poem not in his heart but written on his shirt, in the lion's blood. The uncle relents, conveniently forgetting about those camels, when Bishr slays a serpent and brags unconscionably of his exploits.

A beardless youth appears on horseback and challenges Bishr to surrender his prospective father-in-law. After a suitable exchange of blood curdling insults ("shut of thee be she who shat thee!"), Bishr is roundly trounced and driven from the field, with many pricks to the kidneys. Most unchivalrously, he does give up his uncle, on condition that the youth reveal his identity. In a moment that mocks the poignancy of epic discovery, the boy announces that he is Bishr's son. Exclaiming that he's hardly even tied the knot and already has such a splendid son, Bishr is unceremoniously informed that the youth is his not by his bride-to-be but by the slave who had urged him to marry his cousin. But she became his bride only a day previous! Horseless, hopeless, tangled in anachronism (or other men's wild oats) and covered with exploded conventions, Bishr swears never again to mount a noble steed or wed a fine lady. As the tale ends, he turns over the cousin who was the object of his quest, to the beardless youth.[137]

Pressing beyond his sound appraisal of Hamadhānī's satirical intent, Monroe urges that Hamadhānī wrote the *Maqāmāt* to uphold moral values—to reject the shallowness and "false teaching" of ʿĪsā the narrator. But that would make the ever present but usually transparent persona rather than his encounters with Iskandarī, the focus of the work and would open far more questions that it could answer: Is the heroic age yet alive for Hamadhānī? Do its values still function for him? Can one descend to parody and burlesque yet preserve the values one lampoons? Can a Muslim author parody "*hadīth, sīra* and the lyric" and even mock the Qur'ān, yet escape censure, since he mocks through the mouthpiece of an unreliable narrator?

Part of Hamadhānī's subject is falsity: the pretensions of false piety, the conventions of artificial romance—the same conventions that Cervantes will lampoon when he takes up the picaresque. Don Quixote too will renounce the false conventions of chivalry. Both he and Sancho Panza in their different ways, are profoundly honest. But Hamadhānī loves roguery and finds profound risibility in stupidity. His is not an earnest pen, at least not in the *Maqāmāt*. He does love his own virtuosity. His language, studded with the ornaments and original devices of a literary dandy, constantly calls attention to itself. It would be silly to say that he invented a new genre simply to express conventional thoughts. That could have been done in a sermon.

Hamadhānī does not simply deliver himself, because he does not deliver himself simply. His theses are unstated. His art is indirection. He plays on the foibles that he pinions. But his purpose is as much in the play as in the pinioning. His literary aim is not moral teaching, which he does not readily distinguish from moralism. But neither is he displaying mere verbal agility and erudition. That could be done in courtly rescripts, or a dictionary.

Hamadhānī *uses* language and uses it to effect. It is not his subject. His praise is sincere when he says of Imru' al-Qays: "He gave us his horse, point for point." That is a fact not to be denied, even though it comes from the mouth of the chameleon Iskandarī. Mentioning Imru' al-Qays at the climax of the first *Maqāma*, the "Poesy Encounter" is no accident but a way of saluting literary values that the *Maqāmāt* will revisit. Hamadhānī is claiming a heritage and setting forth some purtenant values as well: originality in art, deviltry in morals, verbal power and precision.

The "Poesy *Maqāma*" is an *homage*, almost a dedication. But it is also a challenge and a melancholy admission—Shaw addressing Shakespeare through a puppet play. One cannot rival originality by emulation. New and more credible settings must be found for the lyric voice. The fluid, sinuous, and mobile prose that was the new toy of the Arabic secretarial class will afford the nest of words in which a new poetry may find its place, just as the urban environment will offer cover and a setting for a new kind of rogue. Mimicry of the surviving remnants of desert poesy, the lyric or elegiac *qaṣīda*, rings false and hollow in the city streets. New themes are needed. We already *have* Imru' al-Qays—his horse, his girls, his hunts. There is not much more to tell there—but so much more to life's twists, encounters, and surprises, the delicately situated conflicts of emotion, between embarrassed honor and angry impatience, between chastened frivolity and astonished discovery, between foolish generosity and sagacious connoisseurship. All of these and many more colorations and collocations of sense and emotion—as vivid as the particolored silks of the young ʿĪsā's dandy friends—are variations and elaborations of Imru' al-Qays's single theme, the classic dandy's theme: of time's passage, the clash of reality with appearance, and the victory that nature gives to time, but appearance, to art.

Time, as in Imru' al-Qays, remains the enemy, destroying appearances and pleasures. Yet art strikes back, through laughter. Hence Abū 'l-Fatḥ's disguises and his spurious stories about his origins, present circumstances and future plans. Repeatedly he justifies his japes as a kind of revenge against time for the tricks it has played on him. His changes of role, posture, and language pass him through all the classes of men and every locale familiar and exotic to Hamadhānī's readers. The satiric imp becomes in turn the type of every overserious or outrageous figure from the imām in the mosque and preacher in the rostrum to the vagabond pauper, *ghāzī*, doomsayer, catchpenny beggar, and extravagant conman. His changes bespeak the instability of time, that is, of fate and fortune, social circumstance, mores, opinions and expectations. In one of the many moments of discovery in which he is found out, now pretending to a noble Qurashite birth and breeding, Abū 'l-Fatḥ tosses off words that would have the ring of truth for many of Hamadhānī's readers, on the ethnic pretenses of their neighbors:

> God's creatures may take on many a form–
> Their mingled lives, often protean.
> By night they are Arabs,
> Clear of birth and of blood
> By day they've become Nabataean![138]

A Nabataean, it helps to know, was a denizen of Iraq or Syria before the Muslim conquest—stereotypically, a peasant. The barb is aimed at pretensions to Arab birth and a lineage in the Prophet's own tribe. Are the *mawālī* really Arabs? Is Islam itself a new disguise?[139]

Hamadhānī's *Maqāmāt* are a sensuous genre, and the sensuous is the root and branch of aestheticism. But there is more. As Richard Ellmann remarks à propos Oscar Wilde:

> Partly because he was himself leading a secret life as a homosexual, Wilde was keenly alive to the disparity between semblance and reality. He saw hypocrisy in various forms around him, as well as in himself, and particularly scorned those who pretended to pity and morality out of a desire to conform. One had, he thought, a duty to oneself as well as to others: the duty of self-discovery and self-expression. This duty made necessary, among other things, the loss of innocence, for innocence too long maintained could be as dangerous as guilt.[140]

It was Wilde, as Ellmann reminds us, who put in the mouth of Miss Prism (misprision) the description of her lost novel: "The good ended happily, and the bad unhappily. That is what Fiction means." And to the innocent Cecily Cardew he assigned the lines: "I hope you have not been leading a double life, pretending to be wicked and being really good all the time. That would be hypocrisy."

Sensualism is the visible counterpart of the dandy's love of discovery and exposé, wit, surface, the play of appearances with realities, and display of appearances *as* realities. And aestheticism is the meeting ground of sensuality with artifice. Wickedness is delicious in its mouth, and the power of art is especially wicked and delicious. When ʿĪsā describes the making of halva, Hamadhānī knows that he can make the reader's mouth water, even now, just as if we were there in the marketplace, alongside Iskandarī's rustic dupe, watching and taking it all in as ʿĪsā spells out his order. This is the poetry of complicity. Its frisson is the *Gotcha!* of Baudelaire, when he catches the reader peeking in at the window of his poetry and crows, then coos: "*Hypocrite lecteur—mon semblable—mon frère.*"

When Abū ʾl-Fatḥ buggers a burglar or ʿĪsā himself runs through a highwayman, we too are expected to participate.[141] The response, visceral, even involuntary, is Hamadhānī's literary triumph. Innovative, arcane and exotic language, unexpected turns of phrase, rhyme, inversion, anagram, barbed wit and evocative meter are the jeweled movement of his art, which celebrates not just the pungency of the sensate but its own command of emotions and sensations elicited by a deftly drawn objective correlative. In few words, intricately disposed, Hamadhānī tells his tale, limning the contexts that generate the emotive punch and set up the poetic punch line.

When Abū ʾl-Fatḥ is recognized as the teller of the tale in the Ruṣāfa Encounter, ʿĪsā asks him to explain one of his more elegant and obscure conceits. The niceties of language are at least as worthy of note as the ribald yarn. Those niceties—figures of speech and thought, tricks of syntax, prosody and pattern—are the pivot points of Hamadhānī's art. He revels in language just as his young men revel in their silks. Like his fictive narrator ʿĪsā b. Hishām, he would travel far "to snare the rare and wild elusive word." For that word, like his place-dropping and local color, is an emblem of his freedom, and of the skill by which that freedom is won.

Here, then, as with other dandies, artful expression betokens more than just itself. Like all satirists Hamadhānī *is* a critic. Like all parodists he is something of a cynic.[142] But his criticism runs wider than disapproval of objects already (even officially) discountenanced. Where would be the novelty in that? What Hamadhānī is about is a transvaluation of sorts. His situations allow him to make explicit what everyone already knows but lacks the words or face to say—what oft was thought, but ne'er so openly expressed?[143] Transvaluation is a mark of decadence and ennui of the sort that we associate with fin de siècle culture. Thus Abū Nuwās had a slave boy that he nicknamed "ugly" because of his beauty.[144] But it is not just the libertines who are tired of the old values and not just the decadent poets who express such ennui. The values themselves may be tired, and the rationales that support them may be growing thin, all but transparent. That leaves room for a Hamadhānī, whose words cut a swath that is both corruptive and cleansing.

Hamadhānī's target is not all values at once, of course. There must always be a standpoint, ground to push off from. But Hamadhānī has learned the cynics' and the skeptics' trick of shifting ground, switching his side drape, lampooning this in terms of that, and that in terms of the other. Only formal virtues like candor are relatively resistant to such testing. Hypocrisy is the most vulnerable of targets, since it pronounces its own denunciation and awaits only exposure. Candor presents a slender target, since it claims only to be what it is and say what it sees. It gains shock value, sometimes taken for verisimilitude, in part from the simple impact of saying what polite convention cannot say. Hence an author's use of sage fools, sober madmen, and precocious children. But the true cynic, although he uses candor, has no use for it when its work is done. Like the mystic who pulls up his ladder after him or the skeptic who renounces a dogmatic skepticism, the cynic will blow up his final charge, if he can, since candor is uncomfortably close to earnestness, which he lampoons, and to hypocrisy, which doth protest too much.

Hamadhānī has just the out he needs, writing in fictions, repeating hearsay, using a persona whose witness proves repeatedly unreliable. So the tissue of fictions falls, leaving—not mere entertainment but also not the unquestioned words of God in the Qur'ān or the sanctified authority of *ḥadīth*.[145] Instead, what remains in the mouth is the bittersweet taste of impostures exposed, and the clean feeling that no new imposition has been set up in their place. As with Boccaccio, this barn cleaning leaves behind a sense of openness, of free access to sensate and expressive values that jostle with their chaster rivals, without apology or guilt.[146] Like Freud, Hamadhānī purges built up anxieties, the products and byproducts of conflicts among values. But his chosen task is more like Nietzsche's, more diagnostic than therapeutic. He would rather mock than weep, and rather laugh than treat—although laughter is a kind of therapy.

Hamadhānī presses further than Freud the conflicts among values in the culture he surveys. But drawing back from earnestness saves him from the madness that overtook Nietzsche. Like Nietzsche he faces a formidable task in the use of language. For one cannot simply tell people that good is not as good as they suppose, or that bad can have a goodness to it. One can reverse the words, of course, keeping connotations as denotations, as in the pop lyric "*Bad, bad Leroy Brown, baddest man in the whole damn town* . . ." But confusions are hard to avoid if this sort of thing is carried too far, and superficiality results if things are kept too general.

One cannot simply *preach* the beauty and nobility of evil or the insipidity of good. It's no good to be doctrinaire about rejecting dogmatism or to charge disciples to emulate one's moral or intellectual audacity and independence. To challenge moral usage is to explode clichés. So it needs poetry–as Rimbaud and Baudelaire understood. Or it calls for fiction, or dramatic writing, where inner voices are allowed to speak, dramatic irony strips away convention, and rhetoric slips off its clothes and slips under the covers to persuade by means of greater immediacy than open argument affords.

In Jacques Tati's film *Mon Oncle* we meet a little boy whose ultramodern house, with its aluminum fountain and stainless steel gate typify the rigidity and sterility of his family's existence. Only an eccentric uncle who inhabits a cockeyed garret perched precariously above the rooftops of Paris offers glimpses of another kind of life. The boy is fed in an antiseptic kitchen by a mother who wears surgical gloves to prepare his toast and autoclaves his cutlery as the child sits down to eat alone. But occasionally the boy takes his bicycle and rides to the edge of town or accompanies his uncle on mad jaunts. His great joy is to spend his pocket change on enormous pastries, covered with sugar and horrid red jam, purchased from a greasy pastryman who is constantly rubbing his hands on his filthy apron. After eating his pastry on a hillside overlooking the suburban street, the little boy conceals himself carefully and with equal gusto catapults good sized rocks at passersby, skillfully ricocheting the projectiles so as to disguise their line of flight but still give a good klonk to the pedestrians, whose bowlers are unfailingly knocked off. The climax comes when the little boy's father (who manufactures plastic tubing and commutes to work in a slow-paced, multilane ballet) agrees to accompany him on one of his jaunts. The film ends with the two, child and industrialist, joyously practicing the deviltry of the catapult on the unsuspecting respectable folk who pass below. This perfect paradigm of innocent mischief finds its types in Till Eulenspiegel and Mullah Nasruddin, the Trickster figures of myth and fable, Loki and his ilk, the confidence men of *The Sting*, and the vast body of popular literature it follows.

Ulysses is a trickster. His deception of Achilles and his hollow horse conspiracy are reflexes of the delight that audiences take in watching a well-turned scheme (or plot) unfold, twist and drive to its conclusion. Also a trickster is Diomedes, Ulysses's comrade in the theft of the Palladium. Homer's audience will delight in hearing how Diomedes duped his younger combatant Glaukos in the name of honor and half-remembered bonds of family hospitality, getting him to exchange his precious armor for a battle weary veteran's set. And Homer himself cannot resist telling at length of the two men's feeling overtures to one another, joining in at the punch line:

> So they spoke, and both springing down from behind their horses
> Gripped each other's hands and exchanged the promise of friendship.
> But Zeus the son of Kronos stole away the wits of Glaukos,
> Who exchanged with Diomedes the son of Tydeus armor
> Of gold for bronze, for nine oxen's worth, the worth of a hundred.[147]

Northrup Frye counts force and fraud as the two chief springs of action and sources of delight in secular literature.[148] Both tilt more toward evil than toward good in the scales of morality and moralism. Both are present in good measure in Hamadhānī: force as an element of the sensate; fraud, in greater measure, since its soul is wit—its language, virtuosity and false appearances, and its outcome, shock of recognition. That gives us truth discovered through exposure of impostures.[149]

Iskandarī enjoys deceiving others. He delights in sending up the stuffy and puffed up, and he relishes the gullibility of his dupes. ʿĪsā b. Hishām is indeed his disciple, not so much for his parodistic sermons—to ape these would be to parody a parody and land back in the realm of the deadly serious and seriously deadly—but as the retailer of his exploits, and their occasional imitator. For it is ʿĪsā, not Abū ʾl-Fatḥ, in the Baghdad Encounter, who gulls the yokel, with a specious appeal to ancient family friendship that is Homeric in antiquity, and traps the country bumpkin into paying for his dinner, and getting slapped around for the privilege. Again, in the Lion Encounter, it is ʿĪsā who bests Abu ʾl-Fatḥ, with a mathematical match for the verbal skill that has stunned him so often. Iskandarī begs a dirhem. ʿĪsā, speaking in extemporized verse, as Abū ʾl-Fatḥ so often does, offers him a dirhem times one, times two, times three . . . "For as long as I husband one breath." But arithmetic is the new math in tenth-century Baghdad, and Abū ʾl-Fatḥ is hungry. ʿĪsā brings the series to twenty, but Iskandarī can't keep up with the expansion and settles for twenty loaves, leaving ʿĪsā to conclude that "there's no luck for the luckless." Hamadhānī's audience enjoys the tickle that the simple man feels when the Devil is outwitted in folktales or in fabular movies like George Burns's *Oh God, You Devil* or Ingmar Bergman's *The Devil's Eye*.

Is Iskandarī the devil? Hardly. His vices and his virtues are all too human. He is a man, but a man who wants to master the human condition before it masters him. His feelings run from hunger and exhaustion with travel (which is painted as a kind of addiction[150] in the *Maqāmāt* and so becomes a metaphor of the unyielding grip of time—Iskandarī must devour the road before it devours him), to terror at death, to delighted guile, to silly wantonness and innocent deceit—deceit made innocent by the credulity or cupidity of the deceived, or their insensate piety (as in Isfahan), or the narrator's own joyful willingness to be bilked, out of youthful extravagance, aestheticism, high spirits, and nobility.

Iskandarī's charm is not the heroic evil of Milton's Satan, cosmic spite worthy of the global theater in which its action is played out. Neither is it the perverse pride that Blake finds in that figure, nobility in defeat, a worthy rival and counterweight to divine majesty. It is not the lordly arrogance of frustrated spite and spleen, renouncing vassalage yet clinging to its appanages. Rather Iskandarī's is an impudent and all-too-human irreverence that mocks at Fate, but winks at God, as much as to expect that He would understand.

What then is there to celebrate in impishness? The answer, I am suggesting, lies in the fact that where arrogance enslaves, impudence can liberate. Hamadhānī chafes at sobriety and all that is dour. When the young revelers return from a drinking bout in Ahwāz, they are halted in their tracks by an ominous figure bearing a bier. In a fitting irony, their sour admonisher proves a fraud, *the* fraud, Iskandarī, who wants only to kick up his heels, and whose parting message, tossed over his shoulder, is to insist that the young men pay no attention to all that he has said. Compare, for effect, the mocking imps that scamper from beneath the great crimson palliums of the stately cardinals that stalk the stage to the strains of the *Dies Irae* in Leonid Massine's choreography of *Symphonie Fantastique.*

The adventurer turned medicine man encountered in Sijistan is the same fraud again. His conversion story is a sham, another swindle, that pays tribute in the end only to Iskandarī's imagination and resource. For Abū 'l-Fatḥ is never a mere *ṭufaylī*, unless that means more than a mere beggar or parasite but an artful dodger, a chameleon of constantly changing wiles, whose language is as unpredictable as his disguises, whose pranks give color to what our journalists call street life. What Hamadhānī celebrates in the *Maqāmāt* is freedom.

The metamorphoses in Iskandarī's appearance and seeming condition symbolize that freedom. The incongruities about his age in the diverse encounters mark it again. These are emblems of the mocker's battle against time, the one condition that his antics can better only by belying it. Wives can be invented by the *ṭufaylī* as easily as pasts and origins. Infants can be rented for a day's begging or cadging.[151] Front money can be gulled from one pigeon for use on another. What are identities? Iskandarī is rootless, unconnected, unstable of thought and mind. But the conditions of his weakness are sources of his strength. Like the éminence grise in *Diva*, he lives the aesthete's creed, not in any monkish way but by making his every act and utterance a performance and his life itself a work of artifice. He exists only in language, device, and disguise, without solid, answerable frame or substrate of fixed character. He has created complete independence out of perfect dependence. Ḥarīrī (1054–1122), Hamadhānī's greatest imitator, was scored for writing frivolous tales of nonexistent folk. His answer: that Abū Zayd, was no fiction but a man of flesh and blood whom he had met, *preaching in a mosque*.[152]

In inventing Abū 'l-Fatḥ, Hamadhānī has set up a mocking, fun house image that is at once a caricature and a rival to Islamic piety and sobriety. Iskandarī is neither responsible nor respectable. But he is free and gay, with a mad gaiety wholly foreign to veneration or venerability. There is no humility in his abjectness and no bearing in his pride. His figure confronts Islamic gravitas with a rival vision, of insouciance. Yet, like a mummer at carnival, he relieves the more somber colorations of religion. He apes hypocrisy but also offers secular release from the absoluteness of perfect earnestness. In that sense the trickster figure does perform a sort of service to Islam. We can see why Niẓām al-Dīn al-Awliyā' would give himself over to study of Ḥarīrī's *Maqāmāt* and indeed memorize forty of them.[153] For beyond satiric exposure of false piety, false bravado, or false hospitality (as in the *Maḍīra* Encounter), Hamadhānī's Abū 'l-Fatḥ raises a kind of criticism that is hard to voice internally, and perhaps impossible in the language of the law books or the rhetoric of the *minbar*—and yet all the more necessary for that. This is the criticism of the live option, of laughter and verismo, fantasy and whimsy, set against the high seriousness of an ideal that claims exhaustive control and comprehension of the real.

Revived and redefined in the world of the *Maqāmāt* are secular values recaptured from the tribal and heroic age. But the prowess of the warrior has now become Odyssean guile, and the priapism of Achilles, or Imru' al-Qays, has grown rather more indiscriminate. The old enmity with time remains. But the irony that confronts time has become literary—not bookish, perhaps, but detached, focused more on the manner of expression than on its emotive matter. And it has become urbane, not merely self-deprecating, as in Imru' al-Qays' self-portrayal as a once proud hunter and lover reduced to water carrier and pack animal by his own folly, but courtly, mannered, aware of the figure one cuts in fine fabrics or fine words, sharply aware of the social milieu in which those words and fabrics may be all that is visible to announce one's presence.

The secular values that Hamadhānī voices belong to merchants, travelers, members of the secretarial and administrative class. For clerks in his time are not the same as clerics. The mores and notions broached are much older than Islam. Hamadhānī recasts them to reflect his own sense of modernity, setting them at a sharp remove from the heroic past. Their levity tugs against Islamic gravity and leavens Islamic earnestness in ways that I think were valued by the same sort of scholars as those who preserved the pre-Islamic poetry of Arabia.

The official story remains: Studies of the ancient odes met a philological need, in Qur'ānic exegesis. And of course no surer rationale could be offered. In the same way, Eusebius preserved the old philosophy, as a historic propaedeutic to the evangelic message. But Eusebius could not contain the intrinsic interest of his materials. And the Muslim scholars who read the ancient odes, with their celebrations of very un-Islamic values, would naturally find a philologic interest in their rare words and usages, quite apart from their exegetical applications, and could hardly fail to rise to their emotive charms as well.

So the scholars preserved and studied, imitated and reworked the ancient Arab poems in faithful service to the study of the Qur'ān, but also in philologic fascination, and at not without aesthetic and romantic interest. They fed and pleased an urban nostalgia for the desert life and its freedoms, passions, and pleasures, even the sufferings that were more fondly recalled from the middle distance of another age. The old life would naturally seem richer than the life of city enterprise, paperwork and piety. Piety itself seemed less than whole, if piety was all it had to offer. Like these retailers of the old poetry and the anecdotes that surrounded it, Hamadhānī too has fallen in love with language. And like them, he too engages in a construction of alternatives. But his rival world is built not on nostalgia for a lost past but on a sense of currency, wit, and bemused detachment.

Even Muḥammad ʿAbduh (1849–1905), who edited the *Maqāmāt* (with commentary, Cairo, 1889) and bowdlerized them somewhat, removing the most scabrous bits[154] but not effacing their viewpoint or their values, must have felt the need for balance that works like Hamadhānī's can provide. ʿAbduh would go on to serve as *muftī* of Egypt. He would found a college for *qāḍī*s and serve as a trustee of the Azhar. And he founded the *Salafiyya* movement, a pan-Islamic appeal for return to the simplicity of early Islam. For him the *Maqāmāt* of Hamadhānī had become a classic, just as its author had hoped it would be. And a classic it remains, perhaps because it adds a catholicity of its own to a vision already claiming to be catholic. Hamadhānī's fellows, then, besides Imru' al-Qays, would be Chaucer and Boccaccio, and yes, Cervantes and the author of *Lazarillo de Tormes*, but also Apuleius, Swift, and the Defoe of *Moll Flanders* and *Roxana*. I would draw one further comparison here, with that radical mode of Kabbalistic thought that Gershom Scholem called a pursuit of salvation through sin.[155] For the paradox parallels Hamadhānī's own irreverent and unstated thesis that there are kinds of badness that can be good.

Beneath a stereotypic ideal that ignores "the deep inner conflicts" of a life of normative piety,[156] Scholem found a corresponding restiveness with legalism and intellectualism, and a resultant "licentiousness, in the most unlikely places."[157] Such findings enliven our understanding of the Middle Ages and of religious life at large. For figures like Hamadhānī, or Rāzī, or Jābir ibn Hayyān, Ibn al-Rāwandī, or Abelard do not inhabit an age of unquestioned faith. Nor is the religious life in any age a sheer passive placidity. That life has always harbored its doubts, passions, frustrations, anxieties, and inchoate yearnings, sometimes violent, sometimes moving quietly just below the surface of overt expression.

Tensions between the spiritual and the sensate the disciplined and the antinomian, are sometimes salved with magic or mysticism. Other balms, medievally and beyond, were found in art or wealth. But there was also militancy, a two-headed beast that wore its adventurist helmet in the field but found a clerical neckband at home. And there were more pacific outlets, for those whose lives were not engrossed by the sheer struggle to survive—in philosophy, scholarship, the sciences, and the nascent realms of technology best known to the alchemist. But perhaps the greatest alchemy was laughter.

Here is my rendering of one of Hamadhānī's fifty-two *Maqāmāt*:

The Isfahan Encounter

The story was told us by ʿĪsā bin Hishām: I was at Isfahān, set for travel to Rayy, determined to vanish as quick as a shadow. My every glance looked out for a convoy. Every morning I was ready to saddle. But just as the moment awaited arrived, what should I hear but the summons to prayer, a duty demanding an answer, announced as if meant just for me. So I slipped away from my comrades and fell into step with the flock, worried I might miss the caravan I was leaving, but comforted by the blessings that prayer would confer in crossing the desert's dire waste.

I went straight to the front row and took up the position. The imām faced the prayer niche and recited the Opening—in the intonation of Hamza, drawing out every long *a* and pulling up short for every glottal stop, while I seethed and simmered at the thought of my caravan lost, wondering what had become of my horse.

He followed the *Fātiḥa* with the *Wāqiʿa* while I patiently burned, roasting and sizzling with rage, like a steak on the coals. But there was nothing for it but to suffer in silence. That is, if I didn't intend to speak out and keep silence forever. For I knew how raw they are in that place, and there's no cutting prayers short 'til the final *salām*. So I stood as I was, anchored in necessity, until the whole surah was finished and I'd lost all hope of the caravan and given up on my mount and the journey.

Then he bent his bow for prostration, with a humility and devotion that I never before had seen. Slowly he raised up his head and his hands, saying, "God hearken to him who offers His praises." And he waited until I'd no doubts that he slept. Then he struck the ground with his right hand as he fell down in prostration, pressing his face to the floor.

Taking the chance of raising my head, I saw no way out through the rows and went back to my prostrate position, until he'd pronounced "God is great," and we could sit up.

He rose for the second prostration and recited the *Fātiḥa* and the *Qāriʿa*, in a chant stretched to the length of the Judgment Hour, leaving the whole praying throng drained of spirit.

His prostrations were done. He'd confessed his faith in his beard and now turned to the right and the left to salute the two guardian spirits that seemed stuck in his jugular veins. But just as I was saying, "God's given me the perfect moment. Escape is at hand!" up stood a man who said: "Whoever of you loves the Prophet's companions and the House of Islam, lend an ear for a moment!"

Said ʿĪsā bin Hishām, "I stuck to my place, protecting my character."

Said the man: "It behooves me to speak nought but truth and bear witness to that truth alone. I have come unto you with good news from your Prophet, but I shall not disclose it until God cleanse this mosque of any despicable creature vile enough to impugn his command!"

"I saw him," the speaker continued, "in a dream—may God bless him and keep him—like the sun shining out from the clouds, or the moon on a night of its fullness. He traveled with stars in his trail, angels lifting the train of his garment. Then he taught me a prayer, entrusted to me, to teach to this nation. I have written it on these leaves, scented with musk and *khalūq*, saffron and *sukk*, and I offer it freely to whoever requests it. But if you make good the price of the paper, I'll not refuse you."

Said ʿĪsā bin Hishām: The dirhems poured forth so profusely he seemed quite bewildered. But I followed, marveling at the cunning of his con and his art in getting his living. I wanted to ask him of himself but held back, to speak with him but kept silent, pondering his eloquence in impudence, his cunning in cadging, how skillfully he caught men in his snare and how pleasingly took their money—then I caught a glimpse of him—and, of course! It was Abū ʾl-Fath al-Iskandarī.

I said, "How did you ever dream up this dodge?"

He smiled and indited:

Men are asses, ever eager
To form up into a train,
More observant of who passes
Than of what they lose or gain.
You can lead them by their noses
Through their yearning to excel,
'Til you've gotten what you wanted.
Then they all can go to hell!

As Carl Petry remarks, the engaging rogues idealized in picaresque entertainments are not so readily met in the annals of historians.[158] The tricks and effrontery are there, of course. Ibn al-Jawzī tells of Baghdad tricksters who made their living selling rosaries to the Shīʿites, and clay tablets straight from the grave of Ḥusayn.[159] The *Kitāb al-Maghrib* relates with relish how a *ḥajjī* from Iraq told the Ikhshīd of Egypt (who used to weep at the recitation of the Qurʾān) of a dream message from the Prophet, which the traveler had proclaimed at the sacred Zamzam well in Mecca, commanding the release from prison of a certain financial manipulator. Trying to be hardheaded, the Ikhshīd offered the man a generous travel allowance to go back to the well and tell the Prophet that the prisoner would be released when the funds missing and owing were coughed up. But the cadger stood his ground: "I do not make jokes with the Prophet." As he made ready to leave, the Ikhshīd hailed him back and promised the prisoner's release.[160]

Even here the delight remains literary. The medieval counterpart to the police blotter shows a darker picture. Life in the underworld was precarious at best, typically vicious, and as Petry puts it, "fraught with risk of reprisal." Crime was ugly; beggary, desperate; adultery, then as now, dangerous and destructive. Imruʾ al-Qays knew all that. But he made light of the damage and took mournful delight in the hardships and dangers, at least in recollection. Hamadhānī works on a still more rarefied plane. But his goal, we have suggested, is more than satire or exposé.

He repeatedly juxtaposes zeal with insincerity. The knot of men gathered in the mosque in the Ruṣāfa Encounter have come in to get out of the sun. Their talk is not of holy things and sacred practices but of gins and confidence games. ʿĪsā, in Isfahan, peeking out from the rows of worshipers, can scarcely raise his head. He wants only to get to Rayy, and he knows that will have to wait. He is neither as pious as the crowd, whose zeal he fears if he cannot respect it, nor as free as Abū ʾl-Fatḥ, whose abandon he admires, if he cannot fully emulate it. His predicament perfectly situates a central ambiguity for the cultured Muslim. For that man or woman's culture, be it Arab, African, Chinese, or Malay, is not coextensive with Islam. But neither is it separable from the claims of Islam. Piety seems to demand a choice—between *dunyā* and *dīn*, this world and the faith. But for those who are less committed to pure deviltry than Abū 'l-Fatḥ yet less zealous than the credulous mosque crowd, logic does not seem to frame the options quite so starkly.

Faithful Muslims do seek to integrate God's service with a life that is not barren by purely human standards. But individuals differ in what they find fruitful or barren. Secularity is the island or continent where such spirits live, at least part of the time. And that land mass, large or small, is never fully submerged. For Islam, like every religion, harbors its own secular moments and spaces. It fosters secularities that are at once inimical to its claims and yet symbiotic with it. They are dependent on it but also supportive of its worldly presence and self-assertion. And they exact a price in distraction of gaze and diffusion of interests.

To the Arab princes who painted palaces with nudes or rode to hawks, or hounds or cheetahs, to the poets who celebrated the senses and emotions for their own sakes or mapped the landscape of spiritual ecstasy on the topography of the erotic, to the artists who found in figural forms a means of glorifying God and, simultaneously, in that glorying, found a means of celebrating, even titillating human aesthetic sensibilities, to the *ghāzī* and the philosopher who saw Islam as a way of the world and not merely a way *out* of it, Islamic life was more than just an occasional pious moment yet less than an all-engulfing "worldview," a seamless blanket or "blick," through which no light could shine unless from within and in which no discontinuities could be detected, no holes or cross-weaves, admitting alien sunshine or unruly air.

Through hierarchies of means and ends, ploys and symbolisms, a bit of compartmentalization here and a bit of humor there, Islam becomes a way of life coloring every culture reached by the Qur'ān and the Arabic language. In the cosmopolitan civilization that results, communities and individuals find their own tents and awnings, accommodating the sacred and the secular in various modes of coexistence, some intricately devised, some casual or haphazard, some coherent, others restive or unstable, some synthetic or creative, others vapid, stiff, or angry. Many of these shelters are such that those who have lived in their shade could find that they were experiencing something of the best of this world without being deprived of some taste of the next.

2

Humanism and Islamic Ethics

Normative Islam develops in three phases: the Qur'ānic or scriptural phase; its elaboration in the *ḥadīth*, that vast literature of sayings and doings ascribed to the Prophet; and the comprehensive system of law (*fiqh*), which adds new tributaries to the stream, drawing anew on the ancient floodplain of ethical and juridical culture that had from the outset fed the wellsprings of Islamic norms. The first section of this chapter aims to consider the shape that Islamic practical ethics takes under the impress of scripture, tradition, legal theory and practice, and theological theories of action. Having done that, I'd like to focus on two key thinkers. The first is the humanist ethical philosopher, historian, and courtier Aḥmad ibn Muḥammad Miskawayh (ca. 932–1030), a learned and articulate exponent of *falsafa* and *adab*, the Islamic traditions of philosophy and literary culture. The second is the Sufi-inspired theologian, jurist, and philosophic critic of *falsafa*, al-Ghazālī (1058–1111), who spoke up as a friend of music in chapter 1. Ghazālī's ethics builds systematically on Miskawayh's work, but with telling revisions for the fate of Islamic humanism. A word or two first about Sufism, *falsafa*, *kalām*, and *adab*. That will lead us back to some thoughts about Qur'ān and *ḥadīth* and their roles in framing the practical norms of Islam.

To committed Sufis, Islamic mysticism has seemed, since its inception in the contemplative practice of Muslim saints and their appropriation of the mystical traditions of their non-Muslim predecessors, to spring straight from the Qur'ān, the practice of the Prophet, and the life he ordained. Conceived as a meditative quest, Sufism, despite its motivating interest in direct acquaintance with the Divine, has been more a way of life than a way of knowing. Its conceptual and theoretical dimensions are ancillary to its steeply graded experiential pathways and its vivid, if dreamlike, visionary imagery. Sufis themselves, when they schematize their values, place praxis ahead of cognition. And Sufi practice, traditionally, has been communal rather than private. The practical bent and communal shape of Sufism have broadcast Islamic ideas and ideals far more widely than any sheerly speculative or doxastic system could be spread. The Sufi orders articulate and intensify an Islamic ethos, disseminated through channels of transmission and chains of authority that are at once literary and charismatic, transgenerational, and transcultural.

Falsafa, philosophy proper, was grounded in the Arabic translations of the great works of Greek philosophy and science sponsored by the Arab princes and potentates of the eighth to the tenth centuries.[1] As the name suggests, *falsafa* was viewed as a foreign import, a Greek enterprise, although its findings, perspectives, even many of its methods were to be naturalized. The philosophical ideal of individual thought, of walking and working the highwire of metaphysics without a safety net, was just as foreign as the Greek language in the precincts of nascent Islamic traditionalism, and far more threatening. Yet *falsafa*, then as now, was attractive to independent spirits. Most of those drawn to it were confident that reason would lead them more surely by far, if less securely, to the very heights that religion sought—or higher, since religion offered ritual and symbolic surrogates of the truths that only a trusting commitment to untrammeled thought could fully and faithfully deliver.

Kalām, Islamic dialectical theology, was a long-lived endeavor, born, perhaps, in the intercommunal debates that followed the Islamic conquests. It continued on a massive scale among the hundreds of Islamic movements, sects, schisms, parties, factions, divisions, and opinions that reflect the diversity in backgrounds and commitments of the early adherents of Islam.[2] It was *Falsafa* that branded *kalām* dialectical, meaning that it was anchored in stipulative premises extracted from an adversary or (even more suppositiously) from scripture. The *mutakallimūn* or practitioners of *kalām*, for their part, long distinguished themselves from the *falāsifa*, philosophers, by shunning the philosophers' most powerful tool, Aristotelian syllogistic. Perhaps recognizing the naturalism implicit in Aristotle's logical scheme, the *mutakallimūn* relied on hypothetical reasoning that often seemed suspiciously ad hoc. Their approach may hark back to the earlier, Stoic rejection of Peripatetic logic.[3]

Over the centuries the *mutakallimūn* carried their debates from a primitive yet conceptually radical and often exciting doggedness about core theological values to a pitch of high scholastic seriousness addressing a wide range of metaphysical and cosmological issues. The ramifications of these debates included sustained critical discussions of theistic subjectivism and objectivism, voluntarism and determinism, the sanctions and consequences of virtue and vice, obedience and sin, faith, and faithlessness. What emerged were sophisticated, if ultimately etiolated, discussions of moral epistemology and the anatomy of action.

Adab was the literary tradition of the secretarial or administrative class, the culture of the professional literati who looked past the lampoons and boasts, self-deprecations and self-vaunting of the desert poets to the more urbane values of the court and chancery. Arabic prose was their creation. Manners were their mores, and history was their meat. They loved style and relished wit, as we saw with Hamadhānī. They respected refinement and revered statesmanship. But they also had an eye for slumming and a taste for decadence. They knew how high a man could climb in the world, and how fast and far he could fall. Theirs was not the closed world of the Qur'ānic dispensation.

What then of the Qur'ān, the revelation vouchsafed to the Islamic prophet? Orphaned young and reaching maturity in the caravan town of Mecca in inland Arabia, Muḥammad (570–632) gained financial independence with his marriage to the merchant widow Khadījah. His meditations and his moral abhorrence of the rude ways of his contemporaries led him to visionary pronouncements of divine judgment, the first phase of a prophetic message modeled on the admonitions of the Hebrew prophets, whose imagery and idiom he adapted in his Arabic Qur'ān—that is, a Bible, an ecstatically received, liturgically recited revelation of God's word.

The Islamic era is dated from 622, the year of the *hijra*, Muḥammad's emigration from Mecca to the neighboring city of Yathrib, or Medina as it was later called. He was invited, as a spiritual figure, to mediate a tribal feud; but he became the leader of the place, suppressing its tribalized Jews and turning its formerly warring Arab factions against the caravan trade of Mecca, whose denizens had failed to follow his lead or heed his message. After the *hijra* the revelations become more legislative than sheerly hortatory. The visions of apocalypse gradually recede before the delineation of a society ruled under the dispensation of Islam.

Uniting his followers under the banner of their common faith and law, the Prophet made a triumphal reentry into Mecca, which sacred history pictures him as having fled. By the time of his death, just ten years after the *hijra*, he was the ruler of Arabia. His lieutenants, the *khalīfah*s, deputies and successors to the executive and military dimensions of his authority, rapidly brought to heel the fractious tribes who imagined that the Prophet's death had somehow canceled their oaths of fealty. They then turned the united power of the armies of the faithful outward, stunningly overturning the immense Sassanian Persian empire and wresting Egypt and Syria from the Byzantines. Within a century of the Prophet's death the tier of lands from the Indus and Central Asia to the Pyrenees had been brought under Islamic rule.

While Spain, in the course of seven centuries, would ultimately expel the Muslims, the rich lands of Byzantium, after centuries of siege, would finally be subdued. Sicily and much of the Balkans and India would be Islamized. Trade, slaving and missionarism—often hand in hand—extended the faith deep into Africa, China, the Philippines, and Indonesia. The government of all Islamic lands belonged in principle to the Commander of the Faithful, the *khalīfah* or caliph, the *imām* qualified to lead the people, defend the faith, and apply its laws. In practice the many rival and warring Islamic states were led by military governors, dynasts, ambitious vassals, court intriguers, freebooters, slave soldiers (*mamlūk*s), and charismatics.

Despite the fanciful image of the oriental despot, Muslim princes and caliphs did not, of course, wield absolute power. They could be cruel and did exercise a wide discretion. But they were answerable not only to the claims of conscience but also in some measure to the Law, as interpreted by their judicial appointees and by the more independent of the *ʿulamāʾ*, the religious scholars, whose preaching could powerfully move the populace. Muslim princes, like any others, had to answer, in a different sense, to the practical limits that constrain all political claims. They were subject to the pressures of rival rulers, tribal, sectarian, or ethnic rebels, and pretenders, often of their own kin, who might find powerful sponsors in the armies, the ministries, or the harem. Kingmakers might manipulate or depose the caliph or hold him in the harem, at once an ornament of legitimacy and a reproach to the very notion of an unbroken Islamic line.

In principle, Islamic Law, the *Sharīʿa*, was the proper law of any state that laid claim to the heritage of the Prophet. But tensions could hardly fail to arise between the demands of such a state and the ideals of the jurists and legal scholars. Scripture itself did not stand static and alone in that interaction. It was elaborated in systems of morals and codes of law that sought embodiment in the lives of the faithful. The resultant demands readily became maximal, in view of their divine source and sanction. Small wonder that rival dynasts claimed Islamic legitimacy or that charismatic rebels made claims of their own, often apocalyptic, pledging to restore and renew the primal faith that flourished in the days of Islam's dramatic rise. Small wonder too, that the very identity of more than one Shīʿite pretender was sublimated, transforming a vanished *imām* into a cosmic figure or a hypostatic ideal.

Because the Prophet's ecstatic visions and legislative oracles responded so powerfully, even violently, to what he saw around him, Qurʾānic ethics is often presumptive, in much the way that Qurʾānic narrative is allusive.[4] Legislatively, the scriptural foundation will look open textured, like a constitution, ready to be filled in with concrete institutions. But the scope and reach of its claims gives the Qurʾān, like any other monotheistic scripture, an ethical fullness well beyond the sketchiness of mere rules in a law book.

Muḥammad's scripturally inscribed moral vision is a distinctive hybrid of puritan revulsion and earthy permissions: Gambling, alcohol, fornication, and faithlessness are forbidden, anathema in God's eyes. The heedless, who give the lie to the Prophet and reject God's word, await bitter torments in the Hereafter. But believers are allowed four wives (provided they are treated fairly)—and unspecified concubines. Most of the Jewish dietary restrictions (except for the one on pork) are removed, aiding the Prophet in distinguishing Islam from the religion of the Jewish contemporaries among whom he had once sought followers. Of similar effect is the decision to face Mecca rather than Jerusalem in prayer. Muḥammad accommodates the indigenous Arab culture by retaining the Kaʿba as a sacred site, taking over the Arab pilgrim festivals and sacrifices, and even introducing into the Qurʾān verses, soon canceled, that acknowledge pagan goddesses.[5] Never canceled was the peopling of the land with familiar spirits, the jinn.[6] The biblical and rabbinic heritage remains evident in the scriptural and midrashic narratives of the Qurʾān and its laws of inheritance, prayer, charity, and adultery—which last, in Islam, requires four eyewitnesses to the overt act, in view of the gravity of the offense and its capital sanction.

The Qur'ān, to the believing Muslim, is revelation, God's *ipsissima verba*, transmitted to his prophet by the angel Gabriel, capping and sealing the work of all prior prophets. It authenticates God's earlier revelations and is vouched for by them. But should the followers of sister religions balk at the contents or the provenance of Muḥammad's revelatory dicta, they are dismissed as scoffers and deniers. Any disparities between their scriptures and the Qur'ān result from ancient and impious tampering with the texts of revelation.

In the early days of *kalām*, the Muʿtazilite theologians adapted an old Stoic argument, claiming that God's justice made revelation a moral necessity. The argument may have aimed at adversaries who rejected the very idea of special revelation. "Brahmins," in the Muslim sources, are often said to have done just that. But the torque of the recast argument, like so much else in Muʿtazilism, came from theodicy: How could God (justly) punish or reward His servants without warning them of their duties and the consequences of their acts? Later *mutakallimūn*, of the Ashʿarite school, plainly faced a different problematic. They were affronted at the notion that mere humans could assay God's justice, let alone bind the Almighty to some human sense of duty. They denounced the voluntarist Muʿtazilites for making mere mortals the "creators" of their own acts. And they condemned as heresy the view that the Qur'ān was created at all. Borrowing from ancient Jewish notions of God's eternal word or wisdom, as manifested in the Torah, and from the related Christian idea of an uncreated Christ, traditionalists framed an Islamic orthodoxy, in part by making the uncreated Qur'ān an article of faith.[7] They too celebrated the Qur'ānic revelation but spoke of its eternity rather than its moral necessity.

The veneration for scripture attested by both sides in this bitter controversy is shared by all faithful Muslims.[8] Against that background, one might imagine that fundamentalism would be a powerful force in Islam. But strictly speaking that expectation would be mistaken. Fundamentalism as we know it is a modern movement arising in the humanism of the European Renaissance and in the Protestant demand for clarity in theology, plainness in exegesis, and simplicity in Church norms. Fundamentalist biblicism reacted against what seemed overgrown and casuistical in canon law, allegorical interpretation, philosophical metaphysics, and scholastic theology. Even the fundamentalist notions of inerrancy and literalism are the reflex of modernist ideas of the plainness and openness of truth.

Islam, like Judaism and Catholic Christianity, did not reject its own postscriptural elaborations but cherished them as organic supplements to revelation. Subtlety was not the enemy. The early faith, conceived as a pure and ascetic path, has been repeatedly brandished as a challenge to decadence, permissivism, tolerance of non-Muslims and of backsliders, and insufficient rigor in prosecuting the cause and fostering the spread of Islam. But Islamic militancy has not sought to separate the scriptural faith from its juridical elaboration. *Falsafa* may be condemned, but dogmatics is not rejected. Even when suspicious of the dialectic of *kalām*, Islamic theology has remained a scholastic enterprise. Literalism there has been, and simplicity has been an ideal, but the arbiters of practice have turned for guidance far more often to the *ḥadīth* than to the Qur'ān.

Against the expectation that Islamic norms would simply flow from Qur'ān to *ḥadīth*, and thence to the body of *fiqh*, we find the reverse. The Qur'ān retains the highest authority in principle, but the ultimate arbiter of practice, as Brannon Wheeler has shown, is not the highest but the most proximate authority. For "the authority of a canon," as Wheeler puts it, "depends upon its traditional interpretation."[9] In the Islamic case: "The applicability and thus authority of the Qur'ān is fixed by the sunnah, the sunnah by the opinions [of the early jurists], and the opinions by subsequent scholarship."[10] That does not license an arbitrary manhandling of the sources. Far from it. Taking the Ḥanafī school as his model, Wheeler explains:

> The Ḥanafī scholar does not interpret the revelation alone or even directly, but instead interprets how generations previous to him interpreted the revelation. . . . Using previous scholarship as examples of how to apply the revelation, the Hanafī scholar must compare the context in which the revelation was interpreted in precedented cases to distinguish what is specific to each of the cases from what the cases have in common. Through this type of reasoning, the Ḥanafī scholar induces a general principle of the revelation from the different precedented cases. . . .
>
> Postclassical scholarship is primarily a pedagogic enterprise, teaching future Ḥanafī scholars the epistemological and methodological bases of the Hanafī school through a step-by-step commentary on how previous scholarship interpreted opinions. . . . This scholarship focuses upon the notion that the authority of a given definition of practice is less about the interpretation of the revelation than about being able to demonstrate that a given definition is justified in the light of earlier tradition [11]

The same is true, of course, mutatis mutandis, for Talmudic or American constitutional law. Impressions to the contrary are artifacts of analysis: The Constitution or the Torah oversees case law and in that broad sense explains it. But the principles that may warrant or inspire a law always underdetermine the concrete provisions of practice. The dictates of scripture itself will be understood, ultimately, in terms of day-to-day decisions.[12]

Consideration of the disciplines that foster Islamic norms prepares us to assay the content of those norms. For each of these disciplines affirms its own distinctive notion of reason and the reasonable. Reason in Islamic law, as in law everywhere, will mean analogy with precedent. In *kalām* it will mean dialectical, hypothetical inference, anchored in some seeming common ground. In *falsafa* reason will mean something more: rational intuition and its discursive exposition in syllogistic argument.[13] But in *adab* reason will mean sound judgment, deference to experience, that is, to the history, learning, and wisdom of the nations, which Islamic civilization has inherited from its predecessors and made over in new form. And in Sufism, reason itself will be sublimated into a pietist sensibility that trumps the work of philosophy in framing the parameters of a culture.

Islamic Ethics in Theory and Practice

Like biblical Judaism, Qur'ānic Islam does not sharply distinguish between law and morals. Nor does it draw hard and fast lines between ritual symbolism, spiritual expression, and communal engagement. Like biblical Christianity, it places faith in the forefront of piety. Faith is a matter of trust, but even more, of allegiance. Addressing a community of believers—at first a beleaguered minority, later a triumphant authority—it envisions worship as a public exercise and adopts a legalist, rigorist tone in setting out its devotional requirements and ethical expectations, preferences, requirements, distastes, and prohibitions.

Unlike Marx, or even Plato in some moods, but like the scriptural ethics of Judaism and Christianity, Qur'ānic ethics does not countenance breach of its standards in pursuit of its aims. Unlike Aristotle or Nietzsche but like biblical ethics, Qur'ānic ethics is framed in a language of imperatives. Its primal aim is a way of life charted by divine commands. The scriptural law, as in Judaism, will define an ethos; but obedience to God's commands is clearly an end in itself. That opens the door to a kind of legal positivism, which is to say, antirationalism, quite characteristic of scriptural legal systems. Not that Islamic ethics is everywhere inflexible in its development or that scriptural legislation in general is without its inner tensions. But, normatively speaking, the exceptions to scripturally sanctioned rules must be built into the rules themselves. Inner tensions must remain implicit, to be worked out by scholar/jurists, or (for moderns) the conscience of the morally sensitive or ritually scrupulous. The legislative challenge here is not one of adjusting communal norms in the face of new problems but of resolving apparent discrepancies—or submerging the problematics from which they arise.

Seeking to distill the ethos of the Qur'ān, Majid Fakhry focuses on *birr*, piety, godliness, or devotion, the one term "that expresses the moral and religious spirit of the Koran better than any other."[14] An oft quoted verse helps him to help delineate the aim:

> It is not piety to turn your faces East or West. True piety is this: to believe in God and the Last Day, the angels, the Book, and the Prophets, to give of one's substance, out of love of Him, to kinsmen and orphans, the needy, the wayfarer and those who ask, to ransom slaves, keep up the prayers and pay the alms tax. It is those who keep their bond when they have given it and who bear with fortitude misfortune, hardship and danger—these are the faithful. These are the godfearing. (Qur'ān 2:177)[15]

Acts of righteousness and charity join with worship in giving faith and love of God their clearest expression.[16] The immediate circumstances of the revelation highlight those actions that support the needs of the community and the claims of its leader. He presses the bivalent idea of piety, in a manner long precedented among the prophets of Israel,[17] to urge his followers onward from ritual to spiritual, moral, and practical commitment. The proud generosity of the old Arab ideal is channeled to socially preferred and institutionally legitimated uses. It is no longer a noble abandon but a steadfast, even humble response to genuine need.[18] The old Arab sense that life is transitory has become a righteous dread of final judgment. Earnestness replaces what Izutsu calls the desperate hedonism attested in the poetry of the *Jāhiliyya*. Loyalty to the nation of Islam displaces (or supervenes upon) tribal allegiance,[19] The paramount commitment is to a covenant, a spiritual as well as social contract. God is now a party to every undertaking, and good faith means purity of intent, a conscience and consciousness open to His scrutiny.[20] Courage has become steadfastness, and the long-suffering that we saw in Imru' al-Qays is fortified no longer by bitter irony or sweet memories but by hope in visions of the hereafter.[21]

Obedience to God's will is the clearest mark of faith. But faith itself is the Islamic way to salvation. The cardinal sin is *kufr*, faithlessness, unbelief, an ultimately unforgivable ingratitude for God's manifold blessings. Unbelief is arrogance, collapse before the passions and caprices that blind the eyes to understanding and lead on to actual mockery of God's revealed message.[22]

The Qur'ānic ideal of surrender to God's sovereignty raises theological issues at the sensitive border crossing between the realms of divine and human action—issues that the Qur'ān itself only glancingly addresses. For the Qur'ān, as Montgomery Watt rightly notes, is not a work of systematic theology. Many of the problems that would vex the *mutakallimūn* were unseen by the Prophet, or far from the center of his visual field. The Qur'ānic rhetoric of divine immediacy, omnipresence and absolute control butts heads with the equally insistent stress on divine justice and human accountability. But the work of reconciling human choice with God's decree is left to the divines. Their efforts meet with varying success. Often they testify more eloquently to the candor of the theologians' commitments than to their skills at conceptual synthesis.[23]

Just as Islam did not stop at the original audience of the Qur'ān, Islamic ethical teachings do not keep to their Qur'ānic base. But theology was neither the first pathway nor the broadest avenue in their expansion. The medium of *ḥadīth* allowed the appropriation and canonization of a wide range of folk and traditional materials, now heard from the mouth of the Prophet (whereas God was the speaker in the Qur'ān). Moral attitudes, advice, restrictions, and interpretations never voiced in the sacred text find expression here and acquire an authority second only to that of the Qur'ān itself.

The word *ḥadīth* means literally a piece of news, a report of the sayings and doings of the Prophet and his circle, as relayed by his companions and the generations of traditionists. In practice, *ḥadīth* was used to justify the regionally divergent practices of diverse schools of law, projecting back their usages into sacred history.[24] So the repertoires of the great early collectors soon held hundreds of thousands of *ḥadīth*s. Winnowed to its tens of thousands, the corpus grew more manageable in bulk and thematically more coherent. The reports, gathered in collections of varying authority and classified by theme, became a source of ethical, juridical, and ritual exempla and precepts that is still studied for edification and outright implementation and emulation.[25] Indeed, Sunnī Islam takes its name from the claim to orthodoxy embodied in the ideal of adhering to the practice (*sunna*) of the Prophet as discovered in the *ḥadīth*. And Shīʿī Islam, while stressing the inherited charisma of its living or vanished leaders, also upholds the precedent of the Prophet and stoutly maintains its own body of *ḥadīth*s.

The *ḥadīth* speaks in a welter voices. It is far from representing a cult of personality—unless allowance is made for the projection of a prophetic persona that is itself, in some measure, an artifact of the *ḥadīth*. But *ḥadīth* does frame an ethos expressive of the spirit of the Islamic community in its formative centuries. Individual items may echo the Gospels, Midrash, Gemara, Persian wisdom literature, or Arab proverbs of pre-Islamic days. But the nisus emergent from the processes of selection and elaboration is toward the puritan and the supererogatory: Rigor becomes an ideal at a level of detail that no revealed scripture acting alone could enunciate. The expressions of liberality or good humor assigned to the Prophet become striking marks of release of tension and self-demand. Pietist ideals take root and exfoliate, woven about the dicta and events of the Qurʾān. To borrow the image of a recent Talmudist, it is as if the new canon had introduced its own set of categories, making every act and experience a devotional occasion.

From the sea of the *ḥadīth* it is impossible to extract a single essence, but the salt flavor of the whole does pervade every part. There are treatments of faith, knowledge, purification, hygiene (including how to wipe one's shoes, trim one's beard, and clean one's teeth), prayer, funerals, charity, fasting, business, marrying, divorcing, freeing slaves, visiting the sick, paying debts of guilt and honor, making the pilgrimage, and fighting the holy war. Detailed prescriptions are given as to permitted and forbidden foods, clothing and ornaments, modes of address, sitting, standing, laughing, sneezing, yawning, and sexual congress. At the heart of ethics, Bukhārī's collection reports the words of the Prophet: "None of you truly has faith if he does not desire for his brother what he desires for himself." And again, "The Prophet of God said, 'Help your brother Muslim, be he oppressor or oppressed.' People asked, 'Messenger of God, if he is oppressed we shall help him, but what if he be the oppressor?' He replied: 'Prevent him from oppressing.'" The *ḥadīth* here looks back to the biblical and rabbinic formulations of the Golden Rule, but also ahead to political problems undreamed of by Muḥammad. At no time is the Prophet found wanting in teachings of paramount import to the issues of the age.

The Qurʾān itself speaks to the issue of obedience to authority: "O ye who believe, obey God and obey his Messenger and those who hold command among you!" (Qurʾān 4:59). The theme is taken up in the *ḥadīth*. Both Bukhārī and Muslim record the words so often ascribed to Muḥammad: "Whoever obeys me obeys God . . . Whoever obeys the Commander of the Faithful obeys me." In the same vein: "Hear and obey, though an Abyssinian with a head like a raisin be placed over you." But a tradition as rich and varied as the *ḥadīth* will not leave even so categorical a command unqualified. So the caveat is heard, still in Muḥammad's voice: "—But only so long as one is not ordered to disobey God." Then "there is no hearing and no obeying."

Sometimes the Prophetic persona adopts a world-weary tone. Authority, the Prophet advises, is "a good suckler but a poor weaner." That's gentler than Lord Acton's saying that power corrupts and absolute power corrupts absolutely. But it reflects a similar experience and responds by softening the strident call to obedience heard in the Qur'ān. The tension is readily blurred, but not so readily erased. Of course, the faith exhorts its followers to principle. But does that mean resistance to usurped authority? Or do the counsels of prudence join with realpolitik and the claims of peace, tipping the balance toward acquiescence? For the *hadīth*, government (*al-sulṭān*) is the shadow of God on earth; all of God's servants who are downtrodden shall turn to it. When it is just it will be rewarded, and the flock must be grateful; when it is oppressive, the burden of its wrongdoing redounds to its own account, but the flock must bear it patiently. The sentiments smack of Hobbes—just as Ashʿarite theologians sometimes sound like Calvin. For Calvin, like the Ashʿarites, is protective of God's sovereignty, and his theology is caught up in questions of grace. Hobbes, like the *ḥadīth*, is transfixed by the horrors of civil war and anarchy. "If anyone sees something hateful in his commander," the Prophet is made to say, "let him bear it patiently. For no one breaks with the community by even a handsbreadth without dying the death of the *Jāhiliyya*." But then we read the iridescent advice: "If two caliphs are given the oath, kill the second!"

Standards like these left and still leave gaps wide enough to march armies through. Clearly they knit a network of norms that catch hold of the individual conscience and lace the communal ethos with a sense of resignation powerfully seconded by the predestinarian moment in the Qur'ān. But passive obedience is not the only possible response to thoughts of God's omnipotence. "Kill the second!" puts a sharp edge on seeming docility.

Normatively there is no fatalism in Islam, if fatalism means thinking that human choices make no ultimate difference. Even the most predestinarian of Muslim theologians held vigorously to Qur'ānic accountability, the promise and the threat. That seemed to lay the fate of one's immortal soul squarely in one's own hands. Ashʿarites saw the act of faith itself as a gift of grace and an outcome of God's eternal plan. Even so, from a practical standpoint, the belief that God ordains all events is powerfully bivalent. It can urge acceptance but also formidable effort and resistance. All depends on what is seen as the working of God's will. Theologians who called God the creator of our acts could readily explain that God acts through us—creating motion, sin, or sickness in us, not in Himself, yet acting all-powerfully nonetheless, as in the Qur'ānic (8:17) paradigm: "When you shot it was not you who shot but God." We are accountable, the Ashʿarites argued, because we appropriate a choice, not because we "make" it. We remain responsible, even if we do not "create" our actions. But—here is the hidden, distinctively medieval sting—each of us is responsible in his own sphere: Every one of you is a shepherd and must answer for his flock, the Prophet urges: the Imām for the people, a man for his household, a woman for her husband's house and children, a slave for his master's goods.

The Qur'ān (3:104) wraps many of its norms in the broad injunction to "ordain what is right and forbid what is wrong." What is wrong here is called *munkar*, wicked, disreputable—literally, unspeakable (cf. the Latin *nefas*); what is right, *ma'rūf*, is just the opposite: proper, appropriate, respectable.[26] Much of the militancy that has marked Islam stems from this sweeping Qur'ānic mandate in behalf of moral decency. For it is not the law alone that does the ordaining and forbidding. Rather, those who are subject to the law are commanded to do so, the community at large. The rub, as legal positivists would quickly stress, is that what counts as right and wrong is not textually defined but still presumptive here, as are the modalities of enforcement.

The Qur'ānic command, of course, was never abstract in practice. Over time, it was glossed concretely by the juridical schools, who, as we have seen, made the breaking up of musical instruments a paradigm case of what was called for. The open-ended demands of morals and the special expectations of custom, ritual, and propriety now acquire some of the force and stringency of legal statutes, and the law acquires some of the concreteness and open endedness of morals. The Islamic legal schools and traditions array themselves in the diversity of their understandings of just who is responsible for implementing the proper standards, how it is to be done, and how far public authorities and private individuals should press in this regard.

Energy in fulfilling the obligation to institute right and forbid wrong was (and in the most traditional Islamic circles remains) both a standard of legitimacy for governments and a rallying cry for dissent. Rebels found no sharper lance to fling against the states they deemed corrupt than the charge of failing to institute the canons of authentically Islamic practice. And the defenders of a regime found no stouter shield than an image of public piety. A widely cited *ḥadīth* proclaims: "The highest form of holy war is speaking out truthfully before an unjust ruler, and being killed for it."[27] Admiring stories are told of those who died in this way. One such martyr, a goldsmith, was said to have appeared at the court of Abū Muslim (d. 755), the architect of the 'Abbāsid revolution, boldly denouncing the nascent regime. The moderate jurist Abū Ḥanīfa is pictured as warning the outspoken goldsmith that the obligation to ordain the right and forbid the wrong is a public charge, not one that an individual should attempt alone, since that would only mean throwing away one's life. Rebels, Abū Ḥanīfa held, can cause more harm than good. The story may be a back-projection designed to explain why Abū Ḥanīfa did not himself speak out against what was later perceived, at least by the tellers of the tale, as a corrupt and corrupting polity. The fact is that there were rebel causes that Abū Ḥanīfa did approve. But even the quietist dictum ascribed to him, as Michael Cook points out, gave dissidents (or activists) the moral high ground:

> What we see here is the presence, within the mainstream of Islamic thought, of a strikingly—not to say inconveniently—radical value: the principle that the executive power of the law of God is vested in each and every Muslim. Under this conception the individual believer as such has not only the right,

> but also the duty, to issue orders pursuant to God's law, and to do what he can to see that they are obeyed. What is more, he may be issuing these orders to people who conspicuously outrank him in the prevailing hierarchy of social and political power.[28]

Even as a matter of theory the doctrine proved a powerful double edged sword, defending established regimes if they seemed to serve proper Muslim values but assailing regimes that seemed too lax or tolerant. And, of course, the doctrine was never a matter of sheer theory. It was often held forth as a standard for daily life. It was cited, for example, when Egyptian Islamic Jihād issued a fifty-four-page document entitled "The Neglected Duty," aimed at justifying Anwar Sadat's assassination.[29] And, as with the Buddhas of Bamiyan, the doctrine was not confined to human targets or offending regimes. The Ḥanbalites, who took it most seriously, gave the Qur'ānic mandate to enforce the good and suppress wrongdoing concrete application in their war against the lute, the drum, and the *ṭunbūr*, a kind of long-necked mandolin. They used it against wine and other forms of alcohol and against public fraternizing between the sexes. If a young man rode behind a woman or a druggist was seen chatting too freely with a woman customer, or a man divorced his wife but still lived with her, that became a matter for action and reproach. Chess and backgammon are targeted in Ibn Ḥanbal's responsa, as are casual and hasty prayers, the display of images, exchanges of gossip or insults, even noisy and overzealous keening. Everyone, even a slave, must take action against the wrongs he sees: Passersby should break up a fight among boys in the street, and a wife should warn her husband that if he does not keep up his prayers she will pursue a divorce.

The *ḥadīth* assigns the obligation to command the right and forbid the wrong to the hand, the tongue, or the heart. Ibn Ḥanbal prefers the more active of these interventions. He hopes that an unspoken mental condemnation of wrongdoing will satisfy the Qur'ānic demand; but speaking out is better, whether that means counsel, exhortation, censure, direct orders, or shouting at the wrongdoer. With one's hands, one may smash musical instruments and wine bottles, overturn chessboards and scatter the pieces, evict an ex-wife, threaten or beat a youthful offender. But Ibn Ḥanbal draws the line at swords or other weapons, and he cautions those who contemplate coming to blows with adult offenders with the one word reminder, *al-rifq*, civility![30]

Fear for one's personal safety can legitimately keep fulfillment of the obligation pent up "in the heart." But one should not hesitate to seek the help of neighbors, if singing, for example, is persistent. Nor should one be afraid of insults, or of making a scene. The burden of civility, in that case seems to fall on the offenders. But there are bounds of privacy. One doesn't (like some zealots) climb over walls to surprise neighborhood sinners. But if one sees liquor in a jug while visiting a friend's house, one really ought to spoil it, by pouring in salt. Musical instruments left in plain sight should be destroyed, but concealed ones are the subject of various opinions, rather like our own divergent laws about concealed and displayed weapons.[31]

The early Ḥanbalites, Cook notes, did not typically go about reviling or assaulting Muʿtazilite preachers or raiding brothels. Still less did they take on the authorities. A militant but hardly ascendant minority, they kept their heads down. Ibn Ḥanbal's advice was to stay clear of the ruler, since "his sword is unsheathed."[32] Only rarely does this jurist endorse attempts to enlist the state in a campaign for decency—perhaps in opposing the use of frogs or mice as bait, but not in most other cases. Even an incorrigible wrongdoer should be turned in only if one knows that the authorities will apply the statutory penalties and not overreact, as they so often seemed to do.[33]

Later Ḥanbalites swung like a pendulum between the private activism of the master and the Savonarola-like exploits of Barbahārī (d. 941) and his successors, who harassed the Baghdad populace for two and a half centuries, into the Būyid and Seljūq eras, only gradually relaxing their vigilance as the Ḥanbalites came in time to better terms with the state. Ibn al-Jawzī, for example, tones down Ghazālī's activism, requiring government permission before resorting to threats or blows or vigilante action to enforce the standards of decency. Where Ghazālī had commended outspoken censure of slack rulers, Ibn al-Jawzī speaks for tact, arguing that harsh or rude criticism will only provoke its targets and entrench their attitudes.[34]

Ibn Taymiyyah, citing the Qur'ānic (2:217) dictum that *fitnah*, seditious intrigue, is a graver offense than mortal combat, argued that the Islamic state has a divine mandate to suppress unbelievers who obstruct its purposes. *Jihād* here becomes part of the duty to command right and forbid wrong, a notion pursued today by the bloody minions of bin Laden. The goal in any just war, Ibn Taymiyyah holds, is to establish God's will—as he puts it, to render all judgment unto God.[35] The same broad mandate applies in civil affairs, extending, as one modern commentator explains, to "the legislative, judicial and economic affairs of the Community" and to "its religious and moral life."[36] For Ibn Taymiyyah, that means the excommunication of heretics, astrologers, slackers, and, of course, Sufis who ape Christian practice by venerating the graves of their departed saints. The Fāṭimid regime in Egypt came in for particular condemnation, not only for holding heretical views but also for appointing non-Muslim state officials and fostering an atmosphere in which intercommunal celebrations and cross-cultural contacts were all too close, and syncretic influences, all too evident. The remedy, Ibn Taymiyyah argued, was strict enforcement of the so-called Pact of ʿUmar, under which Jews and Christians, as People of the Book, are to be humiliated, albeit not oppressed—protected, but never suffered to forget their abased and inferior status.[37]

Ibn Taymiyyah does weigh the obligation to activism against the risks. He often seems to favor leaving enforcement to the authorities, political, spiritual, or intellectual. But power brings responsibility. The energy and efficiency that leaders show in enforcing public and private decency will bolster or undermine their legitimacy in the eyes of the pious.[38] That thought has not been far from the minds of such modern claimants to Islamic authority as the Wahhābite founders of the present Saudi regime, the Ṭālibān in Afghanistan, and the Ayatollahs in Iran.[39] It was the Afghan Ministry for Promotion of

Virtue and Prevention of Vice that shut down the Kabul office of Shelter Now, a Christian aid organization, and arrested its workers on capital charges of promoting a religion other than Islam.[40]

None of the first four caliphs, writes the jurist al-Māwardī (d. 1058), needed courts of equity. In their day, he explains, the faith was strong; mere admonitions sufficed to halt wrongdoing—aided, in the case of wild beduins, perhaps, with a little strong-arming. But as Islamic society grew larger and more complex and outrages by the great against the small became more frequent, equity courts were established, with their judges, jurisconsults, guards and bailiffs, scribes, and witnesses. The statutory penalties were exacted for apostasy, fornication, theft, wine-drinking, and other offenses. But even the rise of institutional law and order did not exempt the rank and file from their Qur'ānic charge to command what is right and forbid what is wrong. To speak out or take action against individual wrongdoers is the duty of every competent witness. Where the wrongdoing is by a group or is in some sense socially sanctioned, Māwardī explains, most authorities advise discretion: Seek allies, do not squander your life in bootless effort. Bide your time, but countenance nothing that you are capable of ending.[41]

In the same spirit al-Juwaynī (d. 1085), Ghazālī's teacher, classed the obligation to require fit behavior as a public one: Where the wrongdoing is flagrant, the duty to put a stop to it, by word or deed, falls on everyone, as the *Sharī'a* has by now long held. Where a legal ruling is required, the scholars and jurists must act. But at a level of finer detail, a well-ordered society will have suitable officials in every marketplace, to whom it delegates the communal responsibility to enforce decency.[42]

Such an official is called the *muḥtasib*, literally the censor (from the Arabic for counting), a man of upright and incorruptible character, fit to serve as the tongue of the *qāḍī*, as Ibn ʿAbdūn puts it (ca. 1100).[43] The *muḥtasib*'s task is to ensure that what can be mended need not be endured: He sees that beggars are kept from the mosque and that no beast is left to foul its entrance. He regulates schoolmasters and the discipline they mete out. He polices the cemeteries against drinking, depravity, and lovers' trysts. He keeps storytellers and other disreputables out of people's homes, ensures that milk is sold only by honest people, undiluted, and from wooden or crockery vessels, not copper, lest it be tainted by verdigris. He sees that market vegetables are washed in the river, not ponds or pools, that poultry are put up for sale with the tails plucked, and rabbits, skinned—to show at a glance what is fresh or spoiled. He sees to it that eggs are tested when sold; abattoirs, enclosed and sanitary, with proper records of the ownership of slaughtered beasts. His inspections should ensure that market women do not turn town gardens into brothels. He must regulate the sale of grapes, lest they be used for wine, and must oversee the professions, especially medicine, to keep its practice clear of impostors. He must see to it that the baths and bathmen too, are covered up, that no Muslim gives a massage to a Jew or Christian, or does menial work for one. The *muḥtasib* must ensure that Muslim women are not debauched in churches, those dens of wine and fornication, that Jews butcher no meat for Muslims (although they say the name of God in the act of slaughter as the *Sharīʿa* requires), that Christian priests are circumcised—by force if necessary, since they are hypocrites to profess the *sunna* of Jesus yet go about uncircumcised.

Villagers must have their long hair cut or shaved on coming into town, and country youths must be disarmed. Church bells may not sound in Muslim territory, and learned books may not be sold to Jews or Christians. Usury must be suppressed, and foreign currency kept from circulation—lest it cause inflation of the legal tender. Schools must be managed by men of proven piety; and daggers (the handguns of the day), banned from manufacture: "for no one buys them but ruffians, good for nothings, and wicked men." Prostitutes from licensed houses (a telling admission this, in view of the Qurʾānic outrage against fornication) must wear veils when they go out and must be kept from teaching their wiles to married women and from attending wedding parties, even when invited. Catamites must be expelled from the city. Christians, Jews, tax farmers, and police agents must be identifiable by their dress and not allowed to dress as dignitaries. And the *dhimmīs*, as we have seen, must wear a special badge to distinguish and disgrace them as "the party of Satan" (Ibn ʿAbdūn cites Qurʾān 58:20). Boxing and martial arts must be barred to boys, since they foment quarrels; and frivolities like chess and backgammon, to everyone, since they are forms of gambling and, as we have learned, distractions from the thought of God and our ultimate destiny.

It is the *muḥtasib*'s job (somehow) to prevent anal intercourse and other wicked practices and to see that the Qurʾānic demand for public humiliation of the tolerated minorities is implemented institutionally—much as we might delegate to a special office some of our concerns about equal opportunity or nondiscrimination. Fair trade, public health and safety, and private propriety all fall under the same general heading. The idea that personal morals or private dealings somehow escape the reach of law, or the detailed requirements and regulations derived from the unwritten spirit of the law, is clearly foreign to the principles and tenor of Islam—as it is in most traditional polities. But Ibn ʿAbdūn's somewhat idealized job description testifies to the variety of abuses, ranging from privilege and peccadillos to open or secret outrages against public piety that Islam cast into the shadow between normative perfection and day-to-day experience.

Ethics takes on a more speculative cast in the works of the *mutakallimūn*, the Sufis, and, of course, the *falāsifa. Kalām,* for its part, is less concerned with the morals of positive prescription than with the philosophy of action, metaethics—that is, the metaphysic of morals—and the underlying issues of theodicy. Many a *mutakallim* was a *faqīh* or jurisprude, but of all the speculative thinkers of Islam only Sarakhsī was a *muḥtasib.* He wrote on literature, geography, and art history, on music, as we have mentioned, and on the history of the star-worshiping Sabians, among many other subjects, including apparently two works on fraud. Those last are germane to his government post. But he held it for less than a year before falling out of favor.[44] Issues of normative ethics were generally left to the legal schools, where they did not typically elicit the conflicts of metaphysical values that spurred the theologians to action as dialecticians. But *kalām* disquisitions on the theory of action remain fascinating today, even to philosophers who do not share the motivating theological itch of the *mutakallimūn*.[45]

Although the Muʿtazilites were hardly liberals, their *kalām* is, in many ways, a form of humanism. For it preserves human free will and deems human reason competent to judge justice and injustice, even on God's part. On both counts the Muʿtazilite outlook was found objectionable by the defenders of tradition: Human ideas of right and wrong were mere opinion. Better to trust God's good pleasure or steady custom than a will-o'-the-wisp like human moral notions.[46] And voluntarism was an affront to divine sovereignty. How could a human choose between faith or faithlessness, when the faith that promises salvation could only come by grace? In a characteristic twist of terms, the Ashʿarites called their adversaries fatalists (*qadariyya*), on the grounds that their affirmations of human freedom and moral judgment in effect tied God's hands. Real voluntarism was focused on God's freedom.

The Muʿtazilites, and the *falāsifa* in turn, could readily retort that the Ashʿarites made God an arbitrary despot. Indeed there is some evidence that Ashʿarite theology was influenced by a desire not to provoke quarrels with constituted authority.[47] But other values were at stake as well. Abū ʾl-Ḥasan al-Ashʿarī (873/4–932) founded the school in theological reaction to the Muʿtazilite doctrine in which he had been trained and for which he had debated publicly for years before his conversion to the legalism of Aḥmad b. Ḥanbal and to the theological orthodoxy that his own views helped constitute.[48] He and his followers saw Muʿtazilite theodicy, which deduced God's actions and requitals from the a priori given of His goodness, as pollyannaish, a refusal to take seriously the fact of natural evil. In arguing for God's freedom to act and choose at His pleasure, they too, in their own way, were defending human moral perceptions. For to free God's will from human moral notions was also to maintain the internal integrity of those notions: God need not hew to human standards, but we need not pretend that all is well by those standards. Thus the Ashʿarites refused to discover concealed goods behind every apparent evil and held fast by a kind of positivity about the way the world is. For centuries, with varying intent, they argued (even sparring with the great Ashʿarite Ghazālī) to show that this world of ours is not the best that was in God's power to make—or why would the air of the Damascus basin be so impossibly polluted?[49] Even as regards naturalism, the Ashʿarites make welcome contributions. For it was Ashʿarite voluntarism, as applied to God, not humankind, that motivated Ghazālī's critique of the Neoplatonic rationalists' deductivism about causality. That critique may have undercut causal necessity, but it also fostered the idea of a more open universe and a more empiric notion of discovery than was known to the *falāsifa*.[50]

Regrettably, what stuck in the minds of Ghazālī's readers through the centuries, however, was not the potential he left behind for the opening of the universe but the rhetorical emphasis on God's ultimate causality, at the expense of proximate causes. Orientalists, influenced by Averroes's riposte to Ghazālī in behalf of naturalism, tend to read Ghazālī's critique as an outright dismissal of causal judgments. And some Muslim extremists even try to put such a dismissal to practical (or pedagogical) effect. Thus Pervez Hoodbhoy, a Pakistani physicist from Quaid-e-Azam University in Islamabad, complains that educational guidelines once issued by the Institute for Policy Studies in Pakistan urged that physical effects should not be ascribed to natural causes: "You were supposed to say that when you bring hydrogen and oxygen together then by the will of Allah water was created."[51]

The Muʿtazilites held that human beings act and choose by God-given powers—thus that we are justly held accountable for our acts. Naturally the doctrine commends itself to moralists. It was complemented by a sophisticated theory of degrees of freedom: Our choices may limit (or enhance) our future effectiveness and capabilities for choice. A development of Stoic theory, this Muʿtazilite thesis about natural accountability was prominently used by Jewish philosophical ethicists including Saadiah and Maimonides.[52]

The Ashʿarites conceded that we act by capacities, scotching the Aristotelian objection that an act for which one has no capacity must be impossible. But capacities, on the Ashʿarite account, are created by God at the very moment of the action. They have no prior existence (as mere dispositions or unactualized potentialities), and they are not polyvalent. If the capacity for an action predated the act, Ashʿarī argued, then the act would already have taken place. And if capacities were polyvalent, they would yield opposing acts.

Grounded in a strikingly Megarian insistence that only the actual is real, Ashʿarī's dogged counteroffensive against human voluntarism and moral objectivism never quite loses its ad hoc tang. But a welcome by-product was a kind of behaviorism that put a brake on spiritual militancy: The Khārijite predecessors of the Muʿtazilites had denied that grave sinners could be faithful Muslims; as renegades, they must be slain in this world and damned in the next. The Muʿtazilites balked at that extreme and sought a middle ground on the vexed question of the salvation of sinners—again a stance fraught with political meaning. But in the days of Muʿtazilite ascendancy, traditionalists had found themselves beset by a kind of inquisition, the notorious *Miḥna*, which sought to gauge the authenticity of their Islam. The Ashʿarites responded with the doctrine that human inferences from overt actions to the crucial matter of inner faith, once again, would tie God's hands, arbitrarily restraining the dispensation of His grace. Since capacities are coterminous with acts, they argued, a person can be judged humanly only for what he has actually done.

Muʿtazilites might urge that dispositional predicates are well attested in the Qur'ān, as when the daughter of Shuʿayb (the biblical Jethro) describes Moses as "strong and faithful" (28:26). But Ashʿarī responds that Shuʿayb ("the Teacher of the Prophets" in Islamic tradition) did not let her words pass without reproof but immediately objected: "Daughter, you know his strength from what you have seen of him"—for Moses had watered their flock, unfazed by the shepherds whose presence had intimidated the young girl—"but how do you know that he is faithful?" She answered, fittingly, that Moses had said (28:25), "Walk behind me and direct me." He was so pure that he feared to see her figure outlined by the wind if she walked ahead to lead the way. So the virtuous maiden judged only what she had seen.[53]

The fanciful supplements to the austere Qur'ānic narrative, pinned midrashically to the otherwise puzzling "Walk ahead and lead me," are introduced here by Ash'arī solely to support the behaviorism on which the theology of salvation seemed to rest: A simple profession of faith ("There is no god but God, and Muḥammad is His prophet") suffices, as Ghazālī puts it, to "save the necks" of those who utter it. We cannot "pry open the hearts" of those who profess the faith, to test the sincerity of their conviction. Verbal conformity is enough. The higher or deeper levels of faith, beyond or beneath the outer husk of lip service will be judged by God alone.[54]

Sufism develops a dialectical duality of its own, not between voluntarism and predestination but between expansiveness (*inbisāṭ*) and constraint (*inqibāḍ*). The poles here are a sense of elation that seems to engulf the cosmos and a sense of anguish, shrinking and depression bordering on self-extinction. Such moods occur naturally, of course. But they are heightened or deepened by the meditative exercises of *tasawwuf* (Sufi practice). Here arise the rival Sufi life-styles (and theologies) classically described as drunken or sober. Sober Sufism seeks a discipline to curb the conflicting extremes and map the proper place of each along the upward path of Sufi states. It puts each mood to work to set a limit to the other and assign its proper measure. But the intoxicated tradition is no lover of means and moderation. The extreme it seeks, as we have seen, is no mere dying unto self and rebirth to eternal life in God but a dissolution of the boundaries between self and God. Here pantheism takes on the colorations not of a Wordsworthian naturalism but of that deeper immanentism that the heresiographers call incarnationist: The object is not contact or communion but fusion of identities with God.

Mysticism may be personalist in its Hellenistic and romantic phases, but the ancient forerunners and medieval heirs of the tradition organized their quest on communal and corporate lines—Sufi orders in the Islamic case, following the rule and example of charismatic leaders and the train of their successors, a classic routinization of charisma. The Sufi orders pursue a nexus of activities ranging from the *dhikr* and *samā'*, with their meditative repetitions of the names and epithets of God, often accompanied by the whirling, vertiginous dancing of the dervishes, to the feats of self-mortification and wonder-working of the *faqīr* (literally, mendicant), to the exploits of militant and military orders, to the missionary outreach that spread Islam deep into Asia, Africa, and the Pacific, far beyond the reach of the original Arab armies of conquest.[55]

For many Sufis the use of hashish was not excluded. Nor did the metaphysical construction placed on *inbisāṭ* exclude an urge to flout established norms, rebelliously mocking the pervasive, highly structured societal controls. Sufi art and poetry, as we have seen, are enthralled with the symbolic impact of wine, and of gazing at the face of the beloved, figured in poetry and painting as a moon that reflects a still more perfect light. Wine drinking and the sublimated or not so sublimated practice of gazing into the faces of beardless acolytes might signify ecstatic abandon, or serve as a focal point of poetic paradox and ambiguity. But even when such acts became sensuous excursions into libertinage, they might still claim the license of a higher truth and privilege of a higher station. Puritans would fulminate, but they never did wholly put a stop to the abuses or quench the lambent aura of sanctity projected on such semiotically freighted acts—any more than they succeeded in halting all veneration at the shrines of Sufi saints.

Ghazālī spoke for sober Sufism in the institutional and intellectual mainstream of Islam. His guiding lights took Sufi themes in a pietist direction, where mystic monism grounded a life of reliance upon God. Thus Ghazālī argues in his *Iḥyā' 'Ulūm al-Dīn*, Reviving the Religious Sciences, that the highest monotheism—kernel of the kernel, as he puts it—sees nothing in existence but God.[56] Makkī had pioneered in drawing the ethical implications from this sort of monism, which was taught by the great teachers of sober Sufism, al-Junayd (d. 910) and al-Muḥāsibī (781–857):[57]

> Junayd relates on the authority of Yaḥyā b. Abū Kathīr: It is written in the Torah, "Cursed is he whose trust is in a creature no better than himself" (cf. Ps. 118:8). Junayd says that this applies to anyone who says, 'If it hadn't been for so and so I'd have died.' It is said that for a man to say, 'If things hadn't worked out as they did—' is idolatry. And it is said, "Many a time has 'If only—' begun the work of the Devil." . . . If you trust God as He ought to be trusted, God will provide for you as He does for the birds that start out each day empty and return full. The hills will shower you with their bounty. Jesus said, "Behold the birds of the air: they sow not, neither do they reap, neither do they store away, yet God provides for them day by day" (Matthew 6:27).[58]

As the promiscuous quotations from Jewish, Christian, and Muslim sources reveal, Makkī's is a cosmopolitan pietism. Its themes are borne along not only by Ghazālī but by Baḥya ibn Paqūda[59] and numberless other Jewish, Christian, and Muslim mystics for whom the ideal of self-surrender gives a practical meaning to the sense of unity that monistic mystics experience. The idea is close to the heart of Islam. For it means giving over one's will to God's plan, resigning all desires, hopes and fears, with perfect acceptance and implicit trust in God's grace.

Among the philosophers proper of Islam, the *falāsifa*,[60] we find a vibrant interest in ethics, especially in the earlier members of the school, before logic and metaphysics come fully to the fore in the more systematic thinkers. Kindī steps gingerly into ethical philosophy by way of a psychological prescription against anxiety and grief, with the Platonizing advice to attach one's desires only to the permanent, intellectual goods, which alone are ever truly ours.[61] That intellectualist advice stands in striking contrast to the counsels that the mystic pietists were giving at the same time about the proper focus of human hopes and longings. And yet there is more than a passing family resemblance between these two expressions of ethical otherworldliness.

The independent minded Rāzī (d. 925 or 932), like Kindī a physician, re-reduces the ethical counsels of Plato toward a somewhat ascetic Epicureanism, urging that to maximize pleasure is to minimize desire.[62] Fārābī,

Avicenna, and Averroes, the three greatest philosophers of Islam, develop the ethics of Aristotle and the politics of Plato against the cosmological backdrop of the spheres, the physiology of the humors, and the psychology of rational cognition. But the ethical contributions of these men are eclipsed by their larger achievements in metaphysics and logic and, in Fārābī's case, by a sophisticated philosophy of language and culture, in Averroes by a magisterial philosophy of nature, and in Avicenna by a powerful synthesis of Greek rationalism with Islamic mysticism. The best ethical work by a Muslim thinker in the classical age came from the hands of the courtier philosopher and historian Miskawayh, whom we shall encounter again when we turn, in our final chapter, to the emergence of Arabic universal history. Miskawayh is of special relevance to this volume's theme, since he was the most explicit and self-conscious exponent of philosophical humanism in Islam.

Miskawayh's Courtly Humanism

In 945 the caliphs of Baghdad fell under the control of Buyid dynasts risen from the ranks of the Daylamite soldiery. The century that followed climaxed a period of fragmentation for the no-longer-young Islamic state. But it was also an era when ambitious princes and *wazīrs* sought the patina of a higher culture and the trappings of stability through patronage of poets, painters, scholars, scientists, and philosophers. Commercial and administrative skill, military prowess and discipline were avenues to fortune. Such worldly virtues were widely prized, even as pietism and traditionalism were framing a response. The individualism, occasional secularism, rare skepticism, and even rarer liberalism to be found among the pensioners of the Islamic courts support comparisons of the era to the European Renaissances of the twelfth century and beyond.[63] Underscoring the parallel is the systematization of Arabic and Islamic studies during the period. The catalysts and often the seeds for thought in both eras were translated texts of Greek philosophic, scientific, and technical works.

Thinkers trained in Arabic letters and in the Greek sciences laid open by the translation movement took Aristotle seriously. But they were also imbued with the values of the court, the chancery, and the military camp. Theirs was the culture of *adab*, the literature of courtesy and urbanity. Secular values—the distillate of Hellenistic, old Persian, Arab, Byzantine, Jewish, and Syriac traditions, with a leaven of Indian fable and the vivid naturalism of Chinese portraiture and figure painting[64] for critical distance—stood alongside the law and faith of Islam and, like the philosophic outlook of the Greek teachers, claimed the power of interpreting and judging it. The philosophers of the period, a small group, many of them friends, colleagues, rivals, master and disciple, freely invoked a humanistic ethical discourse and ideal. Among the most articulate and long lived (he lived a century by Muslim count), was Miskawayh, described by Khalidi as "a prolific author, a philosopher of very broad interests, an accomplished poet and *adīb*, as well as a universal historian."[65] His *On the Refinement of Character* has been called "the most influential work on philosophical ethics" in Islam.[66] But the influence takes a curiously underground route: Miskawayh's ethics were substantially taken over by Ghazālī, whose polemic against Neoplatonic Aristotelianism in Islam, *The Incoherence of the Philosophers* and monumental *Iḥyā' 'Ulūm al-Dīn* led to his being called the Proof of Islam in traditional Islamic circles. The *Iḥyā'*, a spiritualizing summa that draws on many sources, leans heavily on Miskawayh for its treatment of the virtues. But the slant is altered tellingly.

Miskawayh was born in Rayy near present day Tehran; he died at Isfahan. His ancestors were Zoroastrian Persians. The scion of a wealthy family, he lost his father when young and got on poorly with his stepfather, who was much younger than his mother.[67] Like Fārābī and the Sincere Brethren of Basra, Miskawayh was a Shīʿite. His patrons were Shīʿite princes and potentates, and he wrote in a Shīʿite vein, with respectful reference to the person of ʿAlī. He was also a vocal advocate of Persian culture in its struggle with Arab hegemony.

While still in his teens Miskawayh came to Baghdad. He entered the service of the *wazīr* al-Muhallabī, a self-made man of ancient Arab family, who was now a bilingual maecenas known for his wit and culture, and who sought to recapture the glories of the fabled ʿAbbāsid court in Būyid Baghdad. The patron of Abū 'l-Faraj al-Isfahānī (897–967), author of the celebrated *Book of Songs*, in which were gathered so much of the old Arabic culture and tradition, Muhallabī was a poet and prosodist in his own right. His well-placed benefactions, in Miskawayh's words, "gave new life to forgotten sciences."

Working by day in the chancery, Miskawayh joined the *wazīr*'s salons by night. Here in the *wazīr*'s palace, with its gardens overlooking the Tigris, where eminent *qaḍī*s and other worthies regularly lost themselves amidst the song girls, poetry, and wine, Miskawayh dazzled the assembled literati with his learning. Hard as he worked and played, he was intent on broadening his range. He was immersed in poetry from an early age; now he studied the History of Ṭabarī, under the tutelage of the *qaḍī* Ibn Kāmil, a pupil of the author.[68]

After his patron's death in 963, Miskawayh returned to Rayy as librarian and boon companion to the *wazīr* Ibn al-ʿAmīd, a scholar statesman and warrior whom he calls the Chief Ustadh. Miskawayh remained at his side "day and night" for seven years. Rayy was known as a center of learning, prosperous, well fed, and well watered. Maqdisī, the historical encyclopedist, praises even its police.[69] The poet Mutanabbī called Ibn al-ʿAmīd "an Arab in speech, a philosopher in judgment, a Persian in manners."[70] He was also proud, selfish, temperamental, and power hungry. Miskawayh admired his vast memory, his erudition in philosophy and poetry, his skill in art, verse and engineering, tactics, and administration. Treasured for his command of the ancient sciences, Miskawayh taught the *wazīr*'s son Abū 'l-Fatḥ and presided over some hundred camel loads (twenty to fifty tons) of manuscript folios. After his palace was sacked by Khurasanian raiders, Ibn al-ʿAmīd was left for the time without a chair to sit on or water jug to drink from and had to get by with borrowed furniture and bedding. But his face lighted up when he learned that his books were intact: "All my treasures," he told Miskawayh, "can be replaced but these."[71]

In the *wazīr*'s great library, Miskawayh delved into the works of the Muslim philosophers—Kindī, Rāzī, and Fārābī—and the translations of their Greek predecessors. He read Plato and Aristotle, Porphyry, Simplicius, and Alexander of Aphrodisias. Philosophy joined hands with literary and historical studies in Miskawayh's enlarged conception of the culture of the *adīb*. And the talented *wazīr*'s skills with siege engines, flaming arrows, long distance burning glasses and the like, along with the more civil machinery of administration, gave Miskawayh a living model for his vision of the ideal man, who would unite thought with action, grace, and effectual power.[72]

Ibn al-ʿAmīd, died in 970, and Miskawayh stayed on in the service of Abū ʾl-Fatḥ, who at twenty-three succeeded his father. Although dubbed the "Doubly Competent," for his mastery of the arts of war and peace, Abū ʾl-Fatḥ showed a decadence and extravagance disturbing to his teacher. By 976 the young man had been deposed and imprisoned. His sovereign Rukn al-Dawla died in the same year, and Miskawayh returned to Baghdad in the service of the new ruler, the greatest of the Buyids, ʿAḍud al-Dawla, who was intent on rebuilding and enlarging the fortunes of his house.

As a court favorite, Miskawayh traveled with the ruler in the field and on embassies in his behalf. In 978 he was sent with a treasurer to inventory the goods of a fortress taken from the rival Ḥamdānids, which had been betrayed by its venal officers. Ordered to honor the turncoats and humiliate the captured slave commander, one Ṭāshtam, Miskawayh balked. He was moved by Ṭāshtam's character and piety and pleaded with his prince to take the captive into his own service, for the prince had promised not to harm the man. But ʿAḍud al-Dawla argued that many more forts remained to be reduced; it would not do to favor foes the same as helpers. Ṭāshtam, he insisted, was rightly paraded in disgrace before the holdouts, to scotch any pretense that the fortress was still unconquered. The policy was not unprecedented. Muwaffaq the brother of the caliph Muʿtamid, had similarly displayed the captive leaders who had held out in the Zanj slave rebellion of 870–83, as Miskawayh well knew from Ṭabarī's History. Reminding Miskawayh that he had promised only that Ṭāshtam would not suffer at his hands, not that he would protect him from all others, ʿAḍud al-Dawla sent him back to the master he had served so loyally, and as all three men knew, to certain death at the Ḥamdānid's decree. Neither a Metternich nor a martyr, Miskawayh ruefully acquiesced.[73] The booty of the fortress came to twenty million dirhems.

ʿAḍud al-Dawla founded a hospital at Baghdad in 982, and Miskawayh took advantage of the physicians assembled there to master the art of medicine, which he had probably first studied in Ibn al-ʿAmīd's library. Still serving as a librarian and sometime confidant and secretary to the ruler, he began the universal history that he would dedicate to ʿAḍud al-Dawla.[74] When that ruler died in 983, Miskawayh is said to have gone into hiding, under the protection of his friend and trusted guide in philosophy, the physician Ḥasan ibn Suwār (d. 1017), known as Ibn al-Khammār. Tawḥīdī takes credit for lending him some philosophical works at this time, and Miskawayh seems to have found solace in philosophy, after losing his positions of greatest influence. He went on to serve ʿAḍud al-Dawla's son Ṣamṣām al-Dawla, and after his death, his fractious brother, Sharaf al-Dawla, and his successor Bahā' al-Dawla, who died in 1012. Finally, with a group of friends, he joined the entourage of the Khwarizmshah, ruler of Khiva on the Oxus, as a court physician.

Here he completed his history and composed what F. E. Peters calls "the first systematic rethinking of a humanistic ethic since the Stoics left off the task in the second Christian century."[75] His standing in ethics was hard won. For by his own account he had to overcome the sensuous and cynical values of the court and culture in which he had come of age, the same culture in which Avicenna was now coming to maturity. But the story that Miskawayh answered the young man's disrespect by picking up a copy of *The Refinement of Character* and throwing it at him seems out of character for the refined bibliophile. The story may have been circulated to highlight the one area in which Miskawayh surpassed his formidable successor.

Miskawayh knew the philosopher al-ʿĀmirī (d. 992) and anthologized some of his thoughts, perhaps making a point. For the prickly Tawḥīdī had blamed him for learning little from this valued local source. But it is possible that Miskawayh, like Avicenna after him, did not think overmuch of ʿĀmirī's philosophy.[76] He spoke respectfully of his learning but also observed that ʿĀmirī himself had seen that he had much to learn from the renaissance statesman who was their master.[77]

ʿĀmirī's ethics was a kind of call to higher seriousness,[78] and that will have mattered to Miskawayh. But ultimately such a call must come from within. After all, Miskawayh knew Hamadhānī too, who so brilliantly sang the secular counterpoint to the Islamic figured bass. Miskawayh took up the humanistic text beneath that counterpoint and gave it the dignity and structure of philosophy. His motifs came from in the courtly ethos, epitomized in the image of the scholar gentleman. As Peters writes:

> The old Bedouin virtues of generosity, graciousness and eloquence were still part of the portrait, now urbanized by their contact with Iran and given solid intellectual foundations by Hellenic ethics. More bookish than the Greeks, far more elegant and sophisticated than the contemporary European Christian, the tenth-century Muslim intellectual could still gracefully shuttle between pen and sword, mosque and cup, without notable signs of guilt or self-doubt.
>
> Not everyone was enchanted, of course. On the streets outside the splendid salons were Hanbalites who read only blasphemies in the books of the Greeks and the humanistic ethics of Miskawayh.[79]

To forge a serious ethics, Miskawayh needed to move beyond the superficiality and supercharged sensuality of the salons and rise above the ribaldry that rejected Islamic gravitas but by so doing, paradoxically, acquiesced in the traditionalists' dismissive appraisal of all that was merely humanistic. Just as the Ḥanbalites hijacked the topoi of secular love in their kulturkampf with erotic mysticism, so Miskawayh, without succumbing to their reactionary culture shock, found that he had something of moment to learn from the high seriousness of scriptural ethics.

His mentor here was not ʿĀmirī but Ibn al-Khammār, the best-known Muslim disciple of the Jacobite Christian Yaḥyā ibn ʿAdī (d. 974). Yaḥyā was a translator and commentator of Plato and Aristotle, a disciple of Fārābī and of the Nestorian philosopher Abū Bishr Mattā (d. 940). Like his father, Yaḥyā was a copyist by profession; by avocation, he was a collector of manuscripts. His home was a veritable school of translators and philosophers, Christian and Muslim, including the Boswell of the age, al-Tawḥīdī (d. 1023) and others of his circle—commentators of Greek works, physicians, theologians, litterateurs, even the son of the famous *wazīr* ʿAlī ibn ʿĪsā. The bibliographer al-Nadīm (ca. 936/7–ca. 987/8), a bookseller by trade, relied on Yaḥyā for booklore and for the erudition stored in Yaḥyā's beautifully penned library catalogue. Mattā had been confronted by the Muʿtazilite *mutakallim* Abū Hāshim al-Jubbāʾī (d. 933, the son of Ashʿarī's Muʿtazilite teacher), with the notion that logic, as its name seemed to imply, was just a way of ordering words. The claim was still being bruited in Miskawayh's time. He told Tawḥīdi what Mattā could have said: that if that much could be inferred from etymology, one could equally well conclude that a *mutakallim* was just a talker.[80]

Miskawayh defended the Greek sciences against all forms of parochialism, but the cosmopolitanism he imbibed is perhaps best voiced in a passage from Ibn ʿAdī's ethics urging that our highest perfection lies in the universal love of humankind as a single race, united by humanity itself. The core of that humanity, our crowning glory, is the divinely imparted rational soul, which all men share, and by which indeed all are one.[81] Miskawayh may soft pedal the monopsychism, but he shares with Ibn ʿAdī the view that a chief goal of ethics is control of our natural irascibility, allowing our deeper unity to surface in acts of love and compassion.[82] For Miskawayh the means to that goal is human fellowship, and the most enduring basis of fellowship is virtue.

It was Ibn ʿAdī who brought virtue ethics to the forefront of Arabic ethical writing, arguing that the aim underlying the commands and admonitions of scripture is the refinement of character. That view will be adopted not only by Miskawayh, and Ghazālī in his train, but also by Maimonides. It becomes a significant leaven to the legalism and legal positivism that might otherwise dominate scriptural ethical thinking.

Virtue ethics is an ethics of tendency rather than strict prescription. For the human virtues, classically, are means to happiness, understood as fulfillment of one's nature, or (in the more dramatic imagery favored by the Stoics), of one's calling as a human being. Character, whether virtuous or vicious, reflects the general nisus of our choices and tenor of our acts. Particular acts do matter, but their impact is felt in the aggregate.[83] Thus Aristotle argues, "acting unjustly does not necessarily imply being unjust. . . . a man is not a thief, yet he stole, nor an adulterer, yet he committed adultery."[84] For even acts that enhance or diminish our fulfillment do not suffice to establish or destroy it: "one swallow does not a summer make, nor does one day; and so too one day, or a short time, does not make a man blessed and happy."[85]

The sense of sin recedes into the background here.[86] Ibn ʿAdī has a properly Christian sense of original sin, as witness his discovery of vices like cunning, deceit, cajolery and envy infecting even the use of reason, which Greek philosophers might have supposed, in its purity, to be immune. But the sense of sin is much less prominent in Ibn ʿAdī's ethics than in, say, Augustine or Anselm. It becomes the simple, biblical admission that no mortal man is perfect, or possessed of all the virtues, without a trace of weakness. And as a remedy for human faults, Yaḥyā turns not simply to the Christian redeemer but to the laws and institutions that seek to educate and civilize humankind and rein in our naturally overweening appetites and passions. What humans share in universally is not a corrupted nature but divinely imparted reason.[87] Wrong choices stem not from an externalized Corruptor, but from the (Platonic) vices of concupiscence and irascibility.[88] Miskawayh takes up the thought when he urges that by Satan and the other demons so often spoken of in the utterances of popular piety, what the philosopher means is moral backsliding, a result of conflict between the rational soul and the irrational animal and irascible souls.[89]

Like Aristotle, Yaḥyā prized the spontaneity that arises once virtue is a part of character and thoughtful choices have become a matter of natural and easy habit rather than agonized moral crises. He follows Plato in the belief that just and sound choices must be the work of reason, governing, as Aristotle shows, through the traits of an established character. Even virtues like thrift and mercy reflect the work of reason, holding appetite and irascibility in check and finding the right balance between self-assertion and self-denial. Even vices like levity and rashness reveal the insufficient governance of reason. But, like Aristotle, Ibn ʿAdī finds that what should count as vice or virtue depends in part on one's circumstances. The young, but not the old, should be eager for praise. Adornments are rightly sought after, by women and potentates, but not by monks or clerics. With wealth, the golden mean is to be neither too avid in the gathering nor too stingy in the disbursing, whether in one's own behalf or that of the needy.

By situating the virtues in the thick of their social and cultural context, virtue ethics affects ethical theory profoundly in three ways quite beyond opening it up to more latitudinarian norms than a strict command ethics affords: (1) It creates a scale of attainments (indeed, a number of such scales) by which we may gauge ourselves (and one another) for moral progress or regress, as judged by specific traits that are valued or disvalued socially or personally. (2) The plurality of scales makes way, in some degree, for self-invention and the emergence of individuality, disengaged from a uniform and stereotypic communal ideal, as the members of a culture choose among the constellation of the virtues those that best fit their innate strengths and freely enacted preferences. (3) By the respect it shows for moral wisdom, virtue ethics opens itself to a canon of cultural resources, in literature, history, and life experience, where exemplars are discovered that seem useful in the work of self-cultivation. Those exemplars can be tellingly unparochial.

Virtue ethics tends to the humanistic, then, precisely because the canon of its moral objectivism is pluralistic and potentially cosmopolitan, because its sense of the individual is invested in the idea of personality, and because it values a refinement grounded in learning, social skills, and thoughtful self-development. The philosopher Abū Sulaymān al-Sijistānī (ca. 912–ca. 985), himself a pupil of Mattā and Ibn ʿAdī, boldly captured the humanist ideal when he transmuted a radical monotheist trope about the shoreless sea of the divine, to say: "He who swims in our sea has no shore but himself."[90] It was the humanism of self-cultivation that Miskawayh most clearly valued in Yaḥyā, as is reflected in the traditional assignment to his chief ethical work of the same title as was borne by the ethics of Ibn ʿAdī: *On the Refinement of Character*.

For Miskawayh, clearly, learning was no mere passport to a courtly role and no mere ornament to philosophy. His masters shared his view that statesmen can learn from the actions of past rulers and from the recovered culture that Miskawayh was to lay out in a greater and lesser treasury of ancient knowledge, and in his works on ethics, happiness, moral education, logic, the natural sciences, divinity, arithmetic, alchemy, and cooking. His intellectual savoir faire is still fresh in Tawḥīdī's records of interviews with the learned courtier. Miskawayh's stance toward alchemy, an art that he had looked into with more than casual interest while at the court of Ibn al-ʿAmīd, shows the tenor of his ethics: Alchemy is an esoteric science, taught by hints. So only philosophers have access to it. Its secrets may seem dangerous. For if they fell into the hands of the ignorant, so it is feared, men would abandon cooperation, pursue power only in the form of domination, and pleasures only of the lowest sort. The charge, reflective of a perennial pietist anxiety over *homo faber*, is still made against technology today, and not without cause.

Miskawayh's reply is worthy of a Bacon, a Descartes, or a twentieth-century respondent to Heidegger's alarm at technological nihilism: Real alchemy, of the sort pursued by Rāzī, is simply a branch of mineral science (i.e., chemistry). Its object is not riches but understanding. And it need not be hermetically confined to an esoteric elite. For those who learn are no longer ignorant. Since mastery of the art depends on philosophic understanding, we can be confident that its practitioners will not misuse it. The reassurances reveal a transcendent faith in learning—in the linkage of the natural and human sciences and in the transparency of the will to the goods that illuminate its path. That last, the intellectualist refusal to isolate act from understanding, is authentically Socratic. As for the faith that proper values arise in insight and are prerequisites of scientific understanding, that brings the sciences under the broad tent of the humanities. Our word for the confluence of faiths that we discover here in Miskawayh is humanism. His own word, of course, is *adab*—manners, culture, the root and substance of *ta'dīb,* education, discipline, culture.

Adab in the narrow sense, as literature, was the prime vehicle of the refinement that Miskawayh had counted on from the start of his career. Thus his writings on the pure style in poetry and on usage and manners. But *adab* had long meant much more than literature and had moved far beyond mere usage. The tradition of literary humanism, cultivated, as Joel Kraemer puts it, "by litterateurs, poets, and government secretaries,"[91] was also their means of cultivation. It was the core of a higher secular culture, needful not just to the secretarial class, who were its champions, but also to "rulers, viziers, soldiers, mystics and contemplatives, and even court jesters and raconteurs."[92] As Bosworth explains, it "embraced all the traditional Islamic linguistic, religious and legal sciences, together with the whole stage of human history as it was known to the Muslims."[93] *Adab*, as Miskawayh puts it, is the content of wisdom—knowledge tested by experience about the good life and its means of attainment. Without it, reason is not reason.[94]

The sum of human culture, then, actively assimilated and lived by, now provides the background demanded by Aristotle's phronesis. It broadens experience with the aid of literature, and it disciplines experience by framing a princely science, the study of history. For the lessons of history now underwrite in the language of worldly wisdom the sense of style that is nurtured by the norms of usage and comportment made visible in literature. But Miskawayh's idea of *adab* goes far beyond mere rhetoric, history or belles lettres. Like the Sincere Brethren of Basra, he accedes to the drive for comprehensiveness and supplements literature and history with philosophy and the sciences. He thus transforms polite letters and courtly etiquette by fusing them with what Kraemer calls a "philosophical humanism," a humanism made more acute and systematic by its embrace of "the scientific and philosophical heritage of antiquity as a cultural and educational ideal."[95] It is this wider horizon that enables Miskawayh to become a philosophical alchemist, welding seemingly disparate ideas and values into a coherent ethics and a harmonious way of life. We can see the product of that alchemy most clearly in Miskawayh's work on ethical philosophy. As Majid Fakhry writes: "the subtle way in which Miskawayh has woven together such diverse Stoic, Cynic, Platonic, Neo-Platonic, Aristotelian, Neo-Pythagorean, and Arabic-Islamic elements in his eclectical ethical system could only have been achieved, in the first instance, by a scholar whose knowledge of the Greek ethical tradition must have been very extensive." Fakhry speculates that Porphyry inspired Miskawayh's synthesis, through a work we know of only from the Arabic sources, a lost commentary on the *Nicomachaean Ethics*. But, as Fakhry clearly recognizes, Miskawayh himself was no mere copyist; he carried the work of philosophical synthesis beyond what he received. And he carried his value synthesis beyond the realm of formal philosophy. Hence Fakhry's mention of what Miskawayh gleaned from Arabic and Islamic culture. We can catch a Persian, barberry savor too, as when Miskawayh makes the first Sassanian emperor Ardashir (r. 226–241) a model of political wisdom and practice.[96]

Miskawayh makes the manners and mores of a universal human culture crucial to our fulfillment as individuals and as a species. He places letters and learning in the key role when he calls *adab* (in his expanded sense) the nourishment that gives substance to the mind, as food gives substance to the maturing body. Like Makkī, his pietist contemporary whose spiritual vademecum was entitled *Food for Hearts*, Miskawayh seeks inner sustenance. But Miskawayh does not find the substance he seeks in the devotions of the heart but in the clarity and learning of the mind, the rule of reason, nourished not by the *sunna* of the Prophet but by *paideia*, the *adab* of humanity.

In his traditional foreword, setting out the task of an Islamic ethics, Miskawayh offers a Muʿtazilite, voluntaristic reading of one of the Qur'ān's characteristic oaths: "By the soul and that which shaped it and breathed into it its wickedness and impiety"—the passage might seem to give comfort to predestinarians; but Miskawayh reads on—"he who keeps it pure prospers, and he who corrupts it fails!"[97] Miskawayh reads the verses (91:7–10) as mandating a Socratic tendance of the soul: The same metal might be forged into a perfect or a worthless sword (35). The Creator affords the matter of our humanity, but it is we who must work up that material, through art and culture.

Society, Miskawayh argues, is our means to this end: Each of us is necessary to someone else's perfection, and all of us must cooperate to provide the material base necessary to humanize our existence (14). Once the bare necessities are secured, higher and more intellectual plateaus are sought—each of us advancing in the measure of his capacities and all of us shoring up the weaknesses of the rest (118, 123; cf. 64). The social virtues, then, of friendliness and cooperativeness are necessary to human well being, as Aristotle showed. Ascetics are mistaken in seeking perfection outside human society: The life of the anchorite or vagabond stunts our humanity and thwarts our nature. Such men are neither temperate nor just. Indeed, they lack the social theater in which such virtues might be developed (25–26, 139).

In the spirit of Ibn ʿAdī, and in perfect agreement with Aristotle, Miskawayh argues that love is the basis of all society. Friendship is a more intimate and fellowship a more diffuse form of love (cf. *NE* VIII 9). Humanity itself is named for fellowship (deriving the Arabic *insān* from *uns*), and not, as one embittered poet sarcastically pretended, from *nisyān*, forgetfulness. Even public worship is devised by the religious law to foster human fellowship, neighborhood by neighborhood, city by city, and (in the Pilgrimage to Mecca) among the Islamic community throughout the world. It was with this thought in mind—that religion does not isolate but unites humanity—that the wise Ardashir called religion and monarchy twin brothers (125–28).

In cataloguing the virtues, Miskawayh distinguishes piety from devoutness. The devout honor God and His chosen ones (21–22). But piety is the performance of acts of virtue that enhance and perfect the soul (19). The virtues in general are defined by Miskawayh on the same Aristotelian model, as avenues toward happiness, varying in their demands from person to person and situation to situation. Circumstances must be weighed with the aid of experience and addressed by way of art (22). The virtues are perfections of character. They are not, as a command ethics might seem to suggest, matters of mere adherence to stringent behavioral rules.

Popular religion, Miskawayh argues, is a vulgar attempt to trade self-denial in this world for sensory gratifications in the next—as though a transcendent God would simply serve human appetites and passions (39–40). Like Rāzī, Miskawayh follows Galen in arguing that all sensory pleasures presuppose some prior lack and pain.[98] He goes on to argue that the ethics of the common mass is (on the model he adapts from Plato) conflicted, for it rests on an inner contradiction: Philosophers understand that what is most divine is what furthest transcends the material conditions of pleasure and pain. But popular morality simultaneously celebrates the successful hedonist and abhors the conditions of his success. It is in awe of the seeming ascetic, yet detests his way of life. Without philosophy to reconcile our ascetic and hedonic impulses and direct them toward the higher longings and purer pleasures of the intellectual life, the vulgar oscillate between self-indulgence and shame, never knowing the source of their embarrassment, let alone its remedy (41, 43, 113, 136).

Like Fārābī[99] Miskawayh sees religion platonically, as a mode of poetry and practice that instills the proper ethos in a people. He does not seek literal truth in scriptural rhetoric, just as he does not find categorical commandments in religious laws. Rather, he sees religious symbolism as a hortatory paradigm, and the laws as a discipline, inuring us to virtue. Miskawayh evinces more concern about the quality of a young man's drinking companions than about the fact that young men break the religious law by drinking (53). Before coming to philosophy, he confesses, he himself grew up less in the wholesome ethos of the Qur'ān than in the immoralism of the pre-Islamic poets like Imru' al-Qays and Nābigha, who flaunt the raffish ethos of the desert. When romantic ideals of passion and self-assertion are held up to admiration by one's parents and the spirit of such poets is most prized by one's prince, it is hard to escape their grip. Only gradually, Miskawayh admits, did he break free of the sensuous and wanton values of the *Jāhiliyya* poets and wean himself—with the aid of philosophy—from the way of life their songs instilled (45–46).

Manners, Miskawayh argues, make the man. By nature a boy is bad—a liar, cheat and tattletale, spiteful, meddlesome, importunate, jealous, and malicious—a danger to others and even more to himself. But by training, suitable reading, well-placed praise and private reproof (lest he become shameless under the blast of condemnation before his fellows), proper diet and discipline, decent demeanor, comportment, dress, companions, and play that is neither exhausting nor debilitating, he can be made a man (51–55). Courtesy (*adab* again) is not external but organic to morals—as means serve ends in an organism. Even among the lesser animals, the highest are those that come closest to culture: the sexually reproducing species and those that nurture and train their young (and so are amenable to domestication). Man is the highest of the animals because in him the capacity for education is clearest, allowing human intelligence to reclose the arcing circle from Creator to creatures, reuniting with its Source (61–62).

Like Ibn Zur'a (943–1008), another disciple of Ibn 'Adī's, who called humanity a horizon,[100] Miskawayh makes humanity (*al-insāniyya*) the goal of ethics, to be achieved through the perfection of our identity (*dhāt*) as human beings. The speculative sciences and practical arts of philosophy give us the means to that perfection. Aristotle collected and organized the relevant arts in much the way that physicians have collected and organized the materia medica that God scattered for us around the world.[101] Closely following Fārābī and a tradition that has been traced back to the Alexandrian Peripatetics,[102] Miskawayh catalogues the arts and sciences, showing in detail how theory and practice support one another.

It is sometimes supposed that when Aristotle praises the speculative life and the intellectual virtues as what is most distinctively human he is setting his highest good in the contemplative, over and against the eudaimonia attained through exercise of the moral virtues.[103] But the dichotomy is a false one. Thought is sterile and friendless without action, and action is barbarous and blind without thought. For Aristotle, even the appetites and passions of man must have specifically human forms. So their proper care and feeding demand distinctively human strengths: We can live as befits our humanity only through the use of reason. What that means is that the moral virtues, far from competing with the intellect are both presupposed in its development and dependent on its use.

Since the actual is always ultimately prior to the potential, the properly Aristotelian view is that understanding of the principles necessary to guide the virtues must be present—not necessarily in the mind of every person who acts virtuously or every adolescent who learns virtue, but clearly in the mind of the statesman or legislator who plots the values to be tie dyed into the fabric of a society or ethos of a community. Miskawayh shows his sensitivity to the dovetailing of theory and practice by treating character as the matter to be informed and refined, not by sheer discipline but by the arts and sciences, which articulate the principles behind virtue and train us to use them in the forum of experience. Culture here, literary and philosophical culture, becomes the educator of character that Plato had sought and Fārābī had found, at least for the many, in religion.

Some of the ancients, Miskawayh remarks, recognizing that happiness depends on transcendence of the physical, went so far as to deny that happiness is attainable in this life. It is in this sense, evidently, that Miskawayh reads the notion (which Aristotle takes as a springboard to his holism) that no man may be called happy while he lives. It would be disgraceful, Miskawayh insists, to suppose that a living man who performs good deeds, holds sound beliefs, serves his fellow men, and thus in all ways acts as God's deputy is not objectively happy. Real happiness is possible here on earth, even if transcendent felicity is not. To be sure, intellectual perfection reaches higher than mere moral perfection of our worldly nature; and only intellectual perfection, as Aristotle allowed, endures beyond the grave. But the moral virtues are necessary means to the higher intellectual end. The spiritual goal that is the ultimate aim of philosophy is not attainable by any other means. There are no shortcuts to felicity, bypassing the avenues of moral and intellectual self-perfection, as some Sufis of ecstatic and perhaps antinomian drift might suppose. For the key premise of mysticism, as of all asceticism that pursues a spiritual goal, is that the soul requires purification. And clearly, Miskawayh argues, again citing Aristotle (now on the need for experience), purification is not achieved without living through the stages of our natural human development—undergoing the discipline and acculturation that are the object of our existence in this world (74–83). A school is not life, but life is a school.

Ghazālī's Appropriation

The fate of Miskawayh's ethics is emblematic of that of Greek philosophy in general in the Islamic milieu: The volume of material absorbed is immense, and orthodoxy does not reject it but works the inherited materials into its house, much as the early Islamic builders appropriated the structures and stones of Greek basilicas that had been pagan temples and later used their architectural principles to construct new, distinctively Islamic mosques and palaces. No sentence of Miskawayh's ethics is left unexamined when Ghazālī takes over the work. But Miskawayh's courtly humanism is systematically expunged. Walzer and Gibb showed Miskawayh's influence on Ghazālī, and others have shown his impact on later authors like Naṣīr al-Dīn al-Ṭūsī (1201–1274), the Shīʿite polymath who defected to the conquering Mongols in 1247.[104] But in emphasizing Miskawayh's formative role and Ghazālī's openness to philosophic ethics, Walzer and Gibb rather overstated Ghazālī's dependence, slighting his selective preferences for other philosophers' ideas when they better suited his purposes and glossing over his displacement of Miskawayh's humanistic themes in favor of traditional Islamic sources and Sufi pietists like Muḥāsibī and Makkī.[105] It is as though an archaeologist were so thrilled to find the lineaments of a Greek temple in a mosque that he ignored the Muslim worship going on inside.

The most telling effect of Ghazālī's use of Miskawayh's ethics is the now almost invisible weave of virtue ethics into the fabric of a scriptural command ethics. Indeed, we can see Miskawayh's hand in Ghazālī's pietist affirmation that the study of ethics is more important than *fiqh*, the science of law, because ethics, or as he calls it (avoiding the language of the Philosophers) "the study of the states of the heart" deals with character and not just behavior. For character is the foundation, of which our actions are the outward expression.[106] But, while Ghazālī appreciates the powerful methods and edifying conclusions he finds in Miskawayh, he discards the fruit along with the argumentative branch that sustains it when the conclusions are not to his taste. In general, he likes to use traditional texts to support and thereby naturalize philosophic ideas. Perhaps the most impressive instance is his book-length Neoplatonizing gloss of the Qur'ānic Light and Darkness verses.[107] But his deracinating of Aristotelian ethical theses, excising their argumentative nerve, has a more systemic impact.

Rejecting Miskawayh's polemic against Sufi austerity, Ghazālī suppresses Miskawayh's Aristotelian rejection of the life of solitude as subhuman or superhuman—although he follows Miskawayh closely in the passages that precede and follow. He rejects Miskawayh's social rationale of public worship and suppresses his Platonizing proposal that happiness requires the youthful study of mathematics, to accustom us to truth and truthfulness. In all, Muhammad Abul Quasem estimates that about a third of Miskawayh's ethics was unacceptable to Ghazālī and dropped as quietly as the rest was adopted.[108] Walzer mentions the changes but calls the elements of *adab* that are dropped "merely formal and superficial."[109] Hardly. Whatever was outspokenly humanistic or secular in Miskawayh was dropped by Ghazālī, just as he took issue with the Muslim philosophers where he found their metaphysics too naturalistic.

Ghazālī follows Miskawayh and the Platonic tradition in identifying wisdom, courage, and temperance as the virtues of the rational, irascible, and appetitive faculties and in treating justice as the master virtue that integrates the three; he follows the later Greek and prior Islamic tradition in listing the remaining virtues under the four cardinal virtues. It is evidently because justice engulfs the other virtues that Ghazālī does not, as Miskawayh does, assign it subvirtues at the level of family, household, community, and friends. Ghazālī's is not an assertive, rights-claiming theory of justice. But his ethical writings do distinguish a political sense of justice and set out an idea of distributive justice, overseen by the regulative activities of the conscientious ruler.[110] He follows Aristotle in rejecting Plato's claim that justice is no mere compromise and agrees with Miskawayh in describing justice as a mean between doing and suffering wrong—all the while retaining Plato's notion that justice is the sovereign virtue that uses wisdom to assign a proper scope to all other goods. Like Miskawayh, then, Ghazālī does not reject the Aristotelian idea that justice is a social virtue involving give and take—in Islamic terms, proper and improper acquisition. He is as prepared as Miskawayh was to bracket the more radical claims of Socrates about the preferability of suffering injustice to committing it—despite the Islamic admiration for martyrdom and the spiritual disclaiming of worldly ends. For Islam is a polity, not merely an otherworldly quest.

Miskawayh identifies the intellectual virtues subsidiary to wisdom rather cognitively as intelligence, retentiveness, reasonableness (conformance of our notions to reality), inferential power and quickness, clarity with abstract concepts, and capacity to learn (ease in grasping theoretical matters). Ghazālī, as the tenor of his work demands, takes a more spiritual tack: He parts company with Aristotle but follows pietist and mystic tradition, by separating the love of God from knowledge and placing that love ahead of the knowledge that in Aristotle was its very essence. Mysticism siphons off the naturalistic content that had given divine knowledge its scientific and worldly roots. Ghazālī does place speculative wisdom, whose true aim is knowledge of God, above practical wisdom, as Aristotle does. But he treats even practical wisdom as a mean—placing it between the overclever guile that uses cunning for base purposes and the stubborn stolidity that keeps the lower passions from attaining their proper natural goals.

In place of intelligence, among the less rarefied intellectual virtues, Ghazālī lists excellence in deliberation, following Fārābī and Aristotle's account. Like Aristotle he reasons that practical wisdom is not mere cleverness in finding means to ends but a virtue that deduces what is most conducive in the pursuit of noble aims. He ignores Miskawayh's interest in memory and conceptual clarity and substitutes discernment in matters of controversy (cf. *NE* VI 10) and penetration. In place of reasonableness he puts insight, the ability to hit upon the truth without recourse to proof—a virtue of holymen. To cap his list in the *Iḥyā'*, Ghazālī adds an intellectual virtue not found in his earlier ethical work: self-scrutiny, apprehension of the subtle movements and hidden evils of the soul, a pietist virtue par excellence.[111] Without it we would never know our own motives, and even with it they may remain obscure.

Where Aristotle relies on reason, the virtue of practical wisdom, to locate the appropriate mean in concrete circumstances and direct us toward the doable good, Ghazālī argues that without recourse to God in prayer and without God's help we mortals would never succeed in finding, let alone habituating in our characters that disposition toward choice in accordance with a mean that Aristotle defined as virtue. Ghazālī is a follower of the Philosophic school when he reads the *Fātiḥa*, the opening prayer of the Qur'ān, as invoking God's aid in finding the mean, when it beseeches God (1:6) to "show us the Straight Path." But he insists that we are powerless to find and hew to that path by our own insight and virtue. Underscoring the point, he cites the Qur'ānic dictum traditionally held to imply that everyone will spend at least part of eternity in hellfire.[112]

Turning to the moral virtues, we find that under temperance Miskawayh lists modesty, composure (the ability to keep one's soul at rest when the passions are stirring), liberality, integrity, contentment, delicacy or gentility, orderliness, personableness, dignity, godliness, and an accommodating or conciliatory disposition—all virtues of a courtier. He defines contentment as moderation in food and drink; integrity, in terms of licit and illicit gain; piety, or godliness, as steadiness in fair doings, by which the soul is perfected. Ghazālī lists modesty and liberality under temperance, following Miskawayh, Fārābī, and Ibn Abī Dunyā, the author of the censures of worldly things. Compare Aristotle, who treats modesty as an emotional surrogate for virtue, appropriate in the young but not a virtue in itself. Ghazālī also lists forbearance here, the virtue of Job and other prophets. Forbearance is the fruit of steadfastness, the ability to bear sufferings and losses, which Ghazālī locates under courage. Following Miskawayh and Avicenna, Ghazālī defines forbearance broadly—not confining it to its familiar construal, as patience, but enlarging it to include resistance to all the passions, whether of pleasure or of pain. He reserves this Qur'ānic virtue for special discussion among the avenues to salvation. Under temperance again he includes another form of self-restraint, foregoing some of our due, using a definition Miskawayh had included under liberality. But Ghazālī adds that such virtues are relevant only for those who are still attached to worldly things. Similarly with thrift and Miskawayh's virtue of orderliness. Even with liberality we can see the same thrust: Ghazālī dwells on the dangers of preoccupation with a livelihood, to the detriment of concern with our ultimate destiny. If one must choose between poverty and generosity, he argues, citing Muḥāsibī, one must prefer poverty. For it is less entangled with worldly things.[113]

Ghazālī shadows Miskawayh in defining godliness in terms of good action done for the sake of the perfection in it; but he adds: and for the sake of coming nearer to God. The effect is to render Miskawayh's eudaimonism more starkly theocentric. In this he retains, but subtly shifts the balance of Plato's famous exhortation (*Theaetetus* 176) to perfect our humanity by becoming as like to God as humanly possible. Miskawayh himself equates actions done for their own sake with actions done to please God. But that is a symmetry, not a reduction. It means that we are pleasing God when our motive is the goodness intrinsic in an act. In Ghazālī such symmetries are dangerous. In a sense they are the ultimate danger, since they seem to remove the moral gaze from God. God alone, Ghazālī argues, gives without any expectation of a return. We humans can approximate such liberality if we are generous for God's sake, *or for the sake of an eternal reward*. Ghazālī is wary of any merely social object of moral concern; and he is chary of dismissing canonical eschatology, as Fārābī tends to do, as a mere symbol of something higher. He shows no qualms about making divine favor and immortality moral incentives. The deontologist's idea that virtue is its own reward and that it is nobler to choose the right for its own sake rather than for some benefit is foreign to his axiology. For that seems to place virtue, a human good, ahead of immortality, the ultimate value that God Himself sets before us.

In his properly ethical writings Ghazālī follows Miskawayh and Avicenna in defining contentment as a virtue involving moderation. But in the *Iḥyā'* he seizes upon the general Aristotelian proviso that virtues must be exercised in the right way, to make contentment an ascetic principle demanding that we not seek to provide for our needs beyond a single day—a month at most—and give away all that we have beyond that. Even the Aristotelian social virtues of cheer, affability, and good humor, are modified in the same sense—made over to conform to the ideals of sobriety and sedateness: One should not laugh unreservedly but emulate the Prophet, who preferred smiling to laughter.[114] Jesting, Ghazālī urges, again citing the Prophet, leads to falsehood: Muḥammad "did jest, but he spoke only the truth." The saintly Ḥasan al-Baṣrī, Ghazālī reports with admiration, did not laugh for thirty years.

Miskawayh expatiates on liberality, the brightest virtue in a courtier's firmament—and one on which his fortunes depend. He expands liberality to encompass altruism, magnificence, appreciativeness of great achievement, and certain forms of self-denial, as well as beneficence and bounty—which last means spending more than one really should, a favorite virtue of the Arab poets.[115] Ghazālī, for his part, expatiates on the dangers of speech, listing twenty evils of the tongue. He recognizes the Aristotelian mean of cheerfulness and good humor, between the morose and the clownish. But he also notes that exchanging pleasantries at a party or graciously acknowledging the casual remarks of acquaintances can be a duty and a chore. Seclusion is preferable, and we must look to the model of the Prophet to see how social occasions may be borne with good address. Likewise with tact: we must learn to forego contention and find the mean between pettishness and obsequiousness. But Ghazālī complements this advice by reverting to Aristotle for a virtue that neither Miskawayh nor Avicenna included in their catalogues, righteous indignation, here defined as grief at the undeserved good or ill fortunes of those we know or with whom we have something in common. This virtue must be sharply set apart from envy and spite, which are strictly forbidden but similar in appearance. The true guide in distinguishing the virtue from the vice is the intent—worldly versus otherworldly goals. A similar canonization of intention is familiar to philosophers in Spinoza's distinction between piety and ambition. Ambition seeks approbation and emulation, where piety (also called humanity by Spinoza) seeks the genuine welfare of our fellow human beings. As Spinoza intimates, comparable subtle differences of intention run all through the catalogue of moral strengths and weaknesses. And the pietist theme of scrutiny of our intentions remains prominent in the ethics of Kant.

Ghazālī follows Miskawayh in defining delicacy or gentility as an attachment to what is fair or fine; he follows him again in defining personableness, as Yaḥyā ibn ʿAdī does, in terms of dress, the one aspect of outward appearance, beyond demeanor, that one can regulate for oneself—and with clear impact on one's mood. Miskawayh says simply that personableness is a love of complementing the soul with fair adornments. One can almost picture him interviewing would-be aides and explaining the importance of self-presentation, the signs that properly or improperly chosen clothing give about the inner man. But Ghazālī puts *greater* emphasis on clothing. The *Iḥyāʾ* devotes a full chapter to the Prophet's mode of dress: He wore whatever came to hand, saying that he was just a slave and so dressed as a slave. Our clothing is best made of the coarsest stuff, affording just the necessary coverage, and sturdy enough to last no longer than a day and a night—an outward sign of trust in God that brings to the surface of ritual expressiveness the tenor of one's inner state. Few but the most saintly will attain the ideal, but lavish clothes are never acceptable. The mean, presentability without luxury or ostentation, is no longer an optimum but a compromise.

Under courage Miskawayh lists great spiritedness (disdain for the trivial, an Aristotelian ability to bear both honor and humiliation), dauntlessness (confidence in a crisis), fortitude (in bearing and overcoming sufferings, especially those that cause terror). To these he adds *Ḥilm* (Aristotle's mildness or gentleness, now assimilated to the Arabic counterpart of the Roman *clementia*, from which it takes its name—a virtue cultivated by the caliph Muʿāwiya, who said that if a single thread bound him to his fellow he would not relax his grip on it: "If he pulled I would yield, but if he yielded, I would pull"). He also adds steadiness (especially valuable in fighting to defend one's womenfolk or the religious law), gallantry (eagerness to do great deeds and win glory), and perseverance (sustained command of the soul over the body, applying it like a tool to a task).

Ghazālī quotes Wahb b. Munabbih as saying that he had read in the margins of the Torah itself: "No treasure is more beneficial than knowledge" and "No wealth is more profitable than *ḥilm*." These apothegms sound like paraphrases of *Pirkei Avot*, which might loosely be called a set of marginalia to the Torah. For that tractate of the Mishnah ascribes to Ben Zoma the words, "Who is wealthy, he who is contented with his lot," and "Who is mighty, he who subdues his impulse" (Avot 4.1). But Ghazālī's treatment of courage is as much a riposte to Miskawayh as an appropriation: He uses the Aristotelian notion that every virtue has its proper sphere to urge that the Realm of Islam is not the proper arena for the courage that is a mean between recklessness and cowardice and quotes God Himself in support: "Muḥammad is God's Apostle, and those who are with him are strong against unbelievers but merciful among themselves" (Qur'ān 48:29).

Despite the chauvinism, Ghazālī's interest in courage is less military than Miskawayh's. Like others of Sufi persuasion, he shifts the focus away from warfare, where Aristotle had found the paradigm case of courage, and onto the greater *jihād*, against the passions. He omits the martial arts from his educational program and treats sports as means of strengthening the body rather than of teaching valor. Fear is actually a virtue when applied to God. Its proper object is hellfire.

Among the subvirtues of courage, Ghazālī expands on Miskawayh's list, adding magnificence here, perhaps because courage is needed in making great expenditures. He adopts Aristotle's notion that magnificence is properly shown in honoring the divine and in public works—building mosques, roads, hospitals, and bridges—although such activities and the entanglements necessary to support them are not compatible with the self-denying life of the ascetic. He adds nobility and benevolence as well—the former modified from Miskawayh's anatomy of liberality, and the latter defined (as Spinoza will define humanity) as wanting for all men what one desires for oneself.[116] In defining 'dauntless,' Ghazālī follows Aristotle's definition of courage as a mean in facing danger and death—a mean, he says, between recklessness and helplessness or desertion. But he redefines gallantry to make goodness and eternal life its goal, rather than glory.

Ḥilm is a crucial virtue in Ghazālī, as in Miskawayh and Ibn ʿAdī, because it offers control of anger. It can be simulated, but its true nature acts in cooling the blood, whose heat is necessary to life, but harmful in excess. We are attuned, Ghazālī argues, to arousal in defense of ourselves and what is ours; but, if our claims go beyond bare necessity, we must curb our ire and possessiveness over all that is extraneous. Thus self-control is placed in service to abstemiousness and resignation. Similarly, Miskawayh's virtue of dignity, which in his work as in Yaḥyā's means little more than grave demeanor, is redefined by Ghazālī to become a form of self-respect grounded in a proper sense of one's worth. It lies at a mean between vanity and abjectness. All the same, like most medieval ethicists, Ghazālī insists that humility, not pride, is our proper virtue.

In describing greatness of soul, Ghazālī goes back to Aristotle for the recognition that the great man is not beguiled by honors. Recognition may be needed for effective leadership, but the Sufi ideal demands renunciation. Ghazālī dwells on the dangers inherent in the love of fame and condemns avidity for honors. The point was critical in his own life. For the crisis that tested and fired his faith involved his recognition that much that passed for piety, in others and even in himself, was sheer self-seeking. As he wrote, "I examined my motive in my work of teaching and realized that it was not a pure desire for the things of God. Rather the impulse moving me was the desire for an influential position and public recognition. I saw for certain that I was on the brink of a crumbling bank of sand and in imminent danger of hell-fire unless I set about to mend my ways."[117]

In seeking God in place of worldly regard, Ghazālī observes, some pursue apparent humiliation and disgrace. The reference is to Sufi practice, and here too Ghazālī senses the danger of excess. Seclusion, isolation, and migration to lands where one is unknown prove preferable alternatives to what may become a theatrical pose. Again Ghazālī reflects on his own life history. For seclusion and even exile and (temporary) obscurity were his own resort, when his role and reputation threatened to overwhelm him. Humility must displace the quest for greatness. One must choose between this world's goods and those that are more real and more dear.

It is always ambiguous, of course, how far the efforts of a Ghazālī can succeed in extinguishing the sort of worldliness that he found in the spiritual leaders of his day and even in himself. For the closest self-scrutiny can be deluded, mistaking for spirituality what is in fact mere sublimation of social instincts and acquisitive urges. The verbally adept will readily find a new vocabulary of selflessness in which to voice their old ambitions. And the socially adept can similarly devise new spheres for emulousness and self-aggrandizement, even projecting all lack and evil on the other and thus, as we suggested in the introduction, becoming fanatical and hate-filled. Selflessness plainly has self-deceptions of its own. And even the sincerest renunciation bears a price.

Aristotle thought that the great man does claim the honors due for his achievements. Cicero confessed that he would never have undertaken his struggles in the public interest (which did, in the end, lead to martyrdom) without the love of glory and hope of fame. The spiritual gains from Ghazālī's type of abnegation will remain invisible in the nature of the case, but the material harm of the devaluation of glory can be seen in every land that otherworldliness has touched.

Ghazālī is drawn to the idea of the mean. He uses Aristotle's caveats about appropriateness and context to naturalize virtue ethics far more effectively than Miskawayh could by treating it as an exotic offshoot of the rare and foreign plant Philosophy. In Ghazālī's ethics, Ashʿarite worries about volitions, intentions, bivalent capacities, and dispositions resident in human character are quietly forgotten, along with the fact that the ethical gaze of the Qur'ān and *ḥadīth* is fixed not on virtues but on commands and the example of the Prophet. But in making the virtue schematism at home in its new context Ghazālī modifies it both in form and in content: Virtue is redirected back to positive practice, dispositional tendency is deemphasized, and the mean is often made a second best to ascetic extremes of a sort that Aristotle and such medieval successors as Saadiah, Fārābī, and Maimonides actively combated.

The idea of the mean anchors Aristotelian ethics in social and biological naturalism. But Ghazālī senses an insistent tug from the transcendent. And the goals of that higher realm gain specificity from the rejection of the very appetites and impulses that a worldly eudaimonism like Miskawayh's seeks to channel and modulate but never to deny. Thus Ghazālī's commanding urge to suppress the humanism he finds in Miskawayh. It leads him to ransack Fārābī, Avicenna, Aristotle, or Plato, dig deep into the canon of *ḥadīth,* and plumb the oracular verses of the Qur'ān for readings of the virtues more closely in tune with his own Islamic ideal.

The resultant values do take root in a way that Miskawayh's do not. Their pietist colorations mask the foreign origin and structure of the underlying Greek ideas about the mean and the good life and deeply penetrate the ethical thinking of generations of Muslim thinkers of orthodox stamp. The ancient architecture is strikingly preserved—Aristotle's profound and profoundly original conceptualization of the virtues. But, like the mosaics in the Byzantine basilicas, the faces are erased or plastered over: Where the lithe forms of pagan demigods once danced and later the spiritual lineaments and heavenward gaze of late antique piety and paideia could once be seen in the tesserae of the mosaics, the space is filled with painted sayings from the Prophet and his Book.

The humanism of a Miskawayh, like the intellectualism of Fārābī and Avicenna, or the even the prudential and ascetic hedonism of Rāzī are vanished, displaced by Sufi sayings, canonical dicta, and the dialectics of *kalām*. The channels that still run beneath the ground may be of Greek construction; but the classic motifs at the surface of the font are subtly altered, and the waters that flow forth show no sign of how far they have traveled. To the drinker the taste is local. The free spirit of Miskawayh, the musky flavor that his odd Persian name suggests, is gone. Rarely in the later history of Islamic ethics will the like of his humanistic views and speculative excursions be seen again.

In Ghazālī, as in Aristotle and Miskawayh, the aim of ethics remains the perfection of the individual. But the social and cultural milieu so critical in defining and refining our humanity is altered. In the new milieu we find the very ideal of isolation that Aristotle rejected and that Miskawayh so spiritedly fought. The perfected individual is no longer one who directs his life by habits of reasonableness and whose highest aim is contemplation of nature and its transcendental meaning, but the spiritual seeker, who has, as it were, cut away the middle term and reached directly—as Miskawayh warns one cannot do—for the divine. The discipline now is not simply moderation and self-refinement but ascesis; the contemplation is gnostic and ecstatic—a quest more of the heart than of the understanding, leading not to mastery or even self-mastery in this world, nor to a naturalist's inductive synthesis and practical command, but to detachment from the world and ever closer attachment to the supernal realm and preparation for the hereafter.

We are in no position to romanticize Miskawayh as the last best hope of a cosmopolitan humanism in Islam. It was not simply narrowness, ignorance, or backwardness that grounded the acceptance of Ghazālī's ethics and rejection of its more secular and humanistic prototype. Miskawayh's was a courtier's ethic; and, like his life, it shows the biases of his nature and his role. As in his historiography so in his ethics, Miskawayh is a conspicuous ego. He was criticized in his time for name dropping and trouble making; and his penchants for both, alongside a certain tendency to flatter, are still visible in his writing—even though the ability to make trouble can be a virtue in a philosopher, where it is not in a courtier. The flaws of his ethics—its tendency to promote conformity and to breed a cohort of refined but superficial time servers—were as visible to his successors as the character flaws that favored such biases were plain to his contemporaries. It was in part a recognition of such biases that led Ghazālī and others to seek authenticity and depth in the canon, to take refuge in Islam from an ethic that had come to seem to them as empty and superficial as the counsels of the courtier Polonius may seem to us.

Ghazālī too has faults, also mirrored in his ethics. The exile and partial isolation that he made a virtue were in part a necessity for him, and in part a desertion, to use his own terms, when the patron who had sponsored his polemics against the Isma'īlī sect fell to assassination, the tactic that gave that sect the name by which it became best known in the West. Ghazālī's meditative ethics is itself escapist in part. It renounces worldly aims on the eudaimonistic grounds that it knows of something better. But it does not attain perfect selflessness for any living subject of its counsels, and it does tend to leave the world's wounds to fester. Humanistically inclined Muslim and Arab scholars today may look back yearningly to Miskawayh's ideals of culture, community, and individuality. One can see that yearning vividly in Constantine Zurayk, the Lebanese translator of Miskawayh. Its presence is perhaps more muted in Majid Fakhry's learned appreciation of Miskawayh's work. But its sense becomes vocal in Mohammed Arkoun's appraisal:

> One is always agreeably struck by the serenity of Miskawayh's tone, by a very clear, very accessible and at the same time very rigorous style. When he describes the social and economic consequences of Būyid policy, or when he reports an abstract philosophical theory, he always succeeds in avoiding the use of technicalities which discourage the reader and the pedantry which obscures the subject. He also combines philosophical seriousness, scientific competence and concern with didactic communication, to the point that all these writings recall those of the best modern Arab prose writers. . . . It is through philosophical *adab* that religious reason was able to assimilate certain contributions of philosophical knowledge without provoking the rejection constantly

> repeated by the jurist-theologians who were champions of "orthodoxy." From this point of view, Miskawayh and the intellectuals of his generation remain of current importance in Arabic and Islamic thought; faced with militants of religious orthodoxy who are more numerous than ever, the philosophical attitude and knowledge, as in the 4th/10th century in Baghdād, Rayy and Isfahān, would allow one to pass by dogmatic conflicts whose religious vocabulary conceals principally political stakes.[118]

But yearning, of course, does not breathe life into forgotten arguments, or redistill the clarity that dissolves false political pretensions. Juxtaposing Miskawayh's humanistic ethics with Ghazālī's recasting of it into a Sufi mold, one can feel a poignant sense of loss for the values Miskawayh sought to establish in Islam. Ghazālī does preserve much of the structure and some unmistakable relics of the ancient humanism—but as if in amber.

Pietism is not as welcoming a medium as courtesy for the nurture of a new and lively humanism. Arkoun's rather somber appraisal of present circumstances rests on a painful realism, grounded in the recognition that the politics of radical reaction readily outbids and often outguns the humanism of a Miskawayh. Miskawayh has something precious that serious and committed Muslims and non-Muslims too would like to regain. Yet one cannot go back in time. If there is something to be recaptured in the humanism of Miskawayh, it will have to be recast once again, perhaps even re-created. Courtliness has had its say and its day, and if a new humanism is to emerge it will require new voices. Its authors may yet find instruction in Miskawayh's "didactic" writings, but they will also need to build and plant afresh; and if Miskawayh's achievement is to be a model for them, they will learn from his synthetic method, and not just from an echoing of his personal quirks and preferences. Indeed, they will have much to learn by seeking to balance his courtly humanism against its counterpart in Ghazālī. We have the work of Spinoza and of Kant to show us that even mysticism and pietism can anchor a humanistic ethics, if a philosopher of clear enough intelligence undertakes the task of construction.

3

Being and Knowing

Being and Becoming

Being in Arabic is *kawn*. Given the verbal force typical in Arabic nouns derived from verbs, the word develops the connotations of 'becoming,' in Plato's sense of coming to be, *genesis*. It is used to render that term in Aristotle's phrase 'coming to be and passing away.' Its Aristotelian opposite is *fasād*, corruption, again with verbal force, meaning rotting, wasting, decomposing. Thus Bashshār ibn Burd, the eighth-century poet of Basra, wrote: "Wa kullu shay'in li-kawnihi sababun" "Each thing must have a cause of its becoming."[1] ʿAbd al-Jabbār, with studied deference to Arabic usage, similarly understands being dynamically: "The word *ens* is too to static to use it as a translation for *kā'in*; the Arabic verb *kān* expresses both the beginning and the continuation of what we call 'to be.' . . . According to ʿAbd al-Jabbār this word when used without further determination means 'beginning.'"[2] Jāḥiẓ was writing in an easy and idiomatic Arabic when he asked, "What is the cause of the being of cats, or the reason for the creation of swine?"[3] That all things must have a cause was a natural inference when the being of things meant their coming to be. Al-Dimashqī (d. 1327), a cosmographer from the city whose name he bears, speaks of the completion of the *kawn* of the foetus,[4] that is, its development. The doxographer al-Shahrastānī (d. 1153) writes of foreknowledge of a thing before its *kawn*, that is, its coming to be, its occurrence. There is nothing for Process philosophers to complain of here. Even Ibn Rushd writes that man's being, that is, his coming to be, is from another man.[5] But the tension between being and becoming is evident when readers of Arabic find Aristotle saying that, "change is the opposite of perfect being (*al-kawn al-kullī*)."[6] And this tension is never absent in Islamic discussions of being.

True, the word *being* was not discussed in Muslim sources before Greek writings were translated into Arabic. But reflection on the nature of being as such was well founded when the Qur'ān proclaimed: "All things are perishing, except His face" (28:88). The words are still read as a denial of ultimate adequacy in all creaturely claims upon being. The King Fahd Qur'ān comments: "The only Eternal Reality is Allah. The whole phenomenal world is subject to flux and change and will pass away, but He will endure for ever."[7] Plato's argument that change betokens impermanence and so entails the insufficiency of sensory things and their need of a creator chimes perfectly with the Qur'ānic sense that the world's evanescence is complemented by divine perdurance: "Whithersoever you turn, there is the Face of God" (Qur'ān 2:115). The Face of God, that will be seen by the blessed (Qur'ān 18:28, 30:38–39, 6:52, etc.), who open their faces to Him (Qur'ān 2:112, 3:20, 6:79, etc.) is the emblem of His eternity and omnisufficiency.

Ordinary being, the being of things, is the act or work of God, "Creator of the heavens and the earth; when He decreeth a thing He has but to tell it 'BE!' and it is" (Qur'ān 2:117, cf. 3:47, 6:73, 16:40, 19:35, 36:82, 40:68). Here being is an imperative and not abstract but concrete. This "BE!" is the Qur'ānic logos, vehicle and instrument of God's creative act. It is not confined to the absolute origination of the first creation but extended to every moment of God's governance: His miracles (Qur'ān 21:69—"Fire, be coolness and safety for Abraham"), His ordinances (Qur'ān 5:8—"O believers, be you steadfast before God, witnesses for justice"; cf. 4:135, 39:66), even His curses, hurled upon the Jews (Qur'ān 2:65, 7:166—"Be ye apes, despised and hated").

God's being is regnant (Qur'ān 13:16, 14:48, 38:65, 39:4, 40:16). Beneath it tremble the ephemera of creation: forms, shapes, rules, conditions. All creation owes Him absolute allegiance. Men who fail to confess Him will burn in Hell forever. Thus the heading in the *ḥadīth*: "He who accepts Islam on his deathbed, before the agony of death is a Muslim; but it is forbidden to plead for blessings upon polytheists. One who dies a polytheist is doomed to Hell, and no means are adequate to extricate him" (*Ṣaḥīḥ* Muslim, 1:10). Of Muḥammad, we read:

> The Apostle of God said to his uncle (as he lay dying), "Profess that there is no god but God, and I will bear witness on the Day of Judgment that you did." He answered, "But for fear of [my fellow tribesmen of] Quraysh condemning me for doing it out of fear, I would surely have given this pleasure to your eyes." It was then that God revealed: "Thou canst not guide whomever thou lovest; rather God will guide whom He pleaseth. He knoweth best who shall be guided." (*Qur'ān* 28:56)

God's constancy here becomes implacability, and creaturely dependence is read as moral frailty. In *kalām* the Qur'ānic sensitivity to the conditionedness of created being becomes a metaphysic of contingency. The early *mutakallimūn* reasoned that the positing of one thing does not entail the existence of another, or even the persistence of the same thing beyond the instant posited. A substance (*jawhar*), was thus an atom, an unextended point. Any differentiation, as by extension in space, would mean that more was inferred than initially allowed. If God gave being to a thing, it had that being, for that moment. But no more. Its being was *here*, not elsewhere; *now*, not later or forever. The things we see loom larger than a single point because they are aggregates of atoms. If they seem to persist, it is because God is pleased to create successor aggregates, moment by moment. Created beings are born and die with a flickering evanescence faster than we can see. The features of atoms are also created and meted out to them. All are accidental, none essential. For nothing in the posit of a being implies anything about its nature. That is a separate matter. Logical atomism is here pushed to an extreme untested by Hume or Russell: God gives each substance its character, just as He gives it its existence. So nothing acts of its own power. In the words of the Qur'ān (18:39; cf. 2:165), "There is no power but in God."[8]

Imagination, as Maimonides remarks, is the linchpin of the *kalām*. For on the radical *kalām* account, anything that can be imagined is possible.[9] Thus miracles are possible if they involve no logical contradiction. Indeed all events are on a par with miracles. For there is no sliding of what is into what it shall be, but each new state of the world is a new creation, whose sole reference to the past lies in the sheer will (or customary grace) of the Creator.

The denial of power to any being but God commended to the early *mutakallimūn* the Megarian elenchus against potentiality. For any disposition resident in things is a power imparted to nature, and so, as it seemed, denied to God. Megarians had held that real potentiality violates the law of contradiction, or its Parmenidean archetype, a crudely stated version of the law of the excluded middle: 'Either it is or it isn't.' To say of a thing that it is not ϕ and yet that it is ϕ potentially is, in their view, to fudge logically. *Kalām* occasionalists, as if in deference to Zeno's Eleatic paradoxes, devised a world in which motion and change were absent. Phenomenal change was simply the sequential appearance of a series of freeze-frames, in which nothing was other than it was.

Ashʿarī, who admitted and required capacities, since he acknowledged that an agent is sometimes capable and sometimes incapable of a given action, rejected durable dispositions. Capacities do not exist before the act they render possible. That means a telescoping of potentiality into actuality, as we saw in chapter 2: This cotton tuft is flammable only at the moment that it burns. If the capacity to burn existed sooner, Ashʿarī argues, that capacity would have vanished in the instant, like everything else, leaving the kindling we observe to occur by a nonexistent capacity.[10] So the stark Megaric contrast of being and nonbeing is preserved. There is no latent potentiality to compromise God's absolute creative act, now, as in the beginning.

The radical contingency of created being in the *kalām* seems to aim a sharp riposte at Aristotle's naturalism. For Aristotle, knowledge is science, and its aim is to discover why things must be as they are. Necessities are everywhere. Matter is eternal, ungenerated, indestructible. Form is immutable, although things do put off one form to take on another. Being is not the mere facticity of a thing but its essence, those specifics that make a thing a member of its kind. These cannot be lost or altered without destruction. But destruction, for Aristotle, does not mean annihilation, as in the *kalām*, but denaturing, loss of the features that make a thing a member of its kind. Natural kinds themselves never lose their essences. They are eternal, like the heavenly bodies. Species, then, the natural kinds whose members are visible to the eye, and celestial substances, the bodies whose motions reveal an immutable pattern in the heavens, make special claims upon reality. Being changeless and indestructible, they are the most fitting and responsive objects of scientific study. They are also the hallmarks of the divine Intelligence that animates the cosmos. That intelligence acts not from without, like a deus ex machina in a bad play,[11] but from within, through the powers and dispositions, energies and affinities that are the natures of things. Metaphysically brash the *mutakallimūn* may have been. But they were not naive. They well knew what they were combating.

The earliest Muslim thinkers to call themselves philosophers, *falāsifa*, using the transliterated Greek term, sought accommodation with Greek cosmology. They relied on the arguments and authority of Plato and Philoponus (490–570) to counterbalance the vigorous eternalism of Aristotle and the strident anticreationism of the pagan Neoplatonic reaction to Christian monotheism. Reading the Arabic rendering of Galen's summary of Plato's *Timaeus*, lost in the Greek original, we can look over their shoulders and perceive the methods and the motives of the Arabic translators, and those who sponsored and used their work:

> Galen says: Plato's aim in the *Timaeus* was to argue for the coming to be (*kawn*) of the world and all the living beings within it. He makes no distinction here between speaking of the world and of the heavens, meaning the body that surrounds and circles the earth.
>
> The book opens with the account of a discussion between Socrates and Critias about politics and the ancient denizens of Athens, and about the people of the island of Atlantis, of whom Critias will have much to say once Timaeus has finished speaking. But now Plato shifts from the questions and answers familiar in his Socratic writings, turning the discourse over entirely to the theologian (*mutakallim*) Timaeus. We shall not summarize the ideas put forward by Timaeus in this work as we have with Plato's thoughts in other works of his. For in those other writings his argument is very diffuse. In this book it is extremely pithy, a far cry from the cramped and obscure expositions of Aristotle, and from Plato's own dilated discourse elsewhere. If you find the argument here somewhat constrained and obscure, you should understand that it's really very little so. If you put your mind to it you'll see that the cause is not any obscurity in argument itself but in one's failure to recognize on reading it just what sort of argument it is. For an argument that can be understood only by one with the relevant training might well be opaque, but not intrinsically.
>
> So much by way of introduction to the argument of Timaeus. What he says is this: "What is it that exists eternally and has no coming to be (*kawn*) and what is it that is constantly coming to be and never *is* at any moment whatever?" (27D) To one schooled in Plato's other works, the answer is obvious.

> For Plato divides substances that are understood by the mind and are not bodies from those that are sensory, which he habitually calls "becoming," rather than substances at all. Socrates in the *Republic* is often found speaking of sensory things in this way. He does not think that they deserve the name of substances. So he has to speak in this fashion, labeling whatever is perceived by the senses as 'that which is always becoming' and whatever is understood by the intellect alone as 'eternal being.' Since Plato speaks in this way in the book at hand, I cannot summarize what he is saying here as I have done with his other books, by simply recapping his argument. Here, in this book of mine, I can summarize the ideas he puts forward in the *Timaeus* only by conjoining his earlier thoughts to his later ones.
>
> This, then, is what I say: Having laid down as a premise that there are two primary sorts of being, one eternally existent and the other constantly coming to be, Timaeus proceeds to argue that: "Whatever comes to be must necessarily come from some cause" (28A). This he affirms without proof. For it is one of those truths that are plain to reason. The point is that if anything remains just as it is, neither coming to be nor passing away, then there is no cause of its becoming. But whatever has come to be must have had a cause to make it do so. And whatever is in a state of becoming must have a cause in the present that makes it change as it does.
>
> Timaeus determines categorically that the world itself is in a state of becoming (28B). For Socrates had made this clear to him in earlier exercises. Whether the world had an origin or has always existed he specifies further on: He says that its becoming did have a beginning. And he says that the true nature of the world's creator is hard to find, and if found impossible to reveal to all mankind (28C).[12]

The lively Platonic fiction of a Socratic conversation gives Galen the room he needs to supplement the elliptical argument of Timaeus with premises, definitions, and distinctions drawn from elsewhere in Plato's oeuvre. Timaeus, here, is a faithful disciple of Socrates, whose conversations are training exercises (*riyāḍiyāt*). He is also a *mutakallim*, taking his posits from authority. The reader is a diligent student of Plato, familiar with the theory of Forms from other dialogues. So Plato's distinction of being from becoming and his equation of those two tiers in the ontic hierarchy with the intellectual and the sensory—the division charted by the Line in the *Republic*—here become premises, philosophical counterparts to the doctrines that the *mutakallimūn* appropriate from scripture. The argument remains, even if only in the background or offstage. Obscurity results only from a possible unfamiliarity with its tacit premises, or perhaps its ultimate goal. The conclusion sought is the world's origination, whence its need for an originator would seem to be self-evident. The argument rests on an inference from change to transiency and from transiency to origination.

The trouble is that change itself does not logically presume an origin. One needs more premises: not just the division of all things into the changeable and the immutable, nor even the Platonic thesis that the immutable must be intellectual, but also the idea that the changeable, being sensory, must be incapable of eternal existence and so must have a beginning. Galen finds a hint at the reason why no changeable thing can be eternal in the notion that all change depends on external causes. But that in itself does not bridge the gap from change to creation. For change might be externally sustained without cessation, as the Neoplatonic philosophers presumed it was. Indeed, given the modern idea of inertia, it is possible for motion, say, to continue indefinitely with no external cause. Nor is it a matter of logic (as Galen, supporting Plato, here presumes) that changelessness needs no cause. In the modern dynamic and interactive universe, changelessness is probably the hardest thing to sustain. Recovery of Plato's argument and thus of the scriptural values it was invoked to uphold, then, is not as easy as might appear. The missing premise to be supplied in ʿAbd al-Jabbār and later in Ghazālī is that whatever is inseparable from events that have an origin must itself have an origin.[13] But even the idea that the changeable, being evanescent, must have had a beginning comes at a cost. For the underlying Platonic division of the sensory from the ideal draws the would-be scriptural philosopher into a dualism and an intellectualist idealism whose full costs in implications could not possibly be gauged from the outset by a reader who was, shall we say, inexperienced enough in philosophy to need Galen's explanations.

For Kindī, the first major philosopher to write in Arabic, creation was one variety of change, added to Aristotle's traditional list. It meant bringing something out of nothing.[14] Perfect being is found in God alone. It is shared out with creatures in the measure of their capacity, and some taste of its perfection is available to us through our intellectual awakening to the Platonic Forms, our sole enduring and inalienable possession.[15]

We know that God exists, because changeable things are transitory and cannot cause themselves.[16] Behind all change and perishing lies the One, indivisible and unique, indescribable and eternal, whose constancy nourishes all mutability. No quantity can be infinite, so time itself must be of finite duration; and the bodies whose existence is presupposed by the passage of time will perish in the change that marks its passing. For Aristotle is right that time is the measure of motion. Yet his own arguments against creation seem to Kindī to serve better in its behalf: Where Aristotle had argued from the continuity of time to its everlastingness, and from there to the everlastingness of motion and the cosmos, as the clock that marks unending time, Kindī argues in the opposite direction, inspired by the idea of evanescence: The notion of unending motion is incoherent, he argues. It makes the transitory eternal. But "what is eternal does not move."[17]

Kindī puts to work Plato's perfect division of being from becoming in behalf of a scripturally endorsed creationism. But he sidesteps *kalām* antinaturalism, reconciling his creationism with Aristotelian naturalism—on the Platonic grounds that the nature known to us through the intellect is no mere opposite to the eternal. On the contrary, it is the temporal expression of eternal ideas. Unity and intelligibility *are* found in natural objects, not absolutely but derivatively. So even the lesser reality that we know bespeaks the perfect being of God. As in Plato, unity and intelligibility allow us to glimpse the being hidden in things, which we cannot descry in isolation.

Whatever unity we see in nature, Kindī argues, must have a cause. Natural objects are never without some degree of unity, and this is not ascribable to chance. For in nature multiplicity is always accompanied by unity. (And, as Aristotle reasoned, chance relationships are never uniform.) Nor is the unity in things ascribable to their inner natures. For unity is never of the essence in an aggregate, class, or whole. Even essential properties must be distinguished from that of which they are the properties. So their presence in the essence of a thing cannot be credited to the being of that thing. On the contrary, that being is due to their presence, which must stem, in every case, from a higher source of unity. For "everything which is an accident in one thing is essential in another . . . the unity which occurs in a thing by accident is acquired from that in which it occurs by essence. Thus there is a one, true, of necessity uncaused unity."[18] Kindī stands here at the threshold of the *via eminentiae*: Man is man precisely through what he derives from Above, where all perfections are most truly and most properly discovered.

As the translation of Greek texts advanced, the coherence of metaphysics and the consensus of the Aristotelians made powerful claims to authority. Naturalism gained a firm beachhead through its association with logic and its achievements in medicine, astronomy, and technology. Aristotle's claims for the invariance of the celestial motions seemed vindicated by observation and by the ancient Sanskrit records of the *Siddhānta*, made over into Arabic in the mid eighth century and given a reliable text by the late ninth—along with the *Almagest* and *Tetrabiblos* of Ptolemy.[19]

Kindī was a physician, as well as a philosopher and music theorist, as were most of the major Muslim philosophers. The folly of ignoring and the profit of studying the causal nexus became vivid through the work of the physicians whose art was grounded in Arabic translations from the Greek. Avicenna, long the doyen of medieval medicine, will argue, using Greek geometry against the atomist occasionalists, that dimensionless atoms are demonstrably absurd, fraught with geometrical paradoxes. Maimonides (1138–1204), a practicing physician and the author of ten medical works apart from his writings in Jewish philosophy and jurisprudence, will hold that *kalām* atomism breaks the continuity of solid objects and ignores the scores of mechanical devices that could not work without solidity. Philosophers were not ready to sacrifice naturalism to the idea of creation. Yet the appeal of creation was not lost. Rāzī, another great clinician, holds to a more Epicurean atomism, assigning the atoms solidity and size but retaining the Democritean void and still taking refuge in Plato against the Aristotelian notion that naturalism entails the eternity of the cosmos.

Only by positing five eternal principles, Rāzī argues, can monotheists refute the eternalists (*al-dahriyya*), whose view seemed just one remove from atheism. Eternal Time, Space, Matter, Soul (the world soul), and God, Rāzī argues, are preconditions of the world we know. Challenged by a more conventional creationist at a courtly salon, he declared:

> I hold that five things are eternal, but the world has an origin. The cause of its origination was the longing of Soul to be incarnated in this world. It was this passion that moved her, and she did not know what disastrous consequences would befall her as a result of her embodiment. She thrashed about in bringing forth the world and set Matter into a turmoil of chaotic and disordered motion, unable to achieve what she had intended. But the Creator, glory and exaltation be to Him, pitied her and helped her to bring this world to its inception and to impose order and stability on its motions. He did so out of mercy for her, knowing that once she had tasted the troubles in which she had embroiled herself she would return peaceably to her own world; her thrashing about would cease, and her passionate yearning for embodiment would cool and be calmed. Thus she began the world, with the help of the Creator. Without that help she could not have done it; but without this cause the world would not have come to be. We have no stronger proof against the eternalists than this account. If this is not how it happened, we have no argument at all against them. For we shall not be able to find any other explanation of the origin of the cosmos that will sustain proof and demonstration.[20]

Rāzī descends into the maelstrom of quasi-gnostic descants on the cosmogony of Plato's *Timaeus* for reasons that remain transparent even through the hostile reports of his well-attested views. He is convinced that God is the creator and that nature could not simply cause itself. Indeed, no power but God's could originate the cosmos. An eternal world would be, in effect, its own cause. God would become otiose, and the natural order, self-sustaining. That seemed a wholly untenable view. Yet Greek metaphysics has now so penetrated Arabic thought that absolute creation seems too much to expect of God. For the core idea of Greek metaphysics, from its foundation in the thinking of Parmenides, was the idea that being *must* be, that there is a contradiction in denying the existence of what is real. And Rāzī respects that theme. Each of his Democritean or Epicurean atoms cannot fail to exist. The atoms are not created and cannot be destroyed. But they are powerless to order themselves. They need time and space. But, like Kindī's nature, they cannot move of their own accord. In themselves they are inert. Motion will come only when imparted by Soul, the principle of life. The reasoning is like that of the occasionalist *kalām* in its effort to strip down each posited being to the barest given, and like the *kalām* view again in temporalizing the logical sequence from that barest beginning to the world we know. But, unlike *kalām* atoms, Rāzī's sheerest substances never originate—for that would mean that they change. Rather, at the beginning, they exist without motion. The time in which they endure is unending and unbegun, an absolute, since there is, as yet, no motion to serve as its measure. Its passage does not need a measure. Space too is absolute. The seeming paradox of the being of the void makes way for motion. So space is no longer relative, as in Aristotle. It is not the place of some body. Rather, it is a set of dimensions, that might or might not hold a body.

If God's wisdom is needed to give being to the world, and if God's power suffices in ordering that world, Rāzī still must ask *why* God would do so. He surveys the options with a jaundiced eye, half thinking that creation was a disaster which the world has yet to overcome. He does not agree that finitude is an evil. But he does argue, in Epicurean fashion, that evils outweigh goods in this world. For sufferings, in the end, will always outrun the successes of the subtly ordered complexes of atoms that make up living bodies. These, of course, include the fragile human frame, which the physician struggles to repair, working against the corrosion and decay that will inevitably undermine all that robust health and medical art can shore up. Why would God allow Soul, the life principle, to ensnare herself in matter? Gnostics answer in terms of *tolma*, the audacity that led to the Soul's fall. Rāzī espouses a Neoplatonic version of the story. But wouldn't a God great enough to frame the cosmos have the power, the goodness, and the knowledge to prevent so obvious a disaster? Rāzī answers in a carefully constructed allegory, addressed not to an imaginary but to an actual adversary, who is, in fact, our source for the story:

> "Tell me now,' [his adversary asks,] "What you say is that the Soul longed to be incarnated in this world, but lost control when she was bringing it forth and was assisted by God because He pitied her?"
>
> "Yes."
>
> "And did God know what troubles she would suffer if she undertook to be embodied in the world?"
>
> "Yes."
>
> "Would it not have been more in keeping with God's mercy to hinder rather than help her—to prevent her embodiment in the world, rather than cast her into all these calamities, as you claim He did?"
>
> "He could not prevent her."
>
> "Are you implying that God is powerless?"
>
> "What I said implies no such thing."
>
> "Didn't you just assert that He could not prevent her? You said 'He could not.' Isn't that powerlessness?"
>
> "I didn't mean that He couldn't because he was powerless to stop her. Let me give you an analogy to show you exactly what I mean. The only real parallel to the case would be a man who has a little boy whom he loves tenderly, compassionately, and protectively. This son of his comes upon a garden and sees all the luxuriant flowers in it. There are also many thorns and stinging vermin in the garden, but the boy does not know of the harms it contains. He sees the only the flowers and the richness of the place. Stirred by desire, his soul strains to get in. His father prevents him, because he knows about the harmful things the garden contains. The boy cries and presses, ignorant of the suffering that the thorns and vermin will cause him. So his father feels sorry for him. He is able to prevent him from going in but knows that he will not let up until he does go in and gets stung by a scorpion or pricked by a thorn. Then his passion will abate and his spirit will be at peace. So he lets him enter. And when he goes in he does get stung by a scorpion. He comes out again, and now his soul is not so eager any longer to go back, and he settles down."[21]

Rāzī's interlocutor finds the story puerile, contradictory, even blasphemous, with its suggestions that the Sovereign of the universe could not keep order in His own house. Was God a mere accessory at the creation? But Rāzī's myth does sharply discriminate between God's Wisdom and our own more discursive intelligence, so dependent on experience. Motion is beneath the dignity of God. His impassivity is untouched by the turmoil of embodiment. But Soul is not immune to the attractive, if ultimately noxious adventures of the flesh.

Existence in the barest sense, for Rāzī, does not depend on God. But order and peace do. Beyond the coercive force of nature and the compelling dictates of reason, he argues, there was a kind of wild spontaneity in the world's origination.[22] Viewed in itself, creation is hardly a success. God saw to it that the world was good, but only by imposing some measure of His wisdom on what Soul had begun, turning chaos into cosmos. But such wisdom was imparted only in the measure that time and space and matter could receive. For Soul, embodiment was on the whole a loss. But it was, or is, a learning experience, wholly appropriate to such timebound beings as we are, who can learn only by experience and seem to need the scent of suffering before we can savor the first whiff of the pathways to our true home.

Rāzī's aim is to demonstrate that creation is indeed possible and not absurd.[23] If creation is possible, one can propose God as the source of order and intelligence in the world. But Rāzī finds that he must concede the impossibility of transforming nothingness into being. He adopts *formatio mundi*—not an Epicurean evolution, where material atoms simply arrange themselves, but God's imparting of design. Hence his denial to the atoms of any intrinsic capability of motion. Animation comes from Soul; order, from God.

Creation here becomes a drama played out among eternal principles, each of which has its role to play. What the story shows, in the face of ever-graver philosophic doubts and denials, is that there is a model for creation that violates no law of logic and indeed preserves what Rāzī takes to be the natures of the essential players: God remains wise and good; matter, indestructible but inert; time and space, absolute; soul, undying, active, animating, but irrational. Stirring restlessly between God and nature, soul is capable of incarnation and thus, of alienation. But she is also open to inspiration and so, to redemption, not by the capricious favor of selective grace or prophecy but through the universal revelation of reason, which God opens up to every human soul.[24]

Rāzī's five eternals do not entail one another. They are not elements in some macrocosmic organism, no part of which is conceivable without the rest. Their interaction is contingent, not just on God's immutable wisdom but on the restiveness of the life principle and the strange complementarity of its ignorance with that wisdom. So, although the five are eternal, the world they make is not. Each of the five, even space and time, is real in its way. But no one of them alone can give rise to nature. Being requires a dynamic. Only so does it acquire a history.

Fārābī (ca. 870–950) has a clear idea of philosophic metaphysics. He knows that theology is just one component of first philosophy. It becomes philosophy insofar as the study of being qua being invites an inquiry into ultimate causes. So Fārābī does not expect a cosmogonic allegory to solve metaphysical problems. Nor does he prescind from the thick givenness of being in an effort to reduce it to its sheerest or merest posit. Partly for this reason, perhaps, Fārābī is committed to the world's eternity. He is intimately cognizant of the arguments Aristotle used in defending his claim (in rivalry to mythic discourse) that it would be absurd to seek an origin for the entire cosmos and time itself. So he can skirmish skillfully with a creationist like Philoponus.[25] To Fārābī scriptural creation is, like the sensuous sanctions of the Qur'ānic afterlife, a paradigm case of the sort of symbolism that prophets invoke in their delicate Platonic task of clothing in the rhetoric of pictorial imagination the truths that philosophers apprehend conceptually. The truth subtended by the creation story is emanation, the timeless dependence of all being on the One. Granted the doctrine is not strictly Aristotelian, or strictly Platonic for that matter, yet Fārābī counts on it for the dynamic, causal link between nature and the divine.

Aristotle had chastised Plato for providing only a logical rather than a genuinely causal linkage between particulars and the Forms. But Aristotle himself, in bringing the Forms to earth and making them the immanent essences of the species of things, assigned a constancy and intelligibility to natural kinds that Plato never conceded in this world. And when Aristotle set about to explain the divine governance of nature, he had only an absolute intelligence to appeal to. *Nous* can think. Indeed, it *is* thought. But its thinking has no content but itself. *Nous* is wholly actual and active, but its efficacy seems limited to the passive attracting of lesser intelligences that express their love of its perfection by a ceaseless piloting of the spheres in their steady rotary courses, the vast and invariant rhythms of the cosmic choric dance. If the aim was to transcend the mythic, what actually has Aristotle achieved by substituting one pictorial symbolism for another?

Successors labored to remedy the situation. Since the chief objections to Plato's Forms arose from arguments designed to show that Ideas cannot exist alone and on their own, it became a powerful desideratum among Platonists to find a home for the Forms. Monotheists like Philo (ca. 25 B.C.–40 C.E.) housed them in the mind of God. That expedient subordinates the Ideas to God and resolves their claim to be divine principles themselves, as they readily seem to be in Plato. Two further benefits accrue directly: God's thought no longer seems so empty. For in thinking Himself God now thinks all ideas. And secondly, these ideas are the very plans and patterns of the world, the archetypes of creation. In knowing Himself, it could now be argued, God knows nature; and in projecting His ideas God projects the natures of things, causing nature to be what it is. God governs nature by bestowing its character.

In the *De Anima* (III 5) Aristotle spoke of a duality found in all things, between the protean potentiality of their matter and the active and productive art or agency that allows them to realize their potentials. A key instance was what he called the Active Intellect, which works with the raw material in our minds, allowing us to transform mere notions into concepts (cf. *Posterior Analytics* II 19, 100a), making the mind actually and not just potentially intelligent. As Aristotle put it, the Active Intellect allows us to comprehend what is comprehensible, much as light allows us to see what is visible. In the *Eudemian Ethics*, Aristotle identifies the Active Intellect with God.[26]

Following up on these thoughts, Alexander of Aphrodisias argues that God is responsible for the existence of all things, since He bestows the essences that give things their definite character and thus their reality.[27] Alexander's (rather Platonic) reasoning is that whatever has a given character must derive it from something that has that character in the highest degree. Aristotle had said that the cause of a character in something else will have that character in a higher and more perfect way. And he suggests, on the analogy of fire, that the ultimate cause of a character will have it in the highest and most perfect way (*Metaphysics* II 1, 993b 24–26). Putting these thoughts together, Alexander could make much richer sense of the Prime Mover than might be conveyed by the mere notion of a self-thinking idea: All beings pursue their own perfection through the action of the divine upon or within them. So God does not just inspire the motions of the heavens. Rather, He is the energizing source of all activity. And that activity is the existence of things, since it defines the essences that make things what they are.

Plotinus (205–70), the founder of Neoplatonism, pursues this train of thought. Borrowing the Stoic idea of a divine presence that enspirits the world, he scrapped the Stoic notion that this spirit was a fiery (if artistically active) sort of matter and restored the Platonic equation of Being and the intellectual with the nonphysical. But he retained the Stoic dynamic. There was still an animating spirit in nature, but not in some sort of physical mixture or chemical solution. Alexander of Aphrodisias had killed and buried the Stoic notion that one physical thing could somehow fill up the same space as another. So the way in which divinity pervades the world must be Platonic: Spirit is a projection of Mind, and Mind comes to the world by bestowing form and unity. It is form and unity, as both Plato and Aristotle taught, in their different ways, that must count as being.

The linkage of Forms to particulars, then, need no longer be described by the merely static logical relation of "participation," as if all that particulars owed to their ideas were class membership. Rather, the linkage, which Plato had always called causal, is dynamic: All things derive their being from above. The vibrant radiation of form, symbolized by the undiminished flow of light from the sun, gave Neoplatonists (locked in ever more strident battle with scriptural monotheists) a way of describing divine creativity without reliance on the suspect notion of creation. For it seemed an affront to divinely constant reason and eternal generosity to claim that the world began at some arbitrary moment a finite time ago.

In the pantheon of Plotinus, Aristotle's *Nous* is no longer the supreme God. For intelligence, Plotinus argued, is not the very best of things. Above Mind stands pure Unity, the Platonic Form of the Good, that is God, the One. *Nous*, filled with the Ideas, which are united under their ever more general exemplars but differentiated in their specificities, is not pure unity but a "one/many." Yet because thought and thinker are identical, as Aristotle saw, *Nous* is the Ideas. So *Nous* is Being, with all the clarity, definiteness, and timelessness of Being. Yet its existence, although eternal, is not self-bestowed but derived, imparted by the One, whose infinite Power transcends every determinacy, even that of Being. Divine power shines forth in emanation, the procession of being from the One, that is, of ideas from the goodness that is the highest God. It is the ideas that give life to the Soul and a share in reality to every species of things.

The theory of emanation allows Neoplatonic philosophers to explain the fact of differentiation: The fullness and generosity of the One imparts being to *Nous*, with its spectrum of Forms, united in the white light of unity on one side of the noetic prism, fanned into the rainbow of cosmic diversity on the other. *Nous* gives life in turn, to Psyche, the world soul; and she, to nature, whose temporality reflects the need of Psyche to think discursively, declining from the timeless reflexivity of pure Intelligence. Proclus will say that the One timelessly generates all that is below it just as the point in geometry generates all figures, or as the number one generates all numbers. The simple here is not primitive but ontically rich and potent.

Fārābī adopted and adapted all of this. The Active Intellect, still a hypostasis, is no longer God. It is now the lowest and least in a train of disembodied intellects descending from God, distinct from Him yet dependent upon Him and united to Him by the focus of their thought on what lies above. Each such intellect after the first bears responsibility for one of the celestial spheres. By its own creative, reflexive, and somehow objectifying thought, each timelessly gives rise to the body of its own sphere and to the intellect beneath it in power and dignity. The cascade continues from the outermost sphere that governs the diurnal motion of the heavens, to the sphere of the fixed stars, down through the spheres that are the eternal settings of Saturn, Jupiter, Mars, the Sun, Venus, Mercury, and finally the moon. But what emerges as the tenth of these intelligences is the Active Intellect, which governs not a celestial sphere but terrestrial nature.[28]

The underlying matter of this lower world in Fārābī's view is a kind of precipitate of the spheres. Its invariant features are dictated by their natures, and its changes are governed by their motions–and the interactions of sublunary bodies with one another. But the formal character of natural things, as they strive after their ends in accordance with the Aristotelian scheme, is imparted by that most proximate of the disembodied minds, the Active Intellect.[29]

Relying on the equation of form with reality, Fārābī, like Alexander, ascribes the very existence of terrestrial things to the Active Intellect. He thus takes a stand on a question long debated among the heirs of Greek philosophy. Proclus (410–485) had criticized Aristotle for pinning his theism to the Prime Mover. Was God responsible only for the motion of the world? Plato seemed to have found higher ground. For even if the creation myth of the *Timaeus* was not taken literally (and Proclus certainly did not take it literally), its symbolism pointed to nature's dependence on the Forms. The Divine, then, was not reduced to a mere engine of the motions of the heavens but placed in intimate contact with all that is.

Simplicius, the eternalist adversary of Philoponus in the sixth century, sought to bridge the gulf that Proclus had opened up between Plato and

Aristotle. He reassured his pagan readers that the work of emanation is not to originate but to sustain the world. And that precisely is the task of the Prime Mover: The motions imparted to the spheres do give order to the cosmos, sustaining all natural regularities, from the cycles of the seasons to the rhythms of the generations. So the Prime Mover is the Creator in the only philosophically viable sense, the sustainer of the cosmic order, who timelessly imparts all that differentiates cosmos from chaos.

Abū Bishr Mattā, from whom Fārābī learned so much, was aware of this Greek discussion. Like Simplicius, he papered over the abyss, arguing that if God is a cause of motion He is a cause of existence: What it means for the world to exist is for it to have the nature that it has, that is, to move in the fashion that it does. The cosmos is rightly identified with its largest parts, the celestial spheres. Their motions give it its nature and govern all the processes below, much as the motions in the members of an organism give it its nature, with the most vital members (heart, head, viscera, lungs) determining the complexion or general health of the whole.

Fārābī takes the hint. Summarizing Aristotle's *Metaphysics*, he substitutes "existence" for motion at the crucial juncture, representing the famous teleological argument for the Prime Mover in Book Lambda as an argument for the Ground of all existence. Abū Bishr's gloss serves Fārābī, by enabling him to make the spheres not merely movers but sources of order.[30] Fārābī goes further by putting the Active Intellect to work as a hypostasis distinct from God, fusing his naturalistic interests with his commitment to divine providence and transcendence. Naturalism is served because the model shares out governance between the Active Intellect and the bodies over which it presides. Natural processes are channeled in steady courses that human inquirers can follow. No room is left for the direct and arbitrary or "customary" governance of the *kalām*. Yet there is governance, not abdication. God's transcendence is preserved by setting His perfection at a remove from the turmoil of nature. But the divine is exalted, not exiled, as in Epicurean philosophy. God's governance flows through the ideas of things and is manifested in their natures. So God acts through nature, not despite it; and the natures of things are constant, like the Wisdom they express.

Fārābī's naturalism supports his humanism, since it assigns a genuine reality to nature. God does not take back or withhold the gift of creation. The stability of nature gives credence to the sciences and the arts and enterprises like medicine and engineering, by which the findings of the sciences are put to human use. The same naturalism sustains Fārābī's vehement affirmation of free will: God does not beetle over nature or hug creation unborn to His breast. Rather, the delegated capacities of natural beings include our human powers to make choices for ourselves and take responsibility for them. Fārābī will not impugn divine omniscience. But the notion that omniscience imparts a necessity to events, he argues, would "eliminate deliberation and free will": "The implication for all religions would be that a person has no choice of actions whatever. Any chastisements he suffers in this world or the next would not be for anything that arose from his will or choice. God, who metes out rewards and punishments, would act unjustly. This too is an unacceptable conclusion, repugnant to all religions and very very dangerous for people to believe."[31] The argument is dialectical, appealing to the Muʿtazilite axiom that it would be unjust in God to hold His creatures accountable for acts they did not control. But Fārābī lays out the *kalām* reasoning only to motivate an incisive piece of logical analysis, based on distinguishing the necessity of an implication from the intrinsic necessity of a fact or act: God's omniscience, he argues, does imply that we humans will act as God knows we will. But, Fārābī insists, the necessity of that implication does not seep into the acts themselves, obviating their natural or volitional causes. What God knows is that natural causes, including human agency, will have their effects. God's knowing what Zayd will decide does not somehow render Zayd any less the decider.[32]

I find a further note of humanism in Fārābī's ascribing the world's existence, rather than just its motion, to his supernal principles. For the approach sustains the human connection, as it were, between God and the world. Fārābī's God will express His bounty and wisdom not just in the celestial motions but in the qualities and dispositions of terrestrial bodies. All things in nature have powers to move, to effect change and interact. That in itself, I think, supports the open future presumed in Fārābī's defense of free will. But Fārābī assigns all beings not just efficacy but worth, as he shows when he turns, metaphysically, to the explanation of change:

> Once things in the world have come to be, they tend to persist. But they do consist of matter and form. Forms are opposed to one another, and any parcel of matter is as suited to one form as to its opposite. So every terrestrial body has a right and entitlement by virtue of its form and another by virtue of its matter. What it deserves by its form is to keep the existence it has. But its right by its matter is to a different and opposite sort of existence. Since these two deserts cannot both be satisfied at once, they must be met successively, in alternation.
>
> Similarly, one parcel of matter is susceptible to two opposite and incompatible forms, neither of which can subsist without it, and neither of which deserves it more than the other. So it's necessary that this matter be given to this form at one time and to that at another. The forms share it in turns. Each form, as it were, makes a claim against the other, as if each had something that belonged to the other and was also owed something by the other.
>
> The justice here is in the taking of matter from one form and giving it to its opposite, and vice versa. Since justice must be done to these beings, no one of them can sustain its individuality forever. All the permanence that a being of this sort can have belongs to its species. And for the species to endure, its members must each exist for a time and then decay, to be succeeded by others of its kind.

Change here stands, by synecdoche, for decay and death, as the explanatory and apologetic nisus of the passage makes clear. The more concentrated area of focus is on the human situation, and the cosmic perspective that frames that focus serves the venerable aims of theodicy and consolation. But we are not left with the cold comfort of the sheer assertion that so it must always be, that change is a fact and decay inevitable. For the argument turns on the moral suasion that (God's) universal justice, which extends throughout nature, accords recognition, even rights, to the lowest and least of inanimate things, deserts grounded in the claims of beings themselves.[33]

Avicenna (Ibn Sīnā, 980–1037) presses further in the line of Fārābī's salient, affirming far more unequivocally the world's existential dependence on God. He is not satisfied with Abū Bishr's type of gloss, that asks us, when we see motion, to read "existence." For if Rāzī's work proved anything, it was that imparting motion, even ordered motion, is not the same as imparting being. Proclus saw a real and profound difference between Plato and Aristotle. Philosophers had to choose between Plato's idea that nature is derivative from the true being of the Forms, and Aristotle's affirmation that being is inalienable in the cosmos, in the heavenly bodies, and in all natural kinds. Avicenna chose Plato. He agreed with Fārābī and the great majority of Neoplatonic Aristotelians that creation stories were myths. They were profound in their symbolism, perhaps. For they were emblematic of nature's dependence on the divine, intellectual world. But their literal sense would not stand up to philosophic scrutiny. Emanation, as Fārābī had proposed, was the philosophically robust meaning behind the myth. But what emanation portends is not the imparting of motion. Fārābī had seen more clearly when he argued that it meant the imparting of existence.

To pursue that theme meant a serious departure from Aristotle: The existence of things could no longer be equated with their essences, if existence is bestowed and not inherent in the natures of things. What was called for was a reaffirmation of the scriptural idea, intuitively grasped if too crudely articulated in the *kalām*, that being is contingent all the way down. Yet Avicenna was not willing to abandon the Aristotelian stability of nature and the essences of things, on which the possibility of science depends.

Recognizing both the stability and the continency of being, Avicenna forged the great synthesis of Islamic metaphysics.[34] He merged the naturalism of Aristotle with the seemingly incompatible scriptural idea of the world's radical dependence on God's act. He achieved this synthesis by recognizing that the *kalām* and Peripatetic views of being expressed rival assumptions that are not logically but only perspectivally opposed. When Aristotle made the being of a thing its essence, holding that the properties of each kind are necessary (since they make a thing what it is), and when he argued that the things that are real in the primary sense (essences, species, celestial bodies) can never fail to exist, he was taking being as a given, *assuming* its presence and seeking its character. At the root of his thinking was the powerful Parmenidean suasion that nonbeing is ultimately an absurdity. When *mutakalimūn* demanded that we infer no more from the posit of a substance than the bare fact of its existence, here and not elsewhere, now and not earlier or later, and by a power that could not possibly be its own, they were taking being not as a fact but as a possibility that might or might not have been realized. Their inspiration, of course, was Scripture, with its God's-eye view of the world as a work that need not have been made, let alone been dealt the character we find.

The two views, I say, were not irreconcilable. Considered in itself, Avicenna argued, any finite being is contingent. For it does not suffice for its own existence. It needs its causes to give it being and sustain it. Yet, considered in relation to those causes, it is necessary. They necessitate it. Taken together, the causes of a thing are the necessary and sufficient conditions of its existence.[35] Natural science is the study of those causes. It is not the study of God's habits or grace but of the natures imparted by the divine. No finite thing, moreover, exists in isolation. Each is embedded, physically, in time and in location. That context hones each being's dispositions to the razor edge that marks the boundary between its potentials and its actuality, its past and its present.

No causal sequence or system, Avicenna argues, can extend to infinity. This does not mean, as Kindī and many another creationist assumed, that the sequence of seasons and generations must run back to a moment of origin. Avicenna was convinced that the world's age is infinite. But he was equally persuaded, on good Aristotelian grounds, that the natural order itself is not self-sustaining. A system in which each member is both a cause and an effect, he reasoned, can never be self-sufficient. There must be an ultimate cause, even for an eternal cosmos. And on good Platonic and Neoplatonic grounds Avicenna sought that cause beyond the transient phenomena of nature, and beyond the celestial intellects and spheres, ultimately in God.

Avicenna grounded his idea of being in the distinction between essence and existence. The distinction itself was not radically new. It was latent in Plato's separation of Forms from particulars and acknowledged by Aristotle when he teased out the question of what a thing is from the question of whether such a thing exists. But in Avicenna the distinction acquired a far more central significance. For when Aristotle distinguished *what?* from *whether?* he pointedly confined the issue to particulars. The existence of a given individual might be problematic—was there or was there not a man or a beast, say, in this forest or in this house. But the being of a species was its essence. One might ask whether a given essence is instantiated in a particular case. But without the eternal essences of things (so it seemed) nothing would exist at all–a plain impossibility. One reason for Aristotle to count species as substances was his view that they do have essences that are constant, intelligible, and identical, in fact, with their existence.

For Avicenna, by contrast, with the seconding his philosophy received from the vision of Scripture and the dialectic of *kalām*, all being but God's was problematic; nothing else was self-sufficient. The cosmos and all natural kinds might conceivably have been other than we find them. They might never have existed. All finite things are contingent, then, as the *mutakallimūn* held. The natures and even the existence of things, globally, are not logical necessities. Considered in itself, any determinate thing is contingent. Its actual existence is necessary only in relation to the causes that bring it about. If we posit a cause, as Aristotle habitually did, we must infer the effect. But we can readily see the dependence of effect on cause when we abstract from the cause and reason that without its action the effect would not exist. That is what *Genesis* asks us to do when it evokes the image of a world not yet created.

What Avicenna draws from the Qur'ānic allusions to that story and from the *kalām* responses to it is not the idea that the world had an origin but the idea that the world is contingent, timelessly dependent on a timeless Cause. *Formatio mundi* is no real alternative. For it presumes beings that are not only eternal but self-subsistent—like Rāzī's matter, time, and Soul. The real scandal in Rāzī's story was not that it made God the mere midwife of the Soul, but that matter, Soul, time, and space seemed to exist without any help at all from God.

What Avicenna asked was how anything finite could be self-sufficing. As the *kalām* analysis of possibility revealed, any determinacy in a being—its definite character or even its having rather than lacking existence—can be denied without contradiction and so must be seen as contingent. Necessity is found only in what cannot be denied, a being whose essence is existence and whose reality it is self-contradictory to deny. God is that being, the ultimate Cause demanded by the contingency of all lesser beings. For they cannot explain or cause themselves. Thus, in a sense far stronger than allowed by Rāzī's story, Avicenna's God can still be called Creator—not that He originates the world, but because He alone is the ultimate Author of all that is.

Avicenna's insistence on the world's eternity, in deference to what he saw as compelling Aristotelian and Neoplatonic arguments, sat ill with defenders of scriptural creation. The difficulty was not simply a literalist backlash in defense of scripture. For, as Maimonides argued, rational theology readily allegorizes scripture when its apparent sense runs up against the firm requirements of reason. Biblical anthropomorphism is a case in point. But the tension between eternity and contingency was not so readily resolved. Ghazālī took to task the entire school of Neoplatonic Aristotelian philosophers, with Avicenna at their head, for assigning to God responsibility for a nature that was eternal. What is eternal, Ghazālī insists, needs no cause. So the Muslim philosophers were atheists in spite of themselves. Their notion of God as the "Author" (*Ṣāniʿ*) of the world made no sense if the world had no origin.

Maimonides softened the blow. He withheld Ghazālī's charge that Avicenna's system was incoherent, and he did not accuse the Philososphers of atheism. But he did view their eternalism as problematic, ultimately untenable. It was a mistake, he argued, to try to prove or disprove the world's creation apodeictically. Such efforts lead only to the absurd overburdening of God in the *kalām*, making Him responsible directly for every action and event, and rendering otiose all natural and voluntary causes. The misguided effort to find demonstrative arguments *against* creation, on the other hand, sprang from the Philosophers' projection onto the remote and unseen past of the notions of time, matter, change, and potentiality that we extract from our study of the settled order of nature as we find it today.

Yet although it was misguided to seek a logical necessity in creation, Maimonides did find grounds for choice between creation and eternity. So he did not reject the project of metaphysics itself, as a human attempt to characterize being at large, particularly in addressing the crucial question of its grounding—its self-sufficiency or contingency. Creation, he argued, was more probable than eternalism, and preferable theologically. It was more probable, because it makes more sense to speak of the world's determinacy (including the determination of existence over non-existence) as requiring a cause if one conceives of a time before which the pertinent determinations have yet to be made. Creation is the preferable view theologically, because only a voluntary cause can be expected to make its determinations without some preexisting grounds for preference. Only by conceiving God as freely choosing to create and allotting rather than simply accepting the nature of the world, Maimonides and Ghazālī agreed, could one conceive how sheer Unity would verge into multiplicity at all. Making emanation a mere mechanism or mathematical implication would yield a stifling determinism. Indeed, the view that things must be as they are, if taken strictly, would exclude change altogether and freeze emanation in its tracks. Without voluntary choice, the world could not proceed from God, and God Himself would lie trapped in the monism of Parmenides.

The project of the Philosophers was from the beginning an explanatory one. Its aim was to find the ontic groundworks of a changing and colorful world. So even the stoutest opponents of creation did not scorn emanation, although it was, after all, a kind of continuous creation that curiously paralleled the instant-by-instant creation of the *kalām*. But if the efforts of the Philososphers to link nature to the divine were given their head and the unity and timelessness of the One were indeed to be projected forth from on high and shot through the spheres with the automatism of the logical, concretized as the natural, change would become impossible, and multiplicity, contrary to every explanatory impulse of the Philosophers, would become an illusion.

Despite their rejection of eternalism, both Ghazālī and Maimonides, for their part, recognized the power of the idea of emanation in making sense of the idea of creation, and, in particular, in addressing Plato's problematic about the emergence of diversity and change from the sheer simplicity of the Allperfect.[36] What these philosophically astute creationists hoped to achieve was a reconciliation of emanation with the free grace of God. Both fault the necessitarianism implicit in eternalism. But both make use of Avicenna's distinctive hybrid of necessity and contingency. They prize his recognition that the *mutakallimūn* were right to hold that finitude cannot determine itself. But they cannot put on the whole cloth of *kalām* occasionalism. Any idea that finite things are not self-sufficient leans, after all, even if only tacitly, on a commitment to causality. So naturalism is hard to avoid. As Maimonides argues, God would seem to act in vain if He made the food we eat as the mere occasion of a nourishment for which it was unneeded.

Ghazālī distances himself from the radical occasionalists' notion that appearances are unconnected to real changes in things. He allows essences to natural objects and denies on logical grounds that the members of a species can lack the properties of their genus. Consciousness, for example, is impossible without life. Evidently, then, bodies and events are not as isolated from one another as the radical occasionalists presumed. Indeed Ghazālī knows and seems to respect Avicenna's arguments against *kalām* atomism. He readily introduces a hylomorphic scheme in its place.[37] As for Maimonides, he defends a vigorous naturalism and voluntarism, which rest on the idea that God delegates the power of action to His creatures, in stable patterns for the lower orders, as well as by rational choice in the case human beings.

Still, natural regularities are not logical necessities. The connection between what is familiarly deemed a cause and what is seen as its effect, Ghazālī argues, in the face of a long tradition of Aristotelian essentialism and Neoplatonic logicism, is not a necessary connection. For the two are discrete events, and neither entails the other. God may intervene to alter or contain the familiar natures of things, confining the power of fire so that it does not burn the flesh of Abraham when that prophet is cast into the furnace by the tyrant Nimrod. There is no contradiction in such a notion, so it is not impossible. And God can create. There is no contradiction in that, and the idea that time has a beginning is not incoherent.[38]

Maimonides, more warmly committed to naturalism than Ghazālī, is no less firm in discriminating causal connections from necessities of logic. Following Avicenna's and Fārābī's lead, he carefully distinguishes hypothetical from categorical necessities, arguing that the regularities observed in nature are indeed necessary, but not by the very logic of being. Rather, they express the essences and dispositions that God imparted at the creation. They are what the scholastics, with their flair for terminological niceties, will later call "ordinary," that is, ordained necessities, stable outcomes of God's free determinations. Maimonides accommodates even miracles to the scheme. He finds a hint of the antiquity of his approach in a midrashic conceit: The mouth of the fish that swallowed Jonah, the mouth of the earth that swallowed Korah, and other miraculous particulars from sacred history were created in the twilight of the sixth day. The course of nature was thus ordained from eternity and it remains so—uniform, in the phrase Maimonides adopts from Artistotle, "always or for the most part."

When Aristotelians imagined that natural necessities could never have been otherwise, they were projecting familiar patterns into a stage of cosmic history that was not yet marked by the patterns we now know. But the familiar determinations should not be imagined to have been eternally so, if the very idea of determination is to retain any robust sort of meaning. The present is not fixed in logical necessity; and the future lies open.[39]

Of all the Muslim philosophers, it was Averroes (Ibn Rushd, 1126–1198), the Cordovan physician, *qāḍī* of Seville, scion of a long line of *qāḍī*s, and author of the great Arabic commentary on the works of Aristotle, who grasped most faithfully and firmly what Aristotle meant by his analysis of being. Averroes saw that being, for a committed Aristotelian, must mean the essence of a thing. Confronting the devastating critique of *falsafa* that Ghazālī mounted in *The Incoherence of the Philosophers*, Averroes saw that he must sever the dependence of Islamic philosophy on Avicenna's synthesis, if he was to save that philosophy for Aristotle. His rebuttal, *The Incoherence of the Incoherence*, repeatedly isolates Avicenna as no true Peripatetic.[40] Averroes recognizes, in effect, that eternity was, as Ghazālī had claimed, incompatible with Avicennan contingency. But he opts for eternalism, not contingency.

Avicenna was wrong, Averroes reasoned, to treat existence as an accident that a given essence might have or lack. The differences among the Aristotelian categories run deeper than mere generic differences, variants on a single theme. Category differences do not merely differentiate the expressions of a single notion that we can tag as Being in itself. For what is meant by the being of a time, a place, a habit, or relation, has no content in common with what is meant by the being of a particular substance, or a species. After long relying on the idea that the cause of motion is the cause of existence, Averroes will fall back on the Prime Mover argument alone, making the motion of the heavens the replacement rather than the surrogate of creation.

In the end, then, Averroes will scuttle even emanation, for its presumption that being is an accident imparted to particulars. Fārābī and Avicenna's quest for a Neoplatonic reading of the idea of creation is abandoned. The purity of Aristotelian philosophy is restored. But Kindī's project of naturalizing metaphysics in Islam is lost. Writing of what he calls "the well-known medieval controversy between those who admitted only purely physical proofs of God's existence like Averroes, and those who would admit none but metaphysical proofs, like Avicenna," Gilson reflects on the import of Averroes's turn:

> Where God and the world stand eternally over and against each other, God is but the keystone of the cosmos and its animator, He is not put forward as the first term of a series, which is at the same time transcendent to the series. Avicenna, on the other hand, represents the Jewish tradition, and the Jewish tradition most fully conscious of itself; for his God, whom he calls strictly and absolutely the First, is no longer merely the first being of the universe; He is first with respect to the being of the universe, prior to that being, and consequently outside it.[41]

Averroes's metaphysical stance is clearly the reflex of the distancing he saw between the spirit of philosophy and the spirit of Islam. The impasse between *The Incoherence of the Philosophers* and *The Incoherence of the Incoherence* is matched in a distancing of God from nature that can be seen not just in Averroes but, in a way, in Ghazālī too. For whether God is an engine or an object of Sufi exercises, His immediacy is undercut. The polarity between naturalism and mysticism rends the middle ground where an Avicenna might have pitched his tent. And the disappearance of that ground unsettles the career of philosophy in Islam. In the East, Persian philosophers will continue for centuries to work at the interface of Avicennan metaphysics with Sufi monism. But in all lands of Islamic culture philosophy, as a self-proclaimed and self-critical method, is increasingly on the defensive after the standoff between Averroes and Ghazālī. Eternalism is the core of the trouble, but many related problems follow in its train, difficulties about causality, miracles, providence, divine will, knowledge and personhood, and personal immortality—let alone physical resurrection. Islamic philosophy has yet to regain the assurance it had in the Middle Ages, and the rise of scientism and materialistic trends has hardly been a help. Few Muslim writers after Averroes openly and confidently offer to declare, out of reason and critical thought alone, the true the character of reality at large.

Yet philosophy never does really die, since the impulse to understand and question, reconcile and create is inextricably human. Surveying modern and contemporary trends in Islamic thought, Majid Fakhry winnows the apologists, derivative thinkers, and political ideologues in search of the rare philosopher. He singles out Muḥammad Iqbāl (1878–1938) as "a poet of profound sensibility and a scholar of vast philosophical culture," who "draws upon the philosophical heritage of the West without reservation" neither to worship nor to scorn:

> The synthesis he attempts in *The Reconstruction of Religious Thought in Islam* may be compared in its magnitude to the synthesis attempted a millennium earlier by al-Ghazālī in his *Revival of the Religious Sciences* (*al-Iḥyā'*). In substance it is more analogous, however, to the syntheses attempted by al-Kindī and Ibn Rushd. . . . The fundamental difference between them is that, whereas the philosophical categories employed by al-Kindī and Ibn Rushd were drawn from Plato, Aristotle, and Plotinus, those employed by Iqbāl are drawn from those of Hegel, Whitehead, and Bergson. The masters have changed, but the problem remains essentially the same, namely, the attempt to bridge the gulf between speculative thought and religion.[42]

Knowledge as a Value

The watershed that Islam sets between itself and the prior condition of humanity, especially in Arabia, is marked by the stark Qur'ānic contrast of knowledge from ignorance. The word for knowledge and its cognates of the root *ʿ-l-m* occur 750 times in the Qur'ān, as Rosenthal notes. The centrality of understanding is voiced in many more passages, calling on Muḥammad's hearers to think and ponder, consider and understand.[43] Cognitive themes are made concrete in many more references to God's book and pen, parchment and ink.[44] They are opened up spiritually by references to light, as in the famous Light verse, cited in this book's introduction. All the same, the content of the knowledge called for on the human side is usually pretty uniform: The bounties of nature and comforts of culture, the events of history and verses of God's book are all portents of God's sovereignty, summoning mankind to repentance and obedience, fealty and faith (e.g. 2:164, 12:111, 31:26–27, 52:1–3, 68:1).

Repeatedly the Qur'ān blames ignorance for sin. But this ignorance does not exonerate. In the face of perennial prophetic warnings, it becomes culpable, bearing grave consequences in this life and graver still in the hereafter. The *Jāhiliyya* was, literally, the Age of Ignorance, but in the sense of barbarism and confusion, steeped in anxiety and self seeking (see Qur'ān 3:154). It was ignorance that led the pagans to flaunt their finery (33:33) and that still leads men to cavil at God's dominion, as if preferring some archaic, heathen rule by which to be judged (5:50). "The unbelievers," we read, at a critical juncture in Muḥammad's career, "got up heat in their hearts, the heat of Ignorance" (Qur'ān 48:26).[45] That ignorance is not mere lack of knowledge but a positive passion. As in biblical usage, the heart is the vessel of understanding, and Muḥammad appeals sixteen times in the Qur'ān to the insight of hearers with hearts (e.g., 13:19–22). Faith imparts knowledge, for faith is trust, and trust in God gives certitude.

Hundreds of times the Qur'ān equates knowledge with belief in God and acceptance of the prophetic message. Hundreds of times more the Prophet's hearers are reminded that God knows what we do not, all that is in land or sea, heaven and earth, the actions and intentions of every man. Knowledge shows us the links between God's act of creation and His constant governance. And that in turn teaches us to expect the denouement of judgment. So knowledge is a gift of grace. For it is only through knowledge that man is lifted up, not above the beasts but above the damned.[46] The salvific coloration imparted here to the idea of knowledge never leaves it in Arabic usage.

From the beginnings of recorded thought in Arabic, knowledge is practical. It does not exclude theory but is never confined to it. And it is valued. Surveying the poetry of the *Jāhiliyya*, Rosenthal finds a celebration of knowledge, not ignorance. "Is ignorance any match for knowledge?" one pre-Islamic poet asks rhetorically. Another answers clearly: "One who is ignorant of a thing is not like one who knows." The thought will be echoed a century later in the Qur'ān (39:9), naturally enough. For the Qur'ān could hardly appeal to values disdained by its first hearers.[47]

The root idea behind *ʿilm*, the Arabic word for knowledge, is, it seems, that of knowing the way. Wisdom (*ḥikma*) runs deeper. It is a special attribute of God and of those who know Him best. But, perhaps for that reason, wisdom is yet more practical than knowledge. When Greek philosophy, medicine, and other foreign sciences become spheres of Arabic learning, their passport is their practical value, and they are called wisdom. For the term still bears its ancient Semitic overtones of craft (cf. Ex. 35:31). The word *ʿilm* is held onto by Islam, in keeping with the Qur'ānic penchant for contrasting the certainty (*yaqīn*) of believers with the shaky notions (*shukūk*) and suppositions (*ẓann*) of deniers (Qur'ān 10:36). So the sciences may be sacred or secular, Arab or foreign, shallow or profound. But "wisdom," is often merely technical or pragmatic. A *ḥakīm* in ordinary Arabic is a wise man; but still more ordinarily, a physician.[48]

What does not so readily take hold is the Greek equation of the technical and critical with the scientific—and of wisdom, even at its highest reaches, with the speculative. The Arabic and Islamic sciences do evolve rules and standards. But they do not become systematically critical of their own methods and assumptions, as mathematics, medicine, the natural sciences, and philosophy can be at their best. Speculation, in the formative purview of Islam, may be exotic, subjective, or suspect. But it is learning and knowing that make one profound. As the ways of knowing proliferate, engulfing vast erudition in the sayings and doings of the Prophet (*ḥadīth*), legal and juridical lore and learning (*fiqh*), and scholarly mastery in the byways of theological disputation (*kalām*), the local standards proliferate as well. But they never become radically reflexive. *Ḥadīth, fiqh*, and *kalām* all develop sciences of their own. But what is valued most in the practice of these sciences (*ʿulūm*, the plural of *ʿilm*) is neither radical creativity nor rebelliousness but learning. A Muslim cleric is simply, or not so simply, an *ʿālim* (pl. *ʿulamāʾ*), one who knows. Mystic experience too is labeled cognitively, as in many another tradition.[49] It is gnosis or intuition (*maʿrifa, dhawq*), a knowing that passes understanding. But the pathmarks along the mystic's way, although called objects of acquaintance and experience, are mapped by tradition and learned through discipleship.

We can gauge the depth of the commitment to knowledge in Islamic culture by catching Hamadhānī in a serious, or combative mood.[50] For even in his jeux d'esprit, play finds its metier in learning and sport with words. Every one of the fifty-two surviving *maqāmāt* is a tour de force, a Fabergé egg of verbal virtuosity on display. Hamadhānī was a critic–like most of us, a better critic of others than of himself. He prized originality and sought currency for his own usages and hated the mere stringing together of set phrases and cliches.[51] Learning for him was alive only when it fed originality; but learning was the only soil from which genuine originality could spring.

Hamadhānī got his love of language from his father, and it was to him that he entrusted his three children when he went off at twenty-two, to seek his fortune at Rayy. There he dazzled the Būyid courtiers with his wit and skill, translating Persian poetry extempore into Arabic.[52] But after just a few months he journeyed on to Jurjān, a Būyid vassal state and buffer against the Sāmānids. There he won both admirers and enemies, and soon set his cap for Nishapur, drawn in part, he claimed, by the fame of a literateur, one Abū Bakr al-Khwarizmī. Setting out on good terms with his Jurjān patron and well provided for his journey, Hamadhānī was waylaid by highway robbers and arrived destitute in Nishapur in 992. The "Lion Encounter," I suspect, may be an effort to compensate, in fantasy, for the ignominy of the robbery. Khwarizmī, to whom Hamadhānī applied for help, was an ardent Shīʿite and as prickly as Hamadhānī, who was a Sunnī. Almost from the start the two men were rivals. They soon developed an enmity that led to an elaborate verbal duel before the notables of the city.

Challenged to choose his weapons: prose or poetry, memory or impromptu invention, Khwarizmī opted for poetry, prepared to extemporize on a model set by their host. But Hamadhānī scoffed. Meaning to run circles around his foe, he offered to spin out, after one breath, a poem of thirty lines, paraphrasing one of Khwarizmī's own, but without any of its language. If the audience could guess which poem was Khwarizmī's, Hamadhānī would concede defeat. Shades of the young Mozart. Khwarizmī held out for more familiar ground rules, but when Hamadhānī promptly indited impromptu verses as required, Khwarizmī refused to recite what he had written down. Probably a wise decision, Hamadhānī later wrote, since even a cat knows enough to cover its turds.

Turning to oral composition, the two savants lampooned one another, but Khwarizmī lost sympathy by offering captious criticisms of Hamadhānī's diction. A song was sung to cool everyone's nerves, and the party dispersed amid partisan arguments over which champion could claim victory. Hamadhānī did seek a reconciliation over dinner at his rival's home, but the dispute simmered on, and a rematch became inevitable.

Again many notables were present. Khwarizmī arrived late, preceded by something of a claque; but Hamadhānī, while waiting, took requests, offering what he called "free samples"of his wares. He delighted the audience by improvising verses calculated to gratify their predilections, on themes and in meters and rhyme schemes of their choosing. The actual competition was delayed by some skirmishing over the genres of the joust. Khwarizmī conceded the field of memory to his young challenger, tried to renege, but stumbled in a round of oral improvisation and could produce only what Hamadhānī dismissed as doggerel when the two turned to written extemporizing. In the genre of the epistle, Hamadhānī challenged his rival to write a letter, which, if read backwards, would become its own reply, or one that would yield verse if read diagonally, or one that made no use of the definite article. Scorning such "jugglery," Khwarizmī offered to compose a letter on a theme set by the audience, and did. The topics themselves speak to the times: debased coinage, barriers to trade, shortages, inflation. Hamadhānī then improvised his own letter, *backwards*, starting with the last word and ending with the first. A clear victory for the round. Then came lexicography, with each contestant naming a chapter from a standard dictionary for the other to reel off from memory. Hamadhānī won and went on to best his rival in mastery of the rules of prosody. As the crowd began to disperse, the principals and the more elite guests sat down to dinner and bouts of alliterative brickbats. Hamadhānī was lionized, and Khwarizmī slipped away. He went into a decline after his humiliating defeat and was dead within the year. But Hamadhānī rebuked those who expected him to crow over Khwarizmī's illness. He voiced respect for the defeated scholar and regret over their quarrel, but he could not restrain a sense of liberation at the vindication of his supremacy in the realm of words.

Hamadhānī's feats won him fame, patrons, and some wealth. But again he had to pull up stakes, driven by rumors and enmities. For, as he confessed, he was a man of modest build, fiery temper, and a dangerous sense of his own worth. If one's learning was not duly valued, he wrote, one should speak out or relocate. With the rise of Maḥmūd of Ghazna[53] and the decay of Sāmānid power, Hamadhānī traveled widely among the courts of Khurasan, Sijistan, and Ghazna, enjoying patronage and adulation. He met Maḥmūd at Sarakhs and was to eulogize him, among many others, but he fled the civil turmoil of Khurasan for Sijistan, where warfare, in time overtook him, and he moved on to Bushanj, and then Herat nearby. There he married a wealthy woman, a *dihqān*'s daughter. He started a second family, acquired rich estates, established a prosperous business and sent for his father and the family of his youth in Hamadhan. They never did join him, but he sent them gifts and letters and lived on for some ten years, before he died at forty, professing his faith in his will in traditional Sunnī terms, a turbulent man in troubled times.

Those troubles, allusively backgrounded in the *Maqāmāt*, are sketched in the *Rasā'il* with the stark vividness of a Goya. They include ruinous and confiscatory taxation, anarchic disorder, dreadful shortages, and lawless depredations. In Nishapur, Hamadhānī took the initiative of helping to organize a militia to restore civil order. More frequently, he used the mordant power of his pen, to call for more responsible exercise of authority. Sometimes the affronts that provoked him might seem trivial. He'd overheard a boy chanting Shīʿite curses on the house of Abū Bakr and ʿUmar. But wasn't that a warning of sectarian troubles ahead? Didn't the Shīʿism of Kufa sprout from innocent mourning over the martyred Ḥusayn? There was urgent need of support for the holy warriors at the frontiers of Islam. Meanwhile, there were crime and corruption everywhere, gambling in the *qāḍī*s' homes, wine in the mosques.[54] Confronting outrages and horrors, some on a public scale, like plague or famine, others affecting friends or neighbors who had been robbed or murdered, perhaps with official complicity or complaisance, Hamadhānī spoke out boldly. The right of petition was no dead letter to him, and he seems to relish the Ciceronian role of advocate, won by his verbal skill. He gamely affirmed that a scholar and his sovereign should be able to converse candidly, on equal terms. For the obverse of his pride was fearlessness. One could always move on. God's earth, he said, is wide; and its belly, ampler than its surface—and gentler. Knowledge here made its claim to moral standing and, in that sense, to power as well.

In his letters, Hamadhānī calls knowledge a treasure, the finest of human attainments. Writing to his father (in the kind of self-conscious Bildungsbrief that famous men have written since antiquity, partly to salve their conscience about sons and heirs, and partly to lay out thoughts on education, to edify posterity—and win their approval), he urges that his son be brought up to "stand tall" in knowledge, firmly anchored in religion. Religion here is the root but not the trunk or fruit of the tree. In thoughts like Miskawayh's, Hamadhānī finds in religion a moral and an intellectual side—both aiming at the perfection of our humanity. Knowledge too is twofold: practical and theoretical. Natural talents must be fostered, by cultivation in the moral virtues. Drink, music, and debauchery impede learning. So does a life of avarice and the pursuit of gain. The priorities are clear here: religious strictures serve a purpose, and the goal is not piety itself but paideia. Erudition demands patience, hard work, and concentration, much travel and risk, sleepless nights, but also thought and sensitivity. Learning, in the end, does not promise gold, but as Kindī or Rāzī might have said, it will transform and transport one's soul.

The Ikhwān al-Ṣafā called words the body of which ideas are the soul.[55] Hamadhānī would not readily stoop to so familiar a trope. But capping and trumping an old image of Plato's (*Theaetetus* 197c), he says that learning is a bird that language alone can capture—or a plant that bears fruit only when rooted in the soul. Morals matter, then, because they condition our soul-soil, to nourish learning. Generosity and protectiveness toward women are the sorts of virtues that count. Impudence and pretentiousness are paradigmatic vices. Hypocrisy and spite are especially vicious, because they are base and mean spirited.

Hamadhānī was the first man to write fiction in Arabic that did not come from the mouths of beasts. He held up the Qur'ān as a model of eloquence but made no attempt to imitate its style or content. Indeed, secularity plays a striking role for him in the avoidance of false pretensions. When accused of false pride, he answered that he knew he had the power to lie so gorgeously that his lies would be taken for truths, but had never expected his words to be inscribed in scriptural tomes or intoned in the *miḥrāb* of a mosque. This candid apologetic bears overtones of mild satire of the sacred word itself—or at least of its thoughtless bandying about. But it also reveals a modesty hidden in the use of fiction: Hamadhānī does not pretend to an absolute or higher truth but is content with the earthy truth that glints from his own, rather sidelong glances at his times. Yet false modesty hardly inhibits his claims to learning or stifles his ambition to frame truths that art alone may seem able to deliver when the robes of sanctity have slipped, revealing the sort of hypocrisy that can tarnish the most sacrosanct authority and palsy the grip of piety.

To the *mutakallimūn*, knowing is an active faculty, and knowledge, a subjective content matched to an objective reality. When the philosophically inclined among them speak of knowledge acquiring the form of things, taking things to be as they are, indeed, having a propositional form and affirming what is so, we can see the impress of Aristotle's hand. When they speak more dialectically, of knowledge as a silencing or resting of the soul (*sukūn al-nafs*), they echo the Stoics and Skeptics. Likewise, when they use the language of acquisition, perception and apprehension. The rationalism inherent in the idea of knowledge comes to the fore when the theologians and mystics talk of clarity, discernment, and discrimination. The Muʿtazilites, under Stoic influence, classed knowledge as a species of belief, since commitment is among its necessary conditions. But traditionalists rejected the view, since it would require God to have beliefs.[56]

The prolific ʿAbd al-Jabbār (d. 1025) develops a Muʿtazilite epistemology of *sukūn al-nafs*, as mental satisfaction.[57] He classifies knowledge as belief that is both true and satisfying, sharply contrasting supposition (*ẓann*) and ignorance (*jahl*), but leaving room (as the Stoic background suggests he should) for the Qur'ānic notion of *ijmāʿ*, consensus, not among the nations of the world but among the community of Islam. Jāḥiẓ may imagine that mental satisfaction can coexist with ignorance, but he is mistaken, ʿAbd al-Jabbār insists. True tranquillity of soul is found only in those who know. This Muʿtazilite extension of the Stoic search for a subjective test that somehow mounts the parapets of objectivity remarkably parallels Stoic moral notions, where intent is made a standard of objective right. In both cases, the privileged access of self-consciousness is pressed to yield a criterion of truth. Morally, the reasoning slides from grasp of one's own intentions (good conscience) to a guarantee of their soundness. Epistemically the case is even harder to make, moving from (subjective) certitude to (objective) certainty. The key Muʿtazilite premise, urged by ʿAbd al-Jabbār, is the soundness of our (God-given) faculties and intuitions, be they sensory or moral.[58]

But ʿAbd al-Jabbār does not extend the same confidence to mystical intuitions. *Maʿrifa*, he insists, just means knowledge. We have direct knowledge of our own mental states, crucially including our own volitions: We know that we make choices, that multiple courses lie open to us. And we do have knowledge by acquaintance, as when we recognize a face. Sensations are reliable (as in the Stoic "hydraulic" account) because they put us directly into contact with things—pace the occasionalists.[59] But God is known inferentially, not by acquaintance. Only primitive presentations are grasped without reflection, and God's existence and character are not among these. Even scripture is known to be true only through reliance on its Source. So it cannot establish (but only confirm) the existence and character of God. All beliefs based on tradition are mere dogma and hearsay (*taqlīd*). They may be true, but they do not bear the confirming seal of certitude; and often they are false, as witness the many conflicting claims made in the name of faith.

ʿAbd al-Jabbār's epistemology is polemical; its criticism, not reflexive but aimed sharply at dogmatic, mystical, and traditionalist adversaries. Yet comparable limitations can be found in many theories of knowledge that are given out today as paradigms of critical epistemology. Clearly more might have been made of the Muʿtazilite essays in epistemology, had the theological schools not turned quite so hard toward traditionalism, partly in reaction to the certitudes of the Muʿtazilites.

Just as the Stoics and Epicureans fought shy of Aristotelian conceptualism and Platonic realism, many Muslim thinkers offered reductionistic, anticonceptual models of knowing, defining knowledge as "mere remembering" or imaging (*khayāl*), or as the shadow and shape of what is known. But if the appeal to shadow and shape was literal, it was plainly false; if it was metaphoric, the metaphor cried out for resolution and naming of the actualities intended, as does the more commonplace image that speaks of knowledge as light. Appeals to memory or imagination are similarly unsatisfying. For memory still needs a subject, an object, and a link between them. That link is what we ask about when we inquire after knowledge.

Imaging, imagining, or fantasy similarly requires a subject and an object, if it is to be cognitive. The image of an image does not tell us how a subject and object meet cognitively. Models anchored here presuppose what they pretend to explain. Memories may prompt or precede conceptual knowledge in particular, but they do not reveal what it is. For anyone who hopes to budge beyond the dogmatic, or the circular, such stopgaps will not block the path to philosophy but only demand embarcation on it.

The same is true of pragmatic, formalistic, and functional definitions that speak of knowledge as an overcoming of ignorance and doubt, or as the object of desire, or (as if to anticipate Dewey or Ryle), as an attribute that enables orderly action. Heideggerians might be charmed by the Sufi claim of al-Ḥakīm Tirmidhī (d. 936) that "knowledge is the disclosure (*tajallī*) of things themselves."[60] But such accounts obscure more than they disclose. The idea of the Active Intellect took hold among Islamic thinkers because it arose in philosophical argument, offered to answer a question, and responded to the need to connect knowing with God.

The theory, as we have seen, stems from Aristotle's thought that in all classes of things there is a matter that is passive and potential, and an active, productive cause, analogous to the art that works up the matter of its medium. In the case of thinking, the prepared mind is the matter. When it acquires the concepts of things, it *becomes* those things in a certain way. Something must actualize the mind, render it actually not just potentially intelligent, as light renders actually visible what is in itself only potentially visible. That something is "another, that is what it is by virtue of making all things," just as the human mind "is what it is by virtue of becoming all things" (*De Anima* III 5, 430a 14–15).

Scholars have debated for centuries whether the Aristotelian mind was activated by an inner faculty or an external agency. But Aristotle's lifelong efforts to overcome the dichotomy between immanent and transcendent causality suggest that the obscurity lies less in Aristotle's vision than in the eye of the beholder. For Aristotle does understand thinking and discovery as acts of our individual minds, yet he denies that the mind simply actualizes itself, and he affirms (*Metaphysics* IX 8, 1049b 24–25) that the actual is ultimately always prior to the potential:

> Potential knowledge is prior in time to actual knowledge; but in absolute terms it is not prior even in time. The mind does not sometimes think and sometimes not think. When set free, it is just what it is and nothing more. This alone is immortal and eternal. We do not remember; for although the mind in this sense is impassible, as passive it is destructible. But without this nothing thinks. (*De Anima* III 5, 430a 20–26)[61]

Human intelligence, in its purity, is immortal. Freed from temporality, it is wholly actual. It is caught up in no progress from potency to act. But our life in this world is grounded entirely in such a process. So we have no Platonic recollection of the pure knowledge that a timeless mind enjoys. For memory comes with temporality. Embodied, as we are, we must learn rather than simply dig to recollect what we timelessly know. But the timeless within us remains at the root of all conceptual thought. Marshaling its powers and ordering its experience, the mind constructs our knowledge, drawing its raw material from experience.[62] Our discursive intelligence does not constitute itself. It does not supply the sensory data it needs, and its pure concepts are not innate. So it cannot fabricate conceptual tools out of sheer sensa. It needs help to initiate even the most practical of thought processes:

> One does not deliberate after first deliberating, which would itself presuppose prior deliberation. Rather there is some starting point. Nor does one think after first thinking about thinking, and so ad infinitum. Thought, then, is not the starting-point of thinking, nor deliberation of deliberation. What then can be except chance? So everything would come from chance? But perhaps there is a starting-point with none beyond it, that can act as it does by being the sort of thing it is. The object of our search is this: What is the start of movement in the soul? The answer is clear. As in the cosmos, so in the soul, it is god. For in a sense the divine element within us moves everything. The starting point of reasoning is not reasoning but something greater. And what could be greater even than knowledge and intellect but god? (*Eudemian Ethics* VII 14, 1248a 18–28)

The Active Intellect here is both external and our own, divine and within us. It activates thought by being what it is. That is, by being pure thought and pure actuality, the divine element within us realizes the mind as mind. By a god-given power we initiate our own deliberative processes and cap our cognitive progress with the conceptual knowledge whose timelessness bespeaks the immortality of the human mind, its affinity with divine intelligence.

Alexander of Aphrodisias, as we have seen, squarely identified the Active Intellect with God, the Prime Mover of the Aristotelian heavens. But he also saw the Active Intellect at work in our processes of thought, anchoring the capabilities that differentiate rationality from mindlessness. To make sense of this work of the Active Intellect, he spoke of a *nous thyrathen*, a mind within us that is externally derived.

Plotinus, in a text preserved in Arabic, returns to Aristotle's argument to explain just why such help is needed: Potentiality does not realize itself.[63] Later Neoplatonists, seeking to preserve the transcendence of the Highest from any compromising engagement with particularity, initiate the demotion of the Active Intellect that we find consummated in Fārābī. Thus a commentary ascribed to Philoponus reports that Proclus's disciple Marinus called the Active Intellect *daimonion*, quasi-divine—angelic, in the language that the Christian commentator prefers, language soon to be adopted by the philosophical translators who made over Greek theories into the idiom of Islam. A commentary preserved in Latin, and most likely from the pen of Philoponus himself cites anonymous thinkers who describe the Active Intellect as a being subordinate to God, "closer to ourselves, which sheds its influence upon our souls and perfects them."[64] Themistius (ca. 317–ca. 388), a pagan philosopher at the Christian imperial court of Constantinople, had enriched the theory by elaborating its imagery: If the Active Intellect is like light it must have a source and must enter human minds according to their varying capacities.

In his paraphrase of Aristotle's *De Anima*, Ḥunayn ibn Isḥāq shows little interest in a hypostatic Active Intellect. The obscure philosopher Bakr of Mosul resists such theories, arguing that it is the task of individual human minds to make universal judgments; the ideas enabling that work are innate. But Ḥunayn's son, Isḥāq, in translating Alexander's term *nous thyrathen*, makes it clear that this derived intelligence (*al-ʿaql al-mustafāḍ*) is the Active

Intellect, as received by the individual: He calls it "the received active intellect."[65] So the immanent and hypostatic aspects of the Active Intellect are present at its entry into Islamic epistemology. But its identity with God has been suppressed.

Kindī is drawn to the Active Intellect, apparently identifying it with the first of the disembodied intelligences that govern the celestial spheres. Some forms, he explains, have no matter or "fantasy" to them (he transliterates the Greek term for an imaginative projection). Such forms and the knowledge they represent are attained by the soul's "making contact" (*bāsharat*) with the higher Intellect that eternally thinks them. That is how a mind that is only potentially intellectual becomes actually intellectual. Just as the mind acquires the form of sensory objects abstracted from their matter and becomes the form it knows, so, in intellectual apprehension, the mind becomes its ideas. But it does not, Kindī insists, fuse with the Active Intellect.[66] The human soul is the form of man within us, Kindī argues. It derives from the very substance of the Creator, as light flows from the sun. It is simple, noble and perfect. Its substance is spiritual, and of immense dignity, as is plain from its antipathy to bodily appetites and passions. Clearly it is immortal, distinct and separable from the body.[67] But this does not mean that it is divine. It derives from God, but its being is not the same as His.

Still, to understand the soul as a spiritual, intellectual being, does explain how it is capable of knowing: It knows because the Active Intellect gives it the ideas of things.[68] The theory is laid out more fully by Fārābī. Like other philosophers who fell under the spell of Plato's arguments, Fārābī saw that the senses alone can never supply the universal and necessary laws that Aristotle found at the heart of science. For sense perception provides none of the terms distinctive to such judgments. Yet sense experience is not irrelevant. All human knowledge depends on it. The theory of the Active Intellect shows how conceptual knowledge is built on the hints provided by the senses: Just as the Bestower of Forms sheds reality on particulars by imparting specificity to matter, so does it give actuality to our minds, by imparting forms to our intelligence. It enables us to frame concepts. And it imparts the enlightenment of mystical awakening and prophetic inspiration.[69]

What gives being is naturally the source of understanding, since being, rightly understood, is the formal essence of things, and that is just what thought apprehends when it rises to the pitch of the universal and necessary. It is the work of the heavens, according to Fārābī's theory, as we have seen, to compound the bodies we find in nature and to govern the rhythms of their motions. But the Active Intellect imparts the forms. It scans the cosmos, and when it finds a being at a certain measure of perfection and separation from matter, that is, a human mind, it purifies it and draws it to itself by lighting up the traces of sensory data, transmuting them into concepts apprehensible to the mind.

It is by such means, as Fārābī argues in his *Principles underlying the Beliefs of the Inhabitants of the Virtuous State* and his *Civil Polity*, that we come to know the fundamental axioms of thought, for instance, that the whole is greater than its part or that equals of the same quantity are equal to each other. Given such axioms, we can construct not only arithmetic and geometry but axiology and all the natural sciences. In his *Essay on the Intellect*, Fārābī takes the primary truths for granted and assigns our knowledge of the truths of practical reason to experience. But he credits the Active Intellect with inspiring our ability to grasp the forms embedded in particulars. Besides being the realities of things, these forms are principles of value and intelligibility. Hence their centrality in knowledge. But primary knowledge of them is by acquaintance (*ṣādafa*). It is not propositional. The shift between Fārābī's two accounts may represent an effort to see the work of the Active Intellect at a deeper level than that of axioms. For Aristotle made terms and concepts the elements of propositions, and Plato argued that what underlies our knowledge, say, of the equals axiom, is an intuitive apprehension of the pure form of equality.

Individuals vary in their receptivity to concepts according to Fārābī. Some, indeed, may specialize, in view of their innate receptivities. But it is possible, not just in principle but in practice, for a human being to receive all the primary concepts and, with their aid, to attain adequate knowledge of all things: of natural things, by grasping the forms that constitute their natures and underwrite the accounts of the senses; and of disembodied things like the celestial Intelligences, by direct acquaintance. For light itself is not invisible.

When the human disposition for thought, the material or passive intellect, which Fārābī also calls our rational faculty or power, becomes an "actual intellect," it can serve in turn as the matter or substrate of the Active Intellect itself, which comes into contact (*ittiṣāl*) with it and is even described, in line with suggestions made by Plotinus (in the text known in Arabic as the *Theology of Aristotle*), Porphyry, and Shīʿite theology, as uniting with it, dwelling within it, or raising it nearly to its own rank. The "nearly" is important, if the ancient pagan legacy and its continuing pantheistic resonances in Sufi theory and Shīʿite immanentist theology are to be kept under control and not allowed to swamp the monotheistic framework. But the elevation of the human mind by the Active Intellect is critical, since it enables Fārābī to explain the possibilities of immortality, mystical experience, and the comprehensive inrush of ideas found in prophecy:

> The Active Intellect is what should be understood by the 'Faithful Spirit' or 'Holy Spirit' (Qur'ān 26:139, 2:87). This is what should be deemed the vehicle of revelation to one who is a prophet, the intermediary between God on high and a man inspired Human felicity would mean the soul's coming under its sway. And the Active Intellect itself should be seen as man's Overseer, giving any human being the basis on which happiness is to be won, guiding us and showing us the way to well being. Or if God is seen as the giver of these things, He does so through the Active Intellect.[70]

Prophets require imagination and its gifts of poetry and rhetoric if they are to translate their universal grasp of reality into the symbols, myths, rituals and institutions that will give ordinary human beings practical access to the higher truths that philosophers have gleaned. But the knowledge underlying true prophecy does not differ from that of the mystic or the philosopher. A lower type of prophet, whose mind is not perfected, may work at the level of images, unselfconsciously influenced by the play of the Active Intellect on the imagination. The higher type is a philosopher whose gifts enable him to translate conceptual knowledge into images, words, and laws. But if the prophecy is real and not just a trick of the imagination, the ideas that inform it are the same as those of the philosopher, even when their mouthpiece does not grasp them conceptually. And prophets from different cultures, whose work is articulated in diverse systems of law, custom, myth, and symbol, all voice one message, if their inspiration is genuine and not self-serving, erroneous or perverse. The images may differ, as languages do, but the underlying truths are the same.

What had been a sentence or two in Kindī's "Essay on the Intellect," and a mere caution in Fārābī has become a key thesis in Avicenna: The soul does not unite with the Active Intellect. Human minds retain their identity even in when disembodied. Platonically that is an issue, since knowing is achieved by the uniting of subject with object, and immortality is attained by knowing. The Platonic soul, through knowledge, reverts to its primal status as an eternal, intellectual being and so would seem to shed not only its links to physicality but also its individuality. But Avicenna insists that the fulfilled or enlightened soul, to have the knowledge that is its immortality, must remain a subject and so must retain its individuality.

Taking a hint from Fārābī, who differentiated disembodied souls by the traces of their former linkage with diverse bodies, Avicenna ascribes an origin and history to every soul. These distinguish souls from one another, and from the Active Intellect. Porphyry was wrong to hold that the enlightened mind unites with the Active Intellect. If there were such a union, Avicenna argues, then either the Active Intellect would be hopelessly divided against itself or one who knew anything would know everything. The persistent temporality of our consciousness indelibly marks its uniqueness and thus protects its individuality. The human mind may *intend* divinity, whether in the Absolute or as mediated by the Active Intellect, but we cannot merge with it.[71]

Avicenna's respect for Fārābī seems undiminished by the need to clarify his predecessor's more sympathetic references to the idea of union. For epistemically at least union is unnecessary. The illumination provided by the Active Intellect will suffice for immortality. And, as Kindī says in the passage that opens the whole issue among the philosophers of Islam, a mind can be identical with its ideas without becoming identical with their Source.

Avicenna's motives in preserving the individuality of the disembodied soul are threefold: First, he retains divine transcendence, avoiding the immanentist pantheism of the more radical Shīʿites and Sufis. Second, he retains individual immortality, overcoming the Platonic risk of losing individuality in the divine totum. Third, and perhaps most importantly for our humanistic quest, he affirms the inviolability of the human subject. The import of this affirmation far outruns the appetite for eternal life. It rests on Avicenna's recognition of the phenomenological primacy and ontic primitiveness of individual consciousness. That recognition is as pivotal in Avicenna's psychology as is his idea of conditioned necessity (or ontic contingency) in his metaphysics. It is as central to the philosophic foundations of humanism as was Descartes's phenomenology. For the I that speaks in its own voice, the I of Augustine or Descartes, Cervantes, Hamadhānī, or Avicenna, the I that situates the world around itself, as in a renaissance painting, and thereby situates itself within the world, is the heart and soul of humanism.

Complementing Avicenna's ontology of the rational soul is his epistemic account of the work of that soul. Here too his deep humanism finds expression. It is still widely supposed that Francis Bacon, in overthrowing the idols of the mind, set the inductive method firmly on the throne too long and too unquestioningly held by a priori deduction. But Aristotle credits Socrates with devising induction as a method, eliciting a common theme or pattern from the seemingly disparate materials of experience. And that method was intimately conjoined with the other great methodological achievements of Socrates: dialogue, dialectic, analysis, and definition. Even Plato's theory of Forms arose through the Socratic inductive method. And it was Aristotle, not Bacon, who first broke clear of Plato's deductivism, replacing definitions and analysis with syllogistic and proposing that the bull's-eye of the syllogism, when logic is viewed as a method of discovery, is not the nominal conclusion of the syllogism but the middle term that links extremes, allowing intelligence to discover what seemingly disparate classes have in common and where things differ that are seemingly alike.

Avicenna himself, despite the seeming deductivism of his appeal to pure concepts, contributed inventively to the growth of inductive logic. He incorporated modal values and propositional terms into Aristotle's syllogistic, guided in part by the logical writings of Galen, the author who most influenced his medical work. Galen took seriously the Stoic propositional calculus; and, following in Galen's tradition, Avicenna elaborates a logic of hypotheticals that absorbs the Stoic theory of signs. The synthesis enables Avicenna to schematize a conditional with multiple antecedents and a common consequent: "If this man has a chronic fever, hard cough, labored breathing, shooting pains, and rasping pulse, he has pleurisy."[72] Here Avicenna lays a groundwork for the idea of a syndrome as he pioneers in the diagnosis of a specific disease.

Following up on the theory of signs, Avicenna's medical writings use the methods of agreement, difference, and concomitant variation that are critical to a scientific method.[73] Indeed, if we add modern notions about the regression of multiple variables and quantified probability, we can find in Avicenna's hypothetical syllogism a basis for risk factor analysis. Yet neither the theory of signs nor the logic of hypotheticals leads Avicenna to the notion of a controlled experiment, any more than his interest in observation in medicine and astronomy leads him to the critical significance of quantitative precision in science, a significance that will one day all but eclipse the Aristotelian and ultimately Empedoclean concern with the qualitative.

While key elements of an inductive method are present in Avicenna, they do not loom large, perhaps because he is not convinced that brute empiricism (the empiricism of enumeration, unaided by thematic concepts) can provide the intellectual content needed in sound theories of nature. Nor does he believe that such theories are the sole or highest aims of inquiry. Avicenna pursues an integrated body of knowledge and seeks an integrated epistemology in service of that aim. So his epistemological achievements complement our own. They balance our faith in empiricism with a complementary faith in reason, as a portal to the kind of totality that allows a theory to be universal and necessary—and a portal, as well, to a comprehensive vision of reality.

Reason here is not an artifact of its own devising, still less a construct of psychic or social bias or power hunger. Quaintly or reassuringly, Avicenna gives little thought to the varieties of relativism that dog the heels of modern epistemologies. Reason, for him, is a divine gift, made effectual through our own responses to its play upon our minds. Rāzī had said all along that rationality is inspired. And, as Kindī expected, the reach of reason extends beyond mere matters of fact to the values that invest all being, and rise (as Melville might have put it) to the topmost heavens. Thus even Rāzī will hold that the least degree of (independent) thinking grants one a share in immortality. And Fārābī is prepared to explain how that can be. For understanding anything, as Fārābī saw, means apprehending its value in its own terms, and in that understanding lies a share in the beatific vision.

Our first certainty, Avicenna argues, is that of the senses. They reveal not just phenomena but being. But the idea of being, which we affix to the objects of the senses, is prior epistemically even to sensation: It is a primitive, supplied to the mind from above. Our second certainty, again prompted by experience, is that being is not necessary in itself but contingent. Aided by the recognition that whatever exists but need not must have a cause, we learn of the Necessary Being, the absolute condition of all that is conditioned.

Beyond the external senses, we have "internal" senses—"estimation," for example, which grasps the "intention" or significance of things (not just "grey mass in motion" but "wolf approaching"), and the *sensus communis*, which integrates our sensory givens. Other faculties regulate our receptivity and retention of percepts and our ability to re-present or project them as images and to combine and separate them in fantasy or dreaming. Avicenna assigns all these faculties to the Aristotelian "animal soul," since they involve our sensibility and reactiveness and all have counterparts in beasts. He also gives them locations in the brain. He uses the language of faculty psychology, but less to explain than to describe, carrying the functional analysis to a high pitch, especially by comparison with theories that routinely identify memory, say, with image making.

The rational soul uses the data of the senses, as integrated and interpreted by the internal senses. But it faces in two directions: downward, toward the body, in its practical role, as a governor; and upward, toward the intellectual realm, in its speculative capacity. With the aid of the Active Intellect, it can transmute sensory images into ideas. Modern notions of abstraction may not do justice to that transformation. It cannot be just a matter of leaving something out (as the word abstraction might suggest). For sensory images do not yet contain ideas. Nor is the notion of generalization of much help. That presumes the concepts to be generalized. What Avicenna wants to know is how concepts come into play at all. His answer seems to be that the mind constructs them on the sketchwork of our sensory images, using the pure ideas and "operators" (as a modern logician might call them) that the Active Intellect makes accessible.

While still uninformed by ideas, the rational soul is called potential or material, as a child is said to have the potential to write, meaning that she can learn to write. Once opened up to the primary ideas or axioms, which are too fundamental to be taught and on which our ability to grasp more complex ideas depends, the rational soul is called *intellectus in habitu*, or actual intelligence. Now it is capable of reasoning. But when actually contemplating the forms, it is called acquired or derived intellect, since these ideas are induced in it by the Active Intellect.

The mind's responsiveness to ideas is *hads*, intuition. When such intuitive receptivity is strong and active, knowledge seems to flow from within rather than emanate from beyond the mind. At its peak, such responsiveness is that rare quality called a spirit divine. For both the sensitivity and the ideas stem from God. They may affect the imagination as well as the intellect; and, as Fārābī explained, they lay the basis of prophecy:

> There might be a man whose soul has so intense a purity and is so firmly linked to the rational principles that he blazes with intuition, that is, receptivity to inspiration from the Active Intellect, regarding everything, so that the forms of all things within in the Active Intellect are imprinted on his soul, all at once, or nearly so. Not that he accepts them blindly. He grasps them rationally, by their logic, comprehending all the middle terms. For there is no certainty in accepting blindly ideas that are to be known through their causes. This is a kind of prophetic inspiration, indeed, the highest, and the one most worthy to be called a divine power. It is the loftiest power a human being can reach.[74]

Prophets are not freaks, nor are they charlatans, as Rāzī supposed. Rather they are thinkers whose minds or imaginations are touched by the source of all rationality in nature and beyond it. Mystics too are not creatures of paradox but thinkers whose minds are flooded with the awareness that flows forth eternally from the Timeless to the temporal. For the Active Intellect does not confine its light to prophetic leaders. Purity of mind can bring glimpses at first and then enduring contact with the intellectual realm. An *ʿaql qudsī*, a sacred mind, is continually lit up by that contact.[75] Here, as Walzer was fond of saying, Avicenna unites the two highest values of Greek and Hebraic thought, intelligence and holiness.

Despite his vehement criticism of Avicenna in *The Incoherence of the Philosophers*, Ghazālī uses Avicenna's explanation of the continued individuality of the soul after death. As we have noted, he accepts Avicenna's view that once it has had a history even a disembodied mind is unique forever. And he agrees that if two minds were one, as the old idea of monopsychism suggests, then (*per impossibile*) they would share one consciousness. So the privacy of consciousness and the fact that you and I know different things are sufficient proof that our individuality endures even after the destruction of the body that has grounded that individuality throughout our natural lives.

Ibn Bājjah, Ibn Ṭufayl, and Maimonides all turn to Avicenna for aid in explaining the soul's individuation. Ibn Bājjah (d. 1139), follows Aristotle, Avicenna, and an insight of his own, to argue that minds (like ideas) can retain their identity even in a larger totum–as the many parts of Ṭabarī's History are united by their common purpose.[76] Ibn Ṭufayl projects the vision of just such a unity of discrete identities at the climax of Ḥayy Ibn Yaqẓān's beatific experience. He argues that once matter is left behind, identity and difference are no longer relevant; disembodied minds are neither the same as nor different from one another. They are a many-in-one, in the source that has inspired them. Difference, Ibn Ṭufayl insists, is a matter of degree, but in essence it is alienation, failure of the mind to break free of the trammels of the body, to apprehension of God's unity. Unitive experience, as Avicenna had held, can steady from the vanishing sparks of its first appearance to a lambent flame. In the light of that flame, all prior knowledge, sensory reports, discursive reason, philosophy itself, are seen to be mere preparations for the consummatory vision, not set aside but transcended. Yet even the purest thought does not make us identical with what we behold.[77]

Maimonides writes that Ibn Bājjah and others of his bent cleared up the arithmetic of disembodied souls, by showing that the notion of multiplicity does not apply to things that are neither bodies nor forces within a body, unless (as with the Intellects of the spheres) one is the cause of another: "But what survives of Zayd is neither the cause nor the effect of what survives of ʿUmar. They form a single totality, as Abū Bakr b. al-Ṣā'igh (Ibn Bājjah) made clear."[78] Maimonides does seem less worried by monopsychism than Avicenna or Ghazālī was. Averroes adopts it.[79] He discards the hypostatic *dator formarum*, faulting Avicenna for splitting natural beings in two, as it were, and not allowing a natural cause to impart substantial forms, as man, for example, engenders man. But, where he naturalizes other beings, Averroes elevates the rational soul, arguing that conceptual knowledge would be impossible for us if the human intellect, insofar as it is active, were not identical with the supernal Active Intellect. As Davidson writes, "Averroes remained firm throughout his career regarding the active intellect's nature."[80] It was a hypostatic being, the precondition of all actual conceptual thinking. With increasing confidence as his thought matured, Averroes found in the Active Intellect the final resting place of the human rational soul and, indeed, that soul's unseen identity.[81]

Averroes's surrender of substantial forms to their natural causes but elevation of the human mind to the realm of timeless, undivided thought, prefigures the Cartesian split between thought and extension. Where Avicenna, much in the spirit of Aristotle, had tried to bridge the gap between rationalism and empiricism, by taking the images of things as hints and cues that pure ideas can raise to the pitch of concepts, Averroes insists that concepts must be given and are not to be constructed. Our access to them points not to the capabilities of the mind but to its ultimate identity, if not with God then with His still necessary hypostasis, the Active Intellect.

Ghazālī too parts company with Avicenna epistemologically, but not in the same direction. Plato's rational intuition and Aristotle's active receptivity are now displaced by Sufi intuition (*dhawq*), direct experience of the divine. Sufi exercises may prepare the mind, but unitive experience is nothing that human acts can promise. It comes by God's grace and is known only to its adepts. Paradox and ineffability mask the abyss at whose edge it plays. For it does dance at the edge of pantheism. Only the sheerest and most subtly woven tissue of mental and linguistic discipline prevents the mystic, who "sees God in all things" from plunging headlong into the blasphemous claim to identity with the Godhead. As Ghazālī writes, appropriating a line of verse: "It *was*—what it was don't ask me to say. / Think the best, but don't make me describe it away."[82]

Mystic experience for Ghazālī is a way of knowing, self-certifying and self-sufficient. It validates and sustains religious faith. What it takes from tradition are the intellectual and practical categories that interpret the experience and assign meaning to the signs the mystic will encounter in his quest. Mystic experience voids the skeptic's doubts, not by answering but by eclipsing them. As mystics have remarked since Stoic times, "One does not need a candle to see the sun."

We find a curious symmetry here. For Ghazālī disempowers nature in just the way that Averroes enlivens it. But Averroes elevates what is intellectual in us, locating human rationality not beside but within the Active Intellect, even as Ghazālī accentuates the distance between the two, by making their contact dependent (as his Ashʿarite theology would require) on God's free grace. In an important sense the difference is sheerly nominal. For, as Ghazālī argues in His mystical writings, God's light never goes out, "He is with everything at every moment."[83] In another sense, the difference is of critical import. For both Averroes and Ghazālī modulate the constancy of human access to that light. But for Averroes it is purity of intellect that makes the difference in one's access to the divine. For Ghazālī what makes the difference is construed confessionally—as Rāzī might have feared. To a humanism that cares rather little whether election is a matter of confessional grace or intellectual receptivity, both sides of that divide may look painfully elitist. What seems most precious, perhaps, is Avicenna's effort to assign intellectual capabilities to the human mind qua human and to impute intellectual fulfillment to the conjoint action of the human mind and the divine reaching out, as it were, toward one another.

That Avicennan moment is lost for the nonce, or frozen, like the poignant moment on the Sistine Chapel Ceiling that might be its emblem, in which God and man reach out toward one another. Averroes too is lost, despite the efforts of a few secularists and one filmmaker to recover him as a culture hero, modeled, perhaps, less on his own ideals than theirs. What holds the ground in normative Islam lies closer to Ghazālī's vision. And if Ghazālī compromised to make his synthesis seem credible, what survives is less his metaphysical detente with Avicenna than his existential entente with Sufism. But the comfort he found in the Sufi way, the *sukūn al-nafs* that gave him respite from his metaphysical doubts, came at a price.

Just as there is a routinization of charisma in the succession of guides that may aid the aspirant along the mystic's path, so there is a scholasticism of mystic experience. Tradition hardens and primogeniture tightens its grip where once there was the glint of inspiration. And tradition is not all that may darken insight and stiffen the dance. If study can be sublimated into ecstasy, it may also displace it, pushing the ideal of contemplation toward a rigidity that only antinomian excess or frenzies of fanaticism may seem able to break.

Learning, as in the erudition of *ḥadīth,* can edge out the warmth of practice or the glow of comprehension. For *ḥadīth* is the gateway to the *sunna* and performance of God's will. Orthodoxy privileges such learning. Even an Ibn ʿArabī will soak his mystic virtuosity in *ḥadīth*.[84] What, then, becomes of the larger learning? Ghazālī leaves a place for medicine, jurisprudence, even astronomy in the pious life, and not just as concessions to the world. For such disciplines provide a background of understanding and analogues of the special knowledge that a prophet brings, which lies closest to the truth we find in dreaming. Astrology, with its pagan premises and shaky conjectures, does not.[85] Nor does the frivolous erudition of those who immerse themselves in poesy or tribal genealogies of the Arabs. But what is precious is the knowledge that holymen possess: "This knowledge is not attained through the various sciences in which people busy themselves. For their knowledge only makes them bolder in defying God. But genuine knowledge makes one more reverent and filled with awe.[86] Here Ghazālī returns to the primal opposition between the teaching and lore of the Prophet and the merely human wisdom of his predecessors. Both realms have been enlarged by conquest and the growth of culture. But the hope that either might illuminate the other has faded markedly, and the contrast between them has grown lurid. Ghazālī still holds ajar a door between the two, but the opening is conditional, even coy: Nothing is of real value but the vision of God's face. All things else are instrumental, mirrors or mechanisms, if not toys, worthless or vicious distractions. The test of knowledge is its use in carrying us toward God, and the height of knowledge is found not in learning for its own sake but in apprehension of God's face.

4

The Rise of Universal Historiography

Arabic history writing itself has a history that graphically testifies to the gradual ascendence of synthetic modes of presentation—and thought. Not that thought inevitably follows exposition. But synthesis, especially of a higher order, demands written exposition, if only as its worktable, and the vast and unmanageable materials of history do need a worktable. Initially, we might suppose, history writing would be linear, represented, perhaps, in ancient chronicles and annals. But in historiography, as with consciousness at large, a linear view of time is itself, as Kant suggests it would be, a signal achievement of synthetic understanding.

The earliest Semitic records of historical awareness, Margoliouth observed, are prose narratives pegged to some surviving bit of poetry that is at once their pretext and their treasure, the object from the past, whose story the narrative sets out to tell and, by explaining, to preserve.[1] Franz Rosenthal instances the striking poesy of the Song of Deborah at Judges 5, and the triumphal hymns of Moses and Miriam at Exodus 15.[2] In each of these, a tiny particle (the *vav* consecutive of Deborah's song, and the analogous *'az*, "then" of the Song of Moses)[3] confirms this understanding: The prose narrative is a setting for the ancient song: "Then it was that Moses (or Deborah) sang . . ." That same *'az* is echoed in the Qur'ānic *'idh*, which introduces biblical tales as case studies in divine world management. As Khalidi writes:

> The Qur'ān pans over a landscape where time is less a chronology than a continuum, where Abraham, Moses, Jesus and Muḥammad are all described in a grammatical tense which one is tempted to call the eternal present The whole of history is present at once to God. Within this design, events are arranged in clusters, repetitive in form. This means that the Qur'ānic *qissa*, or tale is closer in function and meaning to a "case in point," an "affair" or even a "parable" than it is to a story or narrative. "As when (*'idh*) Joseph . . ." or "as when Moses . . ." is a common introductory phrase. . . . To know God is, among other things, to

> recognize the overwhelming evidence of His presence in the past: "Have they not journeyed in the land and seen how those before them met their end." (30:9)[4]

The pre-Islamic *ayyām*, tales of battle-days, and the Islamic *khabar* literature are less monitory, more celebratory. They add a note of secular or sacralized triumphalism, situating events amidst the personalities that made them.[5] But they do not typically situate incidents relative to one another. Genealogy is eminently more sinewy. But genealogical history can make an awfully thin gruel. Thus the stark linkages of Genesis 10. The more ornamented begats of Genesis 4–5 *are* relieved by incident—Lamech's boast, or the lapidary mention of the origins of animal husbandry, music, and metal tools (4:20–21). Here the biblical narrative gains the depth of historical perspective: Techne, like the cosmos, has a history. So do human laws and moral institutions. Thus, in Lamech's boast, the text pinions, without comment, the ethos of disproportionate vengeance that forms the backdrop to its own ethic of law and equity. The vista helps the Torah define its vantage point, setting the scene for the central event in its narrative, the giving of the Law.

Genesis figures human art and industry as continuing where God's creative work left off. Culture heroes are named but not especially celebrated. Their arts are milestones, but not supernatural gifts. The cosmological narrative is progressive, developmental: Land and sky precede the plants; plants are readied before the birth of animals. Likewise with culture, there is a progression, and the emergence of a system. As Cyrus Gordon wrote: "Tubal-Cain, the prototype of the metallurgists, worked with iron and copper (Gen. 4:22). The Hebrew author knows that without iron and copper, the technology of the culture known to the Hebrews would be unthinkable. Tubal-Cain's brother was Jubal (Gen. 4:21), the forerunner of all musicians who play both stringed and wind instruments."[6] But the cultural sequence is not figured on cosmogony. Rather, the epochs are arrayed on the loom of genealogy: Religion arose in the time of Enosh (4:26). Like Adam he is an eponym of humanity. But he is not a child of the earth like Adam but the instigator of a spiritual quest. Again in genealogical sequence, we receive the telegraphic news that Enoch, the eponym of learning and instruction, "walked with God" (5:21–24).[7] Lamech, whose braggart machismo makes him an antitype to the calm and humble Moses, with his trust in law and its due measure, is humanized by mention of the comfort he took in the birth of Noah, reflected in Noah's name, which means repose (Gen. 4:23–24, 5:28–29).[8] Anecdote imparts color, and color begets understanding.

Thus, in the biblical account of David's triumph over Goliath (1 Sam. 17–18), Saul does inquire of David's lineage, once the Philistine challenger has been dispatched. But the pedigree is briefly stated (1 Sam. 17:58), almost anticlimactic. For David will be king not by his birthright but despite it. Yet words do matter, like those the women sang on David's triumph: "Saul has stricken in his thousands; David, in his myriads!" (18:7). That refrain will vex Saul's troubled mind (18:8) and will be parroted by the wily courtiers of King

Achish of Gat (21:11). What counts in anecdotal history is motive, personal intent—Saul's promise of wealth and his daughter to the slayer of Goliath, Jonathan's unwavering love for David,[9] Michal's less steady love for the acclaimed hero. Details matter—young David's scornful dismissal by his brothers (17:28), his fighting experience, with a lion and a bear, the inability of the slender youth to do battle in Saul's armor, his lack of a sword, the language of Goliath's and David's taunts and challenges (17:43–47), the number of stones in David's leather pouch.

David's ancestry will one day be a topic of consequence (Ruth 4:18–22). And even more so, the lineage of his progeny. But the story of his Moabite roots, like the promises of dominion to his descendants, is no part of David's story and is not set in parataxis with it. The occasion of his psalmody, however (Ps. 34:1 and 1 Sam. 21:14), is a matter of moment. Like the song of Moses or Deborah it is remembered as an ancient and inspired utterance.

Anecdotal vignettes are powerful devices in history, as in literature, since they capture the imagination and take hold in memory, painting the nuances of complex or conflicting motives. The reconstructed speeches set down in Thucydides' *History* are as crisp as the latest insider accounts of intrigue, nobility, duplicity, or self-sacrifice. Vividness eclipses mere chronology, but it can also mask the deeper causes of events, even when the anecdotes are wholly veracious. Rarely, of course, are they utterly reliable. Events may be woven from the whole cloth or served up from precooked ingredients. The bricolage of narrative applies and reapplies old topoi to new uses, whether in the zeal of partisan back-projection or simply to extract the narrative juices of a good story. Thus, in Umayyad history, we find noteworthy sayings "attached to the wrong persons; sometimes owing to identity of name, sometimes to confusion of personalities who had something in common. Muʿāwiya and ʿAbd al-Malik were the most eminent of the Umayyad Caliphs, and there was not a little in their characters which was similar; hence the same tale is told of both."[10]

History needs diachronic time just as astronomy needs parallax, to objectify distance and distinguish real from apparent magnitude. Without a firm chronology, the recent past rapidly sinks into the deeper abyss. Social memory, without some transgenerational ordering principle, merges the doings of the last generation with archaic antiquity—as witness the primal myths that some island folklores have attached to events as recent as the crash landing of a World War II airplane. So Ṭabarī marks a turning point when he completes his account of antediluvian history by cataloguing (on the authority of such predecessors as Zuhrī and Ibn Isḥāq) the eras by which historical time has been measured.[11]

Even to carve a single sequence of events from the mass of actual and potential data demands formidable critical and dialectical skills. To treat such a sequence causally, as a chain of related happenings to be followed systematically, calls for inquiries and interests that *khabar* history only begins to educate and stimulate. It needs standards of relevance and definite ideas about agency and destiny.

The Birth of Arabic Historiography

The romantic appeal of *khabar* literature is oral.[12] Each event is a set piece responsive to the marvel or other emotive response of an audience. But even in the earliest documented Islamic *akhbār*, the events surrounding Muḥammad's life have already given a definite focus to what might otherwise have remained a literature of sensation or sheer *ʿasabiyya*, that is, tribalism. Even before the rise of Islam we hear of savants like the Prophet's contemporary Naḍr b. Ḥārith (d. ca. 624), who knew the heroic tales of Iran. And soon after the birth of the new religion the caliph ʿUmar commissioned Makhrama b. Nawfal al-Zuhrī to collaborate with ʿAlī's older brother ʿAqīl on a register of the Arab tribes.

Genealogy was an ancient practice, registering claims to noble birth, patrimony, or a heroic heritage. But it gained a further valence in Islam. In Muʿāwiya's time one Daghfal acquired the surname al-Nassāba, "the Genealogist," in recognition of his work recording the affiliations (and so establishing the entitlements) of the living descendants of those who had aided the Prophet and his successors in winning the Islamic empire.[13] But beyond the romance of ancient lore and the sensitive issues of precedence among Muslims, records and recollections of the Prophet's times acquired a vital significance in establishing Islamic law, ritual, and morals—and, of course, in the armamentum of sectarian struggles, for example, between the Shīʿites and Sunnites.

Abū Dāʾūd registers a tradition that forbids writing down *hadīths*. But cheek by jowl with that, he records another mandating such writing. The latter is the one he heeds, as do all the gleaners of tradition whose work becomes canonical in Islam. Even the Prophet's Companions are said to have kept records. So, not much later than the first attested mention of oral transmitters of Arabic genealogical data and *ayyām*, there are "records, *kutub*, which deal monographically with *akhbār*"—such as accounts of a particular battle. These are "circumstantial evidence that the written monograph or pamphlet was the normal mode of expression from the middle of the 8th century, even if the transmissal is still effected by dictation." The *ijāza*, a written license to "pass on," that is teach, material learned by dictation, rested on written documents, a text to be copied.[14] In the lecture format, orality was notionally preserved. But history was written.

ʿUrwah ibn al-Zubayr (ca. 643/4–ca. 712) seems to have written the first connected accounts of Muḥammad's raids and early career. His accounts include the Prophet's first revelatory experience. He also wrote of later developments: the wars of the Ridda and the battles of Qādisiya and Yarmuk, in the end covering all the important events connected with the rise of Islam–and with good reason. He was the son of the Prophet's companion Zubayr b. al-ʿAwwām and of Asmāʾ, daughter of the first caliph, Abū Bakr. His mother's sister ʿĀʾisha was the Prophet's wife and long surviving widow, and his elder brother was the well-known claimant to the caliphate ʿAbdullāh Ibn Zubayr. ʿUrwah was too young to fight at the Battle of the Camel (656) in his kinsmen's civil war against ʿAlī. He became a man of letters, conveying information from his revered aunt, gathering traditions of historical, juridical and ritual significance, and contributing much that set the tone and tenor of Islamic piety. But he did support his family's dynastic claims and more than once represented their interests diplomatically. When their cause was defeated in 692, he made his way to Damascus bringing the news to the caliph ʿAbd al-Malik, even ahead of the victorious Ḥajjāj.

Pardoned for his role in the rebellion, ʿUrwah returned to learned work at Medina and soon was writing historical narratives in response to the caliph's queries. The letters bearing his replies, preserved in Ṭabarī and Ibn Hishām, are longish and direct, taking advantage of the freedom of the epistolary format, which would evolve into the Arabic essay genre. One describes, in only partly legendary terms, Muḥammad's first pitched battle against Meccan forces at Badr. Lacking absolute dates, the accounts have the flavor of *ḥadīth*, ʿUrwah's forte. But the *isnād*s are rather casual by later standards, or lacking altogether. After all, ʿUrwah did know the principals personally.[15]

Muḥammad b. Muslim b. Shihāb al-Zuhrī (ca. 670–ca. 741), ʿUrwah's chief disciple, is named by Duri as the first true historian of his age.[16] He wrote on genealogy and the reigns of the early caliphs, bringing method and critical scrutiny to the *khabar* and *ḥadīth* materials he collected. Identifying the landmark happenings, he periodized the phases of the Prophet's career, carefully sequencing his materials and dating the key events. He was known for the rigor of his *isnād*s, as gauged by the evolving standards, but he also introduced the "collective *isnād*," citing several authorities for a given account, rather than report numerous variants discretely. For he valued a continuous narrative progression. The earnest of his sobriety is his filtering out of most of the *qiṣāṣ* or fabular materials that others might have used, and his discipline in using the poetry he loved. He does not want his history to become a mere album of literary occasions.

Of ʿUrwa and Zuhrī, Duri writes: "The accounts of these authors are distinguished by their candor and their essentially humane character." Rarely, he adds, do they succumb to the penchant for exaggeration found in later authors. Nor do they indulge the Umayyad court's appetite for an overlay of destiny on the historical account. Indeed, Duri finds in them a naturalism comfortably nestled alongside their excursions into sacred history: "the deeds of the Prophet are sometimes presented as actions of divine inspiration, and yet in other situations are deemed nothing more than practical human initiative, as, for example, in the story of the Battle of the Ditch."[17]

Zuhrī's student, Mūsā b.ʿUqbah (d. 758–59) "collated the raids," compiling what Joseph Schacht saw as one of the first actual books of Islamic history, organized around the military campaigns that marked the rise of Islam.[18] Elements of this work, originally in ten parts, survive as a brief collection of *akhbār*, termed an anthology by Guillaume. The extant samples are tendentious, still reflecting the familial and sectarian interests of Ibn Zubayr. But it is hard to imagine that Ibn ʿUqbah gave the raids any but a chronological order. For they were not disparate episodes but stages in a remarkable course of events with an outcome known to all. Their sequence had the force of a developmental progression.

In shaping the idea of history and priming the historian's canvas, which is time itself, the pivotal figure, however, was the often disparaged Wahb ibn Munabbih (d. 728). Wahb may well have been of Jewish origin. He was steeped in Jewish lore, and in one text, as we have seen, cites the wise sayings he saw written in the margins of a Hebrew Bible.[19] His father had come to the Yemen from Herat, sent by Chosroes, and embraced Islam while Muḥammad was still living. Renowned for his piety and asceticism, Wahb became a *qāḍī* at Sanaa, and his writings show a fierce loyalty to Yemenite traditions. His reading of the Jewish scriptures was said to have turned him away from an early penchant for qadarism, but he was imprisoned and flogged toward the end of his life, perhaps for some lingering sense of commitment to such voluntarism. Like Mūsā, Wahb wrote a book on the *maghāzī*, fragments of which survive.[20] But it was his love of *Isrāʾīliyyāt*, fragments or fabrications of Jewish lore, of biblical or midrashic provenance and often fanciful content, that endeared him to many—and put off many others.[21] For the Isrāʾīliyyāt, like the *ḥadīth* at large, permit a kind of displacement: Materials of a certain sort are assigned to a seemingly suitable source. As Vajda writes:

> The practice of introducing folklore themes (such as the motif of the "three wishes") into narratives set in the time of the *Banū Isrāʾīl* is one which the moralists and men of letters readily adopted. It was the works of pure imagination of this kind, and also the extravagant flights of fancy of the *quṣṣāṣ* in their over-loaded and embellished versions of the histories of the prophets which have caused the *Isrāʾīlīyāt* to be condemned by strict scholars such as Ibn Kathīr.[22]

Al-Sakhawī too(1427–97) deemed Wahb's reports, "unworthy of serious historians," as Duri notes: "Wahb was not a scrupulous writer, and was not above making false allegations. For this reason he is to be regarded as no more than a narrator and storyteller. . . . He articulated a point of view which, compared to the approach of the *ḥadīth* scholars of Medina, was distorted and weak."[23] Gibb echoes similar appraisals. He favors historical narratives that are unsmudged by legendary material. He sharply contrasts methods that entertain elements of the fabulous (or foreign) with the more "empirical" technique of the adepts of *ḥadīth*. Nonetheless, Wahb's *Mubtadaʾ* was the first Arabic essay at universal history. Inspired by the biblical model, Wahb began his story with the creation and projected the entire history of the world, in keeping with the Prophet's own vision of the past, as the unfolding of divine revelation.

As the Hebrew scriptures became somewhat less exotic territory, historians like Ibn Kathīr, Sakhawī, and Ibn Qutayba did not hesitate to establish their own critical standards by trading on the opprobrium of Jewish or Judaizing informants. The near synonymy of midrashic materials with folklore and legend gave the historians a rhetorically safe way of distinguishing factual data from sacred history: Who, they demanded, would draw traditions from the *Isrāʾīliyyāt*? But Ṭabarī's Qur'ān commentary used Wahb's materials freely.[24] And it was traditions like those that Wahb gathered, made welcome and even needful in Islam by the almost riddling allusiveness of the Qur'ānic text, that gave Muslim historians the cosmic framework that would impart grandeur, structure, and direction to their historic vision.

Ibn Isḥāq (ca. 704–768), the biographer of Muḥammad, exemplifies the early movement from the anecdotal to the chronological and thematic. Written at the invitation of the caliph Manṣūr and prepared from an extensive gathering of original sources, including old poems, his *Sīra* found its unity in the powerful interest of its subject. The life and career of the Prophet afforded a clear principle of selection, and the collective *isnād* allowed Ibn Isḥāq to "extract an engaging story,"[25] preserving the sense of drama in what plainly were dramatic events.

Ibn Isḥāq set his story against a cosmic backdrop and gave it a universal perspective by prefacing the work magniloquently with the history of all revelations since the creation. Naturally he used the *Isrāʾīliyyāt*. Later *ḥadīth* scholars did not respect his rigor in what had by then become their special province; in legal matters they did not accept his traditions. Indeed, Ibn Isḥāq earned the enmity of Mālik b. Anas. Some said that was because he (like other authorities on the *maghāzī*) was suspected of Shīʿite sympathies or *qadarite* leanings. Others blamed his reliance on the offspring of Jewish converts to Islam for his accounts of Muḥammad's depredations against their forebears at Khaybar in 628. Plainly, the surviving accounts of inner dissension and desperate defense at that oasis rely on such data. For whatever reason, Ibn Isḥāq's biography was not preserved in its original recension.[26] But the expanded version of Ibn Hishām (d. 833) was built from its matter, and the original was heavily mined by Ṭabarī. The tailings attest to Ibn Isḥāq's faithfulness as a historian. As Muir noted nearly a century ago, Ibn Hishām suppressed what Ibn Isḥāq recorded, as to Muḥammad's brief flirtation with polytheism, an episode preserved in Ṭabarī, attested from independent sources by Wāqidī, and evidenced in the Qur'ān itself.[27]

The early Muslim historians were in general not just retellers but collectors of *akhbār*. In the same spirit, the blind but eloquent traditionist ʿAwānah b. al-Ḥakam al-Kalbī (d. 764 or 770) was a source of ancient poetry, often cited in the *Kitāb al-Aghānī*, the Book of Songs. He is credited with a biography of Muʿāwiya and is a chief source for later accounts of the Umayyads. His son Hishām (d. 819) is said to have ordered his materials, which writers like Haytham b. ʿAdī and Madā'inī quarried. Ṭabarī and Balādhurī cite him often. As with Ibn Isḥāq, the later authors recast what they found in ʿAwānah, perhaps seeing a need to purge a perceived ʿUthmānī slant—a tendency to make fate the historical prime mover and ultimate explanation. ʿAwānah rarely cites his sources, but his writing was clear, and he dates the events in his narrative.[28] As Duri writes, ʿAwānah's "design for the writing of general history based on chronological sequence or on the lives of the caliphs represents a pioneering step in the development of historical writing"—even though his work must still be described as falling "within the tribal perspective."[29]

Abū Mikhnaf Lūt b. Yaḥyā (d. 774), besides his work as a traditionist, which was not later respected, preserved episodic accounts of battles, deaths, and other focal events in some thirty-two works, again used by Ṭabarī. He was valued for his data on Iraq; and despite his episodic technique,[30] he used topical groupings that anticipate the so-called monograph form of Madā'inī. For, from the outset, as we have seen, the sequence of the *maghāzī* was a natural organizing principle.

Al-Wāqidī (748–823), a freedman and former grain merchant from Medina who turned to scholarship in Baghdad after losing a fortune in business,[31] is described by Duri as "systematic and selective," more scrupulous than Ibn Isḥāq about *isnād*s, and prone to list his sources and outline each narrative before elaborating its details.[32] Margoliouth calls him "a more serious personage" than, say, Madā'inī, perhaps in part because he rose to the post of *qāḍī* and was a traditionist, the owner of an enormous library, and a reputed disciple of Mālik b. Anas.[33] Scorned as a liar by Aḥmad b. Ḥanbal, Wāqidī was not generally respected as a traditionist; but he was highly valued for his historical accounts of Muḥammad's career, the rise of Islam, and the suppression of recalcitrant groups.[34] Paying close attention to dates like those of the Prophet's campaigns, he moves far enough from hagiography to tell us who was minding the store back at Medina during those expeditions. In Wāqidī's concern for sources, Duri sees the influence of the Medinan school. But the notion of an outline and the interest in diachrony also suggest a more thematic structure than *khabar* literature or *ḥadīth* is likely to generate.

Madā'inī (752–ca. 843) came from Iraq and studied under a Muʿtazilite master. His best friend and final patron was the learned Isḥāq b. Ibrāhīm al-Mawsilī, a celebrated singer, musician, musical theorist, and composer, who loved the old poetry, criticized the new (as represented by Abū Nuwās and Abū Tammām), and supported as well the philologist Ibn al-Aʿrābī. Madā'inī's narratives expand on *khabar* topoi in dealing with specific battles, or movements like the tribal rebellion against Muḥammad. His writings, more than two hundred in number, address events from the birth of Islam down to the the time of the caliph Muʿtasim.[35]

Known for his vast learning, Madā'inī was an expert on the Islamic expansion into Khurasan, Persia, and India. He is often called a pioneer of the historical monograph, and his writings do range about a topic or focus on the life of an individual, such as the notorious Ḥajjāj. But it would be misleading to call his works in general thematic. Often, it seems, they were bundles of *akhbār* pegged to a rubric that served more as a pretext than a unifying theme. Topics include ancestresses of Muḥammad, hypocrites, traitors, fools, men who married a Parsi woman, men named after their mothers, men who married two sisters, or a wife's daughter, persons who quoted verses on learning of a death, men who preferred beduin women, Men who died defending their wives, women lampooned by their husbands, caliphs who remarried. One surviving work is on women of Quraysh who had more than one husband. Rather than data marshaled in support of a thesis, the groupings suggest recreational, or mnemonic interests. *Adab* here is alive and well. The material has become an end in itself.

Still, Madāʾinī's quest was not for the well-turned phrase or original insight but for historical data, settings, backgrounds. He cared about philology and used the collecting methods of a *muḥaddith*, often tracing back his data to eye witness testimony. He was one of several authors who wrote about Qurʾānic textual variants, but he also wrote on geography, consolations, the lives of poets and singers, animals (especially horses), money and coinage. He gathered and classified data about those who gave the lie to the Qurʾān and those who mocked the Prophet. More than sheer curiosity was at stake when he wrote on the Prophet's land allotments, or his sermons, treaties, verses, emissaries, letters to monarchs, deputations, safe conducts, and scribes.[36] But curiosity seems to outrun the sheerly practical when Madāʾinī writes a work on Arabs who refused alms from Muḥammad. Clearly he is fascinated by the Prophet's career. But the crying need that his oeuvre reveals for Socratic principles of organization will await the translation of Greek philosophical works. Indeed, philosophy is among the few topics of which he seems largely innocent.

The political, social, and religious uses of history demand more systematic arrangement than Madāʾinī could muster. Such needs turn the writers of history away from the anecdotal set piece and toward the annalistic, where incidents find their place in a chronological sequence, and causal explanations emerge increasingly into the light, as matters for discussion rather than presumption. The pioneer of the annalistic form in Arabic, Haytham b. ʿAdī (ca. 738–821/4), came from Kufa. He was a fixture of the ʿAbbāsid court from the time of Manṣūr to that of Hārūn al-Rashīd. Imprisoned when his wife's family gave out that he had spoken ill of the dynasty's eponymous ancestor, he was released by the caliph al-Amīn. His historical writings listed events by their year of occurrence, although preserving set pieces like the murder of ʿUthmān. Haytham wrote on pre-Islamic times, famous lives, genealogy, *ḥadīth*, and the rivalry of Kufa with Basra. He quarreled with the poet Abū Nuwās and was looked down on by later traditionists. But Jāḥiẓ uses him even as he scouts him, and he is also used by Yaʿqūbī, Ṭabarī, and Masʿūdī. His *Kitāb al-Taʾrīkh ʿalā ʾl-Sinīn*, History (or Chronology) Year by Year, may seem a natural enough outgrowth of his genealogical research, but it did treat Islamic history as a unified whole, using clear standards in determining what to record. For chronicling, like counting, demands standards of relevance.

A parti pris, of course, could impart an organizing principle to otherwise disparate *akhbār*, as it did for the Basran scholar Abū ʿUbayda Maʿmar b. al-Muthanna (728–ca. 825). A lover of poetry, somewhat eclipsed as a critic by his rival al-Aṣmaʿī, he brought a philologist's hand to the study of history, organizing his works almost lexicographically. One surviving work, on famous Arab horses, shows his penchant for building typologies. He found a favorite device in the rubric of virtues and vices. Titles like *Faḍāʾil al-Furs*, The Virtues of the Persians, and topics like *mathālib al-ʿArab*, the infamies of the Arabs, were relished by the Persian *Shuʿūbiyya* in its polemic against

Arab hegemony. A *mawlā* himself and an outsider, identified with the Khārijite sect, he clearly had his motives for writing his *Kitāb al-Mawālī* or Book of "Clients." His contemporaries saw depth and balance in his learning, but it was his contrarian slant that gave an edge to his collections of *ḥadīth* and tribal lore.[37]

Naṣr b. Muzāḥim (d. 827), often, but not quite accurately, called the first Shīʿī historian,[38] wrote works about the Battle of the Camel, the Battle of Ṣiffīn, and the murder of ʿAlī. Partisanship again affords an edge. But Naṣr rises above the sheer tribalism (*ʿaṣabiyya*) long prominent in *akhbār* to the larger sense of grievance that coalesces in the ʿAlid cause. Often outsiders, Shīʿītes had a stimulus to adopt a critical perspective on much that they saw and read. As Shīʿite ideology expanded to envelop social and ethnic grievances and as Shīʿite mythology grew to cosmic proportions, Shīʿite visions of history themselves took on a more universal perspective.

Even polemical remarks can rise above mere partisanship. Thus the prolific historian and genealogist Ibn al-Kalbī (ca. 737–ca. 820) finds a cosmopolitan standpoint when he sees the pre-Islamic Arab king Nuʿman b. Mundhir, through the eyes of his suzerain, the Persian Chosroes. When Nuʿmān praises his countrymen, the emperor responds that he has seen "no marks of virtue among the Arabs in matters of religion or state, no wise policy and no strength." Arab lands are overrun with wild beasts, shadowed by carrion birds, polluted by infanticide. Cannibalism, induced by famine, is not unknown. The Byzantines, Indians, and Chinese, "even the Turks and Khazars," are praised severally for their unity, and variously for their religious systems of law and ethics, their monuments and cities, their wisdom, mathematics, medicine, and industries, their chivalry, military and civil crafts, and even the natural resources and burgeoning populations of their lands—marks of prosperity and wise administration.[39] Presumably the Arabs will cut a better figure with the coming of Islam. But the idea of enduring, transcultural standards by which nations may be judged carries a lasting if instructive sting.

Ibn al-Kalbī was a Shīʿite born and bred. His father (d. 763) had already written on universal history and the history of religions, as well as on poetry, genealogy, and ancient legends, not to mention composing the most voluminous Qurʾān commentary we know of, a work that survives only in scattered quotations, since its length made it unwieldy and it relied on sources and methods that later authors deemed unacceptable. The son wrote over 150 works, including one on the pedigrees of great horses and the poetry about them, another on Arab markets, yet another on idols. Vast learning was marshaled here, albeit in a cataloguing mode, as if filed for use by later writers. Thematic organization is still wanting, but the need to preserve may have seemed more pressing than any urge to select that might sacrifice what failed to fit a preconcerted scheme.

Ibn al-Kalbī was a scholar of the first water. His *isnād*s would not always satisfy later writers, but he did have recourse to biblical scholars, experts on the ancient Arab kingdom of Palmyra, archeological data, informants about Christian archives and inscriptions, and his own secretary, who could translate Pahlavi texts for him. His cosmopolitan interests and his learning were intertwined and mutually supporting.

The Roots of Annalistic

None of the classic Greek works of history was translated into Arabic. But the surviving references show that not every Greek history remained a closed book in the realms of Islam. Eusebius (d. ca. 340) was well known to Syrian Christians. Anianus, a Greek chronicler of the fifth century, was known both to Syriac and Arabic speakers. The judge al-Wakīʿ (d. 918), best known for his history of Muslim jurists and their rulings, wrote on history, geography, money and coinage, and penned verses on his love of learning and teaching. He possessed a Greek historical work in translation.[40] Abū ʿĪsā, a ninth-century Muslim historian from the Munajjim family, scholarly courtiers of the ʿAbbāsids, cites Cyril of Alexandria's (d. 444) *Contra Julianum*. Jibrīl ibn Bukhtīshūʿ (d. 1006), a physician of the eminent Christian medical family, quotes the Byzantine *History* of Andronicus (sixth century), known to him from the Greek or Syriac. His work in turn is used by the physician and medical historian Ibn Abī ʿUṣaybiʿah. Sijistānī knows the name of Thucydides and can cite sayings ascribed to him, including one on the bootlessness of learning that is not well founded in the virtues. But more recent historical works perhaps seemed more relevant. Masʿūdī can cite the universal history of Agapius (Maḥbūb b. Qusṭanṭīn, fl. ca. 942), bishop of Manbij, which runs from the creation to 938. And Masʿūdī was friendly with Eutychius (Saʿīd b. al-Biṭrīq, d. 940), who became Melkite patriarch of Alexandria in 933. He cites his friend's Arabic chronicles and emulates his digressive style in his own "passing reflections" (*sawāniḥ*).[41]

Eutychius was not an annalist, but he did produce what Rosenthal calls a "skillfully synchronized" pre-Islamic history,[42] and he lays bare the conceptual roots and motives for the idea of universal history that comes to fruition in Masʿūdī's work. Plato and Aristotle, Eutychius writes, teach us to be critically aware of our methodological foundations in every science: "The Torah and similar sound books" are the mainstay of such awareness. Rosenthal regrets that Eutychius did not go on, after that promising introduction, to lay out a general theory of history. But perhaps that seemed unnecessary, if the patriarch found his framework ready made, in Scripture, the acknowledged vantage point of his historical perspective, and the incipit of his chronology.[43]

As for Agapius, he draws on Byzantine sources to weld the biblical sequence of events to Greek scientific cosmology and geography. His mode of exposition is clearly Greek. So is much of his matter. He is not embarrassed to paint a scrim that includes figures from Greek mythology and cultural history, as a backdrop to his accounts of Hellenistic, Roman, and Near Eastern political history. His history is not strictly annalistic, but he does open the door to that mode of writing, often prefacing his account of an event with the phrase, "in this year."

Arabic references to Greek annals are not found before the form appears in Arabic histories.[44] So Gibb, following a hint from Margoliouth and with a touch of vicarious chauvinism, speaks of Arabic historiography as though it cropped up by spontaneous generation or rose like a jinni wraith from behind some sand dune: "It is worth pausing for a moment to note the surprising fact that within 200 years from the rise of Islam the Muslim community had assembled this enormous archive of materials on its pre-history in Arabia, its genesis, and its subsequent development. Moreover, it had done this out of its own resources; there is not a trace to be seen in it of either Byzantine or Persian inspiration."[45] Yet the method and the matter of *ḥadīth* are precedented in rabbinic usage. The devices of Arabic poetry and anecdote, with their framing narratives, are linked with the larger world, and so is annalistic. No culture thrives in isolation, and Arabic history writing, along with the larger Islamic culture of which it was one vital expression, thrived precisely when and where such isolation was overcome. A typical Muslim history would hardly dwell on Greek content. Eutychius, who uses Muslim sources inter alia, similarly, pays scant attention to Islam. But Greek forms and scientific interests are taken up in the Islamic environment, along with the biblical matter and framework.[46] Together these spur the search for a unified view of history.

The annalistic form was widely used in Greek histories and well suited to addressing the organizational problem that confronted Muslim historians acutely by the reign of Ma'mūn. Naturally the model was used. As Rosenthal writes, "Greek chronicles of the period when Islam came into being represent exactly the type of annalistic historiography we find in later Muslim works."[47] A parallel tradition was at hand in Syriac. Drawing on the fruits of his own and Joseph Schacht's researches, Rosenthal writes: "There can be little objection to the assumption that Muslim annalistic historiography in its beginning was indebted to Greek and Syriac models. It was not a particular work that served Muslim authors as an inspiration, but the idea of the annalistic arrangement that came to early Muslim scholars through contact with learned Christians or Christian converts to Islam."[48]

The Byzantine historian Theophanes was using the annalistic form a century before Ṭabarī, and even in Spain Byzantine histories were being written right down to the time of the Arab conquest. There was not the heated market for Arabic translations of the extensive chronicles of other nations that there was for works of philosophy, mathematics, medicine, engineering, alchemy, and astrology. Translating was hard work, and readers pursued what they found most useful. But historical works could be useful. In 948 ʿAbd al-Raḥmān III, the Umayyad caliph in Spain, received from the Byzantine emperor a copy of Paulus Orosius's *Against the Pagans*, along with a priceless Materia Medica of Dioscorides. Born in Tarragon, Orosius (ca. 385–420) was a loyal follower of Augustine's. He settled in North Africa after a mission from Augustine to Jerome, since his homeland had been overrun by the Vandals. Intended as a continuation of the *City of God*, Orosius's seven-volume *Adversus Paganos* was the first continuous world history written from a Christian point of view. It became a standard textbook of universal history, prized in Europe for its reading of historical events as confirmations of biblical prophecy. It was translated into Anglo Saxon for Alfred the Great; and, with some difficulty, translated into Arabic and expanded for the Umayyad court.[49] The Arabic text was used by Ibn Juljul, Ibn Khaldūn, and Maqrīzī.[50]

So there were Greek histories available in Arabic. But long before turning to such texts, historians writing in Arabic found it natural and useful to adapt Greek modes of exposition, just as others were adopting Greek modes of organization in theological writing, book keeping, and administration. Because the new tools and methods both served and fostered new ways of thinking, none of them simply sprang to life in Arabic in a day and a night. *Khabar* literature was fixated on what Margoliouth calls "thrilling scenes." But there was call for a rival approach. Gibb finds a certain historical value in the "tribal traditions," as he labels them, "though partial and one-sided." But "their vivid detail and their bold handling of episodes offer a marked contrast to the annalistic of their own and later times."[51] For annals answer to a different market. As Rosenthal puts it, they were meant to lay out "facts, bare facts, which were, or at least were in theory, recorded by contemporary sources and could not be corrected, improved, or enlarged by any later writer."[52]

Theologians often frowned on the secular, tribal spirit of the *akhbariyyūn*. But the new chroniclers were often theologians themselves, traditionists and jurists,[53] who turned to history in search of sound normative traditions. As scholarly tastes were whetted among these men, whose lives, after all, were the stuff of books and learning, curiosity sparked a quest not just for information but for understanding. The synthetic approach was now too useful to be ignored. Gibb sees the appetite for knowledge for its own sake as "a fresh intellectual element" entering Arabic history writing in the late ninth century, partly through "that legacy of Hellenistic culture which was penetrating all branches of intellectual activity in Islam."[54] Organic form and thematic structure are hallmarks of that legacy.

The *Tabaqāt Fuḥūl al-Shuʿarāʾ* by Ibn Sallām al-Jumaḥī (756–845/6),[55] a selective miscellany of biographical notes and anecdotes on poetry and poets, opens with an introduction, a mark of thematic writing. The linkages are still associative, even in that introduction, but Ibn Sallām, spurns the obsessive collecting impulses of the *ḥadīth* and *khabar* masters. Connoisseurs of ancient poetry like himself, he urges, can distinguish authentic from forged poetry. Ibn Isḥāq infuriates him by professing perfect innocence of poetry and promising to pass on whatever he has received. Ibn Sallām ridicules him for embedding in his work poems ascribed to women, to men who wrote no poetry, even to the legendary tribes of ʿĀd and Thamūd. The traditionist's scrutiny of *isnād*s is of little use here, and Ibn Sallām is proud to have in his quiver literary skills that offer an alternative to what he sees as the uncritical compiling of folklore.[56]

Linking *khabar* with *taqlīd*, uncritical reportage, Muslim historiography first flexed its muscles by leaving to the aficionados of *ḥadīth* the project of *ʿilm al-rijāl* and *jarḥ wa ʾl-taʿdīl*, the biographical studies that sought to render the study of tradition into a critical science by scrutinizing the reliability of the transmitters. For the chains of authorities, the *isnād*s, that mimic the linkages of genealogy, have a similarly mythic function. Where the aim is normative, the links of transmission that fill the role of argument naturally become prominent, and the *matn*, or matter of a tradition, wanes, its narrative elements etiolated and isolated, as the focus sharpens on the legal, ritual, or ethical moral of each story. But when the interest is the story itself and normative questions are not center stage, details that might seem critical in a *ḥadīth* become peripheral, and anxieties recede over the standing of transmitters. We know the pattern well in the rabbinic distinction between *aggadah* and *halakhah*. In matters of history, to quote Petersen, "Even such scrupulous authorities as Sufyān ath-Thawrī (d. 777/8) and Aḥmad b. Ḥanbal (d. 855) considered absolute accuracy obligatory only where the case relates to a right or a wrong, whereas other matters, including the recording of history, did not call for the same care."[57]

Balādhurī's Narrative Strategy

Thus Balādhurī (ca. 810–ca. 892) is asserting a historian's prerogative when he breaks away from traditionalism. When not citing strict prophetic *ḥadīth*s he will use collective *isnād*s, an anonymous "they say," or no *isnād* whatever. The earliest *akhbariyyūn*, after all, did not tag their reports with such pedigrees. The convention came into prominence in eighth- and ninth-century legal work, responding to the rise of rationalism and foreign ways of knowing.[58] Balādhurī will none of it. An admirer of Persian culture, he is credited with a verse translation of the Persian "Testament of Ardashīr," presumably a book of political wisdom. A boon companion of the caliph Mutawakkil, he still cut a figure in the court of Mustaʿīn but fell out of favor in Muʿtamid's reign.

His *Kitāb Futūḥ al-Buldān*, arrayed as a series of brief articles, relies on information and observations gleaned in his travels. Masʿūdī praises it as the best there is on its subject. It may well have inspired him in his own extensive travels. Dunlop calls it "indispensable," if "not particularly well adapted for consecutive reading."[59] Taking the Islamic conquests as its theme, it is arranged geographically rather than chronologically and moves rapidly (being abridged from the author's longer work on the subject) from the wars of the Prophet to the conquests of Syria, Armenia, Egypt, the Mediterranean islands, southern Italy, Spain, and the West. Within each section Balādhurī does proceed chronologically. He does not confine himself to military and political history but takes careful note of cultural and social conditions and documents in detail the Arabs' gradual displacement of Greek and Persian administrative structures.[60]

Unlike many a later historian, Balādhurī here values concision. He abridges the texts of documents and avoids shaggy dog stories.[61] Such efforts at discipline can be frustrating to modern readers, who value his accounts of the Khawārij, for example, and would treasure more circumstantial detail. But although he saw the impact of citing original documents,[62] he could not know how rare a source of primary data his work would become. His quest was for an appropriate narrative mode and scale.

His immense, unfinished *Ansāb al-Ashrāf*, Genealogies of the Nobles, collates lives of the Prophet, his kin and companions, and their descendants. Nominally laid out on a loose genealogical scheme, it follows the contours of dynastic history but ranges far and wide geographically. Ilse Lichtenstadter calls it Arabic genealogical history at its best, because it reveals continuities and changes of outlook among the members of the various constituencies of the Islamic polity–although the narrative technique has the drawback of breaking up the story of those developments, in the effort to stay abreast of parallel developments: "Thus, for example, the death of the Prophet's grandson Ḥusayn in the battle of Kerbala is not discussed in full as one of the events of the reign of the caliph Yazīd ibn Muʿāwiya, of the Umaiyad branch of the Quraysh, during which it occurred, but is recorded among the memorabilia of the family of his grandfather Abū Ṭālib of the Banū Hāshim of Quraysh."[63] For Balādhurī "still retains the ancient attitude which focused its interest on the aristocratic families" of Islam. His underlying system is the *tabaqāt* design of Wāqidī's disciple Ibn Saʿd (d. 845), classifying its subjects by generation. But he does digress pretty freely to expand on certain biographies (e.g., Ḥajjāj) and to relate important events in the reigns of various monarchs.

Balādhurī critically appraises his sources and distinguishes written from oral testimonies, saying *qāla lī* or *ḥaddathanī* (he said to me, he told me) for firsthand reports and *rawā* (he relates) for written accounts.[64] Khalidi finds his tone more jocular and romantic than epic or heroic. Factional and ideological disputes are viewed from the mildly cynical middle distance of a midlevel bureaucrat, and Khalidi detects the same bureaucratic posture in his handling of detail. Where Wāqidī will appeal to a consensus about dates, in the manner of the divines, Balādhurī closes off debate with a "curt and dismissive" bureaucratic "this is solid."[65]

Although he plainly seeks a critical stance toward his materials, Balādhurī rarely stops to reflect on his own methods or criteria, let alone his goals as a historian. His message is unstated. As Khalidi writes, "If the work as a whole has any ulterior argument or purpose, this might well lie in an in-built political moral of the spectacle of powerful dynasties rising and falling, of founding fathers laboriously creating the edifice which less-talented or less-fortunate progeny then proceed to destroy."[66] That sounds almost like the language of Ecclesiastes. If Balādhurī has managed to keep his own counsel and successfully breed his own odd hybrid of the hedgehog with the fox, his aim is perhaps made practicable by the moral vision his readers will bring to his scenes, informed by a Qurʾānic outlook. It will take an Ibn Khaldūn to make explicit in a language credible to worldly ears the idea of moral judgment on the events of history that remains implicit in Balādhurī.

Greek and Biblical Models

The forms of synthetic historiography advance pari passu with the translation movement and the entry of Greek thematic structures into Islamic writings. Increasing awareness of the Hebrew Bible and of Persian, Indian, and other sources conspires with Socratic conceptual organization to make possible that distinctive product or genre of Arabic historiography, the universal history.

Biblical historiography takes a variety of forms. The book of Esther, for example, relates events of the time of the Xerxes, the biblical Ahasuerus (r. 486–465 B.C.E.), the fourth Achaemenian king. He was the son of Darius (r. 522–486), grandson of Cambyses (r. 530–522), and great grandson of Cyrus (r. 550–530). No military genius, he organized his armies ethnically rather than by their weaponry. His reign was marked by his failure to complete his father's conquest of Greece, a traumatic but defining moment for Hellas. His own image builders focused on his more successful campaigns, against Egypt and the rebellious Babylon, where he had once been his father's viceroy. Besides his lavish building projects at Susa, Xerxes completed Darius's magnificent palace at Persepolis and dedicated it to the greater glory of the god of his devotions, Ahuramazda.

In the Book of Esther, Xerxes emerges as an ultimately well-intentioned but self-indulgent bumbler. The narrative technique is uncannily like that of Herodotus: History wheels around palace intrigues, court ceremonial, the whims of monarchs and their viziers. Whether or not Esther or Herodotus preserves the record of actual events,[67] their books confirm one another's impressions of ancient Iranian atmospherics and vividly reveal what their audiences are expected to absorb as historical explanations.

Structural transformations control the exposition in both Herodotus' History and the Esther scroll. Women are exchanged across cultures—Esther in the book that bears her name, Io (Herodotus I 1), Medea (I 2), and Helen (I 3) in Herodotus. A husband boasts of his wife's beauty and seeks to expose it improperly: Candaules, as a result, shares more than he had intended with Gyges, his bodyguard, murderer, and successor (I 8–12).[68] Ahasuerus, in his cups, is too eager to show off Vashti's beauty to his guests. His frustration leads to Vashti's downfall, Esther's fateful elevation—and, in the end, the king's adoption of a far more protective attitude toward his new wife, extended from her to her people, the Jews of the 127 provinces of his empire—which did indeed span territory from India to Ethiopia.

History writing has taken a turn toward the critical with the substitution of prose for poetry, in both Herodotus and Esther. Witness the appeals of the Book of Esther to the official Persian Chronicles and of Herodotus to his own assiduous inquiries and the testimony of local informants. But the criticism expected is that of a listening audience. Herodotus earned his living by reading his histories aloud at Athens, and the letters sent by Mordecai and Esther throughout the Persian Empire denouncing Haman's plot and proclaiming festive celebrations when it was foiled were surely read aloud, as the narrative of their triumph still is in the Scroll of Esther to this day. Orality is still reflected in what both narratives take to be the motive springs of historical events—plots overheard, closeted conversations, royal audiences, and interviews.

Courtly honor and intrigue mingle with irony when Mordecai is treated to the pomp that Haman had designed for himself, and later, when Haman meets the fate he had devised for Mordecai and all Jews. The irony of fate is poetic justice, a reflex of audience response. Fate humbles Croesus, as if to point up Solon's paradoxical moral, that no man should call himself happy until the moment of his death (Herodotus I 30–45). Fate overmasters Haman's plot. The lots cast to fix the date of his final solution in fact presage his downfall, hanged on his own gibbet. Everywhere there is structural symmetry. Croesus must learn from the veiled words of a wise Greek, Bias or Pittacus, that it would be as rash for him to send ships against Greek islanders as it would be for them to come against him with horse (I 27). The elemental irony of fate sets subjective intention against objective fact when Croesus learns from the Delphic oracle that his designs on Persia will fell a mighty empire. He lacks the self-knowledge to see that the empire will be his own.

Herodotus thinks he has said enough of the casus belli between Lydia and Persia when he has fixed Croesus' state of mind. The king wanted territory, but "more than was his portion." Above all, we hear repeatedly, "he trusted in the oracle." Croesus was set up, or set upon by fate. Such are the hinges of destiny. It made no real difference if Thales, as an engineer in Croesus's camp, altered the course of the river Halys to aid the Lydian army. For Croesus crossed the river only to meet what fate held in store for him. As a captive he will repeat to Cyrus what he now grasps of Solon's wisdom. Nearly burnt alive, he will live on as the victor's dependant, humbly acknowledging, in the end, that it was not the gods but he himself who brought about his own and his nation's downfall.

I mark the parallels between Esther and Herodotus not to find some lineal connection with the Arabic historians, but because the historiographic mode shared by the two narratives draws to a fine point the work of anecdotal history, elevating the idea of destiny. Fate is not just impersonal but implacable. This is the fate of Homer and the tragedians. It is also the fate of pre-Islamic poetry. In Herodotus and the tragedians, as in Heraclitus, character becomes fate. But in the poetry of the *Jāhilyya* fate is time itself (*dahr*), viewed as a mortal enemy, indeed, the embodiment of mortality.[69] In Homer, human ignorance and pride are silhouetted sharply against the bright light of divine blessedness, like the figures on an Attic urn. But in Herodotus the numinous is seen only in its transcendence of human wishes. Fate in Esther, similarly, is not personified, like the deities of some pagan pantheon. It lingers offstage. But its all-seeing, unforgiving eye remains, the ironic eye so shrewdly sited in the implacable goggle-eyed billboard mask of Fitzgerald's *Gatsby*. In the worldly court of Susa, as in Gatsby's world, no God is visibly at work, but the irony of judgment oversees and overpowers nonetheless, and all the more palpably for its presence just out of sight. Fate disposes of what man proposes, dissolving the line between outcome and omniscience, and mocking that firm barrier between subjective apprehension and objective fact that is the boundary and threshold of human consciousness and understanding.

Khabar begets irony,[70] irony begets fate, fate begets the tragic sense of life. Man is powerless. He will regain power only when the poets once again allow God to speak, not in the hedged obscurities of an oracle but with the moral clarity of a legislator. Esther is pivotal here, not in some unilinear developmental scheme but conceptually. The absence of the God of Israel from her scroll is not an accident. But it entails no deep irreligiosity. It is emblematic, rather, of the outlook of anecdotal history, examining events as augurs might scan the flight of birds, to find the currents of destiny in details of seeming inconsequence.

The Book of Esther does not embrace a pagan fatalism, but it does accommodate to the language of that outlook, much as Genesis responds to the cosmogonic language of Babylonian myth, or as Ecclesiastes assumes the cynical tone of a world-weary potentate, or the Song of Songs takes on the breathless, panting, frustrate language of adolescent lovers. A few scholars have proposed that Esther and Mordecai, bearing the names of Astarte and Marduk, are somehow cosmic figures. But that reads into the Esther narrative the cosmogonic idiom of Genesis, which is so foreign to Esther's courtly world that the rabbis fencing the scriptural canon debated sorely over whether to include the book at all. The warrant for its inclusion comes not in Esther's fanciful maternity of Darius (making Xerxes the father rather than the son!) but in the recognition that the narrative of Esther faithfully sought the hand of the living and loving God of Israel where familiar forms and popular thinking might find only the power of fate—vindicating the victors as the chosen and singling out the vanquished as the butts of history and the laughter of the gods. Thus the Talmud finds in Esther veiled hints that providence is still active, working its own deeper irony behind the ironies of fate. Here the work of God is experienced, as humanity must generally experience it, in implicit rather than explicit terms. As the Talmud puts it, playing on Esther's name: "Where does the Torah allude to Esther? 'I will surely hide my Face' (*haster astīr panay*—Deut. 31:18)" (Ḥullin 139b).

Genesis evokes a very different perspective, universal and cosmogonic. We can see the impact of its narrative strategy centuries later when Paul addresses the intellectually minded populace of Athens. Urged on by philosophers and meeting pagan localism head on, he appeals to the universality of Genesis, linking cosmology to history:

> Men of Athens, I see that in all things you are too superstitious. For, as I passed by and beheld your devotions, I found an altar inscribed, TO THE UNKNOWN GOD. Whom therefore you ignorantly worship, Him do I declare to you. God that made the world and all things in it, being the Lord of heaven and earth, dwelleth not in temples made with hands. Neither is He worshiped with men's hands, as though He needed any thing, seeing that He giveth to all life and breath and all things and made of one blood all nations of men to dwell throughout the face of the earth, and fixed the epochs of their history and ap-

> pointed the bounds of their territory—that they should seek the Lord, if haply they might feel after Him and find Him, though He be not far from every one of us.[71]

The same topos echoes from the proems spoken by the orators in the delightful philosophical fable *The Case of the Animals vs Man*[72] to the poignant Day of Atonement litany of the *Eleh Ezkerah*, which sets its martyrology against the backdrop of the story of creation. The New Testament wish and veiled warning, "If haply . . ." reverberates in the Qur'ān. The cosmic proscenium arch spread out by the narrative of origins lingers in the preamble to many a work on science, even (or especially) in the age of Darwin or the red shift, when accounts of origins are once again accepted as a legitimate mode of explanation.

In the purview of Genesis, every event has a meaning, not as a portent of the unseen, a signal blinking obscurely from the baleful eyes of a grimly laughing god, but as earnest of the sublimity of a God whose design for creation is goodness and whose plan for humanity finds voice not in an inexorable doom but in a law grounded in freedom and dignity. Here responsibility comes to rest not in the humbling of mortality by fate but in the liberation of humanity through holiness. And holiness now means moral purity and spiritual generosity—the acts of grace and justice that forge God's covenant with humanity.[73]

The irony of fate survives the work of Genesis as prophetic irony. Its target is no longer the mere hubris of those who deny their mortality by seeking to overmaster destiny but the folly of those who mistake violence for power or exploitation for prosperity, imagining that rapacity grants peace, or that boundless lust is satiable. The Psalmist pinions that folly in the phrase, "The fool hath said in his heart there is no God" (14:1, 53:1). What the fool denies is accountability. He misses the nexus between reality and justice that makes the one God universal, the nexus between truth and the good that is the core of the monotheistic idea. The same folly that gnaws away the seeming strength of self-serving undercuts the seeming prudence that finds no lesson in the rise and fall of nations. It undermines the seeming realism that finds no moral in history beyond the fact of human weakness. The worldly maxim is humility before inexorable power. It sees the greatness of the great and the smallness of the small but cannot discern which is which, until fate has cast its die. Moral insight, however, allows a prophetic sensibility to see (sometimes before it is too late for change) what should count as strength and what must be diagnosed as sickness or pollution.

The biblical kinship of all nations (Genesis 3:20) and affirmation of the common wellsprings of all languages (Genesis 11:1–9) evoke a cosmopolitan humanism that chimes with philosophical themes far more harmoniously than does the chauvinism of so many ancient Greeks, and far more suggestively than does the partisanship of the earliest Arabic secular or Islamic sacred history. Indeed, part of function of proems like those spoken in *The Case of the Animals vs Man* is to restore the Qur'ānic narrative to its larger, cosmic setting.

That setting is powerfully evoked in the Hexaemeron genre, the classic format of the six days of creation that Christian authors used, down to the times of Severus bar Shakko (d. 1241) and Bar Hebraeus (d. 1286), to celebrate the panoply of nature and display their scientific learning. The genre is paralleled in the summa of Job of Edessa (d. 814), a translator of Galen from Greek into Syriac,[74] whose Christian lore is situated in the cosmos framed by Greek science and philosophy.

Universal History

It is not surprising, then, that the great Christian translator and Galenist, Ḥunayn ibn Isḥāq (808–73) is credited with a history of the world.[75] The genre of universal history, complete with its cosmological prelude, will find enduring monuments in the work of Yaʿqūbī, Masʿūdī, and Muṭahhar. The format will become so familiar in Arabic historical writing that Washington Irving, who was well versed in Spanish history and its Andalusian predecessors, adapted its structures to his mock grandiloquent *History of New York from the Creation to the Expulsion of the Dutch.* Lichtenstadter sees a continuity between works of Arabic universal history and the *khabar* tradition:

> Once Islam had attained spiritual as well as political power, the historian's interest in its origins and the ways in which it had reached that eminence intensified. Partisan factions that arose among the conquering Muslims and the conquered peoples with axes to grind searched for justification of their claims to preeminence in the records of the past and used the traditions of their forefathers to support their demands. This interest in the origins and growth of the new religion and its political protagonists was in line with the old pre-Islamic tradition; only the central figures had changed. In the *aiyām* literature the events and the personalities that shaped the destiny of the tribes formed the topic; with the widening scope of their experience, the focus shifted from Arabia to the Fertile Crescent and beyond. "World history" began to be felt as relevant; not only the contemporary, but also the ancient world needed to be known, events of the distant past were found to have a bearing on those of the Prophet's time and of the conquests and the creation and consolidation of the Muslim empire that followed. The history of neighboring empires and their rulers, such as Iran, too, entered into that survey, if only to demonstrate their weakness and to glorify the achievements of the conquerors.[76]

There was partisanship among the world historians. But, by that very token, there was a demand for equal time on the part of Iranian partisans, who found voice in the *Shuʿūbiyya.* And if there was partisanship there was also disinterested curiosity, an appetite for information and understanding, the collector's urge for completeness, and the seeker's drive for comprehension.

Aḥmad b. Isḥāq al-Yaʿqūbī (d. 897), in his world history, organized his Islamic materials in the Iranian manner, by the reigns of the caliphs.[77] They extend to the year 872. He accompanied each reign with appropriate astrological data and lists of its influential personalities, giving each regime a character of its own. Yaʿqūbī traveled widely and shows broad interests in philosophy, astronomy, and medicine, the chronologies of ancient civilizations and the character of pre-Islamic religions. Khalidi calls him "probably the first Muslim historian to take almost the entire spectrum of human culture for his object of study."[78] His Shīʿite and Muʿtazilite sympathies[79] underwrite and underscore his universalist and rationalistic efforts. For Shīʿite theology views history as a progressive unfolding of God's manifestation. And rationalism disposes the mind to a belief in progress, as Rāzī explains: Independent minds are keen and of lively interests. They readily master and surpass the achievements of their predecessors, not because they are wiser but because intellectual work (which, for the rationalist, is the real work of human history) is cumulative.[80] Such notions were so far from the consciousness of the early Muslims that in collating the Qur'ānic revelations no arrangement seemed more fitting than that of declining length.

Yaʿqūbī's History lays claim to comprehensiveness by beginning the story of humanity with Adam. It quotes frequently in Arabic from the Old and New Testaments and, as the nineteenth-century editor, T. M. Houtsma recognized, draws on Syriac sources of biblical narrative like the *Meʿarat Gazze* (Cave of Treasures). Yaʿqūbī writes of the rulers of Syria, Assyria, Babylon, India, Greece, Rome, Iran, Europe, China, Egypt, North Africa, Ethiopia, Africa, and pre-Islamic Arabia. He even lists the Khazar kings, not known from other sources. Surveying the scientific and philosophical achievements of the ancients, he devotes generous sections to Hippocrates, Ptolemy, and Aristotle and discusses Pythagoras, Socrates, Plato, Euclid, Nichomachus (of the Arithmetic), Galen, and Aratus. His cosmopolitan scope links naturally with his scientific and philosophical outlook.[81]

Al-Dīnawarī (d. *ca.* 891–902), best known for his work on botany, which uses both Greek and beduin sources, was said by Tawḥīdī to combine "the wisdom of the philosophers with the eloquence of the Arabs." A celebrated stylist, he was ranked with Jāḥiẓ as one of the finest writers of his age.[82] He wrote on astronomy, geography, mathematics, philology, and literary history. His Book of Long Narratives selects favorite episodes from history down to 842, including reports about Alexander the Great, the Sassanian monarchs, the Muslim conquest of Iraq, and the Umayyad era. He is fascinated by ʿAlī and his conflict with ʿUthmān but dispassionate about the early caliphs and sympathetic toward Abū Bakr and ʿUmar and does not allow his ʿAlid sympathies to project Shīʿite dogmas about *naṣṣ* (the Prophet's purported designation of ʿAlī as his successor) onto what he takes to be the facts.[83]

In his sketch of universal history Dīnawarī garnered much information about Byzantine and Persian history. He strove to synchronize the biblical, Persian, and pre-Muslim Arab chronologies[84] and to give fair coverage to both Persian and Arab contributions to movements and events.[85] As the title *Al-Akhbār al-Ṭiwāl* suggests, Dīnawarī still uses the method of the *akhbārī*.[86] But the chronological sequence and thematic elaboration of details show how far he has advanced from the anecdotal mode of his sources.

Dīnawarī cites a good deal of pre-Islamic poetry; and he does include legendary material in his histories, but more from a collector's instinct than from sheer credulity. Margoliouth complains that his history "has little authority," since it quotes letters, speeches, even conspiratorial conversations, that only the principals are likely to have witnessed.[87] But Margoliouth may judge more fairly when he applies the word "dramatization" to this method. For the documents and conversations seem to be embedded in the narrative not as verbatim reports but (as in Thucydides), as interpretive devices: They make motives explicit that would otherwise remain unstated. Once again we see a departure from *khabar*. The device is not wholly foreign to the *akhbarī*. For even ballads use embedded discourse for the insight it affords into intentions. But the idea that events should be explained, not just reported takes us well beyond the sort of history that leaves explanations to be inferred or presumed.

Like Balādhurī, Dīnawarī dispenses with *isnād*s. Like Yaʿqūbī, he relegates alternative accounts of a given event to the end of his report, "almost as footnotes to the main text."[88] Literary style and a sustained narrative are of moment to Balādhurī. They are aesthetic counterparts of his broad interest in culture, letters, and the sciences. Once again the historian has declared his independence from the craft of the *ḥadīth* scholar, even as his interest in veracity and a connected narrative removes him from the realm of the sheer literary connoisseur.

Ṭabarī's Synthesis

Muḥammad b. Jarīr Abū Jaʿfar al-Ṭabarī (839–923) may seem at first a retrograde figure. His *Chronicle of Apostles and Kings* is a triumph of the annalistic on a grand scale. But its method may grow tedious, as he dwells with loving patience on variant accounts of the same event and painstakingly lists his sources. Ṭabarī seems at times to risk losing his narrative thread. But that he does not do.[89] He has a sense of vivid narrative, as found among his sources; and he uses even his verbosity and deference to his matter to lend drama as well as authority to his accounts, studding them with documents, speeches, and (in the ancient manner) poetry representative of the eras of which he writes.[90] As Rosenthal says, "Aṭ-Ṭabarī brought to his work the scrupulousness and indefatigable longwindedness of the theologian, the accuracy and love of order of the scholarly jurist, and the insight into political affairs of the practicing lawyer-politician.[91]

A theologian, ethicist, jurist, and traditionist, Ṭabarī reportedly studied for forty years and wrote for forty years at the rate of forty sheets a day. His expositions contrast strikingly with those of Miskawayh, who heavily uses him as a source. Miskawayh is cool to sectarian issues, strong on thematics, long on current affairs, but highly derivative for events before his time.[92] Of Ṭabarī, Margoliouth writes: "He was too decidedly a man of letters to possess some of the qualifications of a historian: hence when he has to deal with the affairs of his own time, he is defective, gives no intelligible account of the progress of events, omits important details, whence the all-powerful viziers and Caliphs of his time are shadowy figures."[93]

Ṭabarī sought rigor in an exclusive reliance on well-established traditions. His History, as originally conceived would reportedly have filled some thirty thousand leaves, but he pruned it to a mere three thousand. His compendium of *ḥadīth* was said to be on the same scale; and his Qur'ān commentary, again compressed by a factor of ten to one, filled three thousand leaves in its final form.[94] It was the founding source for all subsequent compendia of Qur'ānic exegesis, just as the History was a model of the annalistic form for subsequent writers from Miskawayh, to Abū 'l-Fidā' (1273–1331) and Dhahabī (1274–1348).[95]

Ṭabarī's History treats the *isnād* with the greatest respect, all but eclipsing the *matn* in its variants and its valence of testimonies. It was on the scrutiny of authorities, as Frank Peters puts it, that "whatever critical insight went into the work was lavished."[96] To quote Ṭabarī's own words:

> In all that I say on the subjects I have decided to recount here I rely only on explicitly identified reports (*akhbār*), accounts whose transmitters I cite by name. I do not achieve understanding through rational proofs, nor do I make more than minimal inferences based on thought processes (*fakr al-nufūs*). For knowledge about men of the past and reports about men of the present is obtained only by firsthand experience with those men, not by one whose lifespan does not reach back to theirs.[97]

Empiricism and traditionalism are here set against a rationalism that seems aprioristic and arbitrary.

Ṭabarī's method will look frightfully mechanical by modern standards, that is, those of the Enlightenment—and of Socratic, thematic organization. Events (except for the connected narrative of the Prophet's life) are related year by year, not serially. Within individual years the *akhbār* seem to be set down in order of importance, with variants spread out in loving prolixity, as in the *ḥadīth*. Yet Ṭabarī's method will commend itself to postmoderns, even as it may warn them of the extremes to which worries about the suborning of reason might lead. For Ṭabarī, like our postmoderns, is not a primitive but a man in reaction. He puts a premium on strict documentation and is skeptical of independent judgment (*ray'*) as mere subjective opinion, or worse.

Ṭabarī's traditionalism reacts to the teachings of the Muʿtazilite masters of his youth and to the newfound sciences of logic and mathematics.[98] Yet Ṭabarī was not a rigorist as a jurist or theologian. He studied with both Aḥmad b. Ḥanbal and Dā'ūd b. ʿAlī al-Ẓahirī, but his distinctive methods made him the proud founder of his own juridical system. He was an intellectual adversary of Dā'ūd's son and was violently persecuted by the Ḥanbalites, who resented his critical judgments[99] If we set aside some of our own conventions, we can detect in Ṭabarī (with all his archaizing) a significant advance in synthetic historiography. For he realized the universal history, toward which Yaʿqūbī and Dīnawarī had been moving. The agglutinative structure that absorbs so many prior accounts lends his work a sense of the definitive, and his Annals do bear the power of a consecutive narrative, even if built up from a mosaic of *akhbār*.

Masʿūdī, an aficionado of diverse modes of exposition, knew Ṭabarī and did not miss his strengths. He calls him "the jurist of his age, the godly man of his generation, who mastered the learning of the divers legal authorities and marshaled the lore of the traditionists."[100] Ṭabarī did marshal the vast resources of tradition under the discipline of text and chronology. Thus Qifṭī can roll the authority of all past accounts into the embrace of this one work: "If you want continuous historical information well arranged, you must consult the work of Abū Jaʿfar al-Ṭabarī, from the beginning of the world to the year 309."[101] Rosenthal adds an exclamation point here, since Ṭabarī's History extends only to 302 (July 915 by the Common Era), and near his own time his coverage is markedly parochial, departing from the ideal of universal history for want of suitable sources. Rosenthal justly complains that Ṭabarī took no notice of the widening of historical and cultural horizons going on in his own day.[102] But in one sense, his comprehensive plan is such a notice, and many a later historian found no better scheme than simply to continue Ṭabarī's chronicle.

Peters rightly sees in Ṭabarī "an Islamic traditionist, not an Arab Thucydides."[103] Yet, as all historians know, one never can go back again. Dancers in the West today move with the full extension used in the dance movement of our time. They may find it hard even to imitate choreographies from the past, without importing this element of style and the aesthetic it represents. Historians, in the same way, are writers of their age. Their first subject is themselves and their own times, whether or not they heed the Delphic maxim commending an awareness of that fact. It is when Ṭabarī's History seeks to interweave Persian, biblical, and pre-Islamic Arab history that it shows itself most typically a work of its era. It has a methodological introduction and sets critical standards for itself, distinguishing questions about the character of the purveyor of a report from the value of his testimony. Ṭabarī resists imposing theological schemes and rational patterns on the sheer data of history.[104] But his work is no mere pastiche. Indeed, as we have seen, when Ibn Bājjah wants a paradigm case of unity in diversity, it is Ṭabarī's history that springs to his mind.[105]

What unifies Ṭabarī's work is its vision of its subject, "Apostles and Kings," a pious and somewhat unstructured, if Qur'ānic, vision of the struggle between the righteous and the unrighteous,[106] whose outcome is the rise of Islam as heir to the Persian Empire. *Akhbār* are here not for their own sake nor as mere exemplars to be emulated, rued, or celebrated but as evidence of Ṭabarī's own broad thesis. The *isnāds* serve not as authorities for norms but as factual documentation. Yet evidence will serve only if handled critically and with due deference. Ṭabarī stretches to ensure that deference. Most strikingly, he does not seek to conflate his sources. That, in his view, would be to masquerade as an independent source in his own right. The reports he uses are not chosen out of archival piety, however. They are tesserae offered for critical evaluation, a continuation of Ṭabarī's own selection process, in which the reader must now take part, even as the author himself stands aside, like an artist displaying a work in progress.

Ṭabarī's self-restraint is part of a quest for epistemic rigor. In his History, as in his voluminous *Tafsīr*, he does not pretend to see an escape from the dilemma between editorial laissez faire and the authorial omniscience of an invisible redactor. He wants to hold an even course between the two extremes. So he will not follow Dīnawarī's lead in dispensing with the *isnād*. Attributions are necessary, as labels of provenance, even when norms are not directly at stake. As Sakhāwī put it long after the authority of tradition was firmly established, "Were it not for the *isnād*, everyone would say whatever he liked."[107]

Recognizing Ṭabarī's synthetic work, Khalidi writes:

> In his *History of Prophets and Kings*, Tabari combined the history of creation and prophecy with the history of ancient nations, especially the Persians, adding to them a *Sira* of Muhammad, his *Maghazi*, the conquests, and a history of the community up to his own days. In his methodology, it is possible to find echoes of Ibn Ishaq's universalism, of Waqidi's consensualism and accuracy, of Baladhuri's crisp verdicts and of Ibn ʿAbd al-Hakam's moral epic. And it was Tabari who composed what was by far the most explicit defence of the *Hadith* method in historical writing, while his annalistic arrangement enshrined a style that lasted until modern times.[108]

Ṭabarī's explicitness about his method belies any impression of naivete. His exegetical work moves freely from *ḥadīth* to *qiyās*, to grammatical explication. The traditionalism of his historiography, by contrast, is a discipline self-imposed. His postulate, as Khalidi articulates it: "Knowledge about the past cannot be deduced or inferred; it can only be transmitted."[109] Narratives may become distended, even shapeless; but history is not to be sculpted by sheer authorial technique and audience demand. Only a strict traditionalism can protect it from bias.

We can gauge the worth of Ṭabarī's method by a comparison with the more synthetic Ibn al-Athīr (1160–1233). A denizen of Mosul who often traveled to Baghdad and who, at twenty-eight, was present with Saladin's armies mustered against the Crusaders, Ibn al-Athīr used Ṭabarī's *Annals* heavily (apparently including long passages on the pre-Islamic battle days from the lost original) in composing his *Kāmil fī 'l-Ta'rīkh*, which Rosenthal calls "the high point of Muslim annalistic historiography."[110] The perfection to which his title lays claim is sought in the integration of materials like those culled from Ṭabarī. Vast learning is evident; and the impartiality is notable in Ibn al-Athīr's *Usdu 'l-Ghāba fī 'Ilm al-Ṣaḥāba* (Lions of the Thicket on the Companions of the Prophet), a Who's Who containing some seventy-five hundred biographies of Muḥammad's contemporaries. But Ilse Lichtenstadter trenchantly sums up the cost he paid for narrative continuity in the *Kāmil*: "Ibn al-Athīr used his earlier sources eclectically, synchronizing contradictory dates, following one report and continuing with another without regard to ensuing conflicts and discrepancies in either chronology or historical data."

Seconding R. A. Nicholson's verdict, Lichtenstadter adds her own comparison with Ṭabarī: "The resulting work is, in consequence, far more sophisticated in representing Islamic development, but factually far less reliable."[111]

Ṭabarī's History does not struggle to impose uniformity on the babble of his sources, but he does reduce a vast array to some semblance of coherence, a considerable achievement and a tribute to his energy and distaste for mere economy or literary impact. The survival in medieval libraries of as many as twenty manuscript copies of his monumental work testifies to the value readers found in it. Despite some of the habits of a literary pack rat, Ṭabarī is not "more a collector of traditions than a historian."[112] He is a historian critically aware of the limitations of his authorial role.

Ṭabarī's desire for a universal view of history, *ab initio*, is ultimately biblical in inspiration, as is his notion of history as a succession of prophets and kings. Although no Shīʿite, Ṭabarī is favorably inclined toward the ʿAlids and to the Muʿtazilite theology they often favored.[113] That orientation may help him find a direction and frame a narrative from the sea of data. There is a parallel here with philosophers like Avicenna, and such lesser philosophical lights as Abū Zayd al-Balkhī and Āmirī. All three were accused of Shīʿite sympathies. Avicenna, for one, was pretty clearly no Shīʿite. But the movement was widely followed in his youth, his father came under its influence, and it did play a role in shaping his vision and drawing him toward philosophy and the integrated world view that shows up in his philosophy and even in his medical writings.[114]

The Qurʾān suspends historical time between creation and judgment.[115] But in the biblical text, cosmology is the backdrop to history. It is Ṭabarī's attunement to the resulting vision of history that makes it natural for him to begin his chronicle with a definition of time and a theory of the world's duration. His self-conscious traditionalism sets the form of these introductory comments. For he defines time lexically, citing the poetic texts and Arabic usages that a sound philologist of his day would employ. And the world's duration is deduced from extensive iterations of *ḥadīth*. Yet history now must take its start in cosmology.

Saadiah's Historical Orientation

The impact of Genesis, and philosophy, could not be plainer. Jews and Christians were nursed on biblical historiography, drinking in its subtle blend of historic data with interpretation, the natural and the transcendent. Under Islamic rule, these non-Muslims could share the cosmopolitan values and philosophical inheritance of the empire yet stand clear of the reaction against rationalism and the pressure to become a mouthpiece for dynastic agendas.

Saadiah Gaon, the first systematic Jewish philosopher (882–942), is said to have composed a *taʾrikh* that ran from the creation to his own day. Later a word for history, *taʾrikh* is probably meant here in its original sense, as an ordering of dates, a chronology. Such attempts at order are a primal task of historical synthesis.[116] If Saadiah wrote such a work, it would parallel his efforts to order the ancient rabbinic authorities.[117]

Chronology for Saadiah was a tool in a vital struggle. For it could vindicate the continuity of tradition and thus give the imprimatur of sustained (and sustainable) growth to a tradition whose authority his adversaries, the Karaites and "deniers" like Hiwi al-Balkhī, rejected. Appeals to continuity have a Judaic history at least as old as *Mishnah Avot*, Philo, and Josephus. They extend to the arguments of Judah Halevi and Abraham Ibn Dā'ūd.[118] The great theme of medieval appeals to tradition is not Burke's notion of the trials of experience, the idea that ancient customs and institutions have stood the test of time. It is closer to the claims for organicity that thinkers like Oakeshott and Hayek graft to Burke's claims: Medieval traditionalists call upon a sense of trust to bind together the generations. What is organic is not simply the growth process, the annual rings on the same tree, but the linkage among the members of a community—the ecology of the forest.

But more is at stake here than apologetics. Saadiah was a consummate exegete, and his interest in history finds its philosophical significance in his understanding of the workings of scripture. Writing of religious texts in general (including the Qur'ān, whose language he sometimes echoes in his Arabic biblical translations, giving them a scriptural sound)[119] Saadiah finds a tripartite message, embodying law, sanction, and historical lessons that link the two:

> All the books, however numerous, of the prophets and sages of every nation, are made up of three elements. First in precedence is command and prohibition. That is one rubric. Second, reward and punishment, the fruits of obedience and disobedience. And third, the reports of those who lived virtuously in the land and so fared well and those who lived corruptly and so were ruined For no reformation (*istislāh*) is complete without these three components.[120]

Saadiah's analysis echoes Plato's account of laws. He fuses the Platonic rational "preamble" with scriptural narrative; and the Platonic sanction, characteristic of positive law, with the prophetic understanding of God's requital of obedience and disobedience. That requital, Saadiah argues, springs from our own actions. For he understands accountability on a Muʿtazilite model and in keeping with the rabbinic idea that destiny underscores human choices by promoting the penchant that led to them.[121] Without historical examples, he urges, we might not see the clear nexus of action to outcome. It is by spelling out the inherent or consequential destructiveness of wrongdoing, that scripture achieves its monitory purpose. Saadiah illustrates with a medical example: A good physician does not just say, 'Do this and don't do that,' but 'Do this and don't do that, because it will cure or prevent your headache, as it did for so-and-so.'[122]

Saadiah was the first Hebrew lexicographer. His Hebrew-Arabic dictionary grew out of his pioneering work on the vexing *hapax legomena* and other rare words of the Bible. His exegesis and translation of the ancient text were founded on a conscientiously applied philology and poetics. He ordered the Hebrew liturgy and wrote the earliest known systematic Hebrew grammar. And he mobilized his knowledge of astronomy, mathematics, Talmudic law, and biblical exegesis in settling a bitter calendrical dispute among the Jewish leaders of his day. But historical knowledge proved useful in far broader contexts. A Hebrew work like the *Ta'rikh*, the so-called *Seder 'Olam* or Universal Order, was used by Muslim authors in laying chronological groundworks for their own work in universal history.

Saadiah's efforts in systematic philosophy were organized not just by the problematics of *kalām* but by the Socratic principles of conceptual analysis. His regular use of thematic introductions, for each part of his philosophical summa and each biblical book in his Arabic translations and commentaries of the books of the Hebrew Bible, are hallmarks of the conceptual approach. They are also landmarks in the emergence of the "introduction" as a semi-independent literary form. The genre goes back to the *Eisagoge* of Porphyry, written as an introduction to Aristotle's Organon and to the Aristotelian corpus as a whole. It continues down to the *Muqaddimah* of Ibn Khaldūn and our own practice of writing introductory textbooks, and teaching courses that are introductory to a discipline or field of study.[123]

A drive for order—and for intelligibility through order—runs all through Saadiah's oeuvre. That drive is paralleled, for example, in the works on logic, politics, language, ethics, and culture of his contemporary Fārābī. And compare al-Bīrūnī (973–ca. 1050).[124] The great astronomer, mathematician, and anthropologist of India, who corresponded in his youth with the even younger Avicenna, composed a chronology in his maturity, based on his calendrical and cosmological researches. Bīrūnī calculated the earth's diameter, based on the measure of a degree in the solar arc. Earlier workers, in Ma'mūn's reign, had applied a method devised by the Hellenistic polymath Eratosthenes (ca. 275–ca. 195 B.C.E.) to form a good estimate, using observers stationed miles apart. But Bīrūnī contrived to achieve the same end from a single observation point. The project is emblematic of all strivings to find the place of the human subject in the cosmos. To Saadiah such efforts are more than symbolism. Reasonings about the sun's course, the seasons, the polar night, the earth's cycle of evaporation and rainfall, are prominent in his thinking. Others might compare man's place to that of some worm in the bowels of the magnificent organism of the macrocosm, whose eyes are the stars and whose limbs are the spheres. But for Saadiah humanity is at the heart of things: The earth's centrality in the cosmos and man's rank among earth's living creatures bespeak the dignity of humankind and the centrality of the human calling in God's plan.

But even that moral does not exhaust the significance of the quest. The work of situating ourselves in time and space has an intrinsic interest, and the dignity that the sciences impute, along with the sense of intellectual control they impart, would vanish without the larger curiosity and the more detailed responses to it that factual knowledge can provide. Saadiah draws on all the sciences for his reading of Scripture and on Scripture for his vision of history. Like his Muslim contemporaries, he is seeking orientation. Chronology blossoms in his time, along with geography, geodesy, and astronomy, for parallel reasons. The new interest of authors and their readers in situating themselves enlarges the usefulness of historical work and sets a premium on clarity, accuracy, and synchrony. A well-marked geography and a credible chronology allow readers to relate not just physically but morally and intellectually to the great events and epochs of other times and places. So such work expands the specious present beyond the moment of phenomenal immediacy. It allows historiography, through its potential to enlarge the human sensibilities of its readers, to assert itself as a humanistic discipline.

Masʿūdī

Masʿūdī (ca. 890–956) advances the global perspective and thus the humanistic project of history writing. Educated in the Greek sciences, he was well read in the translated works of Plato, Aristotle, Alexander of Aphrodisias, Themistius, Proclus, Philoponus, and the philosophers of the Islamic school.[125] He cites some 165 sources by Pellat's count, including Arabic versions of Plato, Aristotle, and Ptolemy, and of Pahlavi classics as well.[126]

Most of Masʿūdī's writings, some thirty-six works in all, are lost.[127] But the extant text of an early version of *The Golden Meadows* (completed in the winter of 947), reveals how sensitive he was to thematic arrangement. Organizing his materials by caliphal reigns rather than years, he uses geography along with geology, geodesy, ethnography, and ethology to frame a backdrop to his history. He cites the precedent of Christian authors for this approach, and we know its use in Agapius for one. The same pattern was to be followed by other Muslim writers including Muṭahhar. It was richly elaborated by Ibn Khaldūn. But, as Shboul pointedly remarks, Masʿūdī does not relegate his settings to a preface. His aim is to integrate geographical with historical discussions, "to use his historical knowledge as evidence for verifying a geographical hypothesis, and, conversely . . . to employ geographical considerations for explaining a historical detail or situation."[128] He used facts about the Russian attack on Muslim settlements on the Caspian, for example, to discredit the notion that the Black Sea and the Caspian were a single body of water. He offered details about Khālid b. Walīd's campaigns in southern Iraq as evidence of the recession of the Gulf of Basra. He ascribes the linguistic diversity and political fragmentation of the Caucasus to the mountainous terrain and relates the political power of Byzantium to the strategic location of Constantinople. Similarly, his ethnography is geographically oriented, pursuing an environmental determinism that he had broached in biology[129] and that will be much prized by Ibn Khaldūn.

In a strange phrase that Khalidi notes with interest,[130] Masʿūdī described himself as "a woodcutter by night (*ḥāṭib layl*)." The expression might hint at a random mingling of grave with trivial matter. But Masʿūdī seems to mean it, with some ironic self-deprecation, to suggest the values that guide him in choosing his material, not least of which is the need to keep his audience awake. Partly as a result, his work survives where many more are lost. Holding a mirror to the minds of his audience, he tells of the antiquities of Egypt—its pyramids, canals, nilometers, bridges and dikes, and of black Africa to the south, as described by an old Copt at the court of Ibn Ṭulūn.[131] The monarch's curiosity stands in for the interests of the audience, and the Coptic persona shades the patina of antiquity with the curious ambivalence of the exotic.

Masʿūdī's ideal is an "integrated" (*manẓūm*) history, preserving and interrelating achievements in the arts and sciences, with the wisdom of the sages, and the broad experience of humanity in law, ethics, rhetoric, theology, and government. The records of war and politics are part of his story, of course. But history has a larger charge, as the memory of human culture. Without it, mankind would forget the foundations acquired through centuries of struggle; and the arts and sciences would lose their cumulative edge. History bears implicit lessons, to be grasped through critical study. For statecraft can learn the causes of the rise and fall of states and nations. But more largely, history can explain the growth and decline of the sciences and the arts.[132]

Masʿūdī had no specialized, professional training. He reveled in being a generalist. Bearing no official post or title, he traveled far more widely than his erudite and well-traveled contemporaries; and he learned far more eclectically. Born in Baghdad, he journeyed to most of the Persian provinces and saw Syria, Oman, Khurasan, Armenia, Azerbaijan, Sind, and other parts of the Indian subcontinent. He was more than once in East Africa, but finally settled in Egypt, where he did most of his writing and where he died. He has heard tell of Paris and shows a knowledge of Ceylon and China, and of Korea or Indochina, evidently gleaned at secondhand, just as he learned about Byzantium by questioning others during his travels in Syria near the Byzantine frontier.[133] His desire to situate himself in time is as visible in his surviving writings as his desire to situate himself culturally and spatially.[134]

Masʿūdī may have been a merchant or a Shīʿite missionary, or both. Regardless of his means of support, he made knowledge—later to be dispersed in his writings—the overriding aim of his itinerant life. Everywhere he lived or traveled he sought out Muslim savants of all persuasions and traditions and interviewed sea captains and admirals, *ghāzī*s, ambassadors, merchants, and other travelers, systematically seeking information. But he put no special premium on oral accounts, and his written sources go far beyond those that come in for particular mention. Often they are exotic. He took his list of Frankish kings, for example, from a work he found at Cairo in 947–48, only a few years after its composition (in 939–40) by Godmar, the bishop of Gerona, at the behest al-Ḥakam, the Umayyad prince (and later caliph) at Cordova.

From his own references to his lost writings, it seems pretty clear that Masʿūdī was a Twelver Shīʿite, not an unusual concomitant of his Muʿtazilite outlook.[135] He debated with all manner of Muslim sectarians and adherents of rival faiths but always eagerly probed their beliefs. Sabians, Zoroastrians, Manichaeans, Mazdakites, Khurramites, Carmathians, Samaritans, Masoretic Jews, and probably Hindu Brahmins were among his interlocutors.[136] He visited Magian fire temples,[137] consulted the Bible (*al-Tawrāh*) for himself, and knew his Baghdad contemporary Saadiah Gaon personally, as well as Saadiah's teacher Abū Kathīr of Tiberias. He rates Saadiah's Arabic translations and commentaries of the Hebrew Bible the best he knows.[138]

Besides the *Murūj al-Dhahab*, Meadows of Gold, only his *al-Tanbīh wa 'l-Ishrāf*, Notice and Overview, survives to represent his writings. It is a late work, meant as a summary, update, advertisement, and guide to his others.[139] Dunlop details how Masʿūdī expanded and corrected his European geographical and historical information here, relying on such authors as the Maronite Qays, the Melkites Agapius and Eutychius, and a monk named Athenaeus, the Nestorian Yaʿqūb b. Zakariyyā' al-Kaskarī, and the Jacobite Abū Zakariyyā' Dankhā, whose purview extended to Greek philosophy as well as political history.[140]

Masʿūdī's great work, by his own account, was a universal history entitled *Akhbār al-Zamān*, Reports of the Ages. In thirty sections, it dealt with history and geography, including much ancient history—biblical, Egyptian, Greek, Roman, and Byzantine. Characteristically, Masʿūdī does not confine his treatment of Europe to an appreciation of ancient Greek achievements. He was, as Shboul points out, "the only known Muslim author to deal systematically with Byzantine history after the rise of Islam and up to his own day. . . . One could perhaps add that seldom has an author discussed the affairs of a hostile nation with such fairmindedness."[141] The lost magnum opus included sections on the history of Africa and Persia. It dealt with the pre-Islamic Arabs and, of course, with the rise of Islam. It concluded with an account of Shīʿite rebellions in ʿAbbāsid times.[142] It was from his studies of history that Masʿūdī extracted the general sketch of the history of the world that gave him the loom on which to weave the *Meadows of Gold*.

Despite a fascination with the ideal of an integrated historiography, "the general impression we get from what Masʿūdī himself says," Dunlop comments, "is that his writings were not very systematic." They were composed, it seems, from information gathered on the fly and revised as new data came to hand in the course of his travels.[143] But Khalidi finds a pattern and method nonetheless. Anecdotes persist, to be sure, by the universal vitality that a good story can always command. But they are arranged by reigns. Circumstantial data about each caliph's names, birth and ancestry, regime, counselors, and death make the monarchical figures focal points, about whom the anecdotes sketch the image of a personality and the spirit of an age.

The titles of his lost works, cited in his surviving texts, reveal Masʿūdī's experimentation with varying formats,[144] and his own testimony confirms the playful spirit behind that experimentation. As Shboul reports,

> The idea of writing a book that would contain a miscellany of historical traditions without any chronological framework, or single theme, seems to have taken shape in Masʿūdī's mind in the course of writing the *Murūj*, for towards the end of the *Murūj* he expresses his hope to write such a book 'if circumstances allow it.' Giving the title of this forthcoming compilation as *Waṣl al-Majālis* (Combination of Assemblies, or roughly Collection of Traditions

> for Literary Assemblies), he describes its proposed contents as a "collection of historical information and traditions with no particular framework or system of compilation, but rather according to occasion."[145]

The *Tanbīh* reveals that Masʿūdī did write such a work, and another on similar lines, appropriately entitled *Masʿudian Reports*. Here is no naif, innocent of thematic principles, but a sophisticate on the subject, adopting a disarming conversational tone, but laboring behind the scenes, as Plato did, to bring the digression to the level of high art.[146] As man of letters (*adīb*), Masʿūdī is fascinated by the kaleidoscope of experience and well aware that the colors that dance in his own mind's eye might also fascinate an audience.

The spirit of play is evident in the *Murūj al-Dhahab* and reflected in the title: The fields of gold and mines of gems that the title promises offer their nuggets and jewels where we find them. If one's own tillage, as the old homily has it, hides acres of diamonds, Masʿūdī reasons that one never knows what might lie further afield. Adopting a sober tone, he is careful to state, "I had not thought it fitting to busy myself with such studies as this or to devote myself to this [generalist historical] branch of literature (*adab*) until I had written my books on religious beliefs and doctrines . . . jurisprudence . . . the Imamate . . . politics . . . astronomy and cosmology . . . the sensory and nonsensory world."[147] Having fulfilled these obligations, the work of a lifetime for a man of lesser energies and interests, the mind was free to range where it would and, in Masʿūdī's case, to carry the body with it.

Even in its fragmentary state, Masʿūdī's historical work shows clear marks of method: a reliance on specialists and eyewitness accounts, a respect for authors of broad vision and sophistication, a distaste for dilettantes, for uncritical reportage and unconfirmed reports (*taqlīd*). Masʿūdī admires Ibn Khurradādhbih (ca. 820–25–911) for his skill in composition, his learning and scope—and relies on him for data, especially for early history. But he smiles at his conveying information that might be heard from court messengers and mail carriers. The dig is ad hominem. For Ibn Khurradādhbih's *Kitāb al-Masālik wa 'l-Mamālik* or Book of Roads and Realms, reflects his work as a postmaster and intelligence director in the province of Jibāl.

Like Saadiah, Masʿūdī applies explicit standards of credibility and possibility.[148] He anticipates Ibn Khaldūn's dislike of sheer guesswork about numbers. He values technical modes of ascertainment (*taḥṣīl*) and corroborated testimony, as in assuring the authenticity of quoted verses—thus heeding the sort of concerns that Ibn Sallām voiced. Like Ṭabarī, Masʿūdī favors empirical inquiry (*baḥth*) over appeals to the "self-evident," or "obvious" (*badīhī*). Presumption, he argues, can verify only the most trivial of facts and discredit only the rankest errors.

In place of intuition (and quite unlike Ṭabarī), Masʿūdī uses induction and reasoning (*istidlāl, qiyās*) to check reports, especially when they are uncorroborated (*akhbār al-āḥād*). Like Saadiah, then, he puts his data to the test (*miḥna*), using the natural sciences, causal regularity, and experience (*al-ʿādāt wa 'l-tajārub*) to confirm, discredit, or suspend judgment about received accounts, but also to understand or rationalize unusual phenomena. He explains the magnetic properties of the earth, for example, by analogy with the magnetism of iron.[149] His cosmology stems from Aristotle, whom he calls "the author of the *Logic*." But the Greek worldview is enlarged by the work of Kindī, Sarakhsī, and Thābit b. Qurra, whose book on the influences of the sun and moon Masʿūdī received from Thābit's son Sinān. His naturalism and skeptical tendencies are moderated by deference to God, the ultimate sovereign, whose "custom" we observe in nature's familiar course.[150]

Masʿūdī's critical spirit stands in tension with his storyteller's love of fantasy and fables. Respecting well-corroborated traditions and revering the revelation on which human welfare depends,[151] he seeks a middle path between sheer mistrust or scientism and the credulity of the anthropomorphists, which he finds typified in the *Isrāʾīliyyāt*, and in all popular fables, romances about marvels, and gullible *akhbār*. He finds his middle ground in the notion that even wonders need enough explanation to make them conceivable. Otherwise, he leaves them in limbo, cited, but with a formulaic shrug: *Allahu aʿlamu*, "God knows best."

Even stories of the creation of the jinn are held at arm's length, with the remark that although they are widely credited, most scientific people reject such tales.[152] Masʿūdī labors in the *Tanbīh* to extricate a kernel of fact from the matter of the Alexander Romance, encrusted with wisdom literature, popular fable, and Qurʾānic allusions to the figure of Dhū ʾl-Qarnayn. He prunes sensational details from the account of Cleopatra's suicide and corrects the *Murūj al-Dhahab* as to the identities of Octavius and Anthony. He also corrects his earlier confusion of Claudius Ptolemy with the Ptolemid dynast, recognizing, from texts he has now seen, that the astronomer/geographer was not a monarch but a scholar living in the reign of Antoninus Pius.[153]

Masʿūdī's yen for system does overlay his empirical receptivity with a schematism, or several, beyond the sheer discipline of critical thinking, logic, and naturalism. He struggles to fit the nations he knows—including the Indians and Slavs—into the genealogies of the seven nations sprung from Noah. Persian, Chinese, and Indian traditions do not readily dovetail with the presumption of a universal flood. That means trouble in making Noahids of these nations.[154] Masʿūdī's aim, especially as he matures, is accuracy, even at the expense of the literary values that entranced him in his early work. So the problems about Genesis are loyally but dispassionately noted. But, like Cicero, Masʿūdī is ready to set apart what is upheld on religious grounds from what reason and experience would otherwise have persuaded. Contact with the traditions of other nations has prepared him, as it did Herodotus long before and Isaac LaPeyrère long after,[155] to view orthodox chronologies and genealogies with a measure of skepticism. Often voiced as a tactful pluralism, acknowledging, say, that others tell another story, Masʿūdī's questioning is fostered by scientific cosmology, empirical geography, and an experiential anthropology, that as yet has no method to call its own. But it is nurtured as well by the very comprehensiveness of the biblical cosmology whose mythic topoi are now called into question.

Like Hegel or Toynbee, Masʿūdī tries to sum up the contributions of the great civilizations in terms of some particular national genius: Indians have wisdom and virtue, perfected among them, since they (at least at the start) retained the memory of Adam but had no revelation (as the stereotypic "Brahmin" rejection of special revelation drove home). The Indians took human capabilities to their human limits, developing in their caste system and their astrology the perfect images of the natural hierarchy found in the heavens. The Greeks (including Romans, Byzantines, Slavs, and Franks) have wisdom and philosophy, typified in the texts now translated into Arabic—most especially, Euclid's geometry, Ptolemy's *Almagest*, and the thoughts of Socrates, Plato and Aristotle. Masʿūdī cites with admiration the meteorology, astronomy, musical theory, medicine, political philosophy, geography, biology, and cosmology, but above all the logic of the Greeks.

The Persians and Chinese have statecraft, typified in the idealized rule and administration of the ancient Persian empires,[156] the fabled justice of ancient Chinese monarchs, the natural religion of the Chinese, and the allying of religion with politics in both civilizations. Masʿūdī's commercial interests show through in his discussions of China and India. Beyond the naturalist's description of flora and fauna, he dwells on the trade goods and especially the artistry of Chinese craftsmen. For the Turks (including the Khazars, among others), the national genius is warfare—a projection of the most visible role of the otherwise rather marginal-seeming nomadic northern tribes. For the Chaldaeans (understood to include all the old Syriac speakers of Syria and Iraq—the Ninevans, Babylonians, Aramaeans, Assyrians, Nabataeans, and others) the national genius[157] is agriculture and the kind of urban and rural development that made the first cities and roads, canals and mines, as well as the astrology that the ancients associated with the Chaldaean race.[158] This last group is of special interest to Masʿūdī. His remarks on the superiority of the "Babylonian" clime and his resistance to Arab commonplaces about Nabataean peasants betray his identification with these "Syrian" peoples. He traces their history from biblical Assyria to the Mosul of his day and locates the cradle of civilization in their midst.[159] For the Egyptians (including Maghrībīs and the black nations of Africa), although Egyptian monuments of art and engineering remain to be marveled at, the dominant themes are astrology and magic.

As for the Arabs, the early nomads were free and self-reliant[160]—an image amply developed in Ibn Khaldūn. Their spiritual sensitivity made them seers and soothsayers and so prepared them to be the first recipients of the Qurʾān. Masʿūdī records a tradition that aligns the Arabs with the Greeks, as descendants of the brothers Qaḥṭan and Yūnan, making the Arabs proper heirs to the Greek legacy when the decline of Hellas orphaned the sciences and the arts.[161] But, as Shboul remarks, Masʿūdī does not seem to give this tradition much weight.[162]

Masʿūdī's vision of history contains a clear sense of cultural progress. But that sense runs counter to his observations of palpable decline. And it is hardly seconded by the general Islamic tendency to assume that the world has never regained the purity it had in the earliest days of Islam, when Muḥammad's revelations were still falling fresh and fast on the startled ears of his first hearers. There was a gradual advance, Masʿūdī argues, up to the Prophet's arrival. For until then humanity was unready for the full revelation of God's light and plan. Thereafter, the divine effulgence was preserved and spread (often esoterically) through the work of the Shīʿite *Imāms*.[163] Yet the world *is* trapped in an inexorable downward slide, from the perfection of its creation to the final execution of God's judgment.

The clashing movements reveal the interplay of opposing forces: Spiritual light does shine ever more brightly, as Shīʿite doctrine teaches. It is the source of all inspiration and ultimate redemption. But the impetus given nature at the outset slows inevitably, and material substance, pristine as it was at the creation, inevitably erodes. Thus the loss of human vigor and longevity since the days of the Flood. Political conflict and linguistic fragmentation, the weakness of even the best of kings, expose the fragility of worldly history, the story of what Augustine (unbeknownst to Masʿūdī) had called the City of Man.

In the realm of the spirit, and so of the mind as well, progress remains a proper hope. Modern poetry and learning do outshine their early counterparts, and "the sciences progress without end." History is the register of such progress, the standard and celebration of human achievement and the chapbook of those qualities and values that make it possible. Not least of these is awareness of the very distinction, which we have seen taken up by Kindī and Rāzī from Plato, the distinction of the world, where loss is inevitable, from the spiritual realm, where progress can be won, through vigilance, diligence, and creativity.[164] Masʿūdī's has temporalized the Platonizing distinction, transforming the warring tendencies it represents from an internal tension to a torrent of crosscurrents that mark the entire course of history. But he holds fast to the Platonic thesis that all moral decline is a turning toward the physical, away from the intellectual and spiritual. He finds that general thesis instantiated not only in the case of the Umayyads, where any Muslim writer might have sought it, but even in the history of the Chinese.

Viewed from where Masʿūdī stands, what is distinctive in Bacon, we must note, is not the idea of progress per se but the linking of science with technology that shifts the idea of progress from the purely intellectual or spiritual into the material realm. Viewed from our own standpoint, what is perhaps most distinctive is Masʿūdī's rescue of the idea of moral and intellectual progress from the entropy of inevitable decline—by its linkage to the realm of the spiritual. But, then again, for us today, the advance of technology, now freed from the thrall of magic and armed with the aegis of Athena, makes the lack of moral or spiritual progress the striking fact of history.

The Triumph of Synthetic History

The high tide of Greek learning all but engulfs the matter of Arabic and Islamic history with its flood of ideas and eddies of thought. Sinān b. Thābit b.

Qurra (d. 943), the Sabian physician charged by the caliph Muqtadir with licensing the physicians of Baghdad, moors his biographical history in the ethics and politics of Plato.[165] Muṭahhar b. Ṭāhir al-Maqdisī (d. 985), "a keen and remarkably unbiased student of religions, writing in Bust, Eastern Persia,"[166] enriches his history with science, philosophy, theology, and doxography. Eloquent and clearly interested in ideas for their own sake, his *Kitāb al-Bad' wa 'l-Ta'rikh*, the Book of Creation and Chronology (ca. 966), discourses on God's attributes and offers rich accounts of geography, early thought and civilizations, the Islamic sects, and the achievements of naturalists and philosophers. It does not reach the Muslim era until its fourth volume, the midpoint of the work. Muṭahhar gives precedence to Islam, but shows broad respect for the contributions of its predecessors and rivals. Like Saadiah, whose theological summa opens with an epistemological introduction, Muṭahhar anchors his work in a discussion of knowledge and the mind. Only then does he take up the now familiar sequence, from the creation to the Prophet and the Muslim dynasties.

Muṭahhar's gusto for literature and ideas matches Masʿūdī's humanistic ideal. But, as Rosenthal notes, Muṭahhar's work does not find a use for all its explorations of intellectual history in explaining what more conventional thinkers might call historical events.[167] The fault is not unique to Muṭahhar—nor to writers in Arabic for that matter. Part of the blame may lie with the makers rather than the writers of history. But the disconnect with more pragmatic interests, along with Muṭahhar's independence and tendency to free thinking, may have contributed to making his work all but unknown in later ages. Yet in the heyday of the Sāmānids, the same dynasty that nurtured Avicenna, Bīrūnī, and Firdawsī, Muṭahhar's cosmopolitan humanism was welcomed and warmly supported by his courtier patron.[168]

Hamza al-Isfahānī (ca. 893–ca. 970) was a brilliant philologist, a collector and classifier of proverbs and superstitions, a connoisseur of poetry, and the author of a universal history. He edited and commented on the *diwān* of Abū Nuwās—thus firmly enlisting with the "moderns" in poetry.[169] Like Muṭahhar, he sought chronological assistance in astronomy, as Bīrūnī too would do, masterfully. Fascinated by orthography and its ambiguities, he was fond of devising etymologies, often far fetched and Persianizing. His *Shuʿūbī* biases show through in his historiography. Yet he does not expatiate on the glories of ancient Iran. Nor does he slight Arabic history, but only seeks its context in the Byzantine, Persian, Lakhmid, Coptic, Ghassānid, Yemenite, Jewish, and Graeco-Roman past.

Isfahānī knew Ṭabarī personally and was well known in his native Isfahan, admired for his learning—although branded a "drivel monger" by his detractors. His history, in Dunlop's words, is "not a historical masterpiece but rather a textbook for practical use."[170] But that gives an idea of just what now seemed useful: not concepts but chronology, ethnographic and dynastic history. Hamza's readers want to know the sequence of the world's monarchs, the genealogies of the Persians, Arabs, Chaldeans, and Chinese, and the routes taken from their pagan origins to their present Muslim, Jewish, Christian, Sabian, or Buddhist faiths.

Hamza details eight manuscripts he had before him in listing the Persian shahs. For the history of Israel, he consulted a learned Jew, who, Dunlop writes, "appears to have had most of the Hebrew Bible by heart."[171] In matters Byzantine, he used a *History of the Greeks* translated into Arabic by Ḥabīb b. Bahrēz, metropolitan of Mosul in the time of Ma'mūn. He arranged for two Greek war prisoners, father and son, to translate a Byzantine history for him. In the list of kings included in Wakī''s history, Hamza found a sequence at odds with the prisoners' report. He recorded both versions but gave preference to the soldiers' account, since the old text may have been marred by the Arabic translator's misreadings.[172]

The historians of the mid tenth century struggled to balance form with matter, theory with data. They did not succeed in every way. But, then, even their contemporary Fārābī did not produce a complete and free-standing Islamic philosophy. His ideal was a systematic and rigorous metaphysics and cosmology, integrated with ethical, social, cultural, linguistic, and political theory. But, as he writes, almost confessionally, some thinkers can follow a sound argument even when they cannot always mount one. Often Fārābī writes in aphorisms. The most original statement of his philosophy brackets his ideas not in any demonstrative framework but as a body of principles underlying the received beliefs of the people of a virtuous society.

A great deal more in the way of philosophical integration and synthesis remained to be achieved by Avicenna, Ibn Bājjah, and Averroes. Here the material was as Greek as the method. But in history the great mass of data was local in content and not thematic in its raw state. To marshal it into significance demanded synthetic work of the highest order. And that task was not made easier by the unfolding of events, which made it ever clearer that history was not simply the realization of God's plan on earth, as the propaganda of the more thoughtless or ruthless dynasts might have wished it to be. Only compare the triumphalism of a Juwaynī or a Bābūr (among the apologists and celebrants of Mongol hegemony) with the soul searching of Maqrīzī (1364–1442) over the deeply troubling turns that he found Islamic history to have taken.

For generations, as Stephen Humphreys explains,[173] Muslim historians had aspired to write "salvation history." But widespread revulsion with the Umayyad reign and the triumphalism of its apologists led not just to revisionism and a quest for more critical standards but to the search for a metaphysic of history that would allow the winnowing of empiric events from divine decrees. Thus Yaʿqūbī, spurred by his Shīʿite interests, abandons the dogma of communal infallibility to blame the early *umma* for the rise and presumptive wickedness of ʿUthmān.[174] But Maqrīzī was no Shīʿite. He could boast study with no less than six hundred masters, including Ibn Khaldūn, with whom he was on friendly terms. Before retiring to Mecca to work as a historian, he had served as a judge, hospital financial officer, and sometime *muḥtasib*, as well as a professor. Perhaps as a result, his historical writings mingle a certain somber detachment with a deep sense of engagement.[175]

Seven centuries after the ʿAbbāsid revolution, eight after the battle of Ṣiffīn, Maqrīzī, living in Damascus and Mamluk Cairo, will ponder for years how the twists of providence allowed the Umayyads not only to claim but to win the caliphate.[176] The question resonates with his life experience and a moral sensibility sharpened by personal and public tragedy. The Umayyads here might stand for powers in his own time and much closer to home.

Maqrīzī outlived all his children, including an only daughter, who may have died of the plague. He witnessed the recurrent famines that beset Egypt between 1394 and 1405,[177] and he blamed the food shortages on poor government. He could not have been wholly wrong. For Egypt, as we know, was once the granary of the Roman Empire. Mobilizing the resources of universal history, Maqrīzī researched similar calamities in the past and applied what he had learned from Ibn Khaldūn about the interplay of politics and economics. He blamed governmental neglect of the most basic human needs for the high rents, inflation, and debased coinage.[178] Looking back to the founding moments of the caliphate, he sought that first fork in the road that led to misgovernment in the dominions of Islam.

His explanation, forecast in Masʿūdī and in Kindī's philosophical consolations, turns on a dualism that rejects the naive expectations that first sparked his anxious quest. Sorrowfully, he turns to what we would call an Augustinian, two worlds approach. Muḥammad himself, Maqrīzī must acknowledge, was a politician as well as a prophet. He needed to conciliate the worldly Umayyads, to win them over and bring the force of their military and administrative skills to his cause, and that of God. Muḥammad knew what would ensue. But it was he, not just the later community but the Prophet himself, who gave the Umayyad clan power in Mecca and confirmed their grip after the rise of Islam, effectively marginalizing the faithful Medinan *anṣār*. By relegating these early followers to an intellectual role, he elevated them spiritually. But worldly governance was no longer theirs. Even the ʿAbbāsid regime, for which Maqrīzī had once been a fulsome apologist, could now be seen as one more outcome of the Prophet's fateful compromise with history. Bosworth sums up Maqrīzī's conclusions:

> Everything which happened in these formative decades of the Islamic community must have been part of God's inscrutable plan for His creation. The Prophet knew that the caliphate would fall into the hands of unworthy successors, i.e., the Umayyads. . . . Yet because God had marked out Hāshim above all the rest of the Arabs by selecting Muḥammad as the channel for His revelation for the Arabs and then for all mankind, and because Muḥammad, though a prophet, had chosen to live a humble life rather than the life of a monarch, the Prophet's family could not subsequently be demeaned by their involvement in secular affairs like governorships and military commands.[179]

The degrading, often brutal business of collecting taxes—winning and holding the power that allowed them to be collected, and administering the system by which they were collected and disbursed—was far too base for the house of the Prophet. Inevitably, wisely, in fact, it was turned over to what must now be acknowledged, with distaste but some lingering sense of legitimation, as a necessary and divinely ordained evil, the secular arm.

The critique is profound. But so is the sense of resignation. In the long struggle for the historian's eye, the struggle between facts and ideals, theory has now found a way of accommodating not only the plethora but the cruelty of facts—but only by consigning the most unwelcome of those facts to a realm of positivity beyond the reach of moral judgment, conceding the flow of history to powers beyond the reach of God's fullest command and most perfect will.

Miskawayh's Historiography

In *The Experiences of Nations and Outcomes of their Endeavors*, Miskawayh, as we have noted, follows Ṭabarī down to his own times and then (for the years 951–83) turns strikingly to firsthand experience and eyewitness reports of military, diplomatic, and court events, recorded with insight and élan. The interest, as in Ṭabarī, remains moral. But the morality is now more secular and pragmatic. History has become what Khalidi calls "a long parable on the art of government."[180]

So the multivolume work, full of matter and incident, does have a theme. Miskawayh scorns most Arabic historical writing as idle talk, useful only for entertainment, or as a soporific.[181] Small wonder that the ancient philosophers did not rate history a science—if its uses merge with those of fiction.[182] Serious history demands clearer standards of fact and a mode of organization that will highlight the lessons to be learned. Those lessons, for Miskawayh, are not captured in the old triumphalist scheme. He shifts his gaze, as Bosworth puts it, from the "unfolding of God's plan on the general stage of history" to "human actions and the temporal causation of events."[183] These are matters of interest, but not mere casual interest. As Frank Peters writes:

> Earlier students of *adab* had filled their books of "Table Talk," "Culture of the Vizier," and related subjects with richly moral anecdotes about the great and near-great in Islamic government circles. The stuff of Miskawayh's own history was not so much anecdotes as richly detailed reports, his own or those of other eyewitnesses and incisive moral judgments. By bringing together the *ta'rikh* and *adab* techniques in composition, Miskawayh rendered both of them more genuinely historical. Against the traditionalists' atomistic approach to history, Miskawayh argued the historian's responsibility to provide organic causal explanations for events. *Adab* history, on the other hand, lacked precision, rigor, and a detached view of its subject. Miskawayh successfully supplied all three, controlled by his own point of view. He did not possess, as Ibn Khaldūn did, a philosophy of history, but he was the first Muslim successfully to locate history *within* philosophy.[184]

Miskawayh breaks with the convention of opening with the creation, finding data from before the Flood neither sure enough nor useful enough to warrant inclusion, even in a universal history. Tales of miracles are also avoided, for they are often distorted and do not contribute to the direction of human activity. Such judgments would rather shock the recipients of prophetic visions, and those most receptive to such accounts. They consider such stories the quintessence of guidance for every age. But the idiom has lost if not its ultimate power then certainly its moral punch for Miskawayh. Even the early victories of Islam are left out of his history, on the grounds that providential and miraculous events provide no models for ordinary mortals. But scientific data are welcomed, and the conventional correlations of temperaments with climatic zones find a place, since they are seen as aids to understanding of human history and mores.[185]

Miskawayh's demand of practical value in the study of history parallels the view of many of the sponsors and users of Arabic translations in natural science, medicine, and metaphysics. Beyond the idea that history should be relevant lies a pointedly political idea of what counts as relevance. In his ethical work, Miskawayh argued that the prudent king and the prudent individual alike will prepare themselves to confront their enemies, internal as well as external. That means doing battle against weakness and vice and not just foreign foes–a striking parallel with the spiritual interpretation of the proper target of *jihād*.

Politically, as Kraemer notes, Miskawayh's History, "gives a brilliant description of [Islamic feudalism] the *iqṭā*ʿ system and its pernicious consequences"[186]—the tax farming, bribery, mulcting of officials, and dependence on mercenaries, slave soldiers, and praetorians. The critique is not radical, but it is all the more telling for that. It fingers mismanagement and wrongdoing in the system's own terms of reference and warmly describes ʿAlī b. ʿĪsā's vigorous efforts at reform. Standing up for the prudential courtier ethic at its best, Miskawayh applies Plato's thesis (*Republic* VIII 567A) that arbitrary and excessive taxation depresses revenues: ʿAlī's tax reforms, he stresses, enhanced revenues, even when they reduced particular exactions. For land owners and other producers did not hesitate to expand their enterprises as they grew more confident that taxes would be assessed fairly and collected uniformly.[187]

History, as Miskawayh sees it, provides models for kings and courtiers, just as literature provides models for us all in making our characters fit for life in this world and worthy of reward in the hereafter. The virtues Miskawayh underscores pertain more to policy than to piety or principle. His case studies highlight prudent management but also ruses, plots, and stratagems.[188] Yet behind his worldliness and anchoring its devices to the yearnings of the ethical philosopher is a conception of *tadbīr*, sound governance. To Miskawayh that means fiscal responsibility, military preparedness, attention to detail, extensive and accurate intelligence. The scheme bears comparison with Machiavelli's ideas about civic virtue and effectiveness. Khalidi praises Miskawayh for sundering historical realism from ethical idealism.[189] But I find the same worldliness and the same tensions with idealism in both the ethical and the historical moieties of Miskawayh's work. It is the old Platonic struggle to yoke two warring horses in the same harness that lends drama to his work. Intriguing, but also poignant, is his (often failing) effort to find a moral footing for practicality and a pragmatic footing for prudence in a precarious environment where he was no outsider but a leading player.

Local Chronicles and Biographical Dictionaries

Later historians, lacking Miskawayh's sensibilities, often revert to more conventional and convenient methods. The linear, annalistic format, from which Miskawayh partially broke free, reasserts itself. So do other modes that have more in common with cataloguing than with any search for meaning in the events of history. Thus Margoliouth can remark: "Gibbon's assertion that the Arabic historian is either the dry chronicle or the flowery orator becomes true after Miskawayh's time."[190] Ibn ʿAsākir (1105–1176), despite his poetic gifts, does not prevent his history of Damascus, the city in which his family had long enjoyed prominence, from degenerating into an (eighteen volume) dictionary of notable Damascenes. He traveled widely in search of learning and *ḥadīth*s, taking instruction, we are told, from thirteen hundred men and over eighty women.[191] There is much of redeeming interest in his accounts. But things get worse. Many other histories become little more than annual registers of local obituary notices.

Ibn ʿAsākir's history is filled with local knowledge, and the same can be said of the works on Mosul by the Khālidī brothers and by Ibn al-Athīr. Under the title *Tarīkh Baghdād*, al-Khaṭīb al-Baghdādī (1002–1071) made a compendium of seventy-eight hundred Baghdad biographies, including those of women, intended mainly to support his core interest in the science of *ḥadīth*. Ibn Ḥajar al-ʿAsqalānī (1372–1449), another major *ḥadīth* scholar, prepared a similar work. But his pious energies grew and broadened, leading him, as Rosenthal remarks, to include biographies of "many men having very tenuous connections with *ḥadīth*."[192] Here traditional learning, local knowledge, and scholarly appetites conjoined. The first motive was tradition, but the thirst for control of the data and the appetite for information went far beyond what legal or theological studies might require. Curiosity became a secular leaven in this, as in many another learned Islamic career.

Even genealogical or scriptural studies could lead back toward Islamic, or human, or cosmic origins. So there is no contradiction but only a natural tension between Hamza al-Isfahānī's writing a universal history and his writing a history of his own Isfahan.[193] The value placed on local history, even when the demand for an overarching structure declines, reflects the new prominence of thematic organization and the privileging of firsthand knowledge. Thus, amongst the alphabetic and anecdotal matter, we now find genuinely thematic collections. Chronicles may break the sequence of years to follow a course of events systematically. Ibn al-Athīr, for example, pursues a four-year sequence connected with the Crusaders in 1217–21.[194] And events are not always simply reported. They may be explained or located in a pattern.[195]

Scholars who follow the Arabic history of philosophy and its allied sciences with almost proprietary interest owe a debt to such compilers of biographical dictionaries as Ibn al-Qifṭī (d. 1248) and Ibn Abī Uṣaybiʿah (1203–1270), and to bibliographers like al-Nadīm, who catalogues hundreds of Arabic works now lost. And general historians of Islamic civilization are indebted to Ibn Khallikān's (1211–1282) *Wafayāt al-Aʿyān wa Anbāʾ al-Zamān*, Obituaries of the Eminent and Records of the Age. Al-Ṣafadī (1296–1363) compiled a biographical dictionary of some thirty, or even fifty volumes. That was too big to be copied readily, but manuscript volumes survive, scattered in Arabic libraries.[196] These authors may favor comprehensiveness over comprehension, but we can see their intelligence struggling beneath the weight of their learning.

Rashīd al-Dīn's Universal History

The drive for universal scope, born of biblical mythopoeisis and Greek science, remains alive and continues to assimilate new materials. The historian and statesman Rashīd al-Dīn (ca. 1247–1318) is an outstanding case in point. Trained as a physician and known as al-Ṭabīb, he knew Hebrew and had a thorough Jewish education, for he did not convert to Islam until he was thirty. Then, as if to establish his bona fides, he acquired a circumstantial knowledge of Islam and wrote a series of works on Islamic theology. Cosmopolitan in outlook, Rashīd al-Dīn was rooted in Persian culture. He was an administrator at heart and an active reformer in the interest of the Ilkhānid regime. But, like Miskawayh, he saw literary culture and historical knowledge as the backbone of sound policy and administrative practice.

In the *Jāmiʿ al-Tawārikh*, or Compendium of Histories, the big historical work that assured his fame long after the intrigues that dogged his political footsteps had been forgotten, Rashīd al-Dīn brought together a rich variety of traditions to form what Rosenthal calls a true world history, incorporating "sketches of Chinese, Jewish, Indian and Western European history." J. A. Boyle speaks in the same sense, as does Bernard Lewis, who calls Rashīd al-Dīn's work "the first genuine universal history of Islam" and probably of the world.[197] As its title implies, the work relied on the researches of many previous historians, among them, the writer of Mongol history Juwaynī. It preserves citations from a precious Mongol history of Genghis Khan, now lost in the original.

Numerous research assistants were enlisted in the writing, begun at the request of Ghazan, the Ilkhānid ruler. Originally intended as a history of the Mongols, the work was commissioned by Ghazan to keep the heirs of his empire mindful of their tribal roots on the Central Asian Steppes and keenly aware of their shared identity and imperial destiny. But that imperial claim itself opened up the work's perspective; and after Ghazan's death, his brother and successor asked Rashīd al-Dīn to expand his history to a global scale, as a memorial. It now became a history of all the peoples the Mongols had encountered. In the pattern of Islamic universal history, it would extend from Adam to the present, including histories of the Arabs, Jews, Mongols, Franks, and Chinese, not just in pro forma sketches but in accounts as circumstantial as available information would allow.

Using his personal wealth and his authority as a co-*wazīr* (for Rashīd al-Dīn never held the reins of the state without a co-minister and rival) the learned statesman built a suburb in the Ilkhānid capital of Tabriz. It was named for himself, the Rashīdī quarter, and comprised some thirty thousand dwellings, fifteen hundred shops, and twenty-four caravanserais. Here he sustained as many as six to seven thousand scholars, their work centered on a library to which he bequeathed sixty thousand volumes, including works of poetry, history and science and a thousand rare and precious Qurʾāns, the handiwork of celebrated calligraphers. He brought fifty physicians from Egypt, Syria, India, and China, assigning each to take on ten medical students.

The contacts with Asia and Europe opened up by the Mongol conquests allowed Rashīd al-Dīn to enlist a cosmopolitan staff in pursuit of his dream of a global history, "including two Chinese scholars, a Buddhist hermit from Kashmir, a Mongol specialist on tribal tradition, and a Frankish traveler, probably a monk who had come as envoy from the Papal Curia." The European traveler gave him access to a Latin chronicle by Martin of Troppau, also called Martin Polonus (d. 1278). Updating the information of that source from his informant's firsthand knowledge of the Holy Roman Empire and the sequence of the popes, Rashīd al-Dīn's opus was able to present current geographical and historical knowledge of exotic Western Europe, the first such excursion since Masʿūdī, and the last until the sixteenth century.[198]

To illustrate his history Rashīd al-Dīn gathered artists who prepared figures of historical personages from the time of Adam down to his own day, portrayed, typically, in Mongol dress. Muḥammad was pictured some eight times—the first known portrait representations of the Islamic prophet.[199] Rashīd al-Dīn made extensive provisions for publication. He endowed funds for two copies to be made annually of each of his many works, one in Arabic and another in Persian. The copyists were to be lodged in the library premises, after their skills had been carefully vetted. It was here, however, that history itself intervened. Charged with the murder of his rival, Rashīd al-Dīn was executed, along with his son; the Rashīdī quarter was plundered and dismantled, its revenues sequestered by the state—although another son later followed his father in the office of *wazīr*.

The thematic approach to history does not die out. Indeed, it can become excessive and foster distortions. The notion that the world has a beginning and an end in a way settles too many questions, and it introduces a sense of drama that can become a force in its own right. Muṭahhar feels moved to describe the end of things in his work, as if to balance the customary accounts of the beginning. Ibn Kathīr actually tries to give equal attention to the beginning and the end of days. After so long a struggle with the weight of historical data, it was perhaps inevitable that there would be instances in which form overpowered matter.

Ibn Khaldūn

A far more credible, if still somewhat tremulous balance is struck by Ibn Khaldūn (1332–1406), in part through the expedient, eschewed by Masʿūdī, of segregating narrative from theory. Yaʿqūbī and Maqdisī had followed Islamic history chronologically. But they gave a more sociological or anthropological treatment to other nations. Ibn Khaldūn turns his anthropological and sociological curiosity toward the civilization he knows best, anatomizing its arts and sciences, trades, crafts, and industries, not as exotic curiosities but as means and modalities of human life. The history itself, when Ibn Khaldūn does get down to cases, is but little more advanced than that of his predecessors. "The *Kitāb al-ʿIbār*," as Dunlop puts it, "is in general what we might expect from an eighth/fourteenth century compiler," although it has its distinctive merits.[200] It does cut loose from the annalistic method, to offer backgrounds about each culture and regime it considers; and it does seek critical distance from the old sources, now viewed with the somewhat jaundiced eye of an old political warhorse. But Ibn Khaldūn becomes a historical thinker of world historical stature when he rises from the quest for a critical historiography to the framing of a general theory of history. His *Muqaddimah*, or Prolegomena to the study of history, fully justifies his claim to have founded a new discipline, a science of civilization. Its argument, drawn from broad and considered observation, works on a scale and to a level of detail that no prior historian in the Arabic language had achieved. To quote from the seasoned judgment of Margoliouth:

> Ibn Khaldūn's Prolegomena is unique in Arabic literature with few parallels in any that existed prior to the invention of printing, in that it embodies the author's generalizations drawn from the study of the records which form the subject of the following volumes. The idea is curiously like that of Aristotle, who drew up or caused to be drawn up accounts of a great number [158] constitutions, and from his observations of what happened composed his great treatise on Politics. Both assume that there is a uniformity in human conduct comparable to the uniformity of nature: that certain modes of life develop certain tendencies; both eliminate so far as possible all elements that are exceptional and draw their inferences from normal occurrences, the repetition of which after the like antecedents justifies them in formulating rules. Ibn Khaldūn does not like Aristotle aspire at creating an ideal state: he is of the opinion rather that human affairs follow a natural course and expects nothing but recurrence of the same series of which his historical studies had furnished so many examples. The result is a philosophy of history far removed from any evolutionary philosophy, because it does not contemplate continuous progress, but strictly limited forms of it, which bear the seeds of destruction; the effete population of the towns must regularly give way to the vigorous immigrants from the wilds. And it might have been possible to foretell the future of North Africa with fair accuracy from the theories propounded by Ibn Khaldūn.[201]

Aristotle himself was a realist, far less radical about history and its potentials than, say, Plato was before the debacle at Syracuse. And Aristotle, like Ibn Khaldūn, held a cyclical view of history.[202] But the real basis for comparison is just this, that in Ibn Khaldūn's reflections, the empiric facts of history have finally come to rest within a mature and systematic body of theory.

The standard complaint is that Ibn Khaldūn does not put his theory to work in the actual writing of his history. In answer, one defender has written, "This is obvious, but it could not have been otherwise. No one man could write alone a universal history according to the demands of the *Muqaddima*."[203] The fact is that Ibn Khaldūn was too much the empiricist to subject every facet of every event to the procrustean discipline of derivation from the same few general principles. His most enduring claim to interest, it is true, is in those principles.[204] Indeed, he can be vague about dates and surprisingly fuzzy on matters of detail, even some as significant as the niceties of Almohad doctrine.[205] The specialists who use his historical work admire its insight and organization, but they are not moved to discard all other sources. If we want to appreciate Ibn Khaldūn's achievement, however, we need to put the shoe on the other foot and consider his history not as the mere implementing of his method but as the empiric base for his larger understanding. It is not the derivation of events from theory, after all, but the eliciting of theory from the record of events, and from the larger patterns of human lives, that properly marks a conceptual achievement in this realm.

The starting point for Ibn Khaldūn's historiography is a critical methodology for the discernment of historical facts. But to this he brings a theorist's regard for pattern and (although he was no reformer), the practical orientation common to the *falāsifa*, physicians, jurists, Sufis, and statesmen of Islam. Holding fast, on a sophisticated plane, to the scriptural vision of history as an array of object lessons, Ibn Khaldūn entitles his history, *al-ʿIbār*, The Lesson. His aim is to weld the practical to theoretical in a single discourse.[206] The *Muqaddimah* makes that weld, whose success Khalidi assays in duly protective style: "The History, considered by many modern scholars to be an unworthy sequel of his celebrated *Muqaddima*, or Prolegomenon, was in fact intended to be a precise and carefully constructed demonstration of the principles of historical change outlined in the *Muqaddima*." Adding specifics to make the case, Khalidi writes:

> Ibn Khaldūn highlighted a dominant concern of the age: the relationship between power and virtue as exemplified in the reign of Muʿāwiya. He argued that power was necessary, that it was in itself neither good nor bad but a special kind of skill to be used badly or well in the maintenance of states. Seen in their historical context, these views seem to emanate from reflections on government and justice adumbrated in the thought and writing of Ibn al-Athīr, Turtushi, and Ibn al-Tiqtaqa. But Ibn Khaldūn startles by both the consistency and the expansion of the vision. . . . The universe of Ibn Khaldūn is a structured whole, with its gradations of reality and meaning. . . . The *Muqaddima* sets out the broad outlines of this scheme, the *History* demonstrates how that scheme operated in time.[207]

Ibn Khaldūn's horizons are marked out by the intellectual ambitions of predecessors like Masʿūdī, whom he calls *Imām li ʾl-muʾarrikhīn*, a mentor and guide for all historians.[208] He does not attain Masʿūdī's geographical scope. He has no personal expertise as to China, India, or northern Europe. But the special alloy of particularity with universalism that was blended by his predecessors still gleams in his accounts of the Berbers of North Africa, or the ancient civilizations of Egypt, Babylon, Greece, Rome, Byzantium, and Iran. He had inquired into Berber and Arab history while he lived in the Maghrib, seeking to understand the political events in which he was a player, with life and fortunes often at risk. In Egypt he looked further into Mamluk history and the ongoing events further east, with the rise of Tamerlane.

His data came from merchants, travelers, and scholars from Khwarizm, Khurasan, and China. He consulted texts on Central Asia like the geographical Book of Roger, which al-Idrīsī (d. 1160) had dedicated to Roger of Sicily, the history of Bayhaqī (d. 1169), and the Travels of Ibn Baṭṭūtah (d. 1377). For the wars of Genghis Khan with the Khwarizmshahs, he used the biography of one of those shāhs, Jalāl al-Dīn Mangubirtī, completed in 1241 by the shāh's constant companion and secretary, al-Nasawī.[209] Similarly, he sought out the sources he needed to write intelligently on Christian history—Eutychius, Epiphanes of Cyprus (whom he calls Abū Fānīyūs), John Chrysostom (d. 407, called Fam al-Dhahab, in a calque on his name), Jirjīs al-Makīn (d. 1273), who wrote a history of the world down to 1260, Ibn al-Rāhib (d. 1282), and one Ibn al-Musabbiḥī. For ancient Israel he relies, as Ṭabarī and Ibn al-Athīr had, on the Pentateuch and the Books of Judges and Kings. But he pursues Jewish history down to the destruction of the Second Temple, using the medieval historian Josippon, whose work, translated into Arabic, he discovered with delight in Cairo, but whom he, like many others, confused with Josephus.[210] We have already mentioned his use of Orosius,[211] whose work he valued not only for its North African base but also for its scriptural outlook. Ibn Khaldūn himself does not indulge in figural historiography. But, more subtly and for that reason all the more faithfully, he does seek a moral significance in historical events. What he finds is less a judgment of moral worth than a judgment upon finitude.[212]

Ibn Khaldūn treats the Pentateuch (*Tawrat*) with the utmost seriousness as a historical document and authority. Like his predecessors, he struggles to fit together biblical and other ancient chronologies, identifying many of the biblical figures with Persian counterparts. Resisting the temptation to dismiss the Hebrew canon as corrupted by Jewish fabricators, he joins the camp of those Muslim scholars who understand the Qur'ānic references to Jewish interference with scripture as allusions to a misprision of its content rather than actual tampering with its text. He is troubled that the Torah contains no mention of ʿĀd and Thamūd, Hūd or Ṣāliḥ, and suspicious, as we have seen, at the notion that the Israel of the Exodus numbered 600,000 men at arms. But he is also skeptical of the fanciful embroideries that Qur'ān commentators have put upon the seeming mention of ancient lost cities. He is comforted that Noah's curse makes no reference to Ham's skin color and pleads that silence in support of his own naturalistic and environmental account of the races.

Still, it is not the naturalism alone (much as this may be prized by modern writers), nor even the moral vision that is distinctive in Ibn Khaldūn. His most lasting value lies in his fusion of the two, his naturalization of the scriptural vision, returning it to the experiential grounds that first gave rise to the prophetic claim that God acts in human history.

We have noted ʿAlid interests and Shīʿite ideologies among many of the makers of Islamic universal history, a telling reminder that the universal perspective is itself a tradition received and an art acquired, not an inevitable accretion. Ibn Isḥāq, Wāqidī, Dīnawarī, Ṭabarī, and Yaʿqūbī were all (at least) accused of ʿAlid sympathies.[213] Whether or not they turned to history to show their contemporaries (and find for themselves) a cosmic meaning that ʿAlid claims had already drawn out for them, the comprehensiveness of Shīʿite ideology and the metaphysical sublimation of Shīʿite legitimist longings gave an edge to the historical record for them. Thus, Masʿūdī has a survivor of the Umayyad debacle speak with almost ghostly confessional hindsight:

> We were distracted by pleasures from devotion to what needed our concern. So we were unjust to our subjects; and they, despairing of justice from us, sought to be rid of us. Those who paid taxes were overburdened and abandoned us. Our domains fell into decay; our treasuries were empty. We trusted our ministers, but they put their private interests ahead of our own and managed the state without our knowledge or control. We delayed in paying our troops, so they cast off allegiance to us. When our enemies made overtures to them, they conspired against us and made war upon us. We pursued our enemies but could not apprehend them, so few were our followers. And among the chief causes of the downfall of our rule: that information was kept from us.[214]

Ibn Khaldūn does not share the ʿAlid slant of so many of his predecessors. For him Shīʿism is not a live option, Muʿtazilism has no living appeal, and even philosophy has submerged itself. As we have noted, it no longer travels under its own name or flies the colors of overt, apodeictic argument. But the residue of naturalism, empiricism, even rationalism still potent in Ibn Khaldūn's method holds his moral vision sharply focused on the acts and practices of the world in which he lives. Like Miskawayh and Masʿūdī, he takes up Plato's claim that extortionate taxation destroys the tax base, a special case of Plato's larger claim, echoed by Masʿūdī (and formalized in the Muʿtazilite theory of action), that injustice is destructive of those who practice it. The moral compass that the ʿAlid sympathizers among universal historians had taken up from their spiritual heritage has not been lost. The more catholic standpoint it acquires when generalized by a cosmopolitan perspective has sharpened rather than dulled its point—as has the naturalism that finds the operative workings of moral judgment in the events of history.

What does dull that compass point in Ibn Khaldūn, as in Miskawayh, is facticity: It is hard for either man to quarrel with the given, not because he is a historian, but because he strives to be a realist. Ibn Khaldūn saw in the Mongols' rise confirmation of his ideas about *ʿaṣabiyya*. In the fathering of many sons by Genghis Khan, he saw an expression of tribal spirit. In the rise of Tamerlane and his house he saw further confirmation of his theories. Their power stemmed in part from their mastery of the tribal code, the Yāsā, which Genghis Khan had codified. Tamerlane himself had pointed to the tribal base of his authority, when he corrected Ibn Khaldūn for calling him a king: He was not a king, he explained, but "a relative of kings by marriage," not the owner but the protector of the throne.[215]

There was a lesson here for the heirs of a civilization ever threatening to go soft. But Ibn Khaldūn is not convinced that human beings can profit ultimately from such historic lessons. And, like the Ashʿarite theologians, he does not expect such bitter lessons as history has to teach to answer to our hopeful or wishful canons of justice. Writing of the devastating fire that Tamerlane set to the picked-over goods of the people of Damascus, he labels the arson an abomination. For the conflagration had spread from house to house, finally reaching the ancient Umayyad Mosque and causing its destruction. Then he adds: "But changes of fortune are in God's hands, who does with His creatures as He pleases and rules in His realm as He will."[216]

Like the biblical prophets and their audiences in later ages, the universal historians of Islam sought a moral meaning in the events of history. Ibn Khaldūn was not the first to call history a lesson. This was as natural to him as it was for Muslim theologians and philosophers to expect to read the world as a book.[217] What is perhaps most powerful in Ibn Khaldūn is the emergent synthesis by which the full, rich content of that book becomes a work of science, without losing its ancient thought and theme. Moral judgment may sag and give way, like the melting lead fittings of the Great Damascus Mosque when the fire reached its timbers, but the historian's clear-eyed vision of the events themselves does not waver. He circumstantially describes how Tamerlane erected catapults and fired naphtha to reduce the citadel of Damascus, how the civilian leaders sued for peace and got safe conduct before that citadel was razed. Himself among those who abandoned the city to its fate, he makes no mention of the execution of the viceroy after his surrender and says little of the final gallantry of the vastly outnumbered Mamluk forces left to defend the ramparts, although he dwells with outrage on the rapine, torture, and murder that the Mongols inflicted on the defenseless men, women and children of Syria. Tamerlane's cruelty was a paradigm case, for Ibn Khaldūn, of the nomadic savagery of which he wrote, ingrained in the culture of war that the Tatar hordes shared with other tribal peoples.[218] The human witness might be outraged morally and terrified personally, but the historian saw a pattern and a harsh but ultimately inevitable judgment.

The vision of the Muslim historians had always borne a practical edge, often tinged with the political, even when it seemed to desire only to record, or to entertain. But as the historians' art came to maturity, the vision of the most thoughtful of them deepened and grew more somber, taking on tones that were at once tragic and triumphalist. The worldly spirituality of that new vision is no mere oxymoron, and its tragic triumphalim is no mere paradox. Rather, it bespeaks a certain humanism—as when Masʿūdī seeks to do justice to Muʿāwiya by celebrating his *ḥilm*, as the virtue of a secular ruler. That concessive celebration is strikingly more open than Augustine's polemical urgency and analytic overkill, responding in *The City of God* to pagan notions of secular virtues.

In Ibn Khaldūn, Masʿūdī's skepticism about numbers and fanciful claims has metamorphosed into a critical methodology.[219] Masʿūdī's interest in environmental geography, of the Hippocratic Airs, Waters, and Places variety, and his desire to relate climate, diet, and topography to the varieties of human life and civilization, emerges as a full-fledged theory that projects a moral character on the beduin and other modes of life—a kind of fourteenth-century frontier thesis. Even Masʿūdī's ideas about social cohesion (*jamʿ al-kalima*, *ḍamm al-shaml*–unity and consensus)[220] are taken up in Ibn Khaldūn's celebrated reflections on the dynamics and problematics of *ʿaṣabiyya*. Absent the proscenium arch of Shīʿite cosmology, Ibn Khaldūn replaces Masʿūdī's countercurrents of material decline and spiritual progress with a cyclicity suggestive of Aristotle's historical cycles. These are anchored in nature, under the higher firmament from which the worldly dynamic of the divine promise and threat remain ever present and active.

A word of caution is, of course, in order when we speak of cyclicity in Islamic historiography. As Julie Meisami remarks: "With the exception of Ismāʿīlī hierohistory (and that chiefly in its later manifestations), Muslim historians do not conceive of history as cyclical: history has a beginning—the Creation—and a terminus—the End of Days. While this terminus constantly recedes into the future, its finality is unquestioned."[221] Meisami concedes that "the linear progression of history may be divided into ages in which certain types of events recur–the most prominent being the rise and fall of states. But she argues that "it is more accurate to speak of successive cycles of power, as one group succeeds another"[222] than of some more absolute sort of cyclicity. The characterization is sound, as far as it goes. And it does extend to the recognition that Muslim historiography, like that of the ancient Greeks, locates the springs of history in human morals and mores, typically to the exclusion of such possible prime movers as economy, demography, social conditions, disease, or technological change. This is both a strength and a weakness in traditional historiography. It is linked with one of the core premises of humanism: the primacy of character, and thus with the humanist's characteristically moral uses for history. It is also linked, as Meisami notes, with the tendency among some of our writers for story and style to overpower explanation and fact.[223] But if we insist too singlemindedly on the Muslim historians' penchant for situating of cycles of power within the overarching cosmological drama we risk obscuring the worldliness of those historians.

Ibn Khaldūn is the historian who both proves and tests Meisami's rule. Granted, there is no Epicurean or Nietzschean eternal recurrence to be found among our historians. And granted that the overarching framework of creation-history-judgment remains unquestioned and unquestionable for the most faithful adherents of Islam. Nonetheless, the idea that creation frames the most fundamental question for the historian and that the Day of Judgment frames the ultimate answer to that question is quietly but decisively set aside by Muslim historical writers. Even where their work rises far above the local and parochial, their standpoint is more earthbound than that. Judgment is sought *within* history, not just at its end. That is true even of Muḥammad and of many others who took on the role of prophet before him. It is also true of our universal historians. Ibn Khaldūn, drawing together the work of many predecessors, takes his problematic from the ways of life that he finds on earth. He finds the meaning that he seeks in history not in any final denouement but in the very cycles of power that fill the span of human life and mark the rise and fall of societies as he knows them.

In Ibn Khaldūn, as in all the best of the Muslim historians of the classic age, the search for a moral shape and thrust in history cunningly intertwines with the naturalism, rationalism, and voluntarism that the Greek philosophical outlook fostered, and with the chronological and ethnographic universalism that grew from the biblical outlook. Muʿtazilism, long the theological ally of Shīʿism, promotes a voluntarism as to human character, a rationalism as to moral judgments, and a readiness for the sciences and philosophy. But the traditionalism that reacts against these trends fosters an empiricism of its own, turning historians back toward their materials, with an eye not just for grand, metaphysical theses, but for the mere or sheer givenness of events.

Ibn Khaldūn naturalizes the Platonic schema of political change by rediscovering the dialectic of generational decline in the milieu that experience had taught him to know as intimately as Plato knew the sicknesses and health of the polis. The dialectic of the desert and the sown replaces Plato's (*Republic* VIII) succession of constitutions. But character types still set their mark on each regime, and the moral judgment of history remains, now sketched with an authority that draws its worldliness from the realm of realpolitik but its sense of certitude from the scriptural paradigm. Citing an Arabic translation, Ibn Khaldūn reads the biblical promise of retribution "to the third and fourth generation" (Ex. 20:5) as confirmation of the parameters traced in his own observation, predicted by his own judgment, and explained by his own theory: We know now, in natural terms, psychologically, economically, culturally, why dynastic power is rarely preserved beyond the fourth generation.[224]

None of Ibn Khaldūn's historical ideas, as Fischel remarks, seems more clearly biblical than "his four-generation theory." But, beyond the provenance marked in Ibn Khaldūn's citation, what is most biblical here is the larger theme that the biblical passage underscores, the moral reading of history: It is character that builds and conquers, and character that loses and falls. The state—or society as a whole—is still the individual writ large.

As in the tragic vision of the Greeks and the moralistic models of the Ikhwān al-Ṣafāʾ, history in Ibn Khaldūn has become an enduring process rather than an inevitable progress. The beduins may be "closer to being good" than city people, but they are also savage, and only city folk can sustain the efflorescence of arts and sciences that Ibn Khaldūn knows and loves as civilization and that Aristotle had so much in mind when he argued that man is a creature of the polis and that civil life alone fully humanizes our existence. For Ibn Khaldūn, no one mode of life attains the adequacy or moral stability to endure, let alone progress indefinitely. Presiding over the inevitable dying falls of history is an implacable but ultimately fair moral judgment, whose sentence is written in our characters, by our own choices and human limitations. In the words of the Qur'ān (48:23; 33:62) repeatedly quoted by Ibn Khaldūn, "This is God's way, established of old. Thou wilt never find change in God's way."[225]

Notes

Preface

1. Ibn Ṭufayl, *Hayy Ibn Yaqẓān*, 160.

Introduction

1. Citing Kneale and Kneale's passage in *The Development of Logic* (Oxford: Oxford University Press, 1962), from Boethius in the sixth century to Abelard in the twelfth, Majid Fakhry remarks, "Historians of medieval and pre-medieval philosophy have tended to take it for granted that, indeed, philosophical learning, including Aristotelian logic, had completely disappeared following the death of the Roman consul and author of the *Consolation of Philosophy*," ignoring the contributions, among others, of Fārābī. "Al-Fārābī's Contribution to the Development of Aristotelian Logic," in Fakhry's *Philosophy, Dogma, and the Impact of Greek Thought in Islam*, chapter 3; and see Shukri Abed, *Aristotelian Logic and the Arabic Language in Alfārābī*.

2. See Goodman, *Jewish and Islamic Philosophy: Crosspollinations in the Classic Age*.

3. See Fārābī, *Fī Taḥṣīl al-Ṣaʿādah*, 45–49 and 39; cf. *NE* VI 12, 1144a 36; VI 5, VII 10; *Rhet.* I 6, 1362a 16–21. In *Republic* VI 495 Plato worries that the philosophically talented will forsake philosophy as they mature, leaving her "forlorn and unwed," as they themselves "live an unreal and alien life, while other unworthy wooers rush in and defile her." He calls the weakling pretenders to philosophy manikins and adds an almost Dickensian vignette "of a little bald headed tinker who has made money and just been freed from bonds and had a bath and is wearing a new garment and has

got himself up like a bridegroom and is about to marry his master's daughter, who has fallen into poverty and abandonment." The alien life of the philosopher beguiled away from philosophy is his loss and the loss to society of the chance of his leadership (for which he had shown his propensity even in boyhood). The perversion in entrusting philosophy to the "manikin" is that he has no capability for leadership but squanders what intellect he has in making philosophy a cunning little craft deserving of its reputation as mere jargon mongering.

4. Plato uses similar language about a ship's pilot at *Republic* VI 488E; and cf. VI 485–86 and *NE* VI 10, 1142b 20–22.

5. Fārābī, *Fī Taḥsīl al-Ṣaʿādah*, 29–34.

6. Ibid., 44 with 29–37. For Fārābī's ideas on imagination and assent, see Deborah Black, *Logic and Aristotle's* Rhetoric *and* Poetics *in Medieval Arabic Philosophy*, 185, 221–35; Salım Kemal, *The Poetics of Alfarabi and Avicenna*, 89–138.

7. Fārābī, *Fī Taḥṣīl al-Ṣaʿādah*, 36.

8. Ibid., 28–30.

9. Ibid. 40; Aristotle, *Pol.* I 8, 1256b, 20–25.

10. Fārābī, *Fī Taḥṣīl al-Ṣaʿādah*, 37. Cf. Kraemer, "On Maimonides' Messianic Posture"; Butterworth, "Al-Fārābī's Statecraft."

11. Fārābī, *Fī Taḥṣīl al-Saʿādah*, 36–37.

12. Ibid., 44.

13. Ibid., 29–30, 38–39.

14. Ibid., 45–47.

15. Ibid., 45; cf. Aristotle, *Pol.* I 2, 1252b 24–27; Maimonides *Guide* I 20, 26, 36, 46, 47, 57; Goodman, *Rambam*, 52–119.

16. See S. H. Nasr, *Three Muslim Sages* (Cambridge: Harvard University Press, 1964), 16, for these traditions; cf. Netton, *Al-Fārābī and his School*, 4–6.

17. Cf. the discussions of Fārābī's politics in Charles Butterworth, "Rhetoric and Islamic Political Philosophy"; Galston, *Politics and Excellence*; Parens, *Metaphysics as Rhetoric*.

18. See *EI* 6.872.

19. Abu ʾl-ʿ Alā Mawdūdī, *Islamic Law and Constitution*, ed. and trans Kurshid Ahmad (Lahore: Islamic Publications, 1967), 148; and Charles Adams, "Mawdudi and the Islamic State," in John Esposito, ed., *Voices of Resurgent Islam*, 99–133.

20. See Abdulaziz Sachedina, "Ali Shariati: Ideologue of the Iranian Revolution," in Esposito, 191–217.

21. See *EI* 9.328.

22. Sachedina, "Ali Shariati," 200.

23. Ibid., 200.

24. Ghazālī, *Munqidh*, ed., Jabre, 10–11, trans. Watt, 20–21. For a contemporary effort to recapture Ghazālī's outlook, see Bakar, *The History and Philosophy of Islamic Science*.

25. Sayyid Quṭb, quoted in Robert Worth, *New York Times*, October 13, 2001.

26. Qutb, quoted in Worth, *New York Times*.

27. Ghazālī, *Ihyāʾ* XXXV. See the new translation by David Burrell.

28. Quṭb, quoted in Yvonne Haddad, "Sayyıd Qutb: Ideologue of Islamic Revival," in Esposito, 82.

29. Haddad, 81.

30. Ibid., 81.

31. Ikhwān al-Ṣafāʾ, *Animals vs Man*, 193–96.

32. Cf. Hamoud al-Shuabī, a Saudi sheikh, in the winter of 2001, when America's campaign against the Tālibān regime was at its height: "It is the duty of every Mus-

lim to stand up with the Afghan people and fight against America." It is apostasy even to pay taxes or sustain allegiance to a government that opposes the methods or the aims of a bin Laden: "There is no difference between someone who approves of the war [against terrorism] or supports it with money and one who is actively fighting." Embattled Islam is set against the world: "Everyone who supports America against Islam is an infidel, someone who has strayed from the path of Islam." Douglas Jehl, "For Saudi Cleric, Battle Shapes Up as Infidel vs. Islam," *New York Times*, December 5, 2001.

33. Deut. 30:12; cf. J. Sanhedrin 22a, B. Baba Metzia 59b: "Even a voice from heaven proves nothing; the law of Sinai commands us to decide according to the majority" (citing Exod. 23:2), B. Yevamot 40a; B. Gittin 10b; Tosefta Sota, 15.10. God is said in the Talmud to rejoice when scholars win an argument by using the principles of the Law to depart from too superficial an understanding of its apparent dicta: "My children have triumphed over Me!"

34. Abdulaziz Sachedina, "Militancy, Peace and Islam," lecture delivered at Vanderbilt University, November 12, 2001.

35. Salman Rushdie, "Yes, This is about Islam," *New York Times*, November 2, 2001.

36. Fazlur Rahman, *Islam* (1966. Reprint. Garden City, New York: Doubleday, 1968), 34.

37. See Goodman, *Jewish and Islamic Philosophy*, 134–43.

38. See *Iḥyā'* XXXV bayān 2, (Cairo, 1312 A. H.) 4.188–91, following Makkī, *Qūt al-Qulūb* II 1 (Cairo, 1310 A. H.) 2.4. For Ghazālī's critique of causality, see Goodman, "Did Ghazālī Deny Causality?"

39. See Norman Hammond, "Cultural Terrorism," *The Wall Street Journal*, March 5, 2001.

40. Barry Bearak, "Over Protests, Ṭālibān Say that They Are Destroying Buddhas," *New York Times*, March 4, 2001.

41. Tim Weiner, "Seizing the Prophet's Mantle," *New York Times*, December 7, 2001,

42. Wilfred Cantwell Smith, *Islam in Modern History*, 32.

43. See pp. 197–99, this volume.

44. Cantwell Smith, 41. According to Emmanuel Sivan, bin Laden's deepest influences are from ʿAbd Allah Azzam, a Palestinian killed by a car bomb in 1989, and Safar al-Hawali, a Saudi militant–both "steeped in the writings of Sayyid Quṭb." See Worth, New York Times, October 13, 2001.

45. The Qur'ānic statute (5:42) is not adequately mitigated by the use of local anesthetics. The Ṭālibān were especially brutal in applying this and the other sanctions mentioned here, but everywhere that they have been applied their severity has led to corruption of the judicial process. This is an area where legal fictions are called for, to allow mending of the fabric of *Sharīʿa* law. Raising the evidentiary and procedural bar, a response already seen in the Qur'ānic shift from two to four witnesses in cases of adultery, is not sufficient.

46. Saad Eddin Ibrahim was arrested in the summer of 2000, along with twenty-seven associates. He was charged with treason and espionage for supporting the registration of women voters and calling for judicial supervision of Egyptian elections.

47. Jan Nattier, *The* Candragarbha-Sutra *in Central and East Asia: Studies in a Buddhist Prophecy of Decline* (Ph.D. diss., Harvard University, 1988); John Ronald Newman, *The Outer Wheel of Time: Vajrayāna Buddhist Cosmology in the* Kālacakra Tantra (Ph.D. diss., University of Wisconsin, 1987).

48. Ikhwān al-Ṣafā', *Animals vs Man*, 202; cf. chapter 4, this volume note 157.

49. As Mohammed Arkoun remarks, "The philosophical literature of the 4th century A.H. brings within reach the premises of a humanism centered on man. But insofar as this new outlook was dependant on particular socio-political conditions, its success could only be uncertain, and its survival precarious." *L'Humanisme Arabe au IVe / Xe Siècle*, 356.

Chapter 1

1. See Claude Levi-Strauss, *The Savage Mind* (1962. Reprint. Chicago: University of Chicago Press, 1966); *Totemism*, trans. R. Needham (Boston: Beacon Press, 1963), 62–66, 77, 80–82, 89; L. E. Goodman, *In Defense of Truth*, chapter 8.

2. *Moby Dick, or the Whale* (1851) chapters 55–57 (Berkeley: University of California Press, 1979), 268–79.

3. See L. E. Goodman, *God of Abraham*, 13–19.

4. See Y. Kawabata, *The Existence and Discovery of Beauty* (Tokyo: Mainichi, 1969). I thank Valdo Viglielmo for the anecdote.

5. See *ED* X and *God of Abraham*, chapter 5. Saadiah's ethics is pluralistic in seeking a proper blend among mutually irreducible values (prima facie goods), but it is not radically pluralistic: It does not hold all ends intrinsically equal or incapable of being judged against one another. Saadiah follows Plato in seeing that radical pluralism is mere rudderlessness. The monisms he rejects all treat relative, partial goods as absolutes. Even renunciation and asceticism fail as monisms. Maimonides makes Saadiah's diverse goods coordinate, subordinate, or superordinate parts of a single good; see "Eight Chapters" 5, "On Devoting the Powers of the Human Soul to a Single End."

6. *Maysir* was a gambling game of the *Jāhiliyya* in which a slaughtered beast was butchered into ten parts of quite different value and distributed by the drawing of notched arrows. As in the modern game of craps, some of the arrows signified good or bad luck. There were pagan overtones in the play, perhaps survivals of the use of arrows in divination. When there were fewer than seven players, someone had to buy the parts not assigned to one of the seven notched arrows. If that person won twice in a row, he was to donate his winnings to his following. Other winners might donate what they won to the poor. Hence, according to some commentators, the Qur'ānic (2:219) concession of benefits in *maysir*. See *EI* 6.923.

7. See Ibn Ṭufayl's *Ḥayy Ibn Yaqẓān*, 142–44; Ḥujwīrī, *Kashf al-Maḥjūb*, 111: "There is no chastisement in Hell more painful than being veiled from God. . . . And in Paradise there is no pleasure more perfect than not being veiled. Similarly (as in the rabbinic sources), profession of God's unity at the time of death assures entry into Paradise: Bukhari 3:49, Muslim 1:43, Ibn Ḥanbal 1:65, 69, 374, 382, 402, 407, 425; and (qualifiedly) in Tirmidhī 38:17. Cf. Wensinck, *Handbook*. Wensinck's system of citation for *ḥadīth* is adopted here.

8. See Hamadhānī's Ahwaz Encounter and Basra Encounter, in the *Maqāmāt*. Kueny, *The Rhetoric of Sobriety*, 102, speaks of Umayyad *khamriyyāt* as "a form of protest against the prohibition of wine." She adds (105) that the preservation of pre-Islamic poetry allowed Muslims to participate vicariously in vinous and other now forbidden pleasures. The participation was hardly always vicarious.

9. See Bukhārī 56:37, 58:1, 64:12,17,27; 81:7,52; Muslim, *Ṣaḥīḥ*, 12:121–3, 43:30–31, 53:6–7; Tirmidhī 34:26, 35:28; Nasā'ī 23:8; Ibn Ḥanbal 2:539, 3:7; Ṭayālisī 2180.

10. Jāḥiẓ, *The Epistle on Singing-Girls*, § 32, 38.

11. See Charles Pellat, *EI* 7.872–73.

12. See Goodman, *In Defense of Truth*, chapter 1; for the Prophet's toe: *Mishkāt* XXIV ix 1, Robson, 2.1000.

13. Muslim, *Sahīh* 41:7–9, tr. Siddiqi, 4.1220–1, nos. 5609–11; Bukhārī 78:92; Abū Dā'ūd 40:87; Tirmidhī 41:81; Ibn Māja 33:42; Dārimī 19.71; Ibn Ḥanbal 1:175, 177, 181, 2:39, 96.

14. For the legitimacy of poetry in defense of Islam, see Ibn Ḥanbal 3:456,460; cf *Mishkāt*, 2.1001. Bukhārī transmits *hadīths* stating that there is magic in eloquence, wisdom in poetry. Other *ḥadīths* take a more judicious stance: Poetry "is speech; what is good in it is good, and what is bad is bad" *Mishkāt*, 2.1004. It is not our purpose, of course, to attempt to use the *ḥadīth* literature to fathom the attitudes of Muhammad toward poetry. On this subject that literature is more a battlefield for later writers than a quarry of prophetic intentions. What matters for our inquiry is that poetry, in one of the most proliferated and participatory elaborations of Islamic ideals in the Arabic language, has become problematic—that eloquence can be condemned along with obscenity as "two branches of hypocrisy" (*Mishkāt*, 2.1002) while modesty and inarticulacy are praised—that poetry is in need of defense, since it is seen as a vehicle of secular (autonomous) values.

15. *Mishkāt*, 2.1000–4; cf. Tirmidhī 41:69, Ibn Māja 33:41.

16. See *Mishkāt*, 2.1000; Muslim, *Saḥīḥ* tr Siddiqi, 4.1220, nos. 5602–8. Ibn Isḥāq *Sīrat Rasūl Allāh*, trans., A. Guillaume, *The Life of Muhammad* (Oxford: Oxford University Press, 1955) 169–70, Arabic 243–45. The lines said to have been sung by Muḥammad's followers as they worked expressed an otherworldly theme. The Prophet reportedly altered the word order, dispersing the rhyme and meter; Guillaume, 229.

17. Tarif Khalidi, *Arabic Historical Thought*, 3–4.

18. See Peter Chelkowski, *Taziye: Ritual and Drama in Iran* (New York: New York University Press Press, 1979); Jalal Asgar, *A Historical Study of the Origins of the Persian Passion Plays* (Ann Arbor: University Microfilms, 1970); and Matthew Arnold's classic "The Persian Passion Play," in *Essays in Criticism*, First Series (New York: Macmillan, 1883) 1.223–64. And see *New York Times*, July 15, 2002, p. B-1, for notice of recent performances of Taziye at Lincoln Center.

19. For the opposition to representational art, see *Mishkāt*, 2.940–43.

20. See, for example Keith Critchlow, *Islamic Patterns—an Analytical and Cosmological Approach* (New York: Schocken, 1976).

21. For the customs of the *ʿĪd*, see Gustave von Grunebaum, *Muhammadan Festivals*, 34–35, 58–59, 63–65. On the Great Festival, designed to replace Yom Kippur, there is a sacrifice (Qur'ān 22:33–38), but fasting is forbidden: "In Lane's day popular entertainment had invaded some of the cemeteries," where "families visit the tombs of their relatives." "Women stay throughout the day and may even spend the night in the cemetery, especially if the family possesses a private and enclosed burial ground with a house that is equipped for just these occasions." The solemnity of this "festival of the dead" contrasts with and complements the atmosphere Lane observed: "many swings and whiligigs are erected, and several large tents; in some of which, dancers, reciters (of popular romances), and other performers, amuse a dense crowd of spectators." The mixture of obsequies with carnival release matches what is found in the O-bon of Japan and in many festivals of European provenance. Yom Kippur itself has been followed by secular festivities in both ancient and recent times, and Lent seems incomplete without Carnival.

22. Bukhārī 13:2–3, 25, 56:81, 63:46; Muslim, Ṣaḥīh 8:16–17; Nasā'ī 19:34, 37.

23. Abū Dā'ūd 40:52; Ibn Hanbal 2:8, 38; cf. Zayd b. ʿAlī no. 1001, Ibn Ḥanbal 2:165, 172, 4:259; Tayālisī, p. 221.

24. Immanuel Kant, *Critique of Judgment* (1790) § 53, translated by W. S. Pluhar (Indianapolis: Hackett, 1987), 199–200.

25. Étienne Gilson, *Forms and Substances in the Arts*, 182–83.

26. Gilson, *Forms and Substances in the Arts*, 78.

27. Niẓām al-Dīn al-Awliyā' apud Amīr Ḥasan's *Fawā'id al-Fu'ād*, quoted in Bruce Lawrence, *Notes from a Distant Flute*, 29.

28. Ibn Abī Dunyā, *Dhamm al-Malāhī*, translated by James A. Robson in *Tracts on Listening to Music* (London: Royal Asiatic Society, 1938). A. Shiloah notes that musical instruments are called *malāhī* in contexts that emphasize the root sense of play. The philosophers, Kindī, Fārābī, and Ibn Sīnā, in a more neutral turn of phrase, call them *ālāt* or *ālāt al-ghinā'*, that is, instruments, or musical instruments—or *alāt al-ṭarab*, stirring instruments, if they wish to highlight the emotional impact of music. Shiloah ascribes to the influence of Ibn Abī Dunyā the rather insistent use of the more loaded terminology in legal contexts. When later authors tried to nuance or roll back what they saw as overly extreme prohibitions, they tended to single out stringed instruments and flutes of a type associated with art music as belonging to the class whose destruction was obligatory. Al-Nābulusī (d. 1731) goes further, arguing that what is banned is not any specific type of instrument, but the *use* of instruments for mere entertainment, as distinguished from spiritual elevation–which is, by definition, quite the opposite of distraction. See "*Malāhī*," *EI* 6.214–16.

29. See Tirmidhī 46:17; Zayd b. ʿAlī no. 1001–04; Ibn Ḥanbal 2:165, 172; 3:449, 4:259; Ṭayālisī no. 1221.

30. See chapter 2 in this volume.

31. See *EI* 8.1018–20, 10.210–11.

32. See Bruce Lawrence, *Notes from a Distant Flute*, 25–26, and Niẓām al-Dīn al-Awliyā', *Morals for the Heart*, translated by Bruce Lawrence (New York: Paulist Press, 1992).

33. Amīr Ḥasan Sijzī (d. 1336), quoted in Lawrence, *Notes from a Distant Flute*, 40; cf. pp. 41, 48, 54 for further examples of defense of the *samāʿ*.

34. For Islamic norms about seriousness, see Charles Pellat, *EI* 2.536–37, "Djidd wa 'l-Hazl." Pellat notes that despite the unease with mockery and the call to gravity, there is no outright prohibition of joking in the Qur'ānic text. Ghazālī "declares jocularity to be forbidden and blameworthy," yet tolerates "a moderate joke," and al-Ishbīhī, who follows a chapter on the prohibition of wine with another on the prohibition of jokes "does not fail to quote favorable traditions at greater length and to repeat a certain number of droll anecdotes." Here, as always, the great ally of secularity is the functional autonomy of ideas, which can often work its way in behalf of the human spirit. The Prophet himself jested, and, despite the juridical prohibitions, which some authorities considered absolute, Medina was the seat of a school of humorists, "who helped raise the amusing anecdote (*nādira*) to the rank of a literary form."

35. Henry Farmer, s.v. *Ghinā'*, *EI* 2.1073.

36. ʿAbdu 'l-Wāhid al-Marrākushī, *History of the Almohades*, Arabic text, ed. R. Dozy (1881; Reprint. Amsterdam: Oriental Press, 1968), 172.

37. See Charles Pellat, "*Ḳayna*," *EI* 4.820–24; Henry Farmer, "*Ghinā'*," *EI* 2.1072–75. Farmer remarks: "Human nature, being what it is, could not accept the bigoted ruling of the pious, and so there arose, in addition to the privately owned *ḳayna* or singing-girl, the professional musician (*mughannī*), the first recorded being Ṭuways (10/632–92/711)." Farmer also remarks on the prevalence of work songs: "Ibn Djinnī (d. 392/1006) has said that the drawer of water will go on working as long as the *radjaz*

chant continues. The water carrier, the boatman, the weaver, the gleaner, and even the women of the tent or household sang at work just as they do today."

38. See Jāḥiẓ, *The Epistle on Singing-Girls.*

39. O. Wright, *Mūsīḳī*, *EI* 7.681–88.

40. See E. Wiedemann, "Ḳutb al-Dīn al-Shīrāzī" *EI* 5.547–48.

41. See Robson, *Tracts on Listening to Music*, 1–13.

42. See Ghazālī, "Book of the Laws of Listening to Music and Singing, and of Ecstasy," *Iḥya' 'Ulūm al-Dīn*, trans. D. B. MacDonald, *JRAS* (1901): 195–252, 705–48; (1902) 1–28. In *EI* 8.1019, J. During remarks on the preference for the tambourine and bamboo flute (*nāy*), or for chanting unaccompanied by an instrument.

43. See Ghazālī, *Munqidh*, trans. Watt, 25–26, 54–55; cf. the treatise ascribed to Aḥmad al-Ghazālī, ed. J. Robson in *JRAS* (1938), and *EI* 2.1041 and 8.841.

44. Ghazālī, "On Listening to Music," 227.

45. Abū 'l-Kalām Āzād, *Ghubar-i-Kabīr*, ed. Malik Ram, 283. I am indebted to Mohammed Adeel for this passage and for translating it for me from the Urdu.

46. See *Hidāya* III 558; cf. Nawāwī, *Minhaj*, 200.

47. See Ghazalī, *On Listening to Music*, 201, for Shāfi'ī's seriousness. We shall return to music in chapter 2, but our present concern is with the interplay of the sacred and the secular.

48. For the translation, see Watt, *Companion to the Qur'ān*, 88.

49. See Yedida Stillman, *Arab Dress*, 23

50. See *Mishkāt* 21. Paradise is for ascetics: Tirmidhī 36:3; its chief denizens are the poor: Ibn Ḥanbal 1:234, 359; 2:173, 297, 4:429, 437, 443, 5:209 f.; Tayālisī nos. 833, 2759.

51. Stillman, *Arab Dress*, 22.

52. Muslim, *Ṣahīḥ*, trans. Siddiqi, 1.277–8; Bukhārī 8:14–15, 10:93, 77:19; Abū Dā'ūd 2:157, 162, 31:8; Nasā'ī 9:12, 20; Ibn Māja 29:1; Ibn Ḥanbal 6:172, cf. Bukhārī 77:93. Other traditions have the Prophet advising the faithful that God is pleased when they show His favor by wearing fine clothes, or arguing that signet rings are only for persons of authority. Yet the preference discovered in the *sunna* for white or striped clothing, modest, simple, even somewhat austere (but not uncomfortable or unwholesome) had a powerful impact on sumptuary practice—and accentuated and assigned a clearer meaning to ostentation in dress. Cf. *Mishkāt*, 2.915–19; Tirmidhī 35:39; Ibn Ḥanbal 3:439.

53. Tha'ālibī lists Korah (Qārūn) as the first person to wear his robes long and trail them on the ground, also the first to wear scarlet and the first to practice alchemy. See *Laṭā'if al-Ma'ārif*, trans. Bosworth, 41.

54. *Mishkāt*, 2.912–13, and 915.

55. Muslim, *Ṣaḥīḥ*, 37:1–4, trans., Siddiqi, 3.1139, nos. 5126–8; Dārimī 9:25; cf. Bukhārī 23:2, 67:71, 70:29; 74: 27–8, 77:25, 27,45; Ibn Ḥanbal 1:321, 5:275; Abū Dā'ūd 25:17. Tirmidhī 24:10; Nasā'ī 21:53, 48:106,110; Ibn Māja 30:17.

56. Naṣībī, a Mu'tazilite disciple of Abū 'Abdallāh al-Baṣrī, who was himself a student of the famous Jubbā'ī, is portrayed by Tawḥīdī as a profligate (and his master as a spy, graced with the sobriquet al-Ju'al, the dung beetle). Tawḥīdī tells of hearing Naṣībī ironically praise the Qur'ānic paradise, where there is nothing to do but enjoy food, drink, and erotic pleasures. Wouldn't they grow bored and depressed in this bestial condition, the Mu'tazilite is said to have asked. The Christian translator Naẓīf al-Rūmī (tenth century), called al-Qaṣṣ, the priest, quotes a philosopher who held that three worldly pleasures cloy: food, drink, and coupling; three do not: perfume, clothing, and music. See Kraemer, *Humanism*, 133, 186.

57. Yedida Stillman, *Arab Dress*, 31. The countertradition comes from Ibn Saʿd, *K. al-Ṭabaqāt al-Kabīr*, ed. E. Sachau, J. Lippert et al. (Leiden: Brill, 1908), 29; cf. Tirmidhī, *Sunan*, *K. al-Istiʾdhān wa ʾl-Ādāb*, bab 87 (Beirut: Dar al-Fikr, 1983).

58. Stillman, *Arab Dress*, 120–37.

59. Ibn Khaldūn, *Muqaddimah*, 3.36, trans. after Rosenthal, 66.

60. Stillman, *Arab Dress*, 131.

61. Ibid., 128–33.

62. Ghazālī, *Munqidh*, 56; cf. Ghazālī, *Fadāʾiḥ*, 24; and see Goodman, *Jewish and Islamic Philosophy: Crosspollinations*, 136. Cf. Sufyān al-Thawrī's complaint (716–778) on the secular uses of sacred learning: "We have become mere commodities to the worldly. . . . A man becomes our disciple to get a name as such and convey our learning. Then he gets appointed a governor or chamberlain or steward or tax collector and says, 'Thawrī related to me.'" Ibn ʿAbbād al-Rundī (d. 1320), *Al-Rasāʾil al-Ṣughrā*, ed., P. Nuwiyya (Beirut, 1941) 41, quoted in Khalidi, *Arabic Historical Thought*, 25.

63. Stillman, *Arab Dress*, 158.

64. A. Rugh, *Reveal and Conceal: Dress in Contemporary Egypt* (Syracuse, N.Y.: Syracuse University Press, 1986) 5; cf. Nesta Ramazani, "The Veil—Piety or Protest?" *Journal of South Asian and Middle Eastern Studies* 7 (1983): 36; Nilüfer Göle, *The Forbidden Modern: Civilization and Veiling* (Ann Arbor: University of Michigan Press, 1996) 5; Stillman, *Arab Dress*, 158–59.

65. Stillman, *Arab Dress*, 111

66. S. D. Goitein, *A Mediterranean Society*, 4.194; Stillman, *Arab Dress*, 110–111.

67. The smallest patch of Paradise is worth more than the world: Bukhārī 56:6, 59:8, 81:2, 51; Tirmidhī 20:17; Ibn Māja 37:39; al-Dārimī 20:108; Ibn Ḥanbal 2:315, 438, 482–23, 3:141, 153, 207, 264, 433 f. 5:330, 335, 337–39. The least share in *jihād* bestows a claim upon Paradise: Tirmidhī 20:17–18, 21,26; Ibn Ḥanbal 2:524 Cf. Pascal's Wager.

68. Kathryn Kueny, *The Rhetoric of Sobriety*.

69. Al-Aʿshā, quoted in F. Harb's translation, by Kueny, *Sobriety*, 94.

70. See Qurʾān 16:66–69; Kueny, *Sobriety*, 10.

71. Qurʾān 22:2, Kueny, *Sobriety*, 14.

72. Qurʾān 76:14–21, 56:18–19, 37:45–47.

73. Kueny, *Sobriety* 15–17.

74. Ibid., 65–66.

75. Ibid., 67–80.

76. See *Qurʾān* 11:106 ff. 22:19 ff., 25:11 ff., 38:57 ff., 40:46 ff., 43:74 ff., 56:41 ff., 78:21 ff. The Ikhwān al-Safā' count some seven hundred verses promising reward in the Hereafter and, for every verse of promise, a corresponding threat or admonition. See *The Case of the Animals versus Man*, 200–201. "Paradise and Hell were presented to me, and I have never seen the good and evil as today. Had you known, you would have wept more and laughed less." Muslim, *Saḥīh*, 4 1257, no 5823.

77. *Qurʾān* 3:184, 24:36–37, 25:43 ff., 79:37–39, 83:14, 102:1–2.

78. Ibn Ṭufayl, *Ḥayy Ibn Yaqẓān*, Goodman, 154; cf. Epictetus *Enchiridion* 13; Philo, ad Deut. 21:15–17 in *Sacr*. 19 ff. and the *ḥadīth*: "God has not put two hearts in you." Cf. Qurʾān 4:129: "Ye will not be able to deal equally between your wives, however much ye wish." See also Nasāʾī *Qisāma* 14, Tirmidhī, *Nikāḥ*, 42, and the modernist discussion of Muḥammad Abduh, trans. in Helmut Gatje, *The* Qurʾān *and its Exegesis* (Berkeley: University of California Press, 1976). For other examples of the structural symmetry of this world and the next almost as objects of exchange: "This world is the dungeon of the faithful and the Paradise of the miscreant," Mus-

lim, *Ṣaḥīḥ*, 53:1, Tirmidhī 34:16; Ibn Māja 37:3; cf. Ibn Hanbal 2:197, 323, 389, 485; "Satiation in this world means hunger in the next," Tirmidhī 35:37.

79. See Majid Khadduri, *War and Peace in the Law of Islam* (Baltimore: Johns Hopkins, 1955) 44–6: "The ultimate aim of Islam was, of course, to win the whole world. . . . The Muslim law of nations recognizes no other nation than its own, since the ultimate goal of Islam was the subordination of the whole world to one system of law and religion . . . rules for foreign relations, accordingly, were the rules of an imperial state which would recognize no equal status for the other party (or parties) with whom they happened to fight or negotiate. . . such a law of nations was not based on mutual consent or reciprocity." Cf. 51–54, 59, 63–5: "The possibility of a defeat is dismissed [by al-Māwardī] as if entirely nonexistent," 134. Khadduri compares Roman Imperial, medieval Christian, and twentieth-century Marxist-Leninist ideas. He remarks (81) that the Qur'ānic standard (8:62) makes "no distinction between offensive and defensive purposes." For *jihād* as an expansionist struggle, consider the usage of the *ḥadīth*: "Whether he has engaged in *jihād* in God's path or remained in the land in which he was born," *Mishkāt*, 1.806; cf. 807, also 813–15.

80. Cf. Khadduri, *War and Peace* 69, 141–42; cf. 91 for the use of "chivalrous poetry" on the battlefield *Mishkāt* 1.816, contrasts the fighter who seeks God's favor, obeys the commander, gives up valuable property, aids his comrade, and avoids mischief with one who fights boastfully and without good discipline. The latter undercuts his claim to divine requital, even though *Qur'ān* and *ḥadīth* are generally unequivocal in their promises to *mujāhidīn*. See Khadduri 61–62, 105.

81. Ikhwān al-Safā, *Animals versus Man*, 193–96.

82. Cf. ʿAbd al-Qādir al-Jilānī (d. 1166), "On Struggling with the Self," in John Williams, *Themes of Islamic Civilization*, 281–22. Self-conquest is traditionally the Greater *Jihād*. The Ikhwān al-Ṣafā' offer a distinctive critique of Islamic militancy when they propose that military *jihād* is a political, and thus a secular, rather than religious institution. Miskawayh's history relates how the Buwayhid Rukn al-Dawla was mercilessly shaken down by an army of Khursanian raiders who demanded the entire land tax of his provinces to make war against the Byzantine and Armenian enemy. *Jihād*, they urged, trumped all other purposes of state. When their demands for money and for forces to support their campaign were declined, they began to rob people in the street and strip them of their possessions and even their turbans, in the name of "commanding what is right." See Miskawayh, *Tajārub*, 5.235–36.

83. See Goodman, *God of Abraham*, chapter 5.

84. Trans. Goodman, 100–101.

85. Ibn Qutayba agrees that Imru' al-Qays was the first to use the theme of the abandoned encampment.

86. See Goodman, "Jewish and Islamic Philosophies of Language."

87. For an evocative analysis of the themes of the *qasīda* and the basis of their unity, see Hamori, *On the Art of Medieval Arabic Literature*, 6–30.

88. Kenneth Clark, *The Nude: A Study of Ideal Art* (London: Murray, 1957) 300–301.

89. See Ignaz Goldziher's landmark essay, "*Muruwwa* and *Din*" in *Muslim Studies*, 1. 11–44. Citation of pre-Islamic poetry to clarify Qur'ānic usage was well established by the ninth century and is attested earlier. See Wansbrough, *Quranic Studies*, 97–98; Khalidi, *Arabic Historical Thought*, 86.

90. See G. E. von Grunebaum, *A Tenth Century Document of Arabic Literary Theory and Criticism* (Chicago: University of Chicago Press, 1950), repr. in Lichtenstadter, *Introduction*, 322–39.

91. Bāqillānī, translated after von Grunebaum, 68–69; Lichtenstadter, *Introduction*, 330–31.

92. In one *ḥadīth* (Ibn Ḥanbal 2:228), Imru' al-Qays himself is seen leading the poets to Hell.

93. In Lichtenstadter, *Introduction*, 337; cf. 332–29.

94. For the warrior's reward: Bukhārī 56:2, 57:8, 97:28; Muslim, *Ṣaḥīḥ* 33:103–4; Ibn Dā'ūd, *Sefer Ha-Qabbalah* 15:9; Tirmidhī 20:1, Nasā'ī 25:14; Ibn Māja 24:1.

95. Martyrs of Islam, among their rewards, can expect seventy-two wives from the ranks of the *Ḥūr*: Tirmidhī: 20:25, cf. Ibn Māja 24:16, Zayd b. Alī no. 855, Ibn Ḥanbal 4:131, 200. Another structural symmetry: For martyrs slain by People of the Book, one *ḥadīth* doubles the rewards: Muslim, *Ṣaḥīḥ* 15:8.

96. Ibn Māja 24:16; Ibn Ḥanbal 2:297, 427 f.; cf. *Numbers Rabbah* XI 7, trans., J. J. Slotki (London: Soncino, 1961), 442. The ridicule of mortal wives is expansive in the dialogues proposed in the ninth century Ismāʿīl b. Hayyān.

97. See Ibn Makhlūf, *Kitāb al-ʿUlūm al-fākhira fī 'l-naẓar fī 'l-'umur al-Ākhirah* (Cairo, 1317 A.H.) 2:129. The use of rhyming titles in works of divinity is a small but characteristic touch marking the symbiosis of worldly charm with otherworldly intent.

98. Tirmidhī and Ibn Māja, from Abū Miqdam ibn Maʿdī, quoted in Williams, *Themes of Islamic Civilization*, 259; and see *EI* s.v. "*Ḥūr*."

99. Charles Wendell, "The Denizens of Paradise," *Humaniora Islamica* 2.29–59; Josef Horovitz, "Das koranische Paradies," *Scripta Universitatis atque Bibliothecae Hierosolymitanarum, Orientali et Judaica* 1 (1923): 1–16, and "Die paradiesischen Jungfrauen im Koran," *Islamica* 1 (1925): 543.

100. Asín Palacios, *Islam and the Divine Comedy*, 59–60, 70, 130–35.

101. See Northrup Frye, *The Secular Scripture*, 80, 173; 70. *Balkafa* is the restriction of inquiry made prominent in Islam by Aḥmad b. Ḥanbal, from the Arabic *bi-lā kayf*, "not asking how." See Wensinck, *Muslim Creed*, 85–86 and p. 64 in this volume.

102. Asín, *Islam and the Divine Comedy*, 55–56, 135. One recalls Soeur Sourire's "Dominique," popular in the 1960s, where saint's companions in Paradise include "Platon, Goethe, Mallarmé"–one humanist's harrowing of Hell.

103. See Henri Corbin, *Creative Imagination in the Sufism of Ibn ʿArabī* (Princeton: Princeton University Press, 1969) 105–75; cf. my review, *IJMES* 2 (1971): 278–90.

104. Introducing his translation of *The Mystical Poems of Ibn al-Fāriḍ*, A. J. Arberry writes:

> Here I would merely stress the close relationship between the images of profane and sacred love in Sufi literature. This correspondence is underlined by Ibn al-Fāriḍ in the free use he makes of quotations from or references to earlier, non-mystical poets . . . one ode is in effect composed in emulation of a poem by al-Mutanabbī . . . in another a *qasīda* of al-Buḥturī is recalled . . . the listener, already keyed up emotionally by the erotic imagery employed, and the passionate excitement of the mystical exercises, will surely have thrilled to recognize familiar lines and phrases torn from their original contexts and given a new and heightened significance in the transformation of material into spiritual beauty. (10–11)

The thrill may not always have been grateful; the effect can border on parody.

105. See Arberry, ed., *The Mystical Poems of Ibn al-Fāriḍ* 81–5; Hamori, *On the Art of Medieval Arabic Literature*, 47–77.

106. See *EI* 3.790-99. H. A. R. Gibb calls Ibn Ḥazm's *K. al-Fiṣal fī 'l-Milal wa 'l-Ahwā' wa 'l-Niḥal* the first known survey of comparative religion. He credits Islamic pluralism for stimulating such work; *Arabic Literature*, 114–15. But Ibn Ḥazm's aim is to narrow not widen the range of options. He urges monotheism, Islam, and Ẓāhirism, refuting all other theories and schools. The Shī'ite, Murji'ite, Khārijite, and Mu'tazilite sects are treated as products of a Persian reaction to the pure spirit of Arab Islam. The four major Islamic legal schools are treated so harshly that few modern scholars express surprise at Ibn Ḥazm's persecution or the burning of his books within his lifetime. Ibn Hazm himself was not of Arab or of Muslim background. He was the grandson of a Spanish convert who fabricated for himself the pedigree of a Persian *mawlā* family. His oeuvre includes a work on the merits of Andalusia and another on the genealogies of the Arabs. Like many another legitimist and romanticizer of authentic national genius, his relation to the nation of whom he spoke was more notional than genetic. His own powerful genius, in fact, was highly personal. Wensinck accurately calls him a "die hard," but his style had and has many followers. One who need not fear their zeal might admire his scope and penetrating analytic intelligence. The attention to detail and drive for comprehensiveness of his writings typify the best of Arabic learned writing and make the *Book of Religions and Sects* worthy of Gibb's encomium: "valuable and original." Ash'arī's impressively dispassionate *Maqālāt al-Islāmiyyīn*, by contrast, is purely a doxography, and it deals exclusively with Islamic theses.

107. Tha'ālibī's witty catalogue essay *Laṭā'if al-Ma'ārif* (trans. Bosworth, 38) cites the devil as the first person to use *qiyās*, logical (or analogical) inference. He quotes Sufyān b. 'Uyayna and others, who ascribed to Iblīs the boastful inference that he, Satan, was better than Adam, being created from fire rather than earth. Whether the objection was to modus ponens or to analogical reasoning, there is some irony in the story, since the inference Sufyān draws from it, that one should beware of *qiyās* depends on both—analogy to generalize the case, and modus ponens to move from the generalization to the warning.

108. Ibn Ḥazm, *The Ring of the Dove*. For Ibn Ḥazm on impossibility, see *K. al-Milal wa 'l-Niḥal* (Baghdad: Muthanna, no date) 2.180–3. Ibn 'Arabī himself followed the Ẓāhirī *madhhab* in law. He incorporated Ibn Ḥazm's concept of the *ẓāhir* or external into his system as a counterpart to the inward dimension of the *bāṭin* or esoteric, against which Ibn Ḥazm had campaigned.

109. Gibb, *Arabic Literature*, 114. Gibb seems to ascribe Ibn Ḥazm's work on love to a youthful phase in his thinking, as if it represented some separate current from his legal and theological work. The mood has surely changed but theologically the agenda is consistent.

110. Von Grunebaum, *Medieval Islam*, 256

111. Ibn Ḥazm, *The Ring of the Dove*, 17–18.

112. See Ibn al-Fāriḍ, *The Mystical Poems*, 40–41.

113. Ibn al-Fāriḍ, 45–50, cf. 77–78.

114. Ibn Ḥazm, *The Ring of the Dove*, 18. Ibn Ḥazm draws a leaf from the pages of the moderns here. Ibn Bassām, a Baghdad poet, lampooned a local singer whose favorite poetic measure was the *Qifā nabki* that opens the *Mu'allaqa* of Imru' al-Qays as well as another of his elegies. The sharp-tongued epigramist dubbed the singer "Goat's Beard" and wrote lines urging him to "cut it short"—"may God not have mercy on Imru' al-Qays."

115. See Goldziher, *The Ẓāhirīs*, 24, 27–29, 104, 205–6; for a paradigmatic permission based on literalism, 40–41. Mundhir b. Sa'īd al-Ballūṭī (878/9–966), chief justice of Cordoba, who introduced Ẓāhirism into Spain, was a poet and an admirer

of the love poetry of ʿUmar b. Abī Rabīʿa. His student Aḥmad b. Muḥammad al-Jasūr (931/2–1011), also a poet, is acknowledged by Ibn Ḥazm as his teacher; Gustave von Grunebaum *JNES* 11 (1952): 237.

116. See J. N. Bell, *Love Theory in Later Hanbalite Islam*, 26, cf. 111. Ibn Dāʾūd's *ḥadīth* is a structural transformation of R. Gebihah's gloss of *Joshua* 15:22 apud R. Ashi, *Gittin* 7a: "Whoever has cause of resentment against his fellow and holds his peace, He that abides for aye shall espouse his cause."

117. See George Makdisi, "Ibn Taymiyya: A Sufi of the Qadiriyya Order," *AJAS* 1:118–29, for Ibn Taymiyya's own Sufi activities. The thrust of his efforts is clear in the tenor of his alliance with Abū ʾl-ʿAbbās al-Wāsitī, whom he called the Junayd of his age. Al-Wāsiṭī was, under Ibn Taymiyya's influence, a moderating force in Sufism, a polemicist against pantheistic doctrines and a defender in Ibn Taymiyya's struggle with other Sufis. He was also the teacher of Ibn Qayyim al-Jawziyya; Bell, 93.

118. Bell, *Love Theory*, 46–50, 56–60 ff., 84–91.

119. Ibid., 92–93.

120. Ibid., 97–100.

121. Ibid., 135–36.

122. Ibid., 100, 117; for Ibn al-Qayyim's differences with Ibn Ḥazm, cf. 112.

123. Ibid. 136–38.

124. Giffen, *The Theory of Profane Love among the Arabs*, 40.

125. Bell, *Love Theory*, 183.

126. Giffen, *Profane*, 48.

127. See Ibn al-Nafīs, *Al-Risālah al-Kāmiliyya*, trans. Meyerhof and Schacht, 61, 65; cf. my review in *Archiv für Geschichte der Philosophie* 51 (1969): 219–21.

128. See Bell, *Love Theory*, 22, 182–3.

129. R. B. Serjeant, *South Arabian Hunt*, 6–9, 23, 31, 36, 38–39, etc.

130. Ibid.,14.

131. Ibid., 14, 19–20.

132. Their nonretractile claws, cranial shape, and loping stride, it is said, ally cheetahs with the canines. They are convergent with the cats by evolution, but closer genetically to the greyhound. See F. Viré, "Fahd," *EI* 2.738–43.

133. Franz Rosenthal, *The Herb*; cf. my review in *Middle East Journal* 28 (1974) 86–87.

134. Charles Pellat, "al-Djidd wa ʾl-Hazl," *EI* 2.536.

135. It was T. E. Lawrence who said that there is no Arab art of parody. But he said it in introducing an anecdote about a jape of his own.

136. James Monroe, *Hamadhānī*, 31–37. M. C. Lyons gathers the materials of the Arabic popular story cycle in *The Arabian Epic: Heroic and Oral Story-telling* (Cambridge: Cambridge University Press, 1997). He ascribes ʿAntar's failure "to produce sympathy or interest in the West," to his "monotonous invincibility."

137. If the son's appearance only a day after his father's marriage is anachronism, it counts, as Monroe (p. 34) points out, as "a deliberate parody of *sīra*." Otherwise, Bishr's first bride was a "single mother." As Frye notes, "realistic displacement is closely related to parody"; see *The Secular Scripture*, 37. Bishr's willing acceptance of the boy as his own, by whichever bride, is matched only by Peter Sellars' Inspector Cluzot, who blandly informs the court that his wife's furs and jewels were of course attainable on a police inspector's salary, since she is very careful with the housekeeping money. Bishr's yielding to his son is a motif echoed in Ingmar Bergman's *Smiles of a Summer's Night*. But the whole *maqāma* revels in ambiguity and incoherence like that used to mock the whodunit genre in *Murder by Death*.

138. The Balkh Encounter.

139. *Mawālī* are the converts to Islam from non-Arab populations, who sought social standing by affiliation as "clients" to Arab tribes.

140. Richard Ellmann, writing in *Punch*, April 17, 1985.

141. In the Lion Encounter and the Ruṣāfa Encounter, respectively.

142. See Martin Green, *Children of the Sun* (New York: Basic Books, 1976), on the subject of uproarious, uncontrollable laughter and the practice of hoax, practical joking, fancy dress, costumes, disguises and of course, parodies.

143. A parallel from Hebrew belles lettres may help make the point. Some of the tales in Ḥarīzī's *Taḥkemoni* are outright imitations of Hamadhānī. But chapter 22, "The Arab Astrologer," tells a different sort of tale: A group of wild and headstrong Jewish youths test an itinerant astrologer, who is making an appearance in the city gates. When, the young men ask, will release come to the children of the oppressed race? Having no answer, the astrologer creates a diversion by angrily exposing the questioners as Jews who have impugned the authority of the state, by seeming to call for its apocalyptic overthrow. The youths are beaten by the mob and dragged before a magistrate, whose liberality and patience save their lives. He quietly frees them the next day. But the question remains unanswered: How long must the oppressed race suffer? And the subtext remains unspoken: That Israel will remain in durance as long as worldly natures rule the world. On the surface readers see that astrology has no answers for life's deepest mysteries. But below the surface, the message is that Israel's exile is among those mysteries, a question that has no answer. Liturgically, philosophically, even historically, that is a thesis that cannot be spoken. But the frame tale allows it to be understood, unvoiced.

144. Thaʿālibī, *Laṭā'if al-Maʿārif*, 63.

145. See p. 148, in this volume.

146. A Mamluk Boccaccio is found in the *K. al-Zahr al-Anīq fī Lubūs wa 'l-Ta'nīq*, The Book of Delicate Blooms on Courting and Kissing, by ʿAlī al-Baghdādī (fl. 1340–50). The author was among those charged with clearing up the estates of victims of the Black Death. His twenty-five bawdy stories of sly and deceiving women masks its intent under a flimsy veil of misogynist moralism. As modern critics remark, the moralism is a perfunctory and cosmetic passport for satire, often aimed at historic personages and the mores of the age, from hashish eating to fornication of all sorts. The work seems more to celebrate than deprecate the wiles of its women characters, typically at the expense of their boorish, concupisent, stupid, and avaricious menfolk. There's more Breughel than Bosch here. See Robert Irwin, "ʿAlī al-Baghdādī and the Joy of Mamluk Sex," in Kennedy, ed., *The Historiography of Islamic Egypt*, 45–57.

147. *Iliad* 6:-232–36, tr. Richard Lattimore (Chicago. University of Chicago Press, 1951).

148. Northrup Frye, *The Secular Scripture*, 65, borrowing the taxonomy from Dante.

149. The *Taxing Woman* movies from Japan use a revenue agent's inquiries to strip away the outward shell of false respectability and even sanctity that hides much crime and ugliness. The more conventional murder mysteries of the Erle Stanley Gardner or Agatha Christi variety use murder investigations in the same way: infidelities, blackmail, embezzlements, and betrayals come to light, often readily confessed, in the exigency of response to more serious charges. In this way the mystery becomes a vehicle of social commentary, often banal (since it trades upon, flatters, and indulges "what everyone knows"). Hamadhānī can be more incisive, since some of what he has to say would not more typically be said.

150. For nomadism as a kind of compulsive response to unstable times, Kraemer, *Humanism*, p. 24. Kraemer cites Robert Mandrou, *Introduction to Modern France 1500–1640: An Essay in Historical Psychology*, translated by R. E. Hallmark (New York: Holmes and Meier, 1976) 208–18; cf. 235–42 for other manifestations of instability.

151. See Bosworth, *Banū Sāsān*, 38–42, where many other ruses of beggars are cited, including false and self-inflicted mutilations, and *ghazī* speeches like those that Hamadhānī echoes. One Ibrāhīm b. Muḥammad al-Bayhaqī (fl. early tenth century) praises the beggar's carefree life in his *K. Maḥāsin wa 'l-Mawsāwī* . The literature tells of a man who won gifts in 942 from Ikhshīd in Egypt by claiming that his amputated hand had been miraculously restored; see Mez, *Renaissance of Islam*, 31. In present day Gujrat, in Pakistan, a Sufi shrine offers healing with the aid of deformed women called *chuchas*, whose small heads and severe retardation are thought to mean that they are touched God. Criminals, well into the twentieth century, are reported to have used metal bands or masks to retard cranial growth to produce the deformity in kidnapped healthy children, sending these and other maimed victims out to beg. See *New York Times*, October 28, 2001.

152. Abdelfattah Kilito, *Les Séances: Recits et codes culturels chez Hamadhani et Hariri* (Paris: Sindbad, 1983) 248–59. The Margoliouth-Pellat article on Ḥarīrī in *EI* 3.221–22 speculates on the identity of the historic Abū Zayd, but that seems to me to miss the point. Authors often have a model in mind, but characters remain artifacts of fiction, and the closest model for Ḥarīrī's work was the *Maqāmāt* of Hamadhānī. Ḥarīrī, as Robert Irwin points out, cited as a precedent for his fictional devices the Qur'ān's resort to legends, which, like his own stories, had a moral purpose. Kennedy, ed., *Historiography*, 53.

153. See Bruce Lawrence's introduction to *Morals for the Heart*, 22; *Notes from a Distant Flute*, 24. As Lawrence remarks, Niẓām al-Dīn's stature was enhanced by his association with the great poets and historians of his day.

154. Abduh suppresses the story that constitutes most of the second half of the Ruṣāfa Encounter, as Prendergast puts it "on grounds of decency"; and Prendergast follows suit, but the story is intact in the MSS and translated in Khawam's French version.

155. Gershom Scholem, *The Messianic Idea in Judaism, and Other Essays on Jewish Spirituality* (New York: Schocken, 1971), 78–141. Cf. my essay in *JAL* 19 (1988): 27–39.

156. Scholem, *Messianic*, 80.

157. Ibid., 80, 89.

158. Carl Petry in Hugh Kennedy, ed., *The Historiography of Islamic Egypt*, 170, and Karen Barkey, *Bandits and Bureaucrats: The Ottoman Route to State Centralization* (Ithaca: Cornell University Press, 1994), 170.

159. See Mez, *Renaissance*, 67 n. 8. Mez remarks that the tablets, placed before the faithful so that their foreheads might touch them at each prostration, were still being sold in the late nineteenth and early twentieth century.

160. See Ibid., 31

Chapter 2

1. For the translation movement, see my chapters in the *Cambridge History of Arabic Literature*, vols. 1 and 2, 1984, 1990.

2. See al-Ashʿarī, *Maqālāt al-Islāmiyyīn*.

3. For the stand off between Stoic and Peripatetic ideas about logic, see Goodman, *In Defense of Truth*, chapter 1.

4. For the nature of Qur'ānic discourse and its exegesis, see Wansbrough, *Quranic Studies*; for the life and thought of the Prophet, Tor Andrae, *Mohammed, the Man and his Faith*.

5. See Qur'ān 53:19–30, the locus of the famous Satanic verses; cf. 22:52–54. Commenting on the Qur'ānic mention of Allāt, Manāt, and al-ʿUzza, three pagan goddesses with shrines near Mecca, Watt writes: "The story is that when these verses were first recited, Muḥammad was anxious to win over the pagan Meccans, and failed to notice when Satan introduced two (or three) further verses permitting intercession at these shrines. This story could hardly have been invented and gains support from sura 22 v. 52/1. At length Muḥammad realized the substitution, and received the continuing revelation as it now is in the the Qur'ān." Watt, *Companion to the Qur'ān*, 245.

6. In the Qur'ān commentary published by the Saudi Royal office of The Presidency of Islamic Researches, Iftā', Call and Guidance, 371–72, ad Qur'ān 6:100, we read: "Both the Qur'ān and the Ḥadīth describe the Jinn as a definite species of living beings. They are created out of fire and, like man, may believe or disbelieve, accept or reject guidance. The authoritative Islamic texts show that they are not merely a hidden force, or a spirit. They are personalized beings who enjoy a certain amount of free will and thus will be called to account."

7. The credo known as *Waṣīyat Abī Ḥanīfa*, dated to ca. 825, affirms the uncreated Qur'ān; a letter of the caliph Ma'mūn from 833 rejects that doctrine as a vulgar and irrational confusion. But the tenet of faith was not without sophistication. For the old credo made careful use of the type/token distinction in identifying just what it was that was uncreated: not the individual copies or utterances or memories of the text, but God's word itself. See A. J. Wensinck, *The Muslim Creed*, 77–78, 127, 151; J. R. T. M. Peters, *God's Created Speech*; 2–5, 278–402. As Peters explains, the idea of the uncreated Qur'ān is not unrelated to Islamic notions of predestination, since it seems to require the predetermination at least of all the events mentioned in the scriptural text. Shīʿites may have favored Muʿtazilism in part because the doctrine of an uncreated Qur'ān left the future open and allowed for the possibility that not every event in history was a direct realization of God's will.

8. Wensinck (*Muslim Creed*, 86) sees God's word exalted in Ibn Ḥazm's eternal Qur'ān and but downgraded in the created Qur'ān. I think that appraisal accepts a bit too dutifully Ashʿarī's polemical account; see *K. al-Ibāna ʿan Uṣūl al-Diyāna* (Hyderabad: Dā'irat al-Maʿārif al-Nizāmiyya, 1903), 33 ff., translated by Walter C. Klein (New Haven: American Oriental Society, 1940), 47: "They [the Muʿtazilites and other voluntarists] maintain the createdness of the Qur'ān, thereby approximating the belief of their brethen among the polytheists, who said, 'it is merely the word of a mortal' (Qur'ān 74:25)." The actual stance of the Muʿtazilites was a reaction against attempts to make the Logos a person of the Trinity. The traditionalists were less worried about such ploys but eager to give cosmic stature to God's word. The issue certainly helped them to define their differences with the Muʿtazilites and thus to create a sense of (embattled) orthodoxy. But note Fārābī's qualifications to the immutability of words, as opposed to principles. For Fārābī and Ashʿarī are contemporaries.

9. Brannon Wheeler, *Applying the Canon in Islam*, 1.

10. Ibid., 13.

11. Ibid., 14–15.

12. See Goodman, *God of Abraham*, 203–10.

13. See Goodman, *Avicenna*, 123–49.

14. Majid Fakhry, *Ethical Theories in Islam*, 13; cf. Toshihiko Izutsu, *Ethico-Religious Concepts in the Qur'ān*, 207–11.

15. I render *ʿalā ḥubbihi*, in keeping with the traditional Islamic understanding, as "out of love for Him," rather than, "however cherished" as in Arberry.

16. Izutsu, *Ethico-Religious*, 184.

17. See for example Isaiah 58.

18. Izutsu, *Ethico-Religious*, 65–67, 76–83.

19. Ibid., 53, 58–63; cf. 45–52, 55–58, which cites numerous poetic expressions of the *Jāhiliyya* ethos.

20. Ibid., 86–104.

21. See Ibid., 108–16.

22. Ibid., 119–55.

23. See Watt, *Free Will and Predestination in Early Islam*. For the Qur'ānic backgrounds to *kalām* discussions of responsibility and accountability, see Hourani, *Reason and Tradition in Islamic Ethics*, 23–48 and Fakhry, *Ethical Theories in Islam*, 14–21.

24. See Joseph Schacht, *Origins of Muhammadan Jurisprudence*, 58–81 and Wensinck, *Concordance et Indices de la Tradition Musulmane*.

25. We cited many of these in chapter 1, in exploring the interactions of the sacred and the secular.

26. As Reuben Levy showed in *The Social Structure of Islam* (Cambridge: Cambridge University Press, 1957), 194, the Muslim ideas of *maʿrūf* and *munkar*, the acceptable and unacceptable, build on ancient foundations. It does no good to gloss these ideas etymologically in terms of what is familiar, "approved" or accepted (see Fakhry, *Ethical Theories in Islam*, 12). For neither the pre-Islamic norm nor the Qur'ānic command urged people to do what was accepted but rather what was acceptable. If there was a moral revolution in Islam it was about what was and was not acceptable. Cf. Izutsu, *Ethico-Religious*, 213–17.

27. Michael Cook, *Commanding Right and Forbidding Wrong in Islamic Thought*, 6, gives numerous citations for the *ḥadīth*, from collections including Ibn Hanbal, Ibn Māja, Bukhārī, Tirmidhī, Nasā'ī, and others.

28. Ibid., 8–10.

29. Robert Worth, "The Deep Intellectual Roots of Islamic Terror," *New York Times*, October 13, 2001.

30. Cook, *Commanding Right*, 87–97.

31. Ibid., 98–100.

32. Ibid., 101.

33. Ibid., 101–3.

34. Ibid., 139–41.

35. See Victor Makari, *Ibn Taymiyyah's Ethics*, 140; Cook, *Commanding Right*, 153.

36. Makari, *Ethics*, 141.

37. Ibid., 127–31.

38. Cook, *Commanding Right*, 153–55.

39. Ibid., 165–92.

40. *New York Times*, August 7, 2001.

41. Cook, *Commanding Right*, 344.

42. Ibid., 345–46.

43. See Ibn ʿAbdūn, in John Williams, ed., *Themes of Islamic Civilization.*

44. Sarakhsī was stripped of his wealth, beaten, imprisoned, and left to die in disgrace. See Franz Rosenthal, *Ahmad b. at-Tayyib as-Sarahsi* (New Haven: AOS, 1943), 23–25. The historian Maqrīzī was also a *muḥtasib*; see p. 197, this volume.

45. See George Hourani, *Islamic Rationalism: the Ethics of ʿAbd al-Jabbar*, and my review in *The Middle East Journal* 25 (1971): 543–45.

46. Hourani defends Muʿtazilite objectivism as a pertinent reading of the Qur'ān, *Reason and Tradition in Islamic Ethics*, 15–48; cf. 67–108; Fakhry, *Ethical Theories in Islam*, 14–58.

47. For the political overtones and undertow of *kalām* discussions, see Watt, *The Formative Period of Islamic Thought*, and *EI* 4.368–72.

48. See Watt, *The Formative Period of Islamic Thought*, 304–6.

49. See Eric Ormsby, *Theodicy in Islamic Thought.*

50. See Goodman, *God of Abraham*, 240–42.

51. Dennis Overbye, "How Islamic Scholars Won and Lost the World Lead in Science," New York Times, October 30, 2001; cf. Pervez Hoodbhoy, *Islam and Science: Religious Orthodoxy and the Battle for Rationality* (London: Zed Books, 1991).

52. Saadiah's critique of Ashʿarism and adaptation of Muʿtazilism emerges brilliantly in his exegesis of the Book of Job; he assigns the Ashʿarite view, that God may do as He pleases, to the as yet unenligthened Job. See Saadiah's *Book of Theodicy.*

53. See Ashʿarī, *K. al-Lumaʿ*, 93.

54. Ashʿarī's vivid exposition of his theory of action is contained in his *Kitāb al-Lumaʿ*. For Ghazālī's inference that one cannot pry open a man's heart to test his sincerity, see *Iḥyā' ʿUlūm al-Dīn*, xxxv 2 (Cairo, 1967), 4.305–6.

55. For Sufi theory and practice, see Ḥujwiri, *Kashf al-Maḥjūb*; J. S. Trimmingham, *The Sufi Orders in Islam*; for *inbisāt*, R. C. Zaehner, *Mysticism, Sacred and Profane.*

56. Ghazālī, *Iḥyā'*, 4.305.

57. See Margaret Smith, *Al-Muhasibi*; A. H. Abdel-Kader, *Al-Junayd.*

58. *Qūt al-Qulūb* (Sustenance for Hearts) (Cairo: Mustafa al-Bābī al-Ḥalabī and Sons, 1961) 2.7, correcting the text according to the edition of 1310 A.H., 2.4. As Massignon remarks, Ghazālī copied "whole pages" of Makkī's work in the *Ihyā'*; see *EI* 1.153.

59. See Goodman, *Crosspollinations*, chapter 3.

60. For the history of philosophy in Islam, see Majid Fakhry's *A History of Islamic Philosophy*, and Seyyed Hossein Nasr and Oliver Leaman, eds., *History of Islamic Philosophy*

61. See Kindī's "Essay on How to Banish Sorrow" and cf. p. 127, this volume.

62. See Goodman, *Crosspollinations*, chapter 2.

63. See Kraemer, *Humanism* and *Philosophy*; Roy Mottahedeh, *Loyalty and Leadership*; Adam Mez, *Renaissance.*

64. Thaʿālibī writes: "The Arabs used to call every delicately or curiously made vessel and such like, whatever its real origin, 'Chinese,' because finely-made things are a specialty of China. The designation 'china' has remained in use to this day for the celebrated type of dishes. In the past, as at the present time, the Chinese have been famous for the skill of their hands and for their expertise in fashioning rare and beautiful objects. The Chinese themselves say, 'Except for us, the people of the world are all blind—unless one takes into account the people of Babylon, who are merely one-eyed.'" *Latā'if al-Maʿārif*, 141

65. Khalidi, *Arabic Historical Thought*, 171. And see Arkoun, *Contribution.*

66. Richard Walzer and Hamilton Gibb, *Akhlāq*, *EI* 1.325–29. Fakhry calls Miskawayh's book "the most important ethical treatise of Islam." *Ethical Theories in Islam*, 130.

67. Ansari, *The Ethical Philosophy of Miskawayh*, 16–17.

68. See Mohammed Arkoun, *L'Humanisme Arabe au IVᵉ/Xᵉ Siècle*, 63–64; Kraemer, *Humanism*, 20.

69. See Ansari, *Miskawayh*, 18.

70. Arkoun, *L'Humanisme*, 67–68.

71. Miskawayh, *Tajārub*, 5.237.

72. See Arkoun, *L'Humanisme*, 68–70.

73. Miskawayh, *Tajārub*, 5.431–32.

74. For Miskawayh's history, see pp. 199–201, this volume.

75. F. E. Peters, *Allah's Commonwealth*, 535. For Miskawayh's career, 503–34.

76. See Goodman, *Avicenna*, 39, 51.

77. See Everett Rowson's introduction to ʿĀmirī's *K. al-Amad ʿalā ʾl-Abad* in *A Muslim Philosopher on the Soul and its Fate*, 5.

78. See al-ʿĀmirī, *K. al-Amad ʿalā ʾl-Abad*; Arkoun, *L'Humanisme*, 44.

79. Peters, *Allah's Commonwealth*, 542.

80. In 932 Mattā debated the grammarian al-Sīrāfī (d. 979) over linguistic relativism versus universality in logic. Yaḥyā pursued the matter in his *Making Clear the Distinction*, 38–50, 181–93. See Kraemer, *Humanism*, 110–14; Margoliouth, "The Discussion"; Mahdi, "Language and Logic"; Tawḥīdī, *K. al-Hawāmil wa-ʾl-Shawāmil*, 265–66.

81. See Yaḥyā b. ʿAdī, *Tahdhīb al-Akhlāq*, ed. Muhammad Kurd Ali in *Rasāʾil al-Bulaghāʾ*. 3d ed. (Cairo: 1946), 517–18. The passage is quoted in Kraemer, *Humanism*, 115. Ibn ʿAdī reveals here the ethical implications, or roots, of monopsychism.

82. Cf. Fārābī, *Kitāb al-Ḥurūf*, 77–80; Walzer, *Greek into Arabic*, 33, 222; Kraemer, *Humanism*, 10, 115.

83. Saadiah, the contemporary of Abū Bishr, bridges the gap between an ethics of tendencies and an ethics of acts by the rabbinic expedient of making one's ultimate salvation depend on the general tenor of one's acts. See *ED* III Exordium, V 1, 4, IX 8.

84. *NE* V 6, 1134a17–23.

85. *NE* I 7, 1098a17–19; cf. Maimonides: "Every one of us is capable of growing as righteous as Moses or as wicked as Jeroboam." *Mishneh Torah*, Laws of Repentance, V 1.2.

86. Indeed, Walzer and Gibb remark that "there are no specifically Christian ideas" to be found in Yaḥyā's *Fī Tahdhīb al-Akhlaq*; *EI* 1.328.

87. Ian Netton writes tentatively, "One may be forgiven for wondering whether Yaḥyā's pessimism about human nature does not reflect in some way the Christian theologians' doctrine of original sin." *Al-Fārābī and His School*, 59. But, if so, reason has become the immanent Logos.

88. Yaḥyā b. ʿAdī, *Tahdhīb al-Akhlāq*, On the Refinement of Character, ed. G. F. Awad (Cairo: al-Maṭbaʿa al-Miṣriyya al-Ahliyya 1913) 15–20, 55 ff.; Kraemer, *Humanism*, 101.

89. Miskawayh, *Tahdhīb al-Akhlāq*, 48; Miskawayh hedges (46–47) on whether these elements of the personality are properly called separate souls or faculties—quite rightly, since Plato, in the end, withdraws the idea that they are inevitably separate, allowing for their unity in an integrated personality; see *Republic* X 611.

90. See Kraemer, *Humanism*, 147. Ghazālī has it that God's unity is "a bottomless and shoreless sea," *Iḥyā'* 35 bayān 2; cf. Plotinus' image of the soul as unbounded, a net encompassing the sea, *Enneads* IV 3.9.11.

91. Kraemer, *Humanism*, vii.

92. Bosworth, Introduction to *Tha'ālibī*, 15.

93. Clifford E. Bosworth, in his introduction to *The Laṭā'if al-Ma'ārif of Tha'ālibī*, 15.

94. Cf. Franz Rosenthal, *Knowledge Triumphant*, 284–87, 320.

95. Kraemer, *Humanism*, vii.

96. See Peters, *Allah's Commonwealth*, 538. Miskawayh, was, after all, an expert on blended flavors. In his medical capacity he is credited with two works on diet—the one on cooking and another on beverages. See Ansari, *Miskawayh*, 20.

97 Miskawayh, *Tahdhīb al-Akhlāq*, 1, cited parenthetically in what follows, by page numbers in Constantine Zurayk's translation, *The Refinement of Character*.

98. Cf. Miskawayh's essay on pleasure, ed. Arkoun, 7–19, esp. 10–12; cf. Goodman, *Jewish and Islamic Philosophy*, 38–39.

99. Farābī, *Mabādı Arā'*, *Fuṣūl*.

100. The remark is offered as a paraphrase of Aristotle; see Sijistānī, *Siwān*, 333.

101. See Miskawayh, *Kitāb Tartīb*.

102. Dimitri Gutas, "Paul the Persian," 232–33.

103. See W. F. R. Hardie, *Aristotle's Ethical Theory*, 12–28, 336–57.

104. See Tūsī, *The Nasīrian Ethics*.

105. See Walzer, *Greek into Arabic*, 220–35; Abul Quasem, *The Ethics of al-Ghazālī* and "Al-Ghazālī's Rejection of Philosophic Ethics"; Sherif, *Ghazalı's Theory of Virtue*.

106. See G. Hourani, *Reason and Tradition in Islamic Ethics*, 136.

107. See Ghazālī's *Mishkāt al-Anwār*. The Light verse is quoted in the introductory chapter, p. 25.

108. Abul Quasem, "Al-Ghazālī's Rejection,"119–120

109. R. Walzer, in *EI* 1.328.

110. Sherif, Ghazālī, 72, and Ghazālī, *Maqṣad*.

111. See Goodman, *Crosspollinations*, 70–76.

112. Watt (in *Muslim Intellectual*, 67–68) argues that Ghazālī must have abandoned virtue ethics after experimenting with it in *The Criterion of Action* (*Mizān al-'Amal*, lit., "The "Scale of Practice")—a work whose authenticity he questions in whole or part. But cf. Wensinck, *La Pensée*, ch. 2. It is true that Ghazālī questions the universal adequacy of the model of virtue as choosing a mean between extremes. But so does Aristotle. Ghazālī also questions the adequacy of reason in locating the mean. But he never rejects the idea of the mean. His understanding that this idea is Qur'ānic undergirds his decision to make virtue ethics the backbone of the moral scheme of the *Iḥyā'*. His insistence on grace should not blind us to his recognition that scriptural deontology is not an end in itself but a means to human felicity in this world and the next. Even at the height of his paeans to Sufi surrender, in the celebrated discussion of *tawakkul* or ultimate trust in God (*Iḥyā'* XXXV), the core and kernel of piety is found not in specific behavioral acts but in what they reveal and foster in our hearts. Behaviors, whose paradigm is lip service to the demands of faith, are, as we have seen, the mere "husk of the husk." But this manner of structuring values is virtue ethics, and its source in Ghazālī is Miskawayh's Aristotelian reading of the Qur'ān.

113. See Sherif, *Ghazali's Theory of Virtue*, 99.

114. Ibid., 185.
115. See Hamori, *On the Art of Medieval Arabic Literature,* 11, 23.
116. See Sherif, *Ghazali,* 183 and Ghazālī, *Al-Maqṣad al-Asnā.*
117. See *Al-Munqidh min al-Dalāl,* in *The Faith and Practice of al-Ghazālī,* 56.
118. Mohammed Arkoun, "Miskawayh," *EI* 7.144.

Chapter 3

1. Bashshār b. Burd, *Diwān,* ed. M. Tahir b. Ashur (Cairo: Matbaʿat Lajnat al-Ta'līf wa 'l-Tarjama wa 'l-Nashr, 1950–57), 1.242, *l.* 5

2. J. R. T. M. Peters, *God's Created Speech,* 109.

3. Jāḥiẓ, *Tria Opuscula,* ed. G. van Vloten (Leiden: Brill, 1903) 102 *l.* 12.

4. Dimashqī, *Kitāb Nuḥbat al-Dahr fī 'Ajā'ib al-Barr wa 'l-Baḥr,* ed. A. F. Mehren (St. Petersburg: Académie Imperiale des Sciences, 1866), 78.

5. Ibn Rushd, *TT,* ed. Bouyges, 21 *l.* 6.

6. Aristotle, *Kitāb al-āthār al-ulwīya,* translated by Yaḥyā ibn al-Biṭrīq in the eighth century, ed. A.-R. Badawi (Beirut: Université Saint-Joseph, 1967), 92 *l.* 4.

7. Presidency of Islamic Researches, *Holy Qurān . . . Commentary,* 1148, n. 3421.

8. For Ghazālī's reading of the Qur'ānic "*Lā ḥawla wa lā quwwa illā bi'llāh!*" ("No might and no power but in God"), see *Iḥyā* xxxv.2.1 (Cairo, 1310 A.H.) 4.200 ff.

9. Maimonides, *Guide* I 73, and Goodman, *Rambam,* 124–55.

10. Ashʿarī, *Kitāb al-Lumaʿ,* 76–81.

11. See Aristotle, *Metaphysics* I 4, 985a 18.

12. Galen, *Compendium Timaei Platonis,* 3–5. The Arabic text derives from the work of Ḥunayn ibn Isḥāq, the Nestorian Christian translator of philosophical and medical works, who catalogues some 129 Galenic works that he and his immediate followers translated from Greek into Arabic, typically via a Syriac intermediary version.

13. ʿAbd al-Jabbār, *Muḥīṭ* 1.55–56; cf. J. R. T. M. Peters, *God's Created Speech,* 112–13; Ghazālī, *Jerusalem Letter,* tr. Tibawi, 98–99. Juwaynī had proposed contingency as the basis of our knowledge of creation, and Ghazālī argued along those lines in *Faḍā'iḥ. al-Bāṭiniyya,* 80–81, but seems to have abandoned the argument in view of its potential for an Avicennan, eternalist reading; see Juwaynī, *K. al-Irshād,* ed. Luciani, ch. 4 and pp. 2, 106. As Ghazālī explains, assuming the world to be eternal, there is no absurdity in an infinite succession of causes and effects; *TF,* Discussion 4, ed. Marmura, 80–81; Goodman, "Ghazālī's Argument from Creation," 75–77, and *Avicenna,* ch. 2, esp. p. 86.

14. Kindī, *On First Philosophy,* 73.

15. Kindī, "Essay on How to Banish Sorrow."

16. Kindī, *First Philosophy,* 65.

17. Ibid., 67.

18. Ibid., 84.

19. See L. E. Goodman, "The Translation of Greek Materials into Arabic," 482. Ptolemy flourished in second century Alexandria.

20. Rāzī, "Munāẓarāt," in *Opera,* ed. Kraus, 308; Goodman trans., 96–97. For Rāzī's philosophy, see Goodman, *Crosspollinations,* ch. 2.

21. Rāzī, "Munāzarāt," in *Opera,* ed. Kraus, 309–10.

22. Ibid., 311–12.

23. See Goodman, "Rāzī's Myth of the Fall of the Soul."

24. See Rāzī, "Munāẓarāt," in *Opera*, ed. Kraus, 295–300.

25. See Fārābī, "Against John the Grammarian."

26. See p. 151, this volume.

27. Alexander of Aphrodisias, *De Anima*, 88–89; Herbert Davidson, *Alfarabi, Avicenna, and Averroes, on Intellect*, 20, 30. As we read in Fārābī's *Arā'*: "Alexander the Commentator, says that Aristotle's view entails that the Active Intellect governs not just man but sublunary physical bodies too, with the support of the celestial bodies. For the celestial bodies impart only motion. The Active Intellect imparts the forms that orient those motions" (54); the translation here is my own.

28. Davidson, *Alfarabi, Avicenna, and Averroes, on Intellect*, 45.

29. Ibid., 47–48; cf. 33.

30. Fārābī, *Maqālah fī aghrāḍ mā ba'd al-tabī'ah*, trans., in "Le Traite d'al-Fārābī sur les buts de la *Metaphysique* d'Aristote," *Bulletin de Philosophie Médiéval* 24 (1982): 43.

31. Fārābī, *On* De Interpretatione, 9, 98.

32. See Ibid., 9, and Goodman, "Al-Fārābī's Modalities."

33. For my own development of the idea of universal deserts, see *On Justice*, *God of Abraham*, and *Judaism, Human Rights and Human Values*.

34. See Goodman, *Avicenna*, chapter 2.

35. Like so much else in Avicenna, the approach came from Fārābī; in this case, from his distinction between what is contingent in itself and what is necessary in relation to its posited conditions. The relationship was first pointed out to me by my friend Alfred Ivry. See Fārābī *On* De Interpretatione, 9 and Goodman, "Al-Fārābī's Modalities."

36. Cf. Richard Frank: "It has long been recognized that while al-Ghazālī rejected some major theses of the Avicennan system he appropriated others. What we have seen on a closer examination of what he has to say concerning God's relation to the cosmos as its creator, however, reveals that from a theological standpoint most of the theses which he rejected are relatively tame and inconsequential compared to some of those in which he follows the philosopher." *Creation and the Cosmic System: Al-Ghazālī and Avicenna* (Heidelberg: Carl Winter, 1992) 86; cf. M. E. Marmura, "Ghazalian Causes in Intermediaries," *JAOS* 115 (1995): 89–100.

37. See Ghazālī, *Maqāṣid al-Falāsifa*, 144–46. Ghazālī is not the wholehearted defender of naturalism and free will that Maimonides is. Theologically, Maimonides builds on Ghazālī's work and moderates it. But what Maimonides seems to find most useful here is Ghazālī's rejection of the extreme occasionalism that is sometimes equated with the Ash'arite position. Ghazālī has the objector to his first proposed response find in it *muhālāt shanī'a,* that is, outrageous absurdities—material rather than formal absurdities, to be sure, but monstrous nonetheless. So when Ghazālī proposes an escape or way out *(khalāṣ)* of these difficulties in his second proposed reply, he is not just calling them vilifications but charges of absurdity. The objections are not just name-calling but challenges that deserve a serious answer. Ghazālī seems to enjoy detailing them, and their content suggests why, for the objections echo Ash'arī's account of the extreme occasionalism of Sālih Qubba and Abū Ḥusayn al-Ṣālihī; see *Maqālāt al-Islāmiyyīn* 309–11, 406–7, and Goodman, "Did Ghazali Deny Causality?" Ghazālī wants to address the charge that extreme occasionalism renders nature and experience incoherent. He concedes that sheer voluntarism (as regards God) would leave one never knowing what to expect:

> Someone who put down a book in the house might find when he returned that it had turned into a bright young servant lad going about his duties, or into an animal. Or if he left a servant at home, he would have to allow that he might have changed into a dog; or if he left ashes, they might turn into musk, or stone to gold, or gold to stone. If asked about any of these things one would have to say, "I have no idea what's in my house right now. All I know is that I left a book there, but perhaps by now it's a horse and has spattered my library with its dung and staling. I left a jar of water, but perhaps it's turned into an apple tree. For God can do anything. And a horse need not be created from sperm, or a tree from seed, or from anything at all. And things might have been created that never existed before." So one should be hesitant on seeing someone one had never laid eyes on before, if asked whether this person had a mother, and should answer: "It's conceivable that one of the fruits in the market turned into a man and this is he. For God can do anything possible, and this is possible. So there's no way of avoiding hesitation in such matters."

Ghazālī's second response avoids the difficulties of extreme occasionalism by relying on an Ash'arite appeal to divine custom. God gives us habits of mind that match His custom; and He can prepare prophets for exceptions to the familiar course of events. Ghazālī goes on to deny that God can do the impossible. Among his paradigm cases of the impossible: bilocation, the combination of black and white, and the transformation of one genus into another—the color black into a cooking pot. Most tellingly, Ghazālī concedes that even miraculous changes must pass through the stages of natural transformation (although God may accelerate those phases far beyond our normal expectations). All of these assertions acknowledge the embeddedness of logic in the fabric of nature. For Ghazālī accepts the idea that the characteristics of things come to them "through their principles," the forms, whether imparted directly by God or by the angels (the Philosophers' Form Giver). He draws the line by insisting that this (divine) imparting of forms must be volitional, not a matter of necessity. To all of this we must add that we can hardly fail to note how utterly ordinary Ghazālī's views on causality and the theory of action become in most of the ethical contexts discussed in our chapter 2.

38. *TF*, Discussion 17.

39. See Goodman, *Rambam*, 183–204; *God of Abraham*, chapter 8.

40. Averroes wrote works specifically calling out Fārābī's and Avicenna's departures, respectively, from the logic and metaphysics of Aristotle; see Fakhry, *History of Islamic Philosophy*, 273.

41. Étienne Gilson, *The Spirit of Medieval Philosophy*, 80.

42. Fakhry, *History*, 349–50.

43. Franz Rosenthal, *Knowledge Triumphant*, 21.

44. Wan Mohd Nor Wan Daud, *The Concept of Knowledge in Islam*, 34.

45. "Heat and passion," might better convey the force of the Arabic. The King Fahd Qur'ān renders: "The Unbelievers / Got up in their hearts / Heat and cant—the heat / And cant of Ignorance." Arberry has: "When the unbelievers set in their hearts fierceness, the fierceness of pagandom." As Watt notes in his *Companion to the Qur'ān*, ad loc., the verses are traditionally assigned to the time of the Ḥudaybiyya pact of 628, when the Prophet was testing his adversaries in Mecca by demanding entry to the city to offer sacrifice at the Ka'ba. For more on the term *Jāhiliyya*, see Rosenthal, *Knowledge Triumphant*, 33–35; Izutsu, *The Structure of Ethical Terms in the* Koran; Mohd, 76–79.

46. For the scriptural nexus, see Kassis, *Concordance of the Qur'ān*, 239–54.

47. The poets are Bishr ibn Abī Khāzim and Nābighah al-Dhubyānī, both of the latter half of the sixth century; see Rosenthal, *Knowledge Triumphant*, 14, 17.

48. Jacob Landau, *A Word Count of Modern Arabic Prose* (New York: American Council of Learned Societies, 1959), 70, s.v. *ḥakīm*.

49. For a contemporary cognitivist/experiential account of Islamic mysticism, see Mehdi Ha'iri Yazdi, *The Principles of Epistemology in Islamic Philosophy* (Albany: State University of New York Press, 1992).

50. See Hamadhānī, *Rasā'il*, ed. Yusra Abd al-Ghani Abdullah (Beirut: Catholic Press, 1987) and the discussion in Wadad al-Qadi, "Badīʿ al-Zamān al-Hamadhānī and his Social and Political Vision," in Mir, ed., *Arabic and Islamic Studies in Honor of James A. Bellamy*, 197–223.

51. Hamadhānī's outlook as a critic is voiced in the Poesy Encounter, and spelled out at many places in the *Rasā'il*.

52. Hamadhānī's patrons at Rayy were the *wazīr* Sāḥib b. ʿAbbād and the *amīr*, Fakhr al-Dawla, who took him on as tutor to his son. Sāhib, a Shīʿite and passionate Muʿtazilite, appointed the Sunnite Muʿtazilite ʿAbd al-Jabbār as Qāḍī of Rayy. See Rowson, "Religion and Politics in the Career of . . . Hamadhānī," 654.

53. In the career of Mahmūd of Ghazna (r. 998–1030), worldliness contests the claims of the spiritual in military and political rather than literary terms. This ruthless conqueror assembled the largest of the many Islamic empires. Presenting himself as a champion of Islam, he prized the learning and the arts of this world but saw them not as ends in themselves but as means of self-aggrandizement. He executed and oppressed heretics and sectaries but also made sectarians his allies of convenience. He persecuted Muʿtazilites but also the orthodox scholar Ibn Fūrak, whom he may have poisoned when the learned traditionist seemed to press too closely the ruler's Karrāmite allies. His blood-soaked campaigns carried the sword and banner of Islam deep into India. But many of his foot soldiers and elephant men were pagans, and his raids and pillaging against Shiʿites and Hindus were prompted more by rapacity than by any sincere religious faith. Booty from the temples of India enriched the mosques of Ghaznā—but also adorned the ruler's palaces and sustained his bureaucracy and the powerful, multiethnic professional army that was the engine of his conquests. See C. E. Bosworth, *EI* 6.65 and *The Ghaznavids*.

54. Thaʿālibī, *Laṭā'if al-Maʿārif*, 45, traces to the days of the Rāshidūn caliphs the first acts of bribery, graft, and oppression under Islam. The oppression, it was said, began with attendants' shouting "get out of the road" when the caliph passed.

55. Ikhwān al-Ṣafā', *Rasā'il*, 1.390–403.

56. For a generous survey of *kalām* and allied definitions and general descriptions of knowledge, see Rosenthal, *Knowledge Trimphant*, 46–69.

57. See J. R. T. M. Peters, *God's Created Speech*, 40–104

58. For ʿAbd al-Jabbār's ethical intuitionism, see G. Hourani, *Islamic Rationalism*, 3, 22, 31–34. For a (somewhat subdued) Jewish parallel to the Muʿtazilite reliance on self-knowledge as an assurance of moral probity, see Saadiah's *Book of Theodicy*, 128; cf. 229 n. 22, 292 n.11

59. For the Stoic plenum and Cartesian hydrostatics, see Stephen Gaukroger, *Descartes: An Intellectual Biography* (Oxford: Oxford University Press, 1995), 84–89, 159–67, etc.

60. Tirmidhī, quoted by Rosenthal, *Knowledge Triumphant*, 68.

61. Here I follow the old Oxford translation of J. A. Smith, which seems to me clearer than the Barnes version.

62. *Posterior Analytics* II 19, 100a 4–14; cf. Goodman, *In Defense of Truth*, ch. 5.

63. Plotinus, *Risāla fī ʿIlm*, ed. Abdurrahman Badawi in *Plotinus apud Arabes* (Cairo: Dirāsat Islāmiyya, 1955) 168; see Davidson, *Alfarabi, Avicenna, and Averroes on the Intellect*, 24.

64. See ad *De Anima* 430a 10–12, in *"Philoponus" On Aristotle's* On the Soul *3.1–8*, trans. William Charlton (Ithaca: Cornell University Press, 2000), p. 114 § 30. Charlton ascribes this work not to Philoponus but to a later sixth century author, Stephanus of Alexandria. Our second citation comes from the commentary thought to be the work of Philoponus himself and preserved in Latin: *Le commentaire de Jean Philopon sur le troisième livre du Traité de l'âme: Traduction de Guillaume de Moerbeke*, ed., G. Verbeke (Louvain: Publications Universitaires de Louvain, 1966) p. 44 § 25.

65. See J. Finnegan, ed., "Texte arabe du *Peri Nou* d'Alexandre d'Aphrodise," *Melanges de l'Université Saint Joseph* 33 (1956): 157–202, see 186–87, 189, 194; Jean Jolivet, *L'Intellect selon Kindī* (Leiden: Brill, 1971) 38.

66. See Kindī, *Risāla fī ʾl-ʿAql*, ed. McCarthy, 122–24; trans. Jolivet, 1–6.

67. "Statement on the Soul Abstracted from the Book of Aristotle and Plato and other Philosophers," *Rasāʾil al-Kindī*, ed. M. Abu Rida (Cairo: Dār al-Fikr al-ʿArabī, 1953) vol. 1, p. 273.

68. See Kindī, *On First Philosophy*, 106.

69. See Fārābī, *Risāla fī ʾl-ʿAql*, ed. M. Bouyges (Beirut: Catholic Press, 1948); translated by Arthur Hyman in A. Hyman and James Walsh, eds. *Philosophy in the Middle Ages* (New York: Harper and Row, 1967) 215–221.

70. Fārābī, *Arāʾ*, 52, 54; the translation here is my own.

71. Emil Fackenheim, Philip Merlan, and others have suggested that in his "Essay on Love," Avicenna at least temporarily made an exception to his outspoken rejections of the doctrine of "union" (*ittihād*). But, as I showed in *Avicenna*, 163–72, the suggestion rests on a mistranslation. Avicenna does not endorse *ittiḥād* but resolves the Sufi references to such union in terms of his own preferred idea of contact, *ittiṣāl*.

72. See Nabil Shehaby, *The Propositional Logic of Avicenna* (a translation from the *Shifāʾ*: *al-Qiyās*) (Dordrecht: Reidel, 1973), 54–55.

73. See Ibn Sīnā, *K. al-Ishārāt wa-ʾl-Tanbīhāt*, trans. Goichon, 56–59; cf. John Stuart Mill, *A System of Logic*, book III, Chapter viii.

74. Avicenna, *Najāt*, 36–37.

75. Avicenna, *Shifāʾ*, 248. Avicenna glosses the Qur'ānic Light Verse in terms of the emanative epistemology of the Active Intellect in *K. al-Ishārāt wa-ʾl-Tanbīhāt*, tr. Goichon, 324–26. The effect is at once to naturalize the idea of inspiration and to re-enchant the conception of human knowledge.

76. Ibn Bājjah, *Ittiṣāl al-ʿAql bi ʾl-Insān* (Man's Contact with the Intellect), ed. Fakhry in *Opera Metaphysica*, 156; see Goodman, *Crosspollinations*, 108–14; cf. Aristotle, *Metaphysics* Zeta 4, 1030b 9, where the reference is to Homer's *Iliad* rather than Ṭabarī's *History*.

77. Ibn Tufayl, *Ḥayy Ibn Yaqẓān*, tr. Goodman, 150–55.

78. Maimonides, *Guide* I 74, ed. Munk 1.121b. Pines writes, ad loc, that Maimonides here supports the idea of "the Unity of the Intellect." But the reference to Ibn Bājjah and others of his ilk suggests that Maimonides actually accepts Ibn Bājjah's and Ibn Ṭufayl's Avicennan thesis that individuality is preserved within that unity.

79. Thomas quotes Averroes as follows: "per rationem concludo de necessitate quod intellectus est unus numero, firmiter tamen teneo oppositum per fidem," that

is: "By reason I infer that mind is arithmetically one, of necessity, although I firmly hold the opposite by faith." Quoted in Friedrich Ueberweg, *History of Philosophy from Thales to the Present Time*, translated from the fourth German edition by G. S. Morris (New York: Scribners, 1890) 1.415. That firm confession of faith, an instance of the notorious doctrine of double truth, is not, in this instance, an admission of hesitancy about the conclusions to which reason has led the mind. On the contrary, it is a bracketing of the traditional view and of the familiar notion of that there are many minds, a bold acceptance of the seemingly paradoxical conclusion, and a rejection of the Avicennan style of Neoplatonic reconciliation of diversity within unity that Averroes's courtly sponsor Ibn Ṭufayl had championed.

80. Davidson, *Alfarabi, Avicenna, and Averroes, on Intellect*, 315.

81. Ibid., 323:

> Averroes may at first have been unsure about the possibility of the human intellect's having the active intellect as an object of thought and conjoining with it. His Epitome of Aristotle's *Metaphysics* exhibits skepticism about the possibility. . . . By contrast, an appendix to the Epitome of the *De anima*, Averroes's Long Commentary on the *De anima*, his Long Commentary on the *Metaphysics*, and his three opuscules on conjunction all affirm the possibility of the twin phenomena. . . . once his initial hesitation passes, he tenaciously upholds the possibility of conjunction in some form or another. If it were legitimate to speak of dogmas in Averroes, the possibility of conjunction with the active intellect would rank high on the list.

Borrowing arguments from Alexander of Aphrodisias, Themistius, and Ibn Bājjah, Averroes works his way to the conclusion that "a time must come when the material intellect finally strips away every facet of plurality," that has linked it to the physical. Now individuality disappears, and all minds unite in a single thought, focused on the Active Intellect, which they become. See Davidson, *Alfarabi, Avicenna, and Averroes, on Intellect*, 325–27. What Davidson takes as hesitancy on Averroes's part Ivry reads as an artifact of the philosopher's tendency "to present the views of philosophers he respects so well as to appear often to be in agreement with them." He sees a firm commitment in Averroes:

> Following a common tradition which has its origins in Alexander of Aphrodisias, the Agent Intellect is accepted without question by Averroes as a separate celestial substance, functioning as a kind of guarantor for the intelligible nature of all forms on earth, including, and especially, the rational or intelligent faculty in humans. That faculty appears to be innate to human beings, but is in fact on loan, as it were, from the Agent Intellect. . . . the material intellect, which represents the potentiality for rational thinking, and as such is the first expression of this faculty in an individual, is connected "incidentally" (*bi ʾl-ʿaraḍ*) to the human soul, belonging "essentially" to the universal Agent Intellect. The material intellect is thus a temporary instantiation of that eternal and always actual intellect, our "first perfection"; even as the Agent Intellect is our ultimate perfection or "final form."

Alfred Ivry, citing Ibn Rushd's Middle Commentary on the *De Anima* in "Averroes' Three Commentaries on *De Anima*," 204–5.

82. Ibn Muʿtazz (861–908), quoted by Ghazālī, in *Munqidh*, 61, and in turn in Ibn Ṭufayl, *Hayy Ibn Yaqẓān*, 96. The context, in both cases, is a hedging effort against the immanentism of drunken Sufism. The thoughts of Ibn Muʿtazz no doubt lay else-

where. The poet, an ʿAbbāsid pretender, was kept at a remove from power, writing poems of wine and love. He celebrated the restoration of ʿAbbāsid fortunes when his cousin Muʿtaḍid became caliph. But when proclaimed caliph himself, after the dethroning of Muqtadir, he was abandoned by his guards and strangled. He is remembered in history as "caliph for a day."

83. Ghazālī, *Mishkāt al-Anwār*, 118–19.

84. James W. Morris proposes that "all of Ibn ʿArabī's writing (and the *Futūḥāt* in particular) are best seen as a single vast commentary on spiritual dimensions of the Qur'ān and *ḥadīth*." See Morris's "Ibn ʿArabī's 'Esotericism': The Problem of Spiritual Authority," *Studia Islamica*, 71 (1990); and for case studies of Ibn ʿArabī's method, "The Spiritual Ascenscion: Ibn ʿArabī and the Miʿrāj," *JAOS* 107 (1987): 629–52; 108 (1988): 63–77.

85. Ghazālī, *Munqidh*, tr. Watt, 65–67, 80–81.

86. Ghazālī, *Munqidh*, ed. Jabre, 55.

Chapter 4

1. See Margoliouth, *Lectures on Arabic Historians*.

2. See Franz Rosenthal, *A History of Muslim Historiography*, 19–20, 66. Baruch Halpern in *The First Historians* shows in detail how the prose narrative of Judges 4 is dependent on the poetry of Deborah's Song, Judges 5. In a more general vein he also argues effectively against the dehistoricizing nisus of some versions of the notion that the Bible should be read as literature. He criticizes, as an artifact of the critical-stratigraphic method, the conception of a "redactor" whose only function seems to be to introduce inconsistencies, redundancies, and other apparent glitches into the scriptural text. The "redactor" in such a case, Halpern argues, becomes not just a bumbler but a mere convenience, a methodological wastebasket, into which unassimilated textual residues may be tossed.

3. This *'az*, as placed here, is a particle about which volumes of homilies have been written. See, for openers, Judah Goldin, *The Song at the Sea: Being a Commentary on a Commentary* (New Haven: Yale University Press, 1971).

4. Khalidi, *Arabic Historical Thought*, 8; cf. note 115 below.

5. Besides Rosenthal, see W. Caskel, "Aijam al-ʿArab," *Islamica* 3 (1931): 1–99; G. Widengren, "On the Early Prose Narratives in Arabic," *Acta Orientalia* 23 (1955): 232–62.

6. Cyrus Gordon, "The Background to Jewish Studies in the Bible and in the Ancient East," *Shofar* 12 (1991): 5.

7. Genesis 4:17 gives an alternative genealogy for Enoch and suggests that this culture hero was the first to build cities. The double genealogies for figures like Enoch and Lamech show how hard linearity is to establish and maintain.

8. See Rosenthal, *Historiography*, 22. The text of Genesis calls attention to the fact that Noah in Hebrew means rest and connotes contentment.

9. For the impact of Jonathan's message warning David to flee, see my comments, *In Defense of Truth*, 137–38.

10. Margoliouth, *Historians*, 55. For efforts to penetrate partisan back-projections and detect the superimposed structures of preexisting topoi in Islamic historiography, see J. Wansbrough, *The Sectarian Milieu*; E. L. Petersen, *ʿAlī and Muʿāwiya in Early Arabic Tradition*; Albrecht Noth, *Quellenkritische Studien zu Themen, Formen*

und Tendenzen frühislamiser Geschichtsüberlieferung (Bonn: Selbstverlag des Orientalischen Seminars der Universität Bonn, 1973).

11. See Franz Rosenthal, ed., *The History of al-Tabarī*, vol. 1, *From the Creation to the Flood* (Albany: State University of New York, 1989), 370–71. Masʿūdī marks a similar watershed when he distinguishes, in effect, between sacred history and the events recorded in the annals of the nations of the world; see Shboul, *Al-Masʿūdī*, 125.

12. See William Graham, *Beyond the Written Word*, e.g., p. 4: "in most major religious traditions, sacred texts were transmitted orally in the first place and written down only relatively recently." Yet a religious tradition will not become "major" as intended here, without the use of writing. Orality tends to the diffuse and variegated. It is writtenness that makes the Ten Commandments canonical and public, and publication that gives canonical status to L. Ron Hubbard's works on Dianetics. Only compare the disarray of, say, the Branch Davidians. Mormon missionaries do work with individuals face to face, but the faith they spread is founded and kept uniform not by orality but by its scripture. Even the rather diffuse militia movement in the United States gains its sense of common identity, common grievance, and common strategy from widely circulated manuals, exposes, internet appeals, and works of fiction. A fortiori the plans of al-Qāʾida, and the rationales meant to give them warrant.

13. See Dunlop, *Arab Civilization*, 70.

14. E. L. Petersen, *ʿAlī and Muʿawiya*, 17–18.

15. See *EI* 10.910–13; A. A. Duri, *The Rise of Historical Writing among the Arabs*, 25–26. Even in his *hadīths*, ʿUrwah is rather casual about *isnāds*. The demand for rigor here was not yet strenuous. On *isnāds* and unreliability, see Julius Wellhausen, *Prolegomena zur ältesten Geschichte des Islams*, in *Skizzen und Vorarbeiten* (Berlin: Reimer, 1884–99) 6.4.

16. Duri, *The Rise of Historical Writing among the Arabs*, 27–29.

17. Ibid., 30.

18. See Joseph Schacht, "On Mūsā b. ʿUqba's *Kitāb al-Maghāzī*," *Acta Orientalia* 21 (1953) 288–300. The surviving fragments of b. ʿUqba's work are translated in Guillaume's rendering of Ibn Isḥāq, *The Life of Muhammad*, xliii–xlvii; cf. Franz Rosenthal, *Historiography* 130–31.

19. See Dunlop, *Arab Civilization*, 71;

20. Carl H. Becker, *Papyri Schott-Reinhardt* (Heidelberg: Carl Winter, 1906), vol. 1.

21. A rule for the use of *hadīth* materials ordains: "Ḥadīthū ʿan banī Isrāʾīl, wala ḥaraja." What is couched here as a permission of Israelite materials is sometimes taken to allow only stories *about* Israelites, rather than traditions borne by them; see Kister, *Studies in Jahiliyya and Early Islam*, 215–39.

22. George Vajda, *EI* 4.212. Omar Dashti's *In Search of Omar Khayyam*, trans. L. P. Elwell-Sutton (London: Allen Unwin, 1971), finds that the canon of Omar Khayyam served similarly as a repository, in his case, of materials deemed suitably cynical.

23. Duri, *Historical Writing*, 30–32.

24. Gibb, "*Tarikh*," in *Studies on the Civilization of Islam*, 109.

25. Duri, *Historical Writing*, 36. Aḥmad ibn Ḥanbal rejected *ḥadīths* reported by Ibn Ishāq precisely on the grounds of their use of the collective *isnād*: "I see him relating a single *ḥadīth* on the authority of a group of people, without distinguishing the words of one from those of another" (*Tanbīh* 9.43). But Ibn Ḥanbal did accept Ibn Isḥāq's authority for the *maghāzī*. See *EI* 3.811b, s.n. Ibn Isḥāq.

26. Numerous stories circulate as to the reasons for the rejection of Ibn Isḥāq's book, ranging from his dallying with women in the back of the mosque to his seeking information from Fāṭimah bint al-Zubayr. But most of these have long been known to be canards. See *EI* 3.810–11; and for Khaybar, 4.1138–39.

27. Muir's comments, from the introduction to his 1912 *Life of Mohammad* are quoted in Dunlop, *Arab Civilization*, 73. See chapter 2, note 5 in this book.

28. Margoliouth, *Historians*, 52, 83; *EI* 1.760; al-Nadīm, *Fihrist* 1.197; Rosenthal, *Historiography*, 89.

29. Duri, *Historical Writing*, 46, 154–55. Gibb ("*Tarikh*," p. 112) notes that a caliphal history is ascribed to Ibn Isḥāq, but adds that "it seems to have been a short and summary work."

30. See D. M. Dunlop, *Arab Civilization*, 79; Margoliouth, *Historians*, 82.

31. Dunlop, *Arab Civilization*, 73.

32. Duri, *Historical Writing*, 37–38.

33. Margoliouth, *Historians*, 92–94.

34. Dunlop, *Arab Civilization*, 73–76.

35. See Ursula Sezgin, *EI* 5.946-48, and for Mawṣilī, J. W. Fück, *EI* 4.110–11.

36. See Nadim, *Fihrist*, 79, 202, 220.

37. See Duri, *Historical Writing*, 56–57, *EI* 1.158.

38. Duri, *Historical Writing*, 47; cf. *EI* 7.1015.

39. For Ibn al-Kalbī see *EI* 4.495–96; for the anecdote, Ibn ʿAbd Rabbihi (d. 940), *Al-ʿIqd al-Farīd*, ed. Ahmad Amin (Cairo: Lajnat al-Taʾlīf wa ʾl-Tarjama, 1940); cf. Khalidi, *Arabic Historical Thought*, 103.

40. Rosenthal, *Historiography*, 79, 508; Nadim, *Fihrist*, 250.

41. Shboul, *Al-Masʿūdī*, 231–32; Khalidi, *Islamic Historiography*, 23; Dunlop, *Arabic Civilization*, 117. Sijistānī's paragraph on the wise sayings of Thucydides, is found in his *Siwān al-Ḥikma*, § 133 in D. M. Dunlop's edition of the *Muntakhab* (The Hague: Mouton, 1979), 84.

42. Rosenthal, *Historiography*, 138.

43. Ibid., 138.

44. Cf. Gibb, *Arabic Literature*, 59.

45. Gibb's bias is evident when (p. 116) he traces the origins of Arabic universal history to Balādhurī, mentioning that he worked to a plan sketched out by Ibn Isḥāq. He speaks puristically of Ibn Isḥāq, acknowledging that he was a *mawlā* "of Mesopotamian origin" but insisting that "it would be absurd to look for any but the most indirect Persian influences in the conception" of his work, contrasting its "true Arabian" inspiration, with the fancies of Wahb (112), and neglecting to mention that Ibn Isḥāq's scheme is rooted in the Qurʾān's own biblical vision of history. Gibb disparages Persian, Syriac, Jewish, and Christian historical materials as filled with legends, that "found a way, under cover of Koranic exposition, into Arabic history" (117). He contrasts with these the spirit of *ḥadīth*: "For, during its apprenticeship to the science of *ḥadīth*, the native credulousness and romanticism of Arabic memories of the past had been schooled by a certain empiricism and respect for critical standards" (117). And he praises Ṭabarī for steering clear of such "intrusive elements"—excepting the Persian materials and the matter of *ḥadīth*, and somehow overlooking his acknowledgment of Ṭabarī's reliance on Wahb (109, 118).

46. See Rosenthal, *Historiography*, 137–38. "The Muslim chroniclers have much to say of the war on the frontiers; the Muslim geographers have ample information, probably drawn ultimately from secret service files, on the topography, administration, and strength of the enemy Empire, and even of the scandals of its court and

capital. But at no time did they attempt to consult Greek historical sources, or to deal in a connected form with the history of the Greek Empire." Bernard Lewis, "The Use by Muslim Historians of Non-Muslim Sources," in Lewis and Holt, *Historians*, 181.

47. Rosenthal, *Historiography*, 76.

48. Ibid., 77.

49. Peters, *Allah's Commonwealth*, 258, n. 33. For Romanus here we should probably understand Constantine VII Porphyrogenitus. Romanus I reigned 919–44, and Romanus II, 959–63. Constantine VII held the throne from 913 to 919 and again from 944 to 959.

50. Rosenthal, *Historiography*, 80–81.

51. Gibb, "*Tarikh*," in *Studies on the Civilization of Islam*, 114.

52. Rosenthal, *Historiography*, 81.

53. See Gibb, "*Tarikh*," in *Studies on the Civilization of Islam*, 115.

54. Ibid., 118.

55. The work seems to survive in rather garbled form, in the recension of the originator's nephew, who was blind; see *EI* 3.927.

56. See Rina Drori, "Cultural Authority in the Making: 'Expertise in Poetry,' paper presented at the Israel Institute for Advanced Studies, Jerusalem, summer, 1995

57. Petersen, *'Alī and Mu'āwyia*, 17.

58. See Muhsin Mahdi, *Ibn Khaldūn's Philosophy of History*, 134–35; Khalidi, *Islamic Historiography*, 48, 54.

59. Dunlop, *Arab Civilizations*, 84.

60. See the translation by P. K Hitti and F. C. Murgotten, *The Origins of the Islamic State* (New York: AMS, 1968).

61. See *EI* 1.971b–972.

62. See Margoliouth, *Historians*, 50, 119.

63. Lichtenstadter, "Muslim Historiography," in *Introduction*, 55.

64. Duri, *Historical Writing*, 63; Margoliouth, *Historians*, 116.

65. See Khalidi, *Arabic Historical Thought*, 60.

66. Ibid., 61.

67. For reflections on the historicity of the Esther story, see Carey A. Moore, *The Anchor Bible Esther* (Garden City, N.Y.: Doubleday, 1971).

68. Herodotus (I 12) cites Archilochus (fragment 14) for the mention of Gyges, much as the Biblical text cites ancient sayings and poetry as proof-texts. But to Archilochus, Gyges is a mere archetype of greed, lust for power, the misguided human desire to be divine, which Archilochus would make the foil of his own more modest appetites and less astral, if no less ardent passions. Plato, redirecting the older uses of the tale and perhaps egged on by dislike for current Lydian policy, turns the story of Gyges's usurpation into an object lesson typifying the difference (long obscured by the Sophists) between external success and genuine virtue. Plato is stimulated not only by the tragic irony of Socrates' virtue misrewarded by the Athenians but also by the benefactions Gyges left at Delphi (Herodotus, I 13), which underlie Plato's allusions (*Republic* II 364) to the specious notion that wicked men can buy their way to good repute and a blessed life in the hereafter. Plato universalizes his response to demand a revision of religion and mythology at least as radical as the reforms he proposed for politics and society. Plato's delegitimation of Gyges's Lydian heirs is paralleled in a story retailed by Safadī on the failure of two cunning Mamluk power brokers to win the sultanate. Safadī pictures the two (speaking in colloquial Arabic!) acknowledging that neither is a true Mamluk, since both had been peddlars who had sold one another into that powerful caste of warrior slaves. See Nasser Rabbat in Hugh

Kennedy, ed., *Historiography of Islamic Egypt*, 72. As Rabbat writes, Safadī spoke fluent Turkish but sought an air of familiarity by reporting the conversation in a rough and low-class Arabic, to convey an impression of familiarity and "to signify the uncouth and uncultivated" manners of the Mamluks, much as "Hollywood films have German, Asian, or Arab villains speak in broken English to show their villainy" (74). The high-flown literary expressions interspersed in the same fanciful dialogue, we might add, would have a comic effect, like the overcautious diction of the gangsters in *Guys and Dolls*.

69. Thus the *Mu'allaqa* of Imru' al-Qays, in section "Dunyā and Dīn" of chapter 1 of this book; and see Goldziher's "Muruwwa and Din" in *Muslim Studies*, 1.11–44.

70. For the biblical uses of irony, see Edwin Marshall Good, *Irony in the Old Testament* (London: SPCK, 1965).

71. Acts 17:22–26. See the discussion in Merkley, *The Greek and Hebrew Origins of our Idea of History*, 28.

72. See Ikhwān al-Ṣafā', *The Case of the Animals vs Man*, tr. Goodman, 53, 54, 118, 124–25, 145, 197.

73. See *God of Abraham*, chapter 1.

74. See Peters, *Allah's Commonwealth*, 348.

75. Rosenthal, *Historiography*, 80.

76. Lichtenstadter, "Muslim Historiography," in *Introduction*, 52

77. See Peters, *Allah's Commonwealth*, 258.

78. Khalidi, *Islamic Historiography*, 29.

79. See Margoliouth, *Historiography*, 125–26.

80. Jāḥiẓ too combined a belief in the possibility of progress with an appreciation of the contributions of past civilizations: "We have attained greater wisdom than they, and those who come after will gain greater wisdom than we." *K. al-Ḥayawān*, 1.86, cited in Khalidi, *Arabic Historical Thought*, 108.

81. See D. M. Dunlop, *Arab Civilization*, 87–88.

82. See Margoliouth, *Historians*, 112.

83. Khalidi, *Islamic Historiography*, 126

84. Bīrūnī, like Saadiah and Dīnawarī, is critically interested in synchronizing historical data from diverse sources. Thus his use of Seleucid dates, which jibes with his expertise in astronomy, geodesy, matters calendrical, and cross-cultural. Rosenthal remarks,

> The presentation of pre-Islamic history by Muslim historians. . . . met with the great technical handicap that the Muslims never invented a system of time-reckoning for the pre-Islamic period. . . . All references to other eras, such as that of the creation of the world or the Seleucid era, are merely incidental in Muslim literature and entered through the works consulted, which were either Christian works or works on chronology such as that of al-Bīrūnī. . . . Whenever a correlation of hijrah dates and pre-Islamic dates is attempted, as, for instance, in connection with the establishment of the lifetime of Galen, Christian influence is unmistakable (p. 90).

85. Duri, *Historical Writing*, 159.

86. Ibid., 69.

87. Margoliouth, *Historians*, 23–25, 61–62.

88. Khalidi, *Islamic Historiography*, 24; see also 82. Dīnawarī too keeps his Shī'ite sympathies out of his account of the 'Abbāsid revolution, perhaps hoping for a reconciliation of moderate Shī'ites with the 'Abbāsids. For he was employed by al-

Muwaffaq, the energetic brother and vice-regent of Muʿtamid. See Petersen, *ʿAlī and Muʿāwiya*, 168–73.

89. See the State University of New York Press translation of its volumes, by many hands.

90. See Dunlop, *Arab Civilization*, 92.

91. Rosenthal, *Historiography*, 135.

92. See Margoliouth, *Historians*, 128, 130.

93. Ibid., 110.

94. The printed text runs to thirty volumes in the 1903 Cairo edition. For the story of the scale of the original project, see Margoliouth, *Historians*, 103.

95. See P. K. Hitti, *History of the Arabs* (London: Macmillan, 1956), 390–91.

96. F. E. Peters, *Allah's Commonwealth*, 258.

97. Tabarī, *Ta'rīkh al-Rusul wa 'l-Mulūk*, ed. M. J. de Goeje (Leiden: Brill, 1879–1901) 1.6–7, translated here after Humphreys, *Islamic History*, 73–74, and Rosenthal, *Historiography*, 170

98. See Mahdi, *Ibn Khaldūn*, 135–36. *Qiyās*, reasoning, meant the syllogism in philosophy, and analogical argument in law. The fear was that it would prove supposititious and opinion-laden.

99. Bosworth reports that Tabarī's "debates and altercations" with Abū Bakr M. b. Dā'ūd "took place on a level of courtesy and mutual respect." But the Hanbalites were "belligerent and uncompromising." That school, as Bosworth explains, "was at this time struggling to carve a niche for itself alongside the existing three main *madhāhib* and its advocates were pugnacious and often unscrupulous, being ready to whip up the mindless Baghdad mob"—although Ṭabarī himself had always regarded the founder of the school with respect and had come to Baghdad to study with him. His break with the Ḥanbalīs centered on his treating the founder as "essentially a *ḥadīth* scholar and not a jurist." But it declined into a dispute over a Qur'ānic verse that the Ḥanbalites held to reveal that the Prophet was seated literally on God's throne. Ṭabarī discussed that view at length in his Qur'ān commentary and in the end seems to have rejected the authority of the tradition on which the literal interpretation rested. See *EI* 10 12. The militant Ḥanbalite preacher Barbahārī, who hounded the presumed heretics of Baghdad for twenty years, so persecuted Tabarī that he had to be buried secretly in the courtyard of his home; see Kraemer, *Humanism*, 61; Cook, *Commanding Right*, 116.

100. See Shboul, *Al-Masʿūdī*, 34.

101. Qifṭī, quoted in Rosenthal, *Historiography*, 81. Ibn Khallikān agrees with Qiftī's estimate as to quality, calling Ṭabarī's History the soundest and most reliable work of its kind. See Dunlop, *Arab Civilization*, 89.

102. Rosenthal, *Historiography*, 134–35.

103. F. E. Peters, *Allah's Commonwealth*, 258.

104. Ṭabarī is perhaps aided in his quest for intellectual independence and objectivity as he understands it by his inherited wealth. His father, who had encouraged his scholarly proclivities from an early age was a wealthy land owner, and the son lived on the rents brought to him annually from his estates in Ṭabaristan. See Margoliouth, *Historians*, 16.

105. Ibn Bājjah, *Opera Metaphysica*, 155–73. The parallel argument in Aristotle mentions Homer, as we have noted. See chapter 3 of this book, note 76 and Goodman, *Crosspollinations*, 109–14.

106. See Khalidi, *Islamic Historiography*, 3

107. See Petersen, *ʿAlī and Muʿāwiya*, 16.

108. Khalidi, *Arabic Historical Thought*, 73.

109. Ibid., 74.

110. *EI* 3.724; cf. Dunlop, *Arabic Civilization*, 129–30.

111. Lichtenstadter, "Muslim Historiography," in *Introduction*, 55.

112. Margoliouth, *Historians*, 16.

113. See Fakhry, *Ethical Theories in Islam*, 16.

114. For Avicenna's reports of his father's Shīʿite interests and their intellectual impact, see Goodman, *Avicenna*, 12. Bosworth vouches for Ṭabarī's orthodoxy in *EI* 10.12. Kraemer relates the suspicions lodged against the philosophers for Ismāʿīlī sympathies: *Humanism*, 87. Āmirī was a student of Balkhī's, who was a geographer as well as a philosopher and himself a student of Kindī's.

115. As John Wansbrough writes in the opening passage of *Quranic Studies*, 1:

> Once separated from an extensive corpus of prophetical *logia*, the Islamic revelation became scripture. . . . By the very achievement of canonicity the document of revelation was assured a kind of independence, both of historical traditions commonly adduced to explain its existence and of external criteria recruited to facilitate its understanding. . . . Both formally and conceptually, Muslim scripture drew upon a traditional stock of monotheistic imagery, which may be described as schemata of revelation. . . . originally narrative material was reduced almost invariably to a series of discrete and parabolic utterances.

116. See Henry Malter, *Saadia Gaon: His Life and Works* (1921. Reprint. New York: Hermon Press, 1969), 171–73. For the earliest Greek efforts at synchronic history, see J. B. Bury, *The Ancient Greek Historians* (1908. Reprint. New York: Dover, 1958), chapter 1; and see Herodotus, II 145.

117. See the discussion in Rosenthal, *Historiography*, 139.

118. See Judah Halevi's *Kuzari*, and my discussion in Leaman and Frank, *History of Jewish Philosophy*, 188–227; Ibn Dāʾūd, *The Book of Tradition*.

119. See Saadiah, *The Book of Theodicy*, 224, n. 1; 409, n. 7.

120. *ED* III 6, Saadiah, trans. Kafih, 130; trans. Rosenblatt, 155.

121. Makkot 10b, Shabbat 104a, Yoma 39a, Berakhot 7a, Sanhedrin 27b; Saadiah on Leviticus 26:39, at Job 21:19; cf. Proverbs 11:3, 11; Goodman, *On Justice*, 137–38. For "preambles," see Plato, *Laws* 4.719–23. As Jowett summarizes the point: "The legislator will teach as well as command; and with this view he will prefix preambles to his principal laws." *Collected Dialogues of Plato*, 4th ed., vol. 4, p. 53. For sanctions, see Plato, *Laws* 6.782–83, 7.793–94, 9.853–54.

122. It is in this vein that Eugene Garver reads Aristotle's *hoste paradeigmatos* at *Rhetoric* I 5, 1360b 7–8: not, "for the sake of giving an example," but "taken as an example," or words to that effect. The point, as Garver reads the passage, is not that we are to consider happiness, or various notions thereof, *for example*, but that happiness is made an example in rhetoric, so that people, an audience, a public, can visualize the impact of the choices they must make. Thus the relevance of Aristotle's remarks at the close of chapter 4:

> It is useful, in framing laws, not only to study the past history of one's own country, in order to understand which constitution is desirable for it now, but also to have a knowledge of the constitutions of other nations, and so to learn for what kinds of nation the various kinds of constitution are suited. From this we can see that books of travel are useful aids to legislation, since from these we may learn the laws and customs of different races. The deliberative speaker

will also find the researches of historians useful. But all this is the business of political science and not of rhetoric.

Cf. *Rhetoric* I 8–9, and see the discussion in Eugene Garver, *Aristotle's* Rhetoric: *An Art of Character* (Chicago: University of Chicago Press, 1994) 86–87.

123. For the birth of the Eisagoge literature as a genre, see F. E. Peters, *Aristotle and the Arabs* (New York: New York University Press, 1968), 79–87.

124. For Bīrūnī, see *EI* 1.1236–38.

125. Masʿūdī knows the work of Kindī and of his disciple Sarakhsī. He shows particular interest in their geographical ideas but cites their work on logic too. He also seems at points to echo Fārābī. As for Rāzī, whom he met and is said to have debated on the topic of cosmogony, Masʿūdī describes him as a Pythagorean, perhaps in reference to Rāzī's atomism. He calls Fārābī's disciple Yaḥyā ibn ʿAdī the only person he knew after Fārābī's death who could really be relied upon in matters philosophical. See Shboul, *Al-Masʿūdī*, 42–43, 64.

126. *EI* 6.784b. Khalidi remarks, *Islamic Historiography*, 94: "The heritage of Greece in science and philosophy is more in evidence in the works of Masʿūdī than that of any other ancient nation. Masʿūdī had extensive knowledge of Greek works in the various branches of science and quotes these works frequently in his extant writings." Masʿūdī himself lists eighty-five authors in the unusual bibliographic introduction to his *Murūj al-Dhahab* and notes that he does not mention the works consulted whose authors were anonymous. He does not bother to cite "the histories of *aṣḥāb al-ḥadīth*, and the books on the biographies of transmitters of *ḥadīths* (*asmāʾ al-rijāl*) which were too numerous to be listed," and he gives short shrift to the traditionists in his biographical/obituary notices as well, having little use for their methods and standards and less for their ideology. See Shboul, *Al-Masʿūdī*, 33, 37, 41.

127. For details on Masʿūdī's topics, see Shboul, *Al-Masʿūdī*, 56–76.

128. Ibid., 69, 78, 82.

129. For Masʿūdī's interest in habitats, see ibid., 65.

130. Khalidi, *Islamic Historiography*, 5–9.

131. See ibid., 100–101.

132. See ibid., 32.

133. For Masʿūdī's travels, see Shboul, *Al-Masʿūdī*, 6–9; for his secondhand knowledge of Byzantium, 15. For Paris, Dunlop, *Arab Civilization*, 104

134. See ibid., *Al-Masʿūdī*, 74–75.

135. See ibid., 41, 56.

136. See ibid., 107. Masʿūdī specifies, for example, that he gathered information from Zoroastrian "mobedhs, herbedhs, and other knowledgeable men." He shows familiarity with the Zendavesta and other Avestan texts, some of which appear to have been accessible to him in Arabic translation.

137. Ibid., 108.

138. Ibid., 98–99. Masʿūdī seems to know two or possibly three Arabic translations of the Hebrew Bible (ibid., 287). His testimony helps confirm the view that Saadiah composed his Arabic writings in Arabic rather than Hebrew characters.

139. For the title and focus of the *Tanbīh*, see ibid., 75–77. For its correction of errors, confusions and overly popular data in the earlier works, see ibid., e.g., 114–18.

140. Dunlop, *Arabic Civilization*, 107–8.

141. Shboul, *Al-Masʿūdī*, xxv.

142. Ibid., 72.

143. Dunlop, *Arab Civilization*, 101

144. His writings in jurisprudence, for example, included titles like *Naẓm al-Adilla fī Uṣūl al-Milla* (The Organization, or System, of Arguments on the Principles of the Religion) and *Naẓm al-A'lām fī Uṣūl al-Aḥkām* (The Organization of Guideposts on the Foundations of Judicial Rulings). See Shboul, *Al-Mas'ūdī*,57.

145. Ibid., 66.

146. See ibid., 70.

147. Translated after ibid., 80.

148. See Khalidi, *Islamic Historiography*, 34–35; and for Saadiah's standards, L. E. Goodman, "Saadiah Gaon's Interpretive Technique in Translating the Book of Job," in D. M. Goldenberg, ed., *Translation of Scripture* (Philadelphia: Annenberg Research Institute, 1990), *JQR* supplement, 47–76.

149. *Mas'ūdī* seems to know of the use of the compass, which Arab travelers gleaned from Chinese sailors as early as the eighth century. See *EI* 5.1168b-69a, s.v. *Maghnāṭīs*.

150. Khalidi, *Historiography*, 36–45. Ibn Khaldūn takes Mas'ūdī to task for accepting 600,000 as the number of Moses's fighting force, apparently not knowing that this is the biblical figure. He faults him again for offering no more than traditional genetic accounts (from Galen and Kindī) to explain the supposed levity of blacks—where Ibn Khaldūn himself will offer an environmental explanation. All in all, he finds Mas'ūdī too dependent on his sources. But the brunt of the criticism arises in a demand for greater consistency: Mas'ūdī should have hewn more strictly to the standards that he himself had set out.

151. The idea that revelation answers to a vital human need, of course, echoes a core Mu'tazilite thesis.

152. See Shboul, *Al-Mas'ūdī*, 101. See chapter 2, note 6 in this book.

153. See Shboul, *Al-Mas'ūdī*, 103, 113–19.

154. See Khalidi, *Islamic Historiography*, 85–87.

155. See R. Popkin, *Isaac La Peyrère (1596–1676): His Life, Work, and Influence* (Leiden: Brill, 1987), and my review, *JHP* 29 (1991): 131–35.

156. Mas'ūdī finds in Ardashir the very model of Plato's philosopher king, making him, indeed, Plato's disciple; see Khalidi, *Islamic Historiography*, 22, 92; for the idealization of Sassanian Persia by Muslim writers, see E. I. J. Rosenthal, *Political Thought in Medieval Islam*, 75. The principles of centralized power and bureaucratized decision making that Mas'ūdī idealizes are exactly what Aristotle rejects when he makes the Persian mode of government the antitype of his own ideal of free and independent *poleis* in which the citizens actively participate in the deliberative life of the body politic. In the *Politics*, a book that was not translated into Arabic, Aristotle gives religion an almost recreational role (See *Politics* VII 9, 1329a 26–34; 12, 1331b 4–6) and assigns to music, drama and the arts the ethos-building and sustaining functions that Plato had seemed (to Muslim authors from Fārābī to Ibn Ṭufayl) to entrust to religion.

157. The Ikhwān al-Ṣafā' gently parallel Mas'ūdī's ethnic typing when they describe their ideal man, in the passage quoted in the introduction of this book, p. 24. Cf. Condorcet's notion that every *era* has its own intellectual virtue and has its own cultural contribution to make. Hegel combines the typing of ages with that of nations, urging that every civilization has its proper theme *and era*.

158. Mas'ūdī is probably influenced by the cultic preoccupations of the so-called *Nabataean Agriculture* of Ibn Waḥshiyya, which appeared in 904, if not by the stereotyping of Nabataeans as Syriac-speaking peasants.

159. See Shboul, *Al-Masʿūdī*, 120–22. For the tendency of writers to identify their own clime as the best, see Ikhwān al-Safāʿ, *The Case of the Animals vs Man*, 120–21, 130. For the tendency to disparage "Nabataeans," recall Hamadhānī's punchline, cited in chapter 1 of this book, p. 71.

160. See Khalidi, *Islamic Historiography*, 89.

161. See ibid., 84–108, 116–19.

162. Shboul, *Al-Masʿūdī*, 114.

163. See Khalidi, *Islamic Historiography*, 60, 63; cf. 122.

164. See ibid., 70–71, 76–77, 107, 110–13, 128–31.

165. Sinān licensed some 860 physicians. His father was the famous Ḥarrānian mathematician, philosopher and scientist Thābit b. Qurra (826–901), who came to Baghdad as a student of the Banū Mūsā, best known, perhaps, for their *Book of Devices*, with its designs for some one hundred ingenious machines. Thābit translated many works, including Apollonius' *Conics*, now lost in the Greek original, and Nichomachus of Gerasa's *Introduction to Arithmetic*. His pioneering mathematical astronomy placed theory ahead of observation, much as Sinān would do in history. See *EI* 10.428; 1.899, 7.640. Ḥunayn b. Isḥāq was another protege of the Banū Mūsā.

166. *EI* 5.330.

167. See Rosenthal, *Historiography*, 114–15.

168. *EI* 7.762.

169. Hamza al-Isfahānī wrote: "What Imru' al-Qays was for the ancients, Abū Nuwās is for the moderns." (MS *Fātiḥ* 3773 fol. 7r, cited in *EI* 1.143b). See Hamori, *On the Art of Medieval Arabic Literature*; Khalidi, *Islamic Historiography*, 20–21.

170. Dunlop, *Arabic Civilization*, 114.

171. Ibid., 115–16.

172. Rosenthal, *Historiography*, 78–79; Peters *Allah's Commonwealth*, 259.

173. R. Stephen Humphreys, *Islamic History*.

174. See ibid., 102–3.

175. Ibn Taghrī Birdī writes that Maqrīzī was so much the historian that his name became a byword. He does criticize his illustrious predecessor for occasional lapses of objectivity, as in blaming the sultan Barqūq for the introduction of three Mamluk disgraces: homosexuality, bribery, and sluggish markets—as though these were unknown earlier. See Amalia Levanoni, in Kennedy, ed., *The Historiography of Islamic Egypt*, 94, 102–3; cf. pp.104–5 for Maqrīzī's sense of mission in exposing the abuses of his day. Maqrīzī's disciple and shameless imitator Abū Ḥāmid al-Qudsī was often more down to earth, partly because of his keen spatial sense, architectural interests, and vivid pictorial representations of everyday realia, but partly because he was alienated from the elite *ʿulama'*, who scorned him for his lack of subtlety and his tendency to borrow too freely from his sources; see Ulrich Haarmann in *The Historiography of Islamic Egypt*, 163–65.

176. See Maqrīzī, *Book of Contention and Strife*, and Bosworth's admirable introduction. For Maqrīzī's historical writings, *EI* 6.193–94 and Dunlop, *Arabic Civilization*, 132–37.

177. Dunlop, *Arabic Civilization*, 135–36.

178. Maqrīzī's analysis of these woes comes in his *K. Ighāthat al-Umma bi-Kashf al-Ghumma*, a Book in Succor of the Nation, Exposing its Distress, a work assembled in a single night, although, no doubt, from materials the author had at hand. See Dunlop, *Arabic Civilization*, 136.

179. Maqrīẓī, *Book of Contention*, 30.

180. Khalidi, *Arabic Historical Thought*, 171; and see D. M. Dunlop, *Arabic Civilization*, 123; Dominique Sourdel, *Le Vizirat ʿAbbaside le 749 à 936* (Damascus: Institut Français, 1959–60), 1.25; M. S. Khan "Miskawayh and Arabic Historiography," *JAOS* 89 (1969): 710–30.

181. See Rosenthal, *Historiography*, 141–42.

182. See ibid., 30 ff.; cf. Maimonides, *Guide* I 2; and Aristotle, *Poetics* 9, 1451b 5; cf. 23, 1459a 22. Yet Aristotle does build the argument of his *Politics* from the matter of history, collated in such works of his as the *Constitution of Athens*.

183. C. E. Bosworth, in his introduction to *The* Laṭāʾif al-Maʿārif *of Thaʿālibī*, 12–13.

184. F. E. Peters, *Allah's Commonwealth*, 534.

185. See, for example, the excursion into environmental racism that Miskawayh relies on, for want of a better anthropology, in *K. Tahdhīb al-Akhlāq*, tr. Zurayk, 42.

186. Kraemer, *Humanism*, 49 n. 54.

187. Miskawayh, *K. Tajārub al-Umam*, 4.30–36. Miskawayh's treatment of the regime of Ibn al-Furāt is similarly pointed, but it points in the opposite direction.

188. See Khalidi, *Arabic Historical Thought*, 174–75.

189. Ibid., 171.

190. Margoliouth, *Historians*, 155.

191. Ibid., 151; *EI* 3.714.

192. *EI* 3.778a.

193. See *EI* 3.156a.

194. See Rosenthal, *Historiography*, 147.

195. See Ibn al-Athīr, *al-Kāmil fī ʾl-Taʾrīkh*, ed. C. J. Tornberg (Beirut: Dar Sadir, 1965–67).

196. Dunlop, *Arabic Civilization*, 120.

197. Boyle calls Rashīd al-Dīn "the first world historian." The actual authorship of the work is disputed, since another scholar claimed it was plagiarized from him, and Rashīd al-Din clearly had assistance in compiling it; some portions were lifted bodily from the work of Juwaynī. See also D. O. Morgan, *EI* 8.443–44.

198. See Lewis and Holt, *Historians of the Middle East*, 183–84; Rosenthal, *Historiography*, 147–48.

199. See Arnold, *Painting in Islam*, 74–75, 93–94.

200. Dunlop, *Arabic Civilization*, 138; Fischel, *Ibn Khaldūn in Egypt*, 79.

201. Margoliouth, *Historians*, 1, 57. For the persistence of patterns described by Ibn Khaldūn, mutatis mutandis, into the modern era., see Ernest Gellner, "From Ibn Khaldūn to Karl Marx," *Political Quarterly* 32 (1961): 386; Goodman, *Cross-pollinations*, 236, n.108.

202. Rosenthal marks (*Historiography*, 89) a cyclical view of history in Arabic writing as early as Kindī; see Kindī's *Risālah fī mulk al-ʿArab*, ed. O. Loth in *Morgenländische Forschungen—Festschrift H. L. Fleischer* (Leipzig, 1875 reprinted, Amsterdam: Philo, 1981); for other writers' views on time and cyclicity, see Khalidi, *Arabic Historical Thought*, 118–22; Goodman, "Time in Islam."

203. M. Talbi, *EI* 3.829.

204. As R. A. Nicholson writes, "No Muslim had ever taken a view at once so comprehensive and so philosophical; none had attempted to trace the deeply hidden causes of events, to expose the moral and spiritual forces at work beneath the surface, or to divine the immutable laws of national progress and decay." *A Literary History of the Arabs* (Cambridge: Cambridge University Press, 1957) 438–39. All

the same, when it comes to the events of his own experience, the reign of Barqūq, he does not cite written sources but relies on firsthand knowledge, as Miskawayh had done.

205. R. Brunschvig, *La Berbérie orientale sous les Ḥafsides des Origines à la fin du XV Siècle*. (Paris: Maisonneuve, 1940–47), 2.385–93.

206. *Qur'ān* 12:111 calls the stories (*qaṣṣās*) of prior times a lesson (*'ibra*) for those with hearts to understand, "no mere invented tale but confirmation of what stands before it, explicating all things, guidance and mercy to folk who believe." For the general idea of *'ibra* as a historical lesson, see Muhsin Mahdi, *Ibn Khaldun*, 68. For the parallels with biblical ideas of history, see Walter J. Fischel, "Ibn Khaldūn. On the Bible, Judaism and Jews," *Ignace Goldziher Memorial Volume* 2.161; cf. L. A. Cook, *Cambridge Ancient History* (Cambridge: Cambridge University Press, 1924), 1.223; R. Flint, *History of the Philosophy of History* (Edinburgh: Blackwoods, 1893), 1.151–71.

207. Khalidi, *Arabic Historical Thought*, 222.

208. See Shboul, *Al-Mas'ūdī*, 56.

209. Fischel, *Ibn Khaldūn in Egypt*, 71, 84–85, 93.

210. See Fischel, "Ibn Khaldūn on the Bible . . .", 2.147–71; *Ibn Khaldūn in Egypt*, 109–55.

211. See p. 173, this volume; and see Fischel, *Ibn Khaldūn in Egypt*, 117–18; Dunlop, *Arabic Civilization*, 138. As Ibn Khaldūn reports, Orosius was translated by the Christian "Qādī" of Cordova Qāsim b. Aṣbagh in the reign of the Umayyad Caliph al-Ḥakam II al-Mustansir (d. 976).

212. For an extended elaboration of this theme, see Goodman, *Crosspollinations*, 201–39.

213. Khalidi, *Islamic Historiography*, 115; cf. 127, 133.

214. Translating after ibid., 129.

215. See Fischel, *Ibn Khaldūn in Egypt*, 88, 103.

216. See ibid., 98.

217. Readers of Umberto Eco should take note: Our medievals thought that the world could be read as a book; but I do not know of any who thought that it *was* a text.

218. See Fischel, *Ibn Khaldūn in Egypt*, 98–100; and see Franz Rosenthal's Introduction to the *Muqaddimah*, lxiii.

219. See Khalidi, *Islamic Historiography*, 70–73. Ibn Khaldūn himself, however, is overwhelmed by the numbers of Tamerlane's troops, which he saw at the siege of Damascus. Some estimate the number of his forces at 240,000 (including some 30,000 fighters), although others put the number as high as 800,000. Ibn Khaldūn declines an estimate but urges that one million would not be excessive.

220. Khalidi, *Islamic Historiography*, 77.

221. Meisami, *Persian Historiography*, 11.

222. Ibid., 11.

223. Ibid., 12.

224. See Fischel, *Ibn Khaldūn in Egypt*, 160.

225. Ibn Khaldūn, *Muqaddimah*, 1.173, 2.99, 134, 377; cf. Goodman, *Crosspollinations*, chapter 7. For Ibn Khaldūn's delight in the efflorescence of civilization, witness his enthusiasm on arriving in Cairo in 1383; see Rosenthal, Introduction to the *Muqaddimah*, lviii.

Bibliography

ʿAbd al-Jabbār, Abū ʾl-Ḥasan. *Kitāb al Majmūʿ fī ʾl-Muḥīṭ bi ʾl-Taklīf,* ed. J. J. Houben (Beirut; Catholic Press, 1965).

Abdel-Kader. A. H. *The Life Personality and Writings of al-Junayd* (London: Luzac, 1962).

Abed, Shukri. *Aristotelian Logic and the Arabic Language in Alfārābī* (Albany: State University of New York Press, 1991).

Abul Quasem, Muhammad. *The Ethics of al-Ghazālī: A Composite Ethics in Islam* (Petaling Jaya, Selangor, Malaysia: privately published, 1975).

———. "Al-*Ghazālī*'s Rejection of Philosophic Ethics." *Islamic Studies* 13 (1974): 111–27.

Alexander of Aphrodisias, *De Anima* (ca. 200). Translated by A. P. Fotinis (Washington, D.C.: University Press of America 1980).

ʿĀmirī, Abū ʾl-Hasan. *K. al-Amad ʿalā ʾl-Abad* (985/6). Edited and translated by Everett K. Rowson, in *A Muslim Philosopher on the Soul and its Fate* (New Haven, Conn.: American Oriental Society, 1988).

Andrae, Tor. *Mohammed, the Man and his Faith.* Translated by T. Menzel (1936. Reprint. New York: Harper, 1960).

Ansari, M. Abdul Haq. *The Ethical Philosophy of Miskawayh* (Aligarh, India: Aligarh Muslim University Press, 1964).

Arkoun, Mohammed. *L'Humanisme Arabe au IVᵉ/Xᵉ Siècle: Miskawayh—Philosophe et Historien.* 2d ed. (Paris. Vrin, 1982).

Arnold, Thomas W. *Painting in Islam* (1928. Reprint. New York: Dover, 1965).

Aristotle, *The Complete Works*, revised Oxford translation, ed. Jonathan Barnes, 2 vols (Princeton: Princeton University Press, 1985).

Ashʿarī, Abū l-Ḥasan. *Kitab al-Lumaʿ fī ʾl-Radd ʿalā Ahl al-Zaygh wa ʾl-Bidaʿ* (Highlights in the Refutation of Heretics and Innovators, early tenth century). Translated by R. J. McCarthy, in *The Theology of al-Ashʿarī* (Beirut: Catholic Press, 1953).

Asín Palacios, Miguel. *Islam and the Divine Comedy*. Translated by H. Sutherland (1919. Reprint. London: Cass, 1968).

Āzād, Abū 'l-Kalām. *Ghubar-i-Kabīr*. edited by Malik Ram (New Delhi: Sahitya Akademi, 1967).

Bakar, Osman. *The History and Philosophy of Islamic Science* (Cambridge, England: Islamic Texts Society, 1999).

Bell, J. N. *Love Theory in Later Hanbalite Islam* (Albany: State University of New York Press, 1979).

Black, Deborah L. *Logic and Aristotle's* Rhetoric *and* Poetics *in Medieval Arabic Philosophy* (Leiden: Brill, 1990).

Bosworth, Clifford E. *The Medieval Islamic Underworld: The Banū Sāsān in Arabic Society and Literature*. 2 vols. (Leiden: Brill, 1976).

———. *The Ghaznavids: Their Empire in Afghanistan and Eastern Iran* (Beirut: Librairie du Liban, 1973).

Butterworth, Charles. "Al-Fārābī's Statecraft: War and the Well-Ordered Regime." In *Cross, Crescent, and Sword: The Justification and Limitation of War in Western and Islamic Tradition*, edited by James Turner Johnson and John Kelsay, (New York: Greenwood Press, 1990).

———. "Rhetoric and Islamic Political Philosophy." IJMES 3 (1972): 187–98.

Cook, Michael. *Commanding Right and Forbidding Wrong in Islamic Thought* (Cambridge: Cambridge University Press, 2000).

Davidson, Herbert. *Alfarabi, Avicenna, and Averroes on Intellect: Their Cosmologies, Theories of the Active Intellect, and Theories of Human Intellect* (New York: Oxford University Press, 1992).

———. *Proofs for Eternity, Creation, and the Existence of God in Medieval Islamic and Jewish Philosophy* (New York: Oxford University Press, 1987).

Dunlop, D. M. *Arab Civilization to A.D. 1500* (London: Longman, 1971).

Duri, A. A. *The Rise of Historical Writing among the Arabs*. Translated by Lawrence Conrad (Princeton: Princeton University Press, 1983).

Esposito, John, ed. *Voices of Resurgent Islam* (New York: Oxford University Press, 1983).

Fakhry, Majid. *Ethical Theories in Islam*. 2d ed. (Leiden: Brill, 1994).

———. *Philosophy, Dogma, and the Impact of Greek Thought in Islam* (Aldershot, Hampshire: Variorum, 1994).

———. *A History of Islamic Philosophy*. 2d ed. (New York: Columbia University Press, 1983).

———. *Islamic Occasionalism and its Critique by Averroes and Aquinas* (London: Allen and Unwin, 1958).

Fārābī, Abū Nasr. *K. Mabādi Arā' Ahlu 'l-Madīnatu 'l-Fāḍila* (The Book of the Principles Underlying the Beliefs of the People of the Virtuous State). Edited and translated by Richard Walzer, *Al-Fārābī on the Perfect State* (Oxford: Oxford University Press, 1985).

———. *Commentary on* De Interpretatione. Edited by Wilhelm Kutsch and Stanley Marrow (Beirut: Catholic Press, 1960); trans. Fritz W. Zimmermann, in *Al-Fārābī's* Commentary *and* Short Treatise *on Aristotle's* De Interpretatione (London: Oxford University Press, 1981).

———. *Kitāb al-Ḥurūf*, ed. Muhsin Mahdi (Beirut: Dar el-Machreq, 1970).

———. "Against John the Grammarian." Translated by Muhsin Mahdi. *Near Eastern Studies* 26 (1967): 253–60; ed. Mahdi Sami A. Hanna, *Middle East Studies in Honor of Aziz S. Atiya* (Leiden: Brill, 1968).

———. *Fī taḥṣīl al-ṣaʿādah*. Translated by Muhsin Mahdi, "On the Attainment of Happiness," in *Alfarabi's Philosophy of Plato and Aristotle* (Ithaca, N.Y.: Cornell University Press, 1962).

———. *Fuṣūl al-Madanī*, Edited and translated by D. M. Dunlop, *Aphorisms of the Statesman* (Cambridge: Cambridge University Press, 1961).

Fischel, Walter J. *Ibn Khaldūn in Egypt* (Los Angeles: University of California Press, 1967).

———. "Ibn Khaldūn: On the Bible, Judaism, and the Jews." In *Ignace Goldziher Memorial Volume*, edited by Samuel Löwinger, Alexander Schreiber, and Joseph Somogyi (Jerusalem: Rubin Mass, 1958).

Frank, Richard M. *The Metaphysics of Created Being According to Abū l-Hudhayl al-Allāf* (Istanbul: Nederlands Historisch-Archaeologisch Instituut in het Nabije Oosten, 1966).

Frye, Northrup. *The Secular Scripture: A Study of the Structure of the Romance* (Cambridge: Harvard University Press, 1976).

Galen, *Compendium Timaei Platonis*, Arabic text and Latin translation by Paul Kraus and Richard Walzer in *Plato Arabus I* (London: Warburg Institute, 1951).

Galston, Miriam. *Politics and Excellence: The Political Philosophy of Alfarabi* (Princeton: Princeton University Press, 1990)

Ghazālī, Abū Ḥāmid. *Tahāfut al-Falāsifa*. 2d ed. Edited by M. Bouyges. (Beirut: Catholic Press, 1962); edited and translated by Michael E. Marmura, *The Incoherence of the Philosophers* (Provo, Utah: Brigham Young University Press, 1997).

———. *Maqāṣid al-Falāsifa* (The Aims of the Philosophers), ed. S. Dunya (Cairo: Dar al-Maʿārif, n.d., ca. 1965).

———. *Faḍā'iḥ al-Bāṭiniyya*, ed. A.-R. Badawi (Cairo: al-Dār al-Qawmiyya, 1964).

———. *Al-Munqidh min al-Ḍalāl*. Edited by Farid Jabre (Beirut. UNESCO, 1959); Translated by William Montgomery Watt, in *The Faith and Practice of al-Ghazālī* (London: Allen and Unwin, 1963).

———. *Mishkāt al-Anwār*. Translated by W. H. T. Gairdner as *The Niche for Lights* (1924. Reprint. Lahore: Ashraf, 1952).

———. *Iḥyā' 'Ulūm al-Dīn* (Cairo, Lajnat Nashr al-Thaqāfa al-Islāmiyya, 1937/8); A. L. Tibawi edited and translated the *Jerusalem Letter* from Book 2 as "Al-Ghazālī's Tract on Dogmatic Theology," *Islamic Quarterly* 9 (1965): 65–122; David Burrell translated Book 35 as *Faith in Divine Unity and Trust in Divine Providence* (Louisville: Fons Vitae, 2001)

———. *Mīzān al-ʿAmal* (Cairo: Dāru 'l-kutab, 1964).

———. *Al-Maqṣad al-Asnā fī Sharh Asmā' Allāh al-Ḥusnā* (Cairo: Azhar Press, n.d.).

Gibb, H. A. R. *Arabic Literature* (1926. Reprint. Oxford: Oxford University Press, 1963).

———. *Studies on the Civilization of Islam*, ed. Stanford Shaw and William Polk (Boston: Beacon Press, 1962).

Gibb, H. A. R., J. H. Kramers, E. Lévi-Provençal, J. Schacht, S. M Stern, B. Lewis, Ch. Pellat, C. Dumont, and R. M. Savory et al., editorial committee, *The Encyclopedia of Islam, New Edition*, 10 vols. to date (Leiden: Brill, 1960–).

Giffen, Lois. *The Theory of Profane Love among the Arabs* (New York: New York University Press Press, 1971).

Gilson, Étienne. *Forms and Substances in the Arts* (New York: Scribners, 1966).

———. *The Spirit of Medieval Philosophy*. Translated by A. H. C. Downes (New York: Scribners, 1940).

Goitein, S. D. *A Mediterranean Society*. (5 vols. Berkeley: University of California Press, 1967–88).

Goldziher, Ignaz. *The Ẓāhirīs*. Translated by Wolfgang Behn (1884 Leiden: Brill, 1971).

———. *Muslim Studies*. Translated by C. R. Barber and S. M. Stern (1888–90. Albany: State University of New York Press, 1977.) 2 vols.

Goodman, L. E. *In Defense of Truth* (Amherst, New York: Humanity Press, 2001).

———. *Jewish and Islamic Philosophy: Crosspollinations in the Classic Age* (New Brunswick, N.J.: Rutgers University Press, 1999).

———. *God of Abraham* (New York: Oxford University Press, 1996).

———. *Avicenna* (New York and London: Routledge, 1992).

———. "Jewish and Islamic Philosophies of Language," in K. Lorenz et al., eds., *Sprachphilosophie*, DeGruyter, 1993, 1.34–55.

———. "Time in Islam." *Asian Philosophy* 2 (1992): 3–19.

———. "The Translation of Greek Materials into Arabic," *Cambridge History of Arabic Literature*. Vol. 2 *Religion, Learning and Science in the ʿAbbasid Period.* Edited by M. J. L. Young, J. D. Latham, and R. B. Serjeant (Cambridge: Cambridge University Press, 1990), 477–97.

———. "The Greek Impact on Arabic Literature," *Cambridge History of Arabic Literature*. Vol. 1. *Arabic Literature to the End of the Umayyad Period.* Edited by A. F. L. Beeston, T. M. Johnstone, R. B. Serjeant, and G. R. Smith (Cambridge: Cambridge University Press, 1984), 460–81.

———. "Did al-*Ghazālī* Deny Causality?" *Studia Islamica* 47 (1978): 83–120.

———. *Rambam: Readings in the Philosophy of Moses Maimonides*, selected and translated with commentary (New York: Viking, 1976).

———. "Rāzī's Myth of the Fall of the Soul and its Function in his Philosophy." Edited by G. F. Hourani, in *Essays on Islamic Philosophy and Science* (Albany: State University of New York Press, 1975), 25–40.

———. "Al-Fārābī's Modalities," *Iyyun* 23 (1972): 100–12; in Hebrew with English summary.

———. "*Ghazālī*'s Argument from Creation." *IJMES* 2 (1971): 67–85, 168–88.

Graham, William. *Beyond the Written Word: Oral aspects of Scripture in the History of Religion* (New York: Cambridge University Press, 1987).

Gutas, Dimitri. "Paul the Persian on the Classification of the Parts of Aristotle's Philosophy: A Milestone between Alexandria and Bagdād." *Der Islam* 60 (1983) 235–59.

Halevi, Judah. *Kitāb al-Radd wa 'l-Dalīl fī 'l-Dīn al-Dhalīl*, known as *The Kuzari*. Edited by David H. Baneth (Jerusalem: Magnes Press, 1977); translated by H. Hirschfeld based on Hirschfeld's edition (Leipzig, 1887) (1905. Reprint. New York: Schocken, 1974).

Halpern, Baruch. *The First Historians: The Hebrew Bible and History* (San Francisco: Harper and Row, 1988).

al-Hamadhānī, Badīʿ al-Zamān. *Maqāmāt* (ca. 990). Edited by Muhammad Abduh (1889; Reprint. Beirut: Catholic Press, 1957, 1965); translated by W. J. Prendergast (1915. Reprint. London: Curzon, 1973); French translation, *Le Livre des Vagabonds: Séances d'un beau parleur impénitent.* Translated by René R. Khawam (Paris: Phébus, 1997).

Hamori, Andras. *On the Art of Medieval Arabic Literature* (Princeton: Princeton University Press, 1975).

Hardie, W. F. R. *Aristotle's Ethical Theory* (Oxford: Oxford University Press, 1988).

al-Ḥarīzī, Judah. *The Taḥkemoni*. 2 vols. Edited and translated by Victor Emanuel Reichert (Jerusalem: Raphael Haim Cohen's Press, 1965); translated by David Simha Segal (London: Littman Library, 2001).

Hoodbhoy, Pervez. *Islam and Science: Religious Orthodoxy and the Battle for Rationality* (Atlantic Highlands, N.J.: Zed Books, 1991).

Hourani, George. *Reason and Tradition in Islamic Ethics* (Cambridge: Cambridge University Press, 1985).

———. *Islamic Rationalism: The Ethics of 'Abd al-Jabbar* (Oxford: Oxford University Press, 1971).

Ḥujwīrī, 'Alī b. 'Uthmān. *Kashf al-Maḥjūb* (Drawing Back the Veil, ca. 1060). Translated by R. A. Nicholson (London: Luzac, 1936; 1967).

Humphreys, R. Stephen. *Islamic History: A Framework for Inquiry* (Princeton: Princeton University Press, 1991).

Ibn Bājjah, Abū Bakr (Avempace). *Opera Metaphysica* (early twelfth century). Edited by Majid Fakhry (Beirut: Dar an-Nahar, 1968).

Ibn Dā'ūd, Abraham. *Sefer ha-Qabbalah* (1160/61). Edited and translated by Gerson Cohen, *The Book of Tradition* (Philadelphia: JPS, 1967).

Ibn al-Fāriḍ, 'Umar b. 'Alī. *The Mystical Poems* (ca. 1206–35). Translated by A. J. Arberry (Dublin: Walker, 1956).

Ibn Hazm, 'Alī b. Ahmad. *Ṭawq al-Ḥamāma* (1020s). Translated by A. J. Arberry, *The Ring of the Dove* (London: Luzac, 1953).

Ibn Isḥāq, M. b. Ishāq. *The Life of Muhammad*. Translated by Alfred Guillaume (1955. Reprint. Lahore: Oxford University Press, 1967).

Ibn Khaldūn, Walī al-Dīn. *Muqaddimah* (first draft completed 1377). 3 vols. Translated by Franz Rosenthal (New York: Pantheon, 1958).

Ibn al-Nafīs, 'Alā' al-Dīn. *Al-Risālah al-Kāmiliyya fī 'l-Sīrati 'l-Nabawiyya*. Edited and translated by Max Meyerhof and Joseph Schacht as *The Theologus Autodidactus* (Oxford: Oxford University Press, 1968).

Ibn Rushd, Abū 'l-Walīd (Averroes). *Tahāfut al-Tahāfut*. Edited by Maurice Bouyges (Beirut: Catholic Press, 1930).

Ibn Sīnā, Abū 'Alī (Avicenna). *Shifā'* (1016–27), Psychology. Edited by Fazlur Rahman, *Avicenna's* De Anima (London: Oxford University Press, 1959).

———. *Najāt II 6* (1026/7). translated by Fazlur Rahman, *Avicenna's Psychology* (Westport, Conn.: Hyperion, 1952).

———. *K. al-Ishārāt wa-'l-Tanbīhāt*, with the Commentary of Naṣīr al-Dīn al-Tūsī. 3 vols. Edited by S. Dunya (Cairo: Dar al-Ma'ārif, 1957) trans. A.-M. Goichon, *Livre des Directives et Remarques* (Paris: Vrin, 1951).

Ikhwān al-Ṣafā' (The Sincere Brethren of Basra). *The Case of the Animals vs. Man before the King of the Jinn*. Translated from *Rasā'il Ikhwān al-Ṣafā'* by L. E. Goodman (1978; Reprint. Los Angeles: Gee Tee Bee, 1989).

———. *Rasā'il* (ca. 970) 4 vols. (Beirut: Dar Sadir, 1957).

Ivry, Alfred. "Averroes' Three Commentaries on *De Anima*." Edited by Gerhard Endress and Jan Aertsen, in *Averroes and the Aristotelian Tradition: Sources, Constitution and Reception of the Philosophy of Ibn Rushd (1126–1198)*, (Leiden: Brill, 1999), 199–216.

Izutsu, Toshihiko. *Ethico-Religious Concepts in the Qur'ān* (Montreal: McGill University Press, 1966).

———. *The Structure of Ethical Terms in the* Koran*: A Study in Semantics* (Tokyo: Keio Institute of Philological Studies, 1959).

Jāḥiẓ, Abū ʿUthmān. *The Epistle on Singing-Girls*. Edited and translated by A. F. L. Beeston (Warminster, Wilts.: Aris and Phillips, 1980).

Juwaynī, Abū ʾl-Maʿālī, *Kitāb al-Irshād*, ed. with French translation, J. D. Luciani (Paris: Leroux, 1938).

Kassis, Hanna. *A Concordance of the Qurʾān* (Berkeley: University of California Press, 1983).

Kemal, Salim. *The Poetics of Alfarabi and Avicenna* (Leiden: Brill, 1991).

Kennedy, Hugh, ed. *The Historiography of Islamic Egypt (c. 950–1800)* (Leiden: Brill, 2000).

Khalidi, Tarif. *Arabic Historical Thought in the Classical Period* (Cambridge: Cambridge University Press, 1994).

———. *Islamic Historiography: The Histories of Masʿūdī* (Albany: State University of New York Press, 1975).

Kindī, Abū Yūsuf Yaʿqūb. *On First Philosophy*. Translated by Alfred Ivry, *Al-Kindī's Metaphysics* (Albany: State University of New York Press, 1974).

———. *Risāla fī ʾl-ʿAql*, ed. by R. J. McCarthy, "Al-Kindī's Treatise on the Intellect," *Islamic Studies* 3 (1964), 122–24; French translation, Jean Jolivet, *L'Intellect selon Kindī* (Leiden: Brill, 1971).

———. "Essay on How to Banish Sorrow." Edited with Italian trans. H. Ritter and R. Walzer, *Uno Scritto Morale Inedito di al-Kindi* (Rome, Academia dei Lincei, 1938).

Kister, M. J. *Studies in Jahiliyya and Early Islam* (London: Variorum, 1980).

Kraemer, Joel. *Humanism in the Renaissance of Islam: The Cultural Revival during the Buyid Age* (Leiden: Brill, 1986).

———. *Philosophy in the Renaissance of Islam* (Leiden: Brill, 1986).

———. "On Maimonides' Messianic Posture," in *Studies in Medieval Jewish History and Literature* 2. Edited by Isadore Twersky (Cambridge: Harvard University Press, 1984).

Kueny, Kathryn. *The Rhetoric of Sobriety: Wine in Early Islam* (Albany: State University of New York Press, 2001).

Lawrence, Bruce. *Notes from a Distant Flute: Sufi Literature in Pre-Mughal India* (Tehran: Imperial Academy of Philosophy, 1978).

Leaman, Oliver, and Daniel Frank. *History of Jewish Philosophy* (London: Routledge, 1996).

Lewis, Bernard, and P. M. Holt, eds. *Historians of the Middle East* (London: Oxford University Press, 1962).

Lichtenstadter, Ilse. *Introduction to Classical Arabic Literature* (Twayne: New York, 1974).

Mahdi, Muhsin. "Language and Logic in Classical Islam." Edited by Gustave E. von Grunebaum, in *Logic in Classical Islamic Culture* (Wiesbaden: Harrassowitz, 1970).

———. *Ibn Khaldūn's Philosophy of History* (Chicago: University of Chicago Press, 1957).

Maimonides, *Dalālat al-Hāʾirīn*, (ca. 1185–90) Guide to the Perplexed. 3 vols. Edited by S. Munk (1856–66: Reprint. Osnabrück: Zeller, 1964).

Makari, Victor E. *Ibn Taymiyyah's Ethics: The Social Factor* (Chico, California: Scholars Press, 1983).

Maqrīzī, Tāqī al-Dīn. *Book of Contention and Strife Concerning the Relations between the Banū Umayya and the Banū Hāshim*. Translated by Clifford E. Bosworth (Manchester: Journal of Semitic Studies Monographs, 1980).

Margoliouth, D. S. *Lectures on Arabic Historians* (1930. Reprint. New York: Burt Franklin, 1972).

———. "The Discussion between Abū Bishr Mattā and Abū Sa'īd al-Sīrāfi on the Merits of Logic and Grammar," *JRAS* (1905) 129–79.

Meisami, Julie. *Persian Historiography to the End of the Twelfth Century* (Edinburgh: Edinburgh University Press, 1999).

Merkley, Paul. *The Greek and Hebrew Origins of Our Idea of History* (Lewiston, Ont.: Mellen, 1987).

Mez, Adam. *The Renaissance of Islam.* Translated by S. K. Bukhsh and D. S. Margoliouth (1937. Reprint. New York: AMS, 1975).

Mir, Mustansir, ed. *Arabic and Islamic Studies in honor of James A. Bellamy* (Princeton: Darwin Press, 1993).

Miskawayh, Abū 'Alī. *K. Tahdhīb al-Akhlāq* (late tenth century). Translated by Constantine Zurayk (Beirut: American University of Beirut, 1968); French translation by M. Arkoun, *Traité d'Ethique* (Damascus: Institut Français de Damas, 1969).

———. "On Pleasure," in Mohammed Arkoun, "Deux Epitres de Miskawayh," *Bulletin d'Etudes Orientales* 17 (1961/2): 7–19.

———. *Kitāb Tartīb al-Sa'ādāt* (Cairo: al-Maktaba al-Maḥmūdiyya 1928).

———. *K. Tajārub al-Umam.* Edited and translated by H. F. Amedroz and D. S. Margoliouth, *The Concluding Portion of the Experiences of Nations.* 7 vols. (Oxford: Blackwells, 1920).

Daud, Wan Mohd Nor Wan. *The Concept of Knowledge in Islam and its Implications for Education in a Developing Country* (London: Mansell, 1989).

Monroe, James. *The Art of Badī' az-Zamān al-Hamadhānī as Picaresque Narrative* (Beirut: American University, 1983).

Mottahedeh, Roy. *Loyalty and Leadership in an Early Islamic Society* (Princeton: Princeton University Press, 1980).

Muslim, Abū 'l-Husayn. *Saḥīh.* 4 vols. Trans. Abdul Hamid Siddiqi (Lahore: Ashraf, 1976).

Al-Nadīm, Abū 'l-Faraj. *Fihrist*, trans. Bayard Dodge (New York: Columbia University Press, 1970).

Nasr, Seyyed Hossein, and Oliver Leaman, eds. *History of Islamic Philosophy.* 2 vols. (London: Routledge, 1996).

Netton, Ian. *Al-Fārābī and His School* (London: Routledge, 1992).

Ormsby, Eric. *Theodicy in Islamic Thought: The Dispute over al-Ghazali's Best of All Possible Worlds* (Princeton: Princeton University Press, 1984).

Parens, Joshua. *Metaphysics as Rhetoric: Alfarabi's* Summary of Plato's "Laws" (Albany: State University of New York Press, 1995).

Peters, Frank E. *Allah's Commonwealth* (New York: Simon and Schuster, 1973).

Peters J. R. T. M. *God's Created Speech: A Study in the Speculative Theology of . . . 'Abd al-Jabbār* (Leiden: Brill 1976).

Petersen, E. L. *'Alī and Mu'āwiya in Early Arabic Tradition* (Copenhagen: Munksgaard, 1964).

The Presidency of Islamic Researches, Iftā', Call, and Guidance, *The Holy Qur'ān: English Translation of the Meanings and Commentary* (Medina: King Fahd Holy *Qur'ān* Printing Complex, n.d.).

Rāzī, Muḥammad b. Zakarīyā'. "*Munāẓarāt bayna al-Razīyayn.*" Translated by L. E. Goodman, "Rāzī vs Rāzī—Philosophy in the Majlis," in Hava Lazarus-Yafeh, Mark R. Cohen, Sasson Somekh, and Sidney H. Griffith, eds., *The*

Majlis: Interreligious Encounters in Medieval Islam (Wiesbaden: Harrassowitz, 1999) 84–107.
———. *Abi Bakr Mohammadi filii Zachariae Raghensis Opera Philosophica fragmentaque quae supersunt*, ed. Paul Kraus (Cairo: Fouad I University, 1939).
Rosenthal, E. I. J. *Political Thought in Medieval Islam* (Cambridge: Cambridge University Press, 1968).
Rosenthal, Franz. *The Herb: Hashish versus Medieval Muslim Society* (Leiden: Brill, 1971).
———. *Knowledge Triumphant: The Concept of Knowledge in Medieval Islam* (Leiden: Brill, 1970).
———. *A History of Muslim Historiography* (Leiden: Brill, 1968).
Rowson, Everett. "Religion and Politics in the Career of Badīʿ al-Zamān al-Hamadhānī." *JAOS* 107 (1987): 653–73.
Saadiah Gaon al-Fayyūmī. *The Book of Theodicy* (translation and commentary on the Book of Job) translated with philosophical commentary by L. E. Goodman (New Haven: Yale University Press, 1988).
———. *K. al-Mukhtār fī ʾl-Āmānāt wa ʾl-Iʿtiqādāt = Sefer ha-Nivḥar ba-Emunot uva-Deʿot*, The Book of Critically Chosen Beliefs and Convictions, Arabic text with modern Hebrew translation by J. Kafih (Jerusalem: Sura, 1970); translated as *The Book of Beliefs and Opinions*, by Samuel Rosenblatt (New Haven: Yale University Press, 1948) known as *Sefer Emunot ve-Deʿot*.
Schacht, Joseph. *Origins of Muhammadan Jurisprudence* (Oxford: Oxford University Press, second edition, 1953).
Serjeant, R. B. *South Arabian Hunt* (London: Luzac, 1974).
Shboul, Ahmad M. H. *Al-Masʿūdī and his World: A Muslim Humanist and his Interest in Non-Muslims* (London: Ithaca Press, 1979).
Sherif, M. A. *Ghazali's Theory of Virtue* (Albany: State University of New York Press, 1975).
Sijistānī, Abū Sulaymān. *Ṣiwān al-Ḥikma*, ed. Abdu ʾl-Rahman Badawi (Tehran: Intishārāt Bunyād Farhang Irān, 1974).
Smith, Margaret. *Al-Muhasibi (781–857): An Early Mystic of Baghdad* (1935. Reprint. Amsterdam, Philo Press, 1974).
Smith, Wilfred Cantwell. *Islam in Modern History* (Princeton: Princeton University Press, 1957).
Stillman, Yedida. *Arab Dress from the Dawn of Islam to the Modern Times: A Short History*, ed. Norman Stillman (Leiden: Brill, 2000).
Tabarī, Abu Jaʿfar. *The History, From the Creation to the Flood*. Translated by Franz Rosenthal (Albany: State University of New York Press, 1989).
Tawhīdī, Abū Hayyān. *Kitāb al-Hawāmil wa-ʾl-Shawāmil*. Edited by Ahmad Amin and Aḥmad Saqr (Cairo: Matbaʿat Lajnat al-Taʾlīf wa ʾl-Tarjama wa ʾl-Nashr, 1951).
Thaʿālibī, Abū Manṣur. *Laṭāʾif al-Maʿārif*, trans. C. E. Bosworth, *The Book of Curious and Entertaining Information* (Edinburgh: Edinburgh University Press, 1968).
Tibrīzī, Walī al-Dīn. *Mishkāt al-Masābiḥ* (1335–36), a revision of Ibn al-Farrāʾ al-Baghawī's *Maṣābiḥ al-Sunna*, trans. James Robson (Lahore: Ashraf, 1975).
Trimmingham, J. S. *The Sufi Orders in Islam* (Oxford: Oxford University Press, 1971).
Ibn Ṭufayl, Abū Bakr. *Ḥayy Ibn Yaqẓān* (1170s), translated by L. E. Goodman (1972, Reprint. Los Angeles: Gee Tee Bee, 1990)

al-Ṭūsī, Naṣīr al-Dīn. *The Naṣīrean Ethics* (1235). Translated by G.M. Wickens (London: Allen and Unwin, 1964).
von Grunebaum, Gustave. *Muhammadan Festivals* (London: Curzon, 1981).
———. *Medieval Islam* (Chicago: University of Chicago Press, 1954).
Walzer, Richard. *Greek into Arabic* (Oxford, Cassirer, 1963).
Wansbrough, John. *The Sectarian Milieu: Content and Composition of Islamic Salvation History* (Oxford: Oxford University Press, 1978)
———. *Quranic Studies* (Oxford: Oxford University Press, 1977)
Watt, William Montgomery. *The Formative Period of Islamic Thought* (Edinburgh: Edinburgh University Press, 1973).
———. *Companion to the Qur'ān: Based on the Arberry Translation* (London: Allen and Unwin, 1967).
———. *Muslim Intellectual: A Study of al-Ghazālī* (Edinburgh: Edinburgh University Press, 1963).
———. *Free Will and Predestination in Early Islam* (London: Luzac, 1948)
Wensinck, A. J. *A Handbook of Early Muhammadan Tradition* (Leiden: Brill, 1960).
———. *La Pensée de Ghazzali* (Paris: Maisonneuve, 1940).
———. *Concordance et Indices de la Tradition Musulmane.* 7 vols. (Leiden: Brill, 1936–69).
——— *The Muslim Creed: Its Genesis and Historical Development* (1932. Reprint. London: Cass, 1965).
Wheeler, Brannon. *Applying the Canon in Islam: The Authorization and Maintenance of Interpretive Reasoning in Ḥanafī Scholarship* (Albany: State University of New York Press, 1996).
Williams, John Alden ed. *Themes of Islamic Civilization* (Berkeley: University of California Press, 1971).
Yaḥyā ibn ʿAdī (d. 974) *Tahdhīb al-Akhlaq*, edited by Naji Takriti (Beirut: Oueidat, 1978)
———. "Making Clear the Distinction between the Two Arts: Philosophical Logic and Arabic Grammar." Edited by G. Endress, *Journal for the History of Arabic Science* 2 (1978): 38–50, 181–93.
Zaehner, R. C. *Mysticism, Sacred and Profane* (Oxford: Oxford University Press, 1971).

Index

Printed in the United States
19977LVS00001B/275